W9-CQY-040

THE MIDDLE EAST MILITARY BALANCE

1989-1990

Joseph Alpher - Zeev Eytan - Dov Tamari
Edited by Joseph Alpher

Library of Congress Catalog Card Number:
86-50920

Library of Congress Cataloging-in-Publication Data

ISBN 0-8133-8300-5

Published for the Jaffee Center
for Strategic Studies
by
The Jerusalem Post
POB 81, Jerusalem 91000, Israel
and
Westview Press
Boulder, Colorado 80301, Frederick A. Praeger, Publisher

Printed in Israel at the Jerusalem Post Press

JCSS Publications

JCSS Publications present the findings and assessments of the Center's research staff. Each paper represents the work of a single investigator or a team. Such teams may also include research fellows who are not members of the Center's staff. Views expressed in the Center's publications are those of the authors and do not necessarily reflect the views of the Center, its trustees, officers, or other staff members or the organizations and individuals that support its research. Thus the publication of a work by JCSS signifies that it is deemed worthy of public consideration but does not imply endorsement of conclusions or recommendations.

Contents

Page

Part I. Tables

Page

Preface

This edition of the *Middle East Military Balance*, covering 1989 and early 1990, was about to go to press when Iraq invaded Kuwait on August 2, 1990. The invasion, and its immediate regional and global aftermath, caused us to delay publication operations for nearly three months, and to introduce a number of changes.

Even prior to the invasion, Iraq had been a central focus of the *Balance*, treated extensively in chapters on the Iraqi Armed Forces, missile and CBW proliferation in the region, the role of expeditionary forces in Arab-Israel wars, and inter-Arab developments. We therefore elected to assess the immediate ramifications of the Gulf Crisis in these and additional realms by adding brief epilogues to no less than six chapters. These are set off in each case by three asterisks. In addition, the opening chapter was expanded to assess the overall backdrop and ramifications of the crisis. All these chapters, then, are updated to mid-October 1990. The chapters in the *Balance* that deal with the *intifada* and terrorism, refer primarily to the 1989 calendar year, but include references to events in the first quarter of 1990 as well.

Another unique aspect of this balance was an attempt, inspired by the advent of a new decade, to provide a long look back at the development of two key military strategic issues that threaten to preoccupy Israel in the '90s. These are Syria's concept of strategic parity, and the role of peripheral Arab states like Iraq in Arab-Israel wars.

Two additional main strategic issue areas — the effect on the Middle East of events in the USSR and Eastern Europe, and, specifically, the ramifications of mass Soviet Jewish immigration to Israel — are dealt with in the chapters on inter-Arab developments and the peace process. Events in Lebanon are also referred to in the inter-Arab chapter, and in the chapters on terrorism. Finally, there is a degree of inevitable overlap, and here and there differences of approach, between the descriptions and characterizations of low-level and individual violence in the two separate chapters on the *intifada* and the analysis of trends in the Palestinian armed struggle. We assessed this to be, overall, beneficial to the reader's understanding of these complex issues.

If these chapters of Part I are somewhat innovative, Part II retains its traditional presentation of updated (June 1990) data, figures and battle order information on all countries in the region.

And Part III offers updated comparative tables (with new graphic elements), glossary of weaponry, maps, list of abbreviations, and chronology, all updated to June 1990.

In addition to the three principal writers of the *1989-90 Balance*, a special word of thanks is in order to a number of additional contributors, all from the JCSS senior research staff. Anat Kurz, head of the JCSS Project on Low-Intensity Warfare, wrote two chapters on terrorism: Palestinian Armed Struggle, and Shi'ite International Terrorism and the Iranian Connection. Brig.-Gen.(res) Aryeh Shalev covered The Second Year of the Intifada. Dr. Shai Feldman contributed a chapter on Middle East Missile and CBW Proliferation: Patterns, Trends and Ramifications. And Dr. Ephraim Kam assessed The Inter-Arab Scene: Key Strategic Developments.

It is a pleasant duty to thank the Documentation Center of our neighboring research institution, the Moshe Dayan Center for Middle Eastern and African Studies, for assisting Ephraim Kam in preparing his chapter on inter-Arab issues; and to thank Ofra Bengio of that Center, and the IDF History Department, for aiding Dov Tamari in preparing the chapter on expeditionary forces in Israel-Arab wars.

Finally, the authors are indebted to all the members of the senior research staff of the Jaffee Center for their tough critical review of drafts of the chapters. In particular, the overall guidance of the Head of Center, Maj.Gen.(res) Aharon Yariv, was invaluable.

J.A.
October 1990

PART I

STRATEGIC DEVELOPMENTS IN THE MIDDLE EAST

1. The Gulf Crisis: Iraq Escalates, then Attacks

by Joseph Alpher

On August 2, 1990, Iraq invaded and conquered Kuwait, thereby setting into motion an American-led intervention effort that seemed likely to alter the face of the Middle East. By mid-October it was impossible to assess how or when the crisis would be resolved. Here we shall attempt to trace the origins of the crisis, and offer an initial assessment of its broad ramifications.

Iraq Escalates

Toward the end of 1989, and particularly during the early months of 1990, Arab-Israel tensions increased as a consequence of a series of dramatic revelations that concerned Iraq's accomplishments and plans for weapons development — particularly of the non-conventional variety — as well as the enemy it appeared to be singling out as the object of these efforts: Israel.

The revelations were of two types. In March and April 1990 western intelligence and customs agencies intercepted sophisticated weapons components destined for Iraq: parts of a "space gun" allegedly capable of firing missiles into orbit or against targets at least as distant as Israel, and US-made capacitors capable of detonating nuclear weapons. Iraqi President Saddam Hussein then issued strident declarations regarding Iraqi achievements in developing binary chemical weapons and missile delivery systems. There were also practical demonstrations — in particular, the launching, apparently with technical difficulties, in late 1989 of some form of a multistage missile designed to place objects into orbit, and the deployment of Iraqi surface-to-surface missiles near the Iraqi-Jordanian border, with the declared objective of deterring Israel.

Preventing Israel from attacking Iraqi plants engaged in developing all this weaponry was indeed the rationale repeatedly offered by Saddam for his aggressive posture. This was usually phrased in terms of the Arabs' inalienable right to obtain and apply sophisticated technologies in general, and the alleged desire of Israel and the West to deny them this right. It was also accompanied by shrill threats — e.g., to "burn half of Israel" (if Israel attacked Iraq with nuclear weapons; later amended to state, if Israel attacked any Arab state), "war with Israel is inevitable" — as well as demands that the United States withdraw its naval presence from the Persian Gulf.

In his most explicit statement, in June 1990, Saddam framed his threats against Israel in classic deterrence terminology: "common sense requires that if you do not wish to involve your enemy, tell him what your reaction will be if he attacks you.... Is it better to prevent the destruction, or to wait for the moment when we use our weapon of destruction? We believe that in this situation it is preferable somehow to make the parties aware of the degree of damage that will be caused by their striking at one another."

But there appeared to be additional explanations as well. True, Saddam undoubtedly did fear an Israeli attempt to repeat its 1981 success, when it demolished Iraq's Osiraq nuclear reactor and caused an extended delay in the Iraqi nuclear program. Yet by now Iraqi efforts were far better dispersed and protected. Thus Saddam may also have assessed that in the post-cold war age he himself was liable to become the victim, like Ceaucescu, of Soviet indifference, or, like Noriega, of an aggressive American initiative. Beyond these fears, he also seemed to be taking the lead among third world military powers in exploring the new limits of maneuver afforded by the demise of the superpower balance of power.

Then too, Saddam's harsh rhetoric was presumably directed as much toward persuading Iran to effect a peace process, as at deterring Israel. By early 1990 a tenuous ceasefire in the Gulf War had existed for a year and a half, yet without any progress toward solving the belligerents' fundamental differences — not so much as a single substantive exchange of POWs had taken place. Significantly, Saddam exploited the impact of Iraqi aggressive posturing toward Israel in order to commence an unprecedented direct correspondence with Iranian President Rafsanjani; according to some reports, he even offered a significant Iraqi concession on the Shatt al-Arab issue. By mid-1990 plans were advancing for a Saddam-Rafsanjani summit.

In retrospect it is now clear that Saddam Hussein was also seeking to enhance the credibility of any threats he might make against regional Arab actors, in addition to Israel and Iran, and against the United States, whose withdrawal from the Gulf he had pointedly demanded. In this sense, he was exploiting a combination of regional developments — Arab fears of massive Soviet Jewish immigration to Israel, destabilization in Jordan, the *intifada*, the stalemate in American and Egyptian efforts to advance a Palestinian solution — to make a quick grab at solidifying a position of inter-Arab leadership. To do so, it was helpful to appear to be the cutting edge of the Arab struggle for technological excellence, as well as chief physical protector of the Arab cause against Israel as well as Iran.

Whatever Saddam's motives were at the time, and despite an evident gap between the level of his rhetoric and any new Iraqi progress in the nonconventional and missile field — there was little revealed about Iraqi weapons development in early 1990 that had not been known in early 1989 — he had apparently succeeded in presenting a threat of some sort of Arab strategic parity or, in his perception, even a primitive balance of terror with Israel. This in turn could afford him a protective umbrella for the further development, throughout the decade of the '90s, of nuclear, advanced chemical, and biological weaponry. It was this prospect of a major evolution in the Arab-Israel balance that appeared, in the early months of 1990, to inject a number of new considerations into the strategic picture.

For one, Israel could not ignore the political-psychological effect of Iraq's apparent success in advertising an immediate missile and chemical threat to the Israeli rear. This, added to an already existing Syrian threat, indeed presented a new constraint upon Israeli military planning. One Israeli response was to seek, rhetorically, to advertise its own deterrent: the prospect of visiting massive destruction upon Iraq.

A second constraint was the Iraqi threat to retaliate against Israel for any attack upon an Arab state. Taken to its logical conclusion, this could even have limited Israel's freedom to retaliate against terrorist bases in, say, Libya, or even Lebanon. Here Israel encountered American and Egyptian pressure upon it to avoid escalation by resisting any attempt to deal with Saddam by force, and to rely instead on political contacts by emissaries of good will seeking to reduce tensions. Israel apparently concurred to the extent of allowing Egypt to relay to Baghdad an assurance that Jerusalem would not launch a preemptive attack. The US, for its part, conspicuously avoided voicing any sharp criticism of Saddam's behavior and his weapons program, while reassuring

Israel that the Iraqi nuclear program was virtually nonexistent.

Iraq's newly aggressive profile also affected the inter-Arab scene. Just as Egypt was reemerging as a pole of moderate Arab leadership, Iraq was challenging it with an alternative concept of the inter-Arab reality. Both Cairo and Washington appeared to be motivated as much by fear lest Saddam drag the region into a disastrous military escalation that would endanger their own specific interests, as by a desire to keep all parties on track for the Palestinian peace process, if it could be revived.

Undoubtedly Israel could take comfort in the fact that many Arab states in the region, such as Kuwait, Saudi Arabia and Syria, not to mention Egypt, were unhappy with the prospect of an Iraqi hegemonic embrace. Yet these same states (with the notable exception of Egypt) also appeared to rejoice in Iraq's success in sending a message of defiance to Israel. Even Iran joined the bandwagon — pledging at one point to support any Iraqi war effort against Israel.

Looked at from a different angle, and again with some hindsight, the Middle East reaction to Saddam's increasingly aggressive profile found only Israel and Syria, alone in the region, aware at an early stage of the Iraqi danger. In contrast, the reactions of Egypt and the Arab pro-western camp, the United States, and Iraq's Soviet and European strategic suppliers, varied from indifference to studied appeasement and even encouragement.

Thus Israel and its neighbors responded to the threat in decidedly different ways. As far back as early 1989 Jordan had commenced a major strategic reorientation by moving into the Iraqi military orbit. King Hussein, feeling beleaguered by internal (Palestinian, Islamic) threats, and perceiving a long- term external threat from Israel, apparently reasoned that Jordan's position of weakness dictated that it embrace, rather than oppose, the 'protection' offered by Saddam. Israel, virtually alone, sought to warn the United States and Egypt and to encourage a firmer stance against Saddam. Syria, increasingly isolated both by Saddam's belligerency and by new Soviet policies, and challenged by the Iraqis in Lebanon, had by mid-1990 effected a strategic rapprochement with Egypt.

From Israel's standpoint, Iraq's emergence as the primary Arab military power, coupled with its aggressive stance, enhanced the importance of Jordan. Particularly as long as Syria remained hostile toward Iraq, a stable Hashemite Kingdom, if it could be maintained, would serve as an effective buffer against any large-scale Iraqi conventional confrontation with Israel on the ground. In contrast, a destabilized Jordan, or one that moved headlong into the Iraqi orbit, could provide the trigger for the reconstitution of an anti-Israel eastern front against the backdrop of continued Israeli-Palestinian conflict or stalemate. Hence, from June onward, the same Israeli leadership (Shamir, Arens) that had for the past year caused King Hussein great concern by its advocacy of the 'Jordan is Palestine' formula as a panacea for Israel's difficulties in dealing with the Palestinian problem, now sought to reassure the King regarding Israel's commitment to Jordan's stability.

Perhaps most significantly, by June 1990 it was impossible to avoid the conclusion that, for the first time since the Arab-Israel peace process began in earnest with the Sadat visit to Jerusalem in November 1977, an atmosphere was developing that raised the risk of an Iraqi-inspired Arab-Israel military escalation. In parallel, after a brief interval of relative tranquility since the end of fighting between Iran and Iraq in mid-1988, the overall military situation in the Gulf region was now in danger of deteriorating due to Iraq's behavior.

Iraq Invades Kuwait

It was the Gulf, rather than Israel, that ultimately formed the focus of Saddam Hussein's strategic initiative, and for fairly cogent reasons from the Iraqi standpoint. We have already noted the deterrent motif in Saddam's threats toward Israel; this implied that he had a fairly clear understanding of the dangers for Iraq involved in any belligerent initiative toward Israel. In contrast, the invasion of Kuwait seemed assured of easy success from a military standpoint. It appeared to provide solutions for two of the key strategic problems that the invasion of Iranian Khuzistan in 1980 was intended to solve, and whose saliency resurfaced as it became clear that even in "defeat" Iran was not budging on the Shatt al-Arab issue. It offered unfettered Iraqi naval access to the Persian Gulf; and it posed the prospect that Iraq would increase its revenues from oil — more liftings, and at higher prices — to fuel its ambitious strategic development plans.

Finally, Saddam assessed — correctly, up to a point — that the inter-Arab system was incapable of organizing sustained political or military resistance to an invasion of Kuwait. The weak and narrow-based nature of the regime structures of Saudi Arabia and the Emirates, reflected in the Saudis' traditional reluctance to take a stand on any inter-Arab issue; Saddam's alliances' with Jordan and Yemen on Saudi Arabia's other flanks; his growing Nasserist image, and the popularity among the Arab masses of the comeuppance he delivered to the haughty Kuwaitis; the latent Egyptian-Syrian rivalry that could be expected to hinder any organized resistance by means of the Arab League; the totality of the strategic surprise he had visited upon the world — all these boded well for his enterprise.

Indeed, Egypt's President Mubarak — the only conceivable leader of inter-Arab opposition — proved unable to convene an Arab League meeting at any echelon for the first week after the invasion. Then his efforts were bolstered by two actors whom Saddam had misread or misunderstood. One was Saudi Arabia. Its leaders became convinced that failure to act decisively meant the certain destruction of their country by the Iraqis, who were now poised on the Kuwait-Saudi border, a mere 300 km from the Saudi oilfields. Hence they accepted an American offer to send troops.

The other was the United States. Washington recovered quickly from its surprise at the Iraqi move, and concluded that Saddam's broad goal of regional hegemony posed a clear and immediate threat to the energy resources of the industrialized and much of the developing world. Moreover, this first challenge to the new world order, if not rebuffed forcefully, could spell chaos for American and Soviet efforts to restructure their relationship, for America's status as principal superpower, and for future North-South relations. Accordingly, and in pace with an air and sealift of troops to Saudi Arabia and the Gulf region, Washington acted to galvanize a military and political coalition of western and moderate Arab forces, with Soviet acquiescence and German, Japanese and Arab financing, to oppose Iraq, and to place an embargo on its imports and exports. The new superpower order enabled it to enlist the backing of the United Nations Security Council in a way unprecedented since the UN's founding. Indeed, the determined initiative displayed by President Bush, and supported virtually worldwide, was without precedent, and reflected a readiness to subscribe to a new set of principles in maintaining world order. Finally, the requirements of molding an instant military alliance with a variety of Arab partners rendered it essential that the Israeli-American strategic relationship be reduced to a low profile — a stance that Israel willingly accepted, however nervous it was about the long-term ramifications of such a move.

The United States spelled out two clear and immediate goals of this enterprise: protecting Saudi Arabia and the Gulf from Iraqi aggression, and expelling Iraq from Kuwait (to this was later added the explicit objective of assuring the safety of thousands of western hostages held by Saddam). A larger, more implicit objective — to defang the Iraqi military threat to regional stability — was hinted at in various statements of purpose, and was encapsulated in the alliance's declared readiness to negotiate the removal of the embargo and the withdrawal of its forces only after Iraq's withdrawal from Kuwait.

Ramifications

Some early assessments of the broader ramifications of the crisis tended to describe it as a radical aberration in a new international political dynamic that was otherwise increasingly rational, liberal and democratic; if the American-led coalition could only overcome the Iraqi challenge, it could get back to the business of establishing a new world order in the post-Cold War era. This approach appeared to ignore, or underestimate — in much the same way that the Iraqi threat had been brushed aside prior to August 1990 — a number of crucial and dangerous issue areas inherent to the Middle East, and perhaps to other parts of the underdeveloped "South" as well, that were activated by the Gulf Crisis.

One was the gross overarming of third world powers, egged on by short-term western economic requirements and easy access to technology. While US and Soviet awareness of the problem existed prior to the crisis, and clearly was sharpened by the crisis itself (American arms supplied to Kuwait fell into Iraqi hands), Washington nevertheless felt it had no alternative in the immediate term but to increase arms supplies to fragile but beleaguered allies like the Saudis.

That fragility pointed to a second danger signal: the inherent weakness of the Middle East state structure in general, and particularly that of the Gulf principalities. Whatever its previous merits, Kuwait proved on August 2 to be little more than a bubble of dollars in the desert. When that bubble burst, there emerged 300,000 or so Palestinians who rejoiced, about a million bewildered Asian refugees and a few thousand marooned westerners, and a minority Kuwaiti population, one-fourth of whose number was on vacation. Incapable of understanding the Iraqi danger, fearful of requesting outside aid, the Kuwaiti leadership more than anyone else bore the blame for the country's demise. The remaining emirates, including Saudi Arabia, were now seen, like Kuwait, to have taken pitifully few substantive steps either to ensure their long-term physical survival or to build genuine nations. Nor had anyone else in the Arab Middle East made significant progress toward adapting to the new world climate. Indeed, by bringing Muslim fundamentalists to the fore, the attempts at democratization in 1989 by Jordan and Algeria merely highlighted the resurgent potential of yet another destabilizing element in the region, militant Islam.

These and similar weaknesses were reflected in the Arab League's paralysis during the first, pre-US intervention, week of the crisis. The League's primary raison d'etre as a mutual defense pact proved meaningless. It seems likely that, without the American push, it would have mounted no effective resistance.

The crisis also, once again, focused attention on the dynamic of power politics in the Persian Gulf. Iran, in particular, found the prospect of an American-Saudi post-crisis hegemony in the Gulf as unpalatable as an Iraqi victory. Accordingly it opted to play both sides for maximum advantage, alternately accepting Iraq's far-reaching concession to cement a quick peace treaty, then pledging to uphold the embargo, then violating it as an encouraging signal to Iraq, then releasing western hostages in Lebanon, and so on. Local power rivalry over sway in the Gulf region seemed almost certain to survive the Gulf Crisis — however it ended.

As a corollary, any prospects for effectively regulating the economic relationship between oil producers and consumers in the post-crisis era appeared as elusive as before. A decade seen by many experts as an era of low and stable fuel prices was now in doubt. If the centrality of the Persian Gulf for world energy stability was at the heart of the American reaction to the Iraqi invasion, the early weeks of the crisis produced little by way of innovative thinking about ways to ensure long-term economic, political and military stability. US Secretary of State Baker's reference to the eventual need for a NATO-like "new regional security structure" merely drove home the elusiveness of the Middle East reality.

Finally, there was the threat that instability in the Gulf would somehow link up with regional issues elsewhere. One prospect was the Soviet Central Asian Muslim regions, where religious and politically-motivated centrifugal tendencies were developing independently of outside influences. This suggested that the very fate of the Soviet Union might be an additional source of Middle East instability in the '90s, just as developments in the Soviet Bloc had undoubtedly acted to encourage Saddam Hussein's uninhibited behavior. Another possibility might involve Turkey, whose water disputes with Syria and Iraq would within the decade reach critical mass. In this sense it was no coincidence that the Turks willingly played a key role in the alliance, at considerable financial cost, from the very beginning: with an eye to possible future conflicts, they wished to fortify their influence with the US power broker.

But the key regional problem with obvious potential for linkage of some sort was the Arab-Israel conflict. Here three issues quickly emerged: the possibility of Israel being dragged by Iraq into an Arab-Israel war; ramifications for the Palestinian issue; and the future of American-Arab-Israeli relations.

The first issue returns us to the series of Iraqi threats against Israel that characterized the early months of 1990. As the Gulf Crisis got underway, Saddam Hussein picked up where he had left off. He charged that Israeli pilots and planes had arrived in Saudi Arabia in the guise of Americans; then he threatened that, if attacked by the alliance, he would retaliate against Israel and the Saudi oil fields; by late September, as the embargo on Iraq began to take hold, he asserted that he would attack Israel and the Saudis merely if and when the embargo became too effective.

The logic behind these threats was, presumably, that Iraqi aggression against Israel, if properly timed and orchestrated, could provoke an Israeli response that might force the hand of Arab members of the alliance, like Syria, and of Arab neutrals like Jordan, to join an Iraqi-led eastern front against Israel. This, in turn, might effectively weaken or neutralize the American-led threat from Saudi Arabia and the Gulf. Iraq could attack Israel by missiles, with or without chemical warheads, or by aerial bombing. It might provoke an Israeli response merely by introducing troops into Jordan, thereby crossing an Israeli-proclaimed 'red line.' It could also invoke Palestinian terrorist attacks against Israeli targets, or exploit some extreme expression of the *intifada* or an Israeli raid into Lebanon as a casus belli.

The weakness of this Iraqi option was that it gambled in a totally unpredictable way on the responses of all the other actors — Israel, the Arab states, and the United States — some or all of whom could react by attacking Iraq. Its strength could conceivably be in its use as a tactic of last resort — if the Baghdad regime were about to collapse anyway, under economic, political and military pressure. While Iraq's involvement in a confrontation with much of the world was in many ways for Israel a vindication of its strong stance, indeed even of its controversial 1981 attack on the Osiraq nuclear reactor, the presence of American and Arab troops in an anti-Iraqi alliance, and the requirements of the low profile in Israeli-American relations, rendered far more complicated Israeli calculations concerning a military response to any potential Iraqi attack or provocation. Certainly the stability of Jordan as a neutral buffer separating the Israel-Arab system from the Iraq-against-the-world system now became paramount in Israeli strategic thinking.

Like the anomaly of suddenly enhanced American arms supplies to the region almost certainly paralleling new pressures for a superpower-enforced arms control program, the Palestinian issue too presented a paradox. At both the grassroots and the PLO leadership level, the Palestinians evinced pro-Iraq sentiments from the very start of the crisis. Saddam's aggressive leadership image, the pan-Arab model seemingly reflected (in Palestinian eyes) by his annexation of Kuwait, strong resentment of Kuwait's wealth, coupled with despair over the deadlock in the peace process — all combined to render the Palestinians Saddam's most enthusiastic Arab backers, and Arafat his biggest apologist (however energetically the PLO leader protested that he was merely trying to mediate an 'Arab solution' to the problem). Taken together with Jordan's equivocal attitude (reflecting the sentiments of its own Palestinian majority) this appeared to place the two principal Arab actors in any Palestinian settlement at odds with the US and Egypt, the two primary potential brokers of a settlement. At a minimum, this suggested that the Palestinian issue would be relegated to the back burner during the crisis, and probably after its conclusion too.

On the other hand, Saddam energetically attempted to link the Palestinian issue to his own campaign in the Gulf. Moreover there was a general sense in the US, Europe and the Arab Middle East that the emergence of a powerful American-Arab alliance against Iraq — supported by virtually the entire world, and in particular enjoying UN Security Council backing — obligated the US to seize the opportunity to carry out a general housecleaning in the Middle East. Most actors, including the US and Egypt, studiously avoided any hint of linkage between the Gulf Crisis and the Arab-Israel dispute — not only because there really was no tangible link in terms of cause, but also because it was imperative to avoid appearing to justify Saddam's claims. Syria, for its part, disparaged the notion of linkage because Saddam sought early on in the crisis to match any possible withdrawal by Iraq from Kuwait with Syrian withdrawal from Lebanon. Yet American spokespersons did emphasize the need to offer the Arab world a convincing alternative vision to that proffered by Saddam — one that focused on Arab-Israel peace in general, and perhaps on the Palestinian issue in particular.

This leads us to the third issue area, that of the future of relations within the American-Arab-Israeli triangle. Clearly, one immediate spinoff of the crisis was an enhancement of the US-Arab strategic relationship, in the form of overt military cooperation and increased arms supplies. While this did not come directly at the expense of the American-Israeli relationship — this was hardly a zero-sum game — it nevertheless overshadowed it, particularly in view of the Israeli 'low profile.'

At the same time, Washington, and perhaps Egypt as well, could not but acknowledge the veracity of several Israeli arguments that had been treated, at best, lukewarmly prior to the crisis. Israel alone had been right not only about the Iraqi threat in a broad strategic sense; it had also, in seeking support for its anti-missile missile program, correctly pinpointed the specific prominence of the missile warfare threat in the emerging decade. Nor could its assertion that peace with additional Arab states required higher priority alongside the Palestinian issue be shunted aside in view of the clear imbalance between the immensity of the Iraqi strategic threat on the one hand, and that posed by the Palestinians, on the other.

Nevertheless, assuming the American-Arab alliance triumphed over Iraq in some significant way, the American attitude toward both Israel and the Arabs would likely undergo change. In practical terms, this would probably mean more emphasis by Washington on strategic collaboration with the Arabs, and on

Israeli concessions over the peace issue. If the Palestinians and Jordan were not available to join the process, or remained *non grata* after the crisis, and Syria stayed the course as an ally, then the near term emphasis could be transferred to an attempt to deal with Syria, the Golan, and the Syrian-Israeli relationship in Lebanon. The arms control issue, and particularly the need to regulate development and deployment of missiles and nonconventional weaponry, would also likely be prominent. These weapons systems were, after all, at the heart of the Iraqi threat. And they were the primary issue that continued to preoccupy the Soviets in addressing the Middle East.

Yet the Palestinian issue, however more thorny it had been rendered by the Palestinian attitude toward Iraq, would not go away. This was implicit in the content and tone of US-Israeli contacts during the early weeks of the Gulf Crisis. And it was virtually explicit in American attempts to reassure its Arab partners, the Europeans and the Soviets that their adherence to an aggressive anti-Iraq alliance would be rewarded.

2. The Inter-Arab Scene: Key Strategic Developments

by Ephraim Kam

General Trends

During the closing years of the decade of the '80s the Arab world underwent change — a slow and gradual change, yet one that was significant nonetheless. In essence, the change was twofold: two regional powers, Egypt and Iraq, free of former constraints, moved to the center of the Arab arena; and an atmosphere of reconciliation and solidarity began to manifest itself in inter-Arab relations.

The main source of this change was internal, as a shift in the balance of power within some Arab states began to emerge. Most Arab countries faced severe economic difficulties; in some, the resultant distress enlarged the circle of dissatisfaction with the regime's policies, and enhanced demands for a share in power. In some Arab communities, such as Jordan, Egypt and Algeria, there was also a growing tendency to return to Islamic sources. The outcome was a growing potential risk of instability for several Arab regimes — though most were still relatively stable. This potential threat, in addition to developments in the Soviet Bloc that were read as a warning by some Arab states, impelled Arab regimes to introduce at least tactical changes in both domestic and external policies.

While these growing internal challenges continued to focus much of the attention of most Arab regimes, they also introduced greater flexibility into inter-Arab relations. This dovetailed with the aftermath of an important development of 1988-89, when two factors that previously had contributed significantly to division within the Arab world — the Egyptian-Israeli peace treaty, and the Iran-Iraq War — lost much of their divisive effect. Hence the outstanding tendency, manifested especially after mid-1988, was a willingness to reconcile political differences and to cooperate, at least in the economic field.

By 1989 this tendency had two main aspects. One was a measure of reconciliation between states formerly hostile to one another — most notably Egypt and Syria, but also Egypt and Libya. A second were the attempts to form institutionalized frameworks for economic cooperation and integration, which were not devoid of political significance. The two frameworks created in 1989 — the Arab Cooperation Council (ACC) and the Arab Maghreb Union (AMU) — in addition to the Gulf Cooperation Council formed in 1981, covered almost all of the Arab world.

The growing interest in cooperation was also evident in 1989 in increasing military collaboration among some Arab states, and in intensive Arab attempts to solve the Lebanese crisis. Arab collective efforts regarding the peace process with Israel, or the *intifada*, were less impressive. Even Arab summit commitments to pay 43 million dollars a month to the PLO for the needs of the *intifada*, were only partially met.

An effort to limit the immigration of Soviet Jews to Israel was also a focus of Arab activity in 1989-90. Many Arab states regarded the immigration as a real threat — one that might change the demographic balance between Jews and Palestinians, affect the qualitative edge between Israel and its neighbors, and enable Israel to tighten its hold on the Territories. Hence the intensive Arab diplomatic effort, led by Jordan and the PLO, to combat the immigration. Notably, Arab statements in this regard were characterized by dualism: at times Arab leaders claimed that they opposed only the settlement of immigrants in the Territories; but quite often they opposed immigration to Israel altogether, suggesting that the immigrants be directed to other states, or even that immigration from the Soviet Union cease. In any case, Arab efforts in this regard had little effect by early 1990.

Our survey of these developments should not imply that the Arab system had changed its nature. In 1989 deep traditional divisions still prevailed, the most important of which was the rivalry between Syria and Iraq, to which a new arena was added in Lebanon. Political cooperation was limited, and suspicions held sway even between political allies. The Arab leaders, unable to convene a regular annual summit conference since 1982, once again had to settle for an extraordinary one in Casablanca. And the poor Arab states continued to become financially more dependent on the rich ones: the 1978 Baghdad Summit's financial commitments to the frontline states and the PLO dwindled significantly, and ended in 1988 without specific renewal. Nor did the limited upturn in the oil market in 1989 seriously affect the long-term financial prospects of the Arab oil-producing states. Hence, the decline in financial aid given to the frontline states and the

PLO — as well as of foreign currency transfers by workers in the Gulf states — continued.

Within the Arab world the so-called pragmatist bloc, headed by Egypt, Jordan, Saudi Arabia and Morocco, represented the leading approach. Its members supported a political solution to the Arab-Israel conflict on the basis of returning territories for peace. The more active participants in the peace process generally coordinated their positions, but disagreements among them emerged quite often. The pragmatist bloc was considerably strengthened in 1989 with the return of Egypt to a leading position in the Arab world. On the other hand, the emergence of Iraq as a more active partner in Arab affairs following the end of the fighting with Iran, and the militant approach of its president toward Israel, threatened new instability in the area. Events of 1989-90 also presaged the ongoing decline of the smaller radical group. Its two leading members, Syria and Libya, found themselves further isolated by the end of the Iran-Iraq War and the intensive efforts to advance the peace process. Their isolation was emphasized by the decline of Soviet support for the radical approach, evident in 1989 more than ever before. The weakness of the radical group was one of the main reasons for the willingness of Syria and Libya to improve relations with Egypt and other moderate Arab states.

Here a few comments are in order regarding the broad implications of developments in the Soviet Bloc for the Arab world. By 1989-90, most Arab regimes had cause for concern, and for several reasons. First, those regimes associated closely with the Soviet Bloc — especially Syria, Libya and South Yemen — now had to take into account a probable significant decline in Soviet strategic support, particularly during times of crisis, as well as in their own ability to maneuver between the superpowers. Secondly, those Arab regimes facing severe or even potential internal problems worried that the upheavals in the Soviet Bloc might encourage opposition groups or even the masses to imitate the new Eastern European model. Third, the PLO and the Palestinians, as well as Arab states hoping to benefit from Israel's troubles with the *intifada*, were concerned that much of the attention of world opinion had moved away from the *intifada* to events in Eastern Europe. And fourth, most Arab states were upset by developments in Soviet policy toward Israel, including the mass immigration of Soviet Jews, and by the resumption of diplomatic relations by East

European states with Israel. This was perceived as the loss of a key strategic allied bloc.

On the other hand, there were in these events at least two sources of encouragement for the Arabs. For one, the Palestinians claimed to view the changes in Eastern Europe as a successful model of national liberation and self-determination by oppressed peoples, that might be emulated in the Territories. And, from the Arab viewpoint, the decline of a Soviet global threat might reduce Israel's value as a strategic asset for the United States, and encourage the American administration to improve its relations with pro-Soviet Arab states, at least partly at the expense of its relations with Israel.

Reconciliation Tendencies: The Main Actors

Most mediation efforts in recent years had focused on *Syria*. Damascus was seen as holding the key to some of the most important schisms within the Arab world — in particular its rifts with Egypt, Iraq and the PLO. Correspondingly, Syria had been at least partially isolated within the Arab world for years: its approach to the Arab-Israel conflict, its Lebanon policy, and its support for Iran in the Gulf War had been widely rejected by most Arab regimes. But Syria retained the power to prevent developments considered damaging to its vital interests, and refused to compromise. Whenever it was difficult explicitly to reject Saudi, Jordanian or Soviet offers of good offices, Syria would, for tactical reasons, agree to participate in mediation efforts with rivals. These usually proved futile.

However, after the mid-1980s, and especially after mid-1988, Syria faced additional constraints that weakened its strategic posture. Above all, it had to cope with severe economic problems that imposed limitations on its capacity to sustain a military buildup, and increased its need for financial aid. The end of hostilities in the Gulf strengthened Iraq and further isolated Syria, the only pro-Iranian Arab state; it also left Iraq relatively free to harass Syria, largely in Lebanon. Nor could Syria prevent the return of Egypt to a leading position — a process that gained momentum after 1987. The PLO, another rival of Syria, was also strengthened significantly by the *intifada*, while Syria found it correspondingly difficult to affect developments pertaining to the Palestinian issue. The intensive efforts made from 1988 to advance the peace process also bypassed Syria, as did the formation (without Syria) of the two Arab economic frameworks in early 1989. And Syria had to cope with new difficulties in Lebanon.

Moreover, Syria's relations with the Soviet Union, a cornerstone of its strategic posture, became increasingly problematic in the Gorbachev era. Disagreements between the two allies regarding issues like military aid and political approach were not new. But in 1989 the Soviets made it clear that they did not support the Syrian interpretation of the concept of strategic parity with Israel, and Moscow adopted policies toward Israel that left the Syrians unhappy. Beyond these specific areas of disagreement, the Syrian leaders probably understood that they could no longer rely on the Soviets for strategic support in case of crisis, at least to the same extent as in the past. Finally, Syria's relations with another ally, Iran, were no less problematic: disagreements emerged time and again, especially regarding Iran's role in Lebanon and its relations with the Shi'ite factions there.

Yet Syria retained very important assets. It held the key to a possible future Arab war against Israel, and continued to allocate high priority to preparations to invoke the military option. And it could still influence the peace process, though perhaps less effectively than in the past. Syria remained the key actor in Lebanon, where any settlement would have to take its interests and influence into account. Indeed, Syria was a central factor in *any* Arab balance of power. Yet despite these basic assets, Syria's maneuverability had been narrowed.

This growing isolation signaled to Syria the need to introduce some changes and flexibility into its inter-Arab policy, in order to return to the Arab mainstream. In January 1989, through Saudi mediation, Syria restored its diplomatic ties with Morocco — they had been severed in July 1986 by Syria to protest against the meeting between King Hassan and Israeli Prime Minister Peres. Then, prior to the Casablanca Summit, convened in May 1989, the Syrians allowed that they would no longer stand in the way of Egypt's return to the Arab League.

The most important development in this regard was undoubtedly the resumption of full diplomatic relations between Syria and Egypt, on December 27, 1989. This in turn led to President Mubarak's visit to Damascus in May 1990 — the first by an Egyptian president since 1977. In view of its political isolation, Syria had concrete reasons to affect a rapprochement with Egypt.

It presumably hoped to obtain more economic aid from the Saudis, and perhaps to improve its relations with the American administration and the Europeans. Then, too, Syria sought to offset the decline in Soviet strategic support, and improve its political maneuverability toward Moscow. Damascus may also have hoped to drive a wedge between Egypt and Iraq, and to mitigate Iraqi pressure, especially in Lebanon. At another level, the reconciliation with Egypt reflected Syria's awareness of a measure of decline in its power to prevent moves within the Arab world, especially regarding the peace process and Egypt's return to the Arab ranks.

By early 1990 the rapprochement between Syria and Egypt remained limited, with important disagreements prevailing between the two regimes. Beyond tactical modifications and a repetition of its willingness to negotiate with Israel on its own terms, the move had not brought about any real change in Syria's position regarding the peace process. Nor was it expected in and of itself to lead to a real change in Syria's stance toward Israel and the Arab-Israel conflict in the near future. For the time being, none of the relevant parties appeared overly interested in Syrian involvement in the peace process, viewing it as, at best, a potential complicating factor. Syria, for its part, indeed hoped for the process to fail, and would presumably oppose any Israeli-Palestinian settlement that neglected its interests. However, one could not now ignore the possibility that Syria might try eventually to put the Golan Heights issue on the agenda.

In contrast with developments in Syrian-Egyptian ties, and despite many attempts at mediation, Syria's desire to break out of its isolation did not bring about any real improvement in its relations with two other rivals, Iraq and the PLO. The rift between Syria and Iraq did not narrow; indeed, it extended to a new front, Lebanon. And fundamental disagreements between Syria and the PLO still existed. However, some contacts between the parties and a few indications of Syrian flexibility toward the PLO became noticeable. By mid-May 1990 the Syrians announced a readiness to meet with Arafat in Damascus. Any further effort by Syria to strengthen its inter-Arab position and affect the peace process might indeed entail improvement in its relationship with the PLO, perhaps through Egyptian mediation.

For *Egypt*, the formal return to Arab affairs, after ten years of isolation following its peace treaty with Israel, was a major success, particularly insofar as it took place on Egypt's own terms, without its making concessions regarding relations with Israel. In fact, the gradual process of Egypt's return had commenced in the mid-1980s: between 1987 and 1990 it reestablished diplomatic relations with all Arab states except Libya and Lebanon. Egypt's reacceptance into the Arab League, and the resumption of its diplomatic ties with Syria, represented the removal of the last formal obstacle to reconciliation with the Arab world.

Even relations between Egypt and Libya improved noticeably. In May 1989 the two countries reopened their border, closed since 1977; Libya promised to compensate the Egyptian workers expelled from its territory in 1985. Mubarak and Qadhafi exchanged visits after October 1989, and agreed to promote economic cooperation and ease border restrictions. In March 1990, a meeting of presidents Mubarak, Assad and Qadhafi at Tobruk symbolized the closing of these circles of controversy between Egypt and its two rivals, even if diplomatic ties between Egypt and Libya were not yet resumed. Moreover, the regime that came to power in Sudan in July 1989 was closer to Egypt than its predecessor, which had canceled the Egyptian-Sudanese joint defense agreement in April 1989.

Internally, reconciliation with the Arab world was important for the regime in Cairo, in that it could prove to its opposition and critics that the peace treaty with Israel had not damaged Egypt's long-term inter-Arab interests. In this regard Egypt's return to the Arab ranks strengthened the structure of peace with Israel. No less important were the external implications: Egypt, with its improved relations with all Arab states, its excellent ties with Washington and the Europeans and, to a lesser extent, with Moscow, and its central role in the peace process, was regaining a leading position in the Arab world. Yet further abroad, in 1989 Mubarak was elected chairman of the Organization of African Unity, thus helping him to become a mediator of African conflicts as well.

Another rising power in the Arab arena in 1989-90 was *Iraq*. Since the advent of the ceasefire in the Gulf in August 1988, quiet largely prevailed on the war front. With few exceptions, the international force policing the ceasefire — the UN Iran-Iraq Military Observer Group (UNIMOG), comprising 350 officers from 15 countries — received complaints of only minor violations. But the ceasefire was the only clause of Security Council Resolution 598 to be carried out. On other relevant issues the parties remained far apart. In particular they differed over priorities: Iran wanted the next step to be the withdrawal of Iraqi troops from 2,600 square kilometers of Iranian territory that they occupied, while Iraq insisted that priority be given to opening up the port of Basra to navigation, which would require the clearing of the Shatt al-Arab waterway. The real issue behind this controversy was the question who would control navigation in the Shatt al-Arab. Minor concessions by both parties regarding order of priorities and the release of a small number of prisoners of war did not effect a breakthrough.

Meanwhile Iraq directed efforts toward internal recovery, while simultaneously reemerging as a prominent actor in inter-Arab politics and a central regional power. Its influence was now based on military strength, including nonconventional capabilities, its economic potential, close political ties with most Arab countries, and the prestige granted to it for containing the Iranian threat. Free from the fighting against Iran, Iraq now enhanced its military ties with allies like Jordan, and exerted efforts to weaken Syria.

Yet significant obstacles were likely to impede this Iraqi effort. For years Iraq would still have to cope with the Iranian threat, its most acute security problem. Iraq's main Arab rival, Syria, still enjoyed a significant capacity to curb much of Baghdad's ambitions. Moreover, the rise of Iraq might collide with the reemergence of another Arab power, Egypt, which enjoyed the support of most moderate Arab regimes. Indeed, disagreements between the two Arab powers were clearly visible in 1989-90, despite their friendly relations: they differed over the peace process, with Iraq not supporting Secretary Baker's initiative and Mubarak's plan; unlike Egypt, Iraq did not support the Taif Accord regarding Lebanon (see below); Egypt was unhappy about Iraqi President Saddam Hussein's militant posture toward Israel, while Iraq was probably concerned about Egyptian-Syrian reconciliation; they differed on issues pertaining to their military industries and economic cooperation; and the brutal treatment of Egyptian workers in Iraq during 1989 also clearly upset Cairo.

Jordan's strategic posture weakened during the period under review. After years of prosperity, it now faced severe economic problems. And after two decades of relative internal tranquility, the regime now had to cope with Islamic fundamentalist opposition as well as limited unrest — both by indigenous Bedouin elements and by Palestinians. Though King Hussein's regime remained relatively stable, the potential for instability certainly increased.

Moreover, Jordan not only lost its central role in the peace process, but the *intifada* posed new risks to the regime, and Jordan saw itself as further threatened by developments in Israel: immigration, and hawkish sentiments. Finally, the return of Egypt to the forefront of Arab ranks, and the end of the Gulf War, denied Jordan some of its inter-Arab assets of the previous decade.

In facing these challenges, the regime's main concern was to consolidate its internal stability on the basis of a new reality — cutting its ties with the West Bank. In the Arab arena, Jordan continued to seek a close relationship with Egypt and — with an eye to containing internal threats and limiting the negative implications of the *intifada* — enhanced its relationship with the PLO. Thus Amman permitted members of Palestinian organizations to return to its territory and reestablish their institutions and operational infrastructure.

But the more interesting development was Jordan's growing economic and political reliance on Iraq. The Iraqis, for their part, viewed Jordan as an important asset in their rivalry with Syria, and in their concomitant bid for leadership in the Arab world. Two key aspects of this developing relationship were the establishment of the Arab Cooperation Council, initiated by Jordan in order to compensate for its strategic weakness and economic difficulties, and growing military cooperation between Jordan and Iraq.

Finally, *Saudi Arabia* maintained its traditional cautious inter-Arab policies. It welcomed the ceasefire between Iraq and Iran, as this reduced tensions and risks of deterioration in the Gulf arena. On the other hand the Saudis were concerned about both the emergence of Iraq as a regional power and the possible increase of radical subversion in the Gulf, now that Iran was free of the war effort. This evidently formed the backdrop to the conclusion of a nonaggression pact between Saudi Arabia and Iraq in March 1989.

Frameworks for Economic Cooperation

Both emerging needs to cope with new challenges and the overall atmosphere of inter-Arab reconciliation were reflected in a trend toward sub-regional Arab communities. In early 1989, two new groupings were formed: the Arab Cooperation Council (ACC), including Egypt, Iraq, Jordan and North Yemen; and the Arab

Maghreb Union (AMU), comprising the five North African states of Mauritania, Morocco, Algeria, Tunisia and Libya. The creation of these frameworks had been preceded in 1981 by the establishment of the Gulf Cooperation Council (GCC), grouping six Persian Gulf countries.

The *GCC*, formed under the impact of the outbreak of war between Iran and Iraq, was aimed at promoting economic and administrative cooperation along the Gulf, and provided a framework for Saudi assistance to the other member states. The formation of the two new blocs was prompted in part by the prospect of greater economic integration in Europe by 1993, which particularly challenged those North African countries with close economic ties to Europe. Both new blocs were intended to generate some form of common market-style economic integration among their member countries.

The concept of the *Arab Cooperation Council* was more limited than that of the Maghreb Union. The ACC agreement, signed on February 16, 1989, regulated economic relations among its members, with an eye to gradually promoting economic integration within the bloc. This would be accomplished by coordinating policies and development plans of its member states and encouraging investments and joint projects. The framework was intended to lead ultimately to the formation of a common market on the pattern of the EEC.

Unlike both the GCC and the AMU, the ACC members emphasized that their aim was merely to coordinate their efforts in the economic and industrial fields, that membership was open to all Arab states, and that it would not constitute an axis directed against anyone. They also stressed that they would not separately initiate joint political activities before coordinating them with other Arab states, and that military coordination was not discussed at all at their meetings.

Nevertheless, the establishment of the ACC had obvious strategic-political implications as well. In fact, leaders of the ACC acknowledged that in their meetings they discussed political issues, like the Palestinian problem and the peace process, the Lebanese crisis, and the relationship between Iraq and Iran. The ACC's formation highlighted the isolation of Syria, which remained, with South Yemen, the only Arab state outside the circle of sub-regional groupings. It worried Saudi Arabia, which feared a strong bloc that incorporated four states on its land or sea borders, and particularly strengthened Iraq. Indeed, Egypt had to reassure the Saudis that the ACC was not intended as a regional counterweight to its influence.

Despite the attention focused on the ACC, its initial impact was limited, and the framework appeared to lack real essence. The early economic achievements of the group were minor. The road to integration of widely disparate and overwhelmingly debt-ridden economies — imbalanced in terms of their wealth, resources and political systems — would be long. Although some agreements were concluded among the ACC members, the scope for constructive cooperation seemed limited.

No less important were the differences between the political approaches of the member states. We have already noted some of the areas of disagreement between Egypt and Iraq. In addition, while Egypt relied mainly on the US in its foreign policy as well as economic and military ties, Iraq was linked to Western Europe and the Soviet Bloc in its arms deals and military production. Egypt appeared to prefer a framework for political-economic cooperation, while Iraq put the emphasis on political-military aspects. Thus Egypt probably had its own reservations regarding military cooperation between Iraq and Jordan. All in all, Egypt seemed to be the least enthusiastic with regard to the prospects of the framework.

The other group, the *Arab Maghreb Union*, created on February 17, 1989, had a wider scope. It constituted a loose federation of sovereign countries with a number of joint bodies and committees, at various levels, for consultation and coordination regarding mutually beneficial economic and social arrangements. While the main purpose of the AMU was to promote economic integration, its members also agreed not to tolerate on their territory any activity or organization aimed at undermining the security or territorial integrity of another member state — thereby implicitly supporting Morocco against the Polisario. They also agreed to consider a military attack on one of them as an attack on all — thus implicitly backing Libya in its disputes in Chad and with the US — and undertook not to join a military alliance hostile to any member state. The Maghreb leaders differed, however, over what form the union would take. While Morocco and Algeria wanted to begin cautiously, Tunisia and Libya preferred rapid moves toward a union similar to the European Community; Qadhafi even insisted that it should be a step toward comprehensive unity.

The formation of the AMU reflected the growing need felt among the Maghreb states to strengthen ties in an attempt to cope with the consequences of European economic unity in 1993. It also appeared to reflect the diminishing impact of old quarrels and tensions that kept North African countries divided. Indeed, the substance of intra-Maghreb politics had changed considerably since 1988. Algeria and Morocco resumed diplomatic relations in May 1988, after a break of 12 years, and reached agreement on ways of ending the Sahara War. Some progress was made, in negotiations between Morocco and the Polisario, toward a solution of the dispute in the Western Sahara. Libya strengthened its bilateral ties with both Algeria and Tunisia and resumed relations with Morocco. Relations between Libya and Chad improved also. In August 1989 they signed an agreement to end their border dispute over the Aouzou Strip, occupied by Libya since 1978. Under the agreement, Libya would withdraw its forces from Aouzou, and the issue of sovereignty would be decided at the International Court of Justice, if the parties could not resolve it bilaterally within a year. Beyond the Maghreb arena, in mid-1990 Libya and Jordan also resumed their diplomatic relations, cut in 1985.

A final remark is in order regarding another union — that between North and South Yemen. Following the bloody upheaval in South Yemen in 1986 its regime — the only Marxist regime in the Arab world — was considerably weakened. Facing severe economic problems as well as internal political pressures, it undertook political liberalization. Internal weaknesses, aggravated by the decline in the late '80s of Soviet strategic and ideological support, obliged South Yemen to accept some North Yemeni conditions for creating a union, rejected by it in the past. Thus, beginning in late 1989, the two Yemens concluded a series of agreements designed to move them toward union. Obviously, a merger of two such different states faced considerable problems. Moreover, Saudi Arabia retained its own reservations about the emergence of a stronger Yemenite entity on its southern border.

Military Cooperation

Military cooperation among Arab states was relatively limited throughout the '80s. The main fields of cooperation were the exchange of intelligence, training and sometimes participation in exercises, some assistance in military production, and the transfer of small quantities of weapons systems for various needs. Most of this cooperation took place, on a bilateral basis, among Egypt, Jordan, Iraq and Saudi Arabia, as well as between Syria and Libya. The military industries of Egypt and Iraq, for example, cooperated on a limited basis during the late '80s, but had apparently broken ties by 1990. This and similar instances of inter-Arab cooperation fell far short of building any sort of military coalition against Israel. Indeed, by early 1990 the Arab states had probably not even taken any initial direct steps toward creating such a coalition.

One important development in this regard did, however, occur in the relationship between Iraq and Jordan. Limited military cooperation between these two neighbors developed throughout the 1980s. It included joint exercises, especially of the respective air forces; transfer to Jordan of military equipment, such as Chieftain tanks captured from Iran and products of Iraq's military industry; Iraqi military briefings to Jordan; cooperation in military training; and visits by Iraqi field commanders to Jordan, including to the border with Israel.

Beginning in 1989, this cooperation developed further, especially between the two air forces. In July 1989 Iraqi planes flew reconnaissance flights along the border with Israel. In late 1989 Iraq deployed surface-to-surface missile launchers close to its border with Jordan — presumably with Jordanian consent. And in early 1990 the Iraqi and Jordanian air forces created a joint squadron, to be located in Iraq and financed by the Iraqi government. Its immediate justification was that it saved money for Jordan and allowed Amman to cease its cutbacks on training hours for Jordanian pilots.

In developing this cooperation, Iraq was seeking to improve its early warning capabilities toward Israel. On the political level, it serves Iraq's interest to manifest more involvement in Arab affairs; by tightening its ties with Jordan, Baghdad played the Jordanian card against Syria. Beyond a likely deference to Iraqi pressure, Jordan's motivation for developing military cooperation was twofold: the hope to obtain Iraqi assistance to ease its economic distress; and a perceived need for Iraqi backing to face what Jordan saw as an Israeli plot to bring about the emergence of a Palestinian political entity in Jordan.

By mid-1990 Jordanian-Iraqi military cooperation remained relatively limited and defensive in nature. For Israel, the 'red line' in this regard might be Jordanian willingness to deploy Iraqi troops — either ground or air forces — on Jordanian territory, especially facing Israel. Such a deployment has traditionally had an offensive potential vis-a-vis Israel, and would thus be perceived as a threat. Jordan was undoubtedly aware of this 'red line,' and in mid-1990 King Hussein reportedly expressed his readiness to observe it. But one could not ignore the possibility that Jordan's growing weakness might change its order of priorities in the longer range, and that military cooperation between Iraq and Jordan could be extended, perhaps to include other Arab countries as well. Certainly, were inter-Arab political conditions to bring about the creation of a military coalition against Israel, Jordanian-Iraqi cooperation would be at the heart of its infrastructure. Indeed, in Jordan there were voices — in the new parliament and in the media — calling for Arab military cooperation against Israel. Clearly then, Iraqi-Jordanian cooperation, if enhanced, bore a potential for future friction with Israel.

Lebanon: Ever-widening Complexity

Several inter-Arab dimensions were directly linked in 1989 to the Lebanese crisis: intensive Arab involvement, Syrian weakness, and Iraq's growing role. This, against a backdrop of an extraordinarily high level of violence.

In late 1988 the Lebanese crisis entered a new, complex phase. On September 23, 1988, his last day in office, President Amin Gemayel nominated an interim military cabinet, headed by the army commander, General Michel Aoun, to fill the functions of the presidency until the election of a new president. The incumbent Muslim prime minister, Salim al-Hoss, did not recognize Aoun's cabinet, and the country found itself with two competing governments. As a result, constitutional institutions ceased functioning, and the partition of Lebanon among sectoral enclaves was deepened. This formed the backdrop for the struggle that ensued in Lebanon from early 1989: between the Syrians, seeking to extend their authority over all of Lebanon, including the Christian enclave, and the Maronite Christians, aiming at formalizing the existing partition between their relatively independent enclave and the rest of Muslim Lebanon, now largely controlled by the Syrians.

The struggle erupted in mid-March 1989, when Aoun imposed a naval blockade on Muslim militia-run ports and launched a "war of liberation" against the Syrian presence in Lebanon. Aoun probably hoped to refocus international attention on Lebanon, bring about western intervention on his behalf, and make the Syrian withdrawal the main issue pertaining to the Lebanese crisis. The outcome was an unprecedented deterioration of violence, initially between Aoun's army and the Muslim militias, followed by the intensive intervention of Syrian artillery in the fighting. The Syrian bombardments were accompanied by a naval blockade and partial ground blockade upon the Christian enclave, to prevent the supply of arms to the Christians.

Syrian-Muslim pressure on the Christians was heavy, but not sufficient to prevent them from further consolidating their independence and establishing separate authorities and organizations. The Christians' main problem was that, beyond the constant siege and daily distress they had to cope with, they were divided internally, mainly between Aoun's army and Samir Jeajea's Lebanese Forces. Aoun's contingent, while stronger, was not able to enforce its authority over the Lebanese Forces. Though the two factions were united against the Syrians and the Muslims, once the immediate Syrian threat seemed to have passed they battled one another over political leadership and control of economic assets.

The struggle over the Christian enclave's autonomy projected further instability into the Lebanese system, and introduced additional actors, for whom Lebanon was a convenient theater in which to act out their rivalries. Moreover, alongside the Christians' conflict, other struggles took place as well — most notably, between the Shi'ite factions, Amal and Hizballah, with the involvement of both Syria and Iran.

Syria's isolation was well reflected in the Lebanese arena. During 1989 Damascus had to cope not only with the Lebanese complex itself, but also with Arab pressures and attempts to undermine its position there. These efforts culminated in the Casablanca Summit, where a group of Arab states headed by Iraq focused attention on the issue of Syrian withdrawal from Lebanon. This was followed by the report of the Arab Tripartite Committee, formed by the summit on July 31, 1989, which explicitly and publicly placed much of the blame for its failure to solve Lebanon's problems on Syria's refusal to agree on a timetable for withdrawing its forces.

Yet despite these constraints, Syria's position in Lebanon did not weaken significantly. Damascus managed to engineer the Taif

Accord, signed by Lebanese Christian and Muslim parliament members under the auspices of the Arab League Peace Plan announced in mid-September 1989. The plan was something of a reversal of earlier proposals, and was much more favorable to Syria. It included political reforms that reduced the traditional privileges enjoyed by the Christians, and it stated that Syrian troops would remain in place for a two-year period after enaction of the reforms and the formation of a national unity government. Only then would Syria be required to concentrate its troops in the Biq'a Valley and negotiate a timetable for withdrawal. The plan did not even explicitly mention Syrian involvement in the fighting around the Christian enclave. In fact, it recognized Syria as the main power in Lebanon and implicitly legitimized the special relationship between Syria and Lebanon and the Syrian military presence at least in the Biq'a.

Still, Syria had to pay a high price for defending its position in Lebanon. The Christian challenge caused it incrementally to increase its military presence in Lebanon, and in November 1989 it came close to launching a ground attack on the Christian enclave. But because of the political and military hazards involved in a Syrian invasion, Damascus demurred, Aoun's leadership did not collapse, and he continued to pose a challenge to Damascus.

Secondly, Syria was obliged to accept the involvement of other Arab actors, and particularly the Tripartite Committee, in Lebanese affairs. And Syria's acceptance of the Taif Accord implicitly involved an indirect commitment to withdraw sometime in the future, even if the Syrians did not claim to understand it this way. Meanwhile, some of Syria's few allies — primarily Iran and Amal — rejected the Taif Accord.

Further, Iraq entered the Lebanese conflict on the side of the Christians, seeking to punish Syria for its alliance with Iran during the Gulf War. The Iraqi involvement in Lebanon had two aspects: Baghdad supplied large quantities of arms to the Christians, and it made a major effort to bring about an Arab decision calling for Syrian withdrawal from Lebanon. The Iraqi effort gained wide support at the Casablanca Summit, but Syrian willingness to support the summit resolution on the Palestinian issue blunted the anti-Syrian draft on Lebanon. After the conclusion of the Taif Accord, Iraqi involvement in Lebanese affairs was reduced considerably; the Iraqis apparently realized that, in light of general Arab support for the Taif Accord, further encouragement of Aoun would be politically too costly.

Iraq's rival, Iran, had a longer history of involvement in Lebanese affairs. In 1989-90 Tehran remained mainly concerned with increasing its influence within the Shi'ite community, partly at the expense of Syria, and with mediating between Amal and Hizballah. Though Iran improved its relations with Amal, the collapse of the Amal-Hizballah Damascus agreement was a setback. Furthermore the fighting between Amal and Hizballah, and Iranian reservations regarding the Taif Accord aggravated the already problematic nature of the Syrian-Iranian relationship.

All in all, Arab involvement in the Lebanese crisis in 1989 was much more intensive than in previous years, and represented the most serious Arab effort to date to effect a solution. Despite initial disappointments and failures, the Tripartite Committee of three Arab heads of state formed by the Casablanca Summit managed to produce a settlement plan, approved by Syria and most Arab states, signed by Lebanese Christian and Muslim parliament members, and backed internationally.

Non-Arab international involvement in the crisis was also more intense than in previous years. The leading power in this regard was France, the Lebanese Christians' traditional protector. When Syria appeared set to attack the Christian enclave in August 1989, France sent a flotilla, including the aircraft carrier Foch, to the Lebanese coast. It followed with its own three-point "peace plan," calling for a ceasefire, political reform and withdrawal from Lebanon of Syrian and Israeli forces. France also took diplomatic steps aimed at preventing hostilities, and at mediating between factions within the Christian community.

The Soviet Union was also active in Lebanese affairs, seeking to promote a joint effort, with Washington or with Paris, to mediate the crisis. And the US administration played a role in restraining Syrian military activity against the Christians, in limiting arms supplies to Aoun, and in encouraging Arab states to intervene in the crisis. Still, the two great powers' influence over events in Lebanon remained relatively limited.

Looking ahead, the chances of implementing the Taif Accord appeared slim. While some parties remained committed to the accord, as it was the only settlement plan on the agenda, several other main Lebanese actors — Aoun, Amal and Hizballah — rejected it. Meanwhile, in the fighting in Lebanon most factions were weakened, yet still hoped to gain additional assets by force.

Conclusion

A number of general implications of these trends are worthy of note. First, by 1990 the main concern of most Arab states remained their internal stability, rather than the Arab-Israel conflict. This concern had generated some changes in inter-Arab relations — mainly, a trend toward reconciliation and developing frameworks for economic cooperation. In parallel, the two key factors in inter-Arab politics during the past decade — the Egyptian-Israeli peace treaty and the Gulf War — were losing their divisive effect. On the other hand, the reemergence of both Egypt and Iraq in Arab politics might encourage open competition for leadership between them, with Syria possibly involved as well. Iraq, in particular, held to an aggressive policy that threatened stability in the Arab world.

Syria itself faced growing problems: economic distress; its relative isolation within the Arab world; the rising power of Iraq and Egypt; efforts to advance the peace process that were viewed as contrary to Syrian interests; and the decline in Soviet strategic support. Moreover the Lebanese crisis, by demanding considerable Syrian resources and energy, further weakened Syria rather than strengthening it. Taken together, these factors reduced Damascus' deterrent and preventive power within the Arab world, and required more flexibility, including toward the peace process. Thus they might somewhat reduce, though not eliminate, the risks of a Syrian-Israeli conflict in the near future.

Finally, the gradually rising power of Islamic fundamentalism contributed to the instability of Arab regimes, and reduced their freedom of action. The combined impact of Islamic radicalism and socioeconomic distress could have severe implications for internal unrest. Moreover, Islamic fundamentalism represented a radical approach in the context of the Arab-Israel conflict, insofar as it refused to recognize Israel's right to exist and rejected compromise. Were the Islamic camp to gather additional strength, this might reduce the dominance of the pragmatic approach in the Arab world and pose another stumbling block to the peace process.

The Iraqi invasion of Kuwait abruptly changed much of the inter-Arab scene. The invasion shocked the Arab world by violating one of its basic ground rules: for the first time, one independent and sovereign Arab state had conquered and annexed another. This caused genuine fear, especially among the Gulf states, that if Iraqi military power were not broken, or at least if Iraq were not forced to evacuate Kuwait, then reliance on military force could become an established pattern of behavior in resolving inter-Arab disputes.

Moreover, the invasion introduced a new and significant divisive element into the Arab arena, just as it was recovering from the effects of the Egyptian-Israeli peace treaty and the Iran-Iraq War. The invasion seriously tainted the atmosphere of reconciliation that had begun to emerge in inter-Arab relations. The attempts to construct a new vanguard around Egypt, Iraq and Jordan, in the form of the Arab Cooperation Council, along with frequent high level consultations, totally collapsed. The implicit rivalry between Egypt and Iraq now came to the surface, as a new realignment began to emerge in the Arab system.

A coalition grouping Egypt, Syria and Saudi Arabia now led most of the Arab world. Syria emerged, to a large extent, from its partial isolation, by increasing cooperation with Egypt and sending troops to Saudi Arabia. Iraq replaced Syria as the extreme militant Arab state, and was largely isolated within the Arab system, though it enjoyed the partial support of Jordan, Yemen, Libya and the PLO. Jordan, weak internally and increasingly dependent on Iraq economically, sought to maneuver between the blocs; its tendency to support Iraq eroded its relations with Egypt, Saudi Arabia and Syria.

Finally, the Arab world faced an unprecedented international military intervention, and the prospect of a military clash in the Gulf and perhaps beyond. While most Arab states sought the collapse of Iraqi power, they were more ambivalent over the possibility of an American-led military operation against Iraq. Hence their attempts, ineffectual in September and October, to end the crisis within the Arab framework; hence, too, the dispatch of Arab forces to Saudi Arabia.

However the crisis ended, it seemed highly likely that its outcome would be a different Middle East in general, and a different system of inter-Arab relations in particular.

3. Middle East Missile and CBW Proliferation: Patterns, Trends, Ramifications

by Shai Feldman

In recent years the Middle East has become an arena of dramatic developments in the realm of missile and chemical-biological weapons proliferation. These developments and their strategic consequences were most blatantly reflected in the use of chemical weapons and surface-to-surface missiles in the Iran-Iraq War. Indeed, the general perception that Iraq's use of chemical weapons was militarily successful in stopping large-scale Iranian infantry attacks, and that Iraq's extensive ballistic missile attacks on Tehran and other cities helped induce Iran to accept a ceasefire, may provide a strong incentive for other states in the region to emulate Iraq's capabilities. The likelihood and possible implications of further proliferation deserve much careful attention.

This chapter begins by examining recent trends in the proliferation of missiles, and chemical and biological weapons, in the Middle East. Next, an attempt is made to ascertain the implications of current and anticipated proliferation trends — for the security of the region's states, for the superpowers involved in the Middle East, and for the region's general stability. This is followed by an effort to assess whether the decade of the 1990s may present mitigating circumstances that might alter current proliferation trends. Finally, we evaluate the likelihood that arms control and confidence-building measures could be designed to limit the flow of such arms to the region, or to diminish the negative effects of this proliferation.[1]

Recent Proliferation Trends

Neither surface-to-surface missiles nor chemical weapons are new to the Middle East. Indeed, the armed forces of Egypt and Syria have been equipped with Soviet-made FROG-7 rockets and Scud B missiles since the 1970s; Syria employed the former and Egypt employed both during the 1973 Yom Kippur War. This was preceded in the mid-1960s by Egypt's limited use of chemical weapons during the war in Yemen.

These precedents notwithstanding, the Middle East witnessed dramatic developments in the realm of missile and chemical-biological weapons proliferation during the 1980s. Until the early-1980s, only missiles of relatively low accuracy, such as the 280 km range Scud B, were supplied to some of the region's states. Since then, however, Syria and North Yemen acquired more accurate 80-100 km range SS-21s. At the same time, missiles with a far greater operational range proliferated in the region. The best example of this is Saudi Arabia's Chinese-made DF-3A missile, estimated to have a range of some 2500-3000 km.

Until recently the Soviet Union was the sole supplier of surface-to-surface missiles to the Arab states, including Algeria, Egypt, Iraq, Libya, North Yemen, South Yemen, and Syria. Lately, other suppliers have made their appearance, such as China with its sale of some 8-12 launchers and 120 DF-3A medium-range surface-to-surface missiles to Saudi Arabia.[2]

If until recently the Arab states could equip themselves with surface-to-surface missiles only by importing them, after the mid-1980s a number of the region's states began to develop a capacity for indigenous missile production. Iraq, for example, deployed its 650 km range al-Hussein and 900 km al-Abbas missiles. The former was employed during the final stages of the Iran-Iraq War; the latter was first tested in April 1988. Both comprised some modification and upgrading of the Soviet Scud Bs, and in this sense their development and production could not be considered entirely indigenous. This was also true of the first instance of a multi-national joint venture for the design of a ballistic missile: Argentinean-Egyptian-Iraqi cooperation in developing the 800-1000 km range Condor-II (designated in Egypt as the Badr-2000) missile in the late 1980s.

Iraq's Al-Abd satellite launch vehicle, first tested in December 1989, and its Tammuz-1 2000 km range ballistic missile, scheduled to be tested on Mauritanian territory, were probably the product of enhanced local design and development efforts. With the assistance of foreign experts, the Iraqis were by 1990 reported to be developing two additional surface-to-surface missiles: one with a range of 250-300 km, and the other with a range of 500-600 km. Both were said to be derivatives of Condor-II technologies.

As noted earlier, first-generation chemical warfare agents, including nerve agents, were employed in the Middle East in the mid-1960s. According to US estimates, Egypt conducted some 32 chemical weapons attacks in Yemen between 1963 and 1967. However, since World War I and the Italian conquest of Ethiopia, the Iran-Iraq War comprised the first instance in which chemical weapons were used on a large scale as an integral part of military operations carried out against regular enemy forces. Indeed, chemical munitions were used by Iraq not only against advancing Iranian infantry forces, but also against civilians, notably in the town of Halabja on the Iraqi side of Kurdistan in 1988.

Until the Halabja attack, which coincided with the final stage of the Iran-Iraq War, world public opinion barely reacted to Iraq's use of chemical weapons. Neither during nor after the war was Iraq sanctioned for violating the 1925 Geneva Protocol by using such weapons. Thus, indirectly, their use was tolerated by the international community.

Turning to delivery systems, until recently none of the Arab states was equipped with sophisticated means for long-range delivery of chemical munitions and biological agents. The delivery of such munitions to enemy population centers therefore depended on the penetration capabilities of these states' air forces. Lately, however, a number of the region's states developed the capacity to fit surface-to-surface missiles with nonconventional warheads.

Until recently the 1973 Yom Kippur War offered the only precedent for the use of surface-to-surface missiles in the Middle East. Yet even that war evidenced only limited and selective employment of FROG-7 rockets, and only a few launchings of Scud Bs, all directed at military targets. In contrast, particularly during the closing stages of the Iran-Iraq War, these missiles, mounted with conventional warheads, were used massively, and primarily against civilian populations.

Finally, the possibility that Iraq's massive missile bombardment of Tehran helped compel Iran to accept a ceasefire implies that for the first time such "strategic" weapons may have made an important contribution to deciding the outcome of a Middle East war.

In the Middle East and beyond, these dramatic developments have left a clear mark. In response, the region's states have adopted various combinations of the following modes of action:

Horizontal proliferation. Clearly, the acquisition of surface-to-surface missiles and chemical-biological weapons by some states propelled others to follow suit. For example, the massive use of surface-to-surface missiles by Iraq and Iran caused Saudi Arabia to import missiles from China; and Baghdad's modification and upgrading of such missiles led Tehran to produce its own Iran-130, Iran-160, and Iran 200 missiles.[3] Hence, the multiplier effect of proliferation.

Vertical proliferation. This refers to the perceived imperative to respond to the growing missile threat by developing missiles of higher accuracy and longer range, as well as more demanding nonconventional capabilities, e.g. in the realms of chemical, biological, and nuclear weapons. Thus the wide scale use of surface-to-surface missiles in the Iran-Iraq War seems to have induced Israel to intensify its efforts in this realm. This was exemplified by the reported testing in 1989 of a 1500 km range Israeli ballistic missile.[4]

Active defense. The growing threat of devastating missile attacks generated considerable interest in erecting defenses against short- and medium-range missiles. In Israel this led to the establishment of an Anti-Tactical Ballistic Missile program, whereby the high-altitude long-range Arrow anti-missile missile was developed — a program that was integrated into strategic cooperation between Israel and the United States, and was largely financed by America's SDI program. Iranian missile attacks on Baghdad are said to have induced Iraq to develop and test, with foreign assistance, the Faw-1 missile, which it claimed was an ATBM.

Passive defenses. This includes measures ranging from the distribution of chemical protective gear to civilians and soldiers, to the hardening and/or sealing of key civilian and military installations against missile and/or chemical/biological weapons attack. For example, Israel is known to have stockpiled protective gear in sufficient quantities to permit its distribution in wartime to the state's entire population.[5]

If properly applied, passive defensive measures are likely to reduce the effects of chemical weapons substantially. This was illustrated by a number of simulations conducted by Israel's defense forces.[6] However, a measure of uncertainty remains regarding the results of a possible interaction between large-scale chemical attacks and passive defense measures in major population centers; the estimates produced by simulations are highly sensitive to the assumptions guiding their calculation.

Preventive and preemptive offense. Fear of the consequences of missile attacks and use of chemical/biological weapons may result in a strong incentive to preempt relevant adversary capabilities or to attack these capabilities before they are fully developed. This may be done by either air bombardment or accurate surface-to-surface and air-to-surface missile attacks against enemy missile sites and/or chemical/biological weapons production or storage facilities. For example, a senior Israeli official stated in 1988 that in a future war, Israel might have to preempt the Saudi DF-3A missile launchers.[7]

The temptation to preempt an adversary's missiles prior to the initiation of hostilities may be heightened by the estimate that destroying these systems afterwards is likely to be more demanding and costly. Locating missile launchers will be more difficult under 'fog of battle' conditions, and after the enemy has taken action to prevent their being targeted by employing mobility and extensive use of decoys. Moreover, after an adversary ground-attack is initiated, one's air force is likely to be presented with numerous competing tasks and missions, some of them enjoying a higher priority. In this sense the initiation of warfare might generate new constraints upon one's ability to muster the assets required to destroy enemy missile launchers and missiles in storage.

Deterrence. This refers to the effort to prevent a combined missile and chemical weapons attack by presenting the adversary with a serious counter-threat. Thus, for example, Israel's extreme vulnerability to such a combined attack against its civilian population led its senior defense leaders to threaten that its response would be tenfold more devastating.[8] Through such statements, Israel permitted its Arab neighbors to ponder the nature of its threat. These speculations were reinforced by a variety of demonstrations of Israel's "long-arm" capacities.[9]

Ramifications

These dramatic developments in the proliferation of ballistic missiles and chemical/biological weapons in the Middle East, coupled with the manifest and anticipated reactions of the region's states, present those states with considerable ramifications. First and foremost, they imply that the human costs entailed in any future Middle East war may be very high, since substantial punishment may be visited upon the respective civilian populations as well as the armies of the states involved.

Secondly, because ballistic missiles allow a "vertical indirect approach," bypassing the battlefield and delivering highly lethal munitions to the adversary's population centers, the capacity to punish is becoming increasingly independent of battlefield results. Indeed, as Carus points out, in such a mode, ballistic missiles — even if conventionally armed — can be highly destructive despite their limited payload and low accuracy. Due to the considerable mass of the missiles themselves upon impact, in the Iran-Iraq War they damaged entire streets of shops and houses in Tehran "seemingly out of all proportion to the size of the warhead used." Thus it now becomes possible to extract substantial costs from an adversary's population despite the manifest poor performance by one's own military in combat.

Then too, the nature of the arms race is changing. By investing disproportionate resources in the development and/or acquisition of missiles and/or chemical/biological weapons, general quantitative as well as qualitative gaps can be closed. Thus Iraq could match the quantitatively superior Iranians through the application of long-range artillery rockets and ballistic missiles. In parallel, Syria might hope to exploit "windows" in Israel's operational plans — such as its dependence on the rapid mobilization of its air force and ground forces reserves — by the selective use of highly accurate surface-to-surface missiles such as the SS-21s, armed with conventional or chemical weapons, against Israeli airfields and mobilization centers.

Further, the extended ranges of some of the missiles entering the Middle East might result in far greater interaction among the region's various conflict arenas. A system entering the region in the context of one conflict might, due to its extended range, present a threat to countries in another conflict arena that is still within the general boundaries of the Middle East. For example, surface-to-surface missiles and chemical weapons originally developed by Iraq in the context of its conflict with Iran, soon comprised a security threat to Israel. Subsequently this led Iraq to judge that Israel might attempt to conduct a preventive attack against Iraqi capabilities. Thus activities in the region's two conflict arenas became interconnected. Consequently, in future it seems likely to become even more difficult to isolate the region's diverse conflicts and to attempt their separate resolution.

On the other hand, fear that a future war in the Middle East might entail enormous costs could cause the region's states to conduct a more careful examination of all possible ramifications before initiating violence. Thus, general deterrence in the region might be enhanced, resulting in a lower likelihood of war.

Conversely, anxieties regarding possible missile and chemical-biological attacks could generate increased incentives to preempt, thus leading to growing fear among the states possessing these capabilities lest their weapons be struck preemptively by their adversaries' first strike. This in turn further strengthens incentives for the early use of such weapons, in an escalatory spiral. Thus general "crisis stability" in the region might diminish significantly.

As a result of the new threats that missiles and chemical-biological weapons present, as well as the new imperatives they create, the costs of national defense for the region's states might also increase dramatically. The incentive to emulate and improve missile and chemical/biological capabilities; the necessity of erecting effective passive and active defenses against such weapons; and the imperative of creating preemptive offensive options and enhancing deterrence, would all entail enormous expenditures.

An excellent example of this trend is the substantial cost entailed in the possible deployment of an effective ATBM system. This is the case despite the fact that defenses against conventional or even chemically-armed missiles need not be leak-proof to be effective. The costs involved are associated not only with the missiles developed in the framework of these programs, but also with the complex command, control, communications, and advanced and sophisticated surveillance and tracking systems required to allow ATBMs to acquire their targets.

The proliferation of ballistic missiles and chemical-biological weapons might also change the distribution of power between the region's states on the one hand, and the superpowers involved in the Middle East on the other. Indeed, as a growing number of the region's states equip themselves with enhanced capabilities that threaten, inter alia, the superpowers' forces and facilities in and near the Middle East, the latter's freedom of action in the region might be curtailed. Moreover, as Middle East states increasingly acquire extended-range missiles, the superpowers seem likely to fear lest their own national security be jeopardized. This was already evidenced in the Soviets' strong reaction to Israel's reported testing in 1989 of a 1300-1500 km range ballistic missile, and in America's more frequent expressions of concern regarding the threat of ballistic missiles and chemical and biological weapons in the third world.

The Threat in the 1990s: Some Mitigating Circumstances

While most of the developments and consequences portrayed above seem likely to continue well into the 1990s, a number of countervailing forces might mitigate their intensity and constrain their ramifications. Some of these mitigating factors already began to affect developments at the close of the 1980s.

Thus in early 1990 most Middle East states were confronting increasing economic difficulties. These resulted from a combination of factors: the decline of oil prices during the second half of the 1980s; numerous faulty investments and expenditures made during the euphoria of the oil boom of the mid-1970s; enormous defense expenditures by the region's states throughout the past two decades; the continued population explosion — particularly in Egypt — and the resulting demand for basic foodstuffs and simple consumer goods; the effects of the enormous costs of the Iran-Iraq War on the economies of both countries; the structural economic crisis in Jordan and Syria, with the particular costs of the latter's occupation forces in Lebanon added to the bill; and the competing pressures on the national budget of the State of Israel, specifically those resulting from the need to absorb a large wave of immigration from the Soviet Union.

In turn, these economic circumstances could place new constraints on the ability of the region's states to maintain the past pace of the Middle East arms race. Accordingly, the propensity to acquire or develop and produce ballistic missiles and chemical-biological weapons might also diminish.

Then too, the region's states seemed to be losing their appetite for some of the most heated conflicts with which the Middle East had been afflicted for quite some time. Thus, by early 1990 many Arab states had come tacitly to accept Israel's existence, however grudgingly, as a permanent feature of the Middle East. Moreover, even as new sources of regional conflict appeared on the horizon — such as Egypt's and Syria's respective concerns regarding the security of their water resources — serious efforts were underway among the parties involved to resolve these problems without resort to arms.

The end of the superpowers' Cold War also affected the modes of their competition in the Middle East. In particular, their propensity to transfer huge quantities of arms to their respective allies as a primary mode of superpower competition began to diminish.

The superpowers' new attitude could be observed clearly in the Soviet Union's approach toward its traditional clients in the region. Thus, Syria was increasingly being urged by the Soviets to replace its quest for strategic parity with Israel, with a more modest effort to achieve "defensive sufficiency;" to abandon its commitment to a military solution of its conflict with Israel; and to join the so-called Middle East peace process. This in turn presumably affected the Soviets' propensity to supply the Syrians with "strategic systems," since such supplies signal quite the opposite message.

Indeed, the Soviet Union's own economic problems might dictate that it restrict its arms exports to cash sales. Given the prevailing economic circumstances in the Middle East, the region's states — Syria, the Yemens — were likely to confront increasing difficulties in meeting Moscow's new demand for hard currency payments.

Finally, if the Gorbachev regime were to survive, the growing cooperation between the superpowers would ultimately affect the Middle East as well. This might be reflected not only in superpower cooperation in the realms of crisis management and conflict resolution, but also in helping the region's states to establish a Middle East arms control regime. In this context, joint attempts to stem the flow of ballistic missiles and chemical-biological weapons to the region could be expected. This is particularly the case since, as we have noted, the Soviet Union perceives its own national security to be affected by such proliferation. One possibility is that Moscow would not only adhere to the stipulations of the MTCR regime but also cooperate with Washington in attempting to expand its scope.

Thus a number of important factors may combine to stem the pace of the proliferation of ballistic missiles and chemical-biological weapons in the Middle East and to mitigate its effects and ramifications. Yet it is just as likely that the trends characterizing the 1980s could continue well into the 1990s. Indeed, most conflicts with which the Middle East was afflicted in early 1990 seemed likely to continue into the 1990s, and new sources of conflict seemed likely to arise.

Also, it is far from clear that proliferation would necessarily be slowed by the growing economic difficulties in the region. Indeed, quite the opposite may be equally plausible: namely, that cuts in costly conventional forces induced by growing economic constraints would, in turn, lead to even greater reliance on less costly nonconventional forces. This may apply particularly to chemical and biological weapons.

Then, too, it is far from clear that the diminished intensity of superpower competition in the Middle East would necessarily lead to a more pacified region. Here, again, the opposite effect seems equally likely: namely, that the end of the Cold War, with its associated 'rules of behavior,' would lead to an increasingly uncertain environment. In turn, enormous miscalculations leading to unintended violence might result. In the aftermath of such violence, the propensity to acquire arms might only increase.

Also, it is not entirely certain that the Soviet Union's new approach would necessarily stem its contribution to the flow of arms to the Middle East. Indeed, in 1989-90 the Soviets continued to provide Syria with state-of-the-art systems such as the Su-24 strike aircraft and the MiG-29 interceptor, and it was also expected to provide Arab air forces in the not-too-distant future with Su-27 strike aircraft and MI-28 Havoc attack helicopters.

Finally, even if the transfer of Soviet arms to the region were slowed by 1990, it was far from clear that the United States, the Western Europeans, and other suppliers such as Brazil and Argentina would match Moscow's new restraint. Indeed, competing interests were likely to encourage these producers to do quite the opposite.

Can Arms Control Help?

The risks entailed in the possible continuation, if not exacerbation, of present proliferation trends, necessarily require that we ask whether the application of arms control measures in the Middle East may help slow the pace of proliferation of ballistic missiles and chemical-biological weapons in the region. Unfortunately, an examination of this issue does not yield excessively optimistic results. The following constitutes merely a preliminary list of the difficulties that would confront any effort to control the flow of weapons and sensitive materiel to the region.

The first concerns the multiplicity of active recipients and actual and potential suppliers and the competition among them. Whether some of these suppliers, particularly the Western Europeans, would be willing to limit their sales of arms, sensitive materiel, and high technologies to Middle East states — thus giving up a critical export market — remains very much an open question.

A related problem concerns the asymmetric and often conflicting interests of the region's potential arms suppliers. Whereas some 30 years ago sophisticated arms could reach the Middle East almost exclusively from the advanced industrial states, such weapons or the relevant technologies are now supplied by third world states as well (e.g., Brazil, Argentina, North Korea and the PRC). The acute financial difficulties of these states, inducing them to pursue every possibility of earning hard currency, makes their cooperation with arms control initiatives extremely difficult to obtain.

This problem is compounded by the multiplicity of weapons systems and subsystems, and the lengthy list of sensitive materials and dual-use items, that must be covered by any effort to limit such arms acquisitions. Hence, tailoring effective Middle East arms control proposals is exponentially more difficult than reaching bilateral US-Soviet nuclear arms control agreements.

Then too, the growing capabilities for indigenous arms production, often involving complex overt or covert multi-national joint ventures and technological transfer agreements, make verification and enforcement of arms control accords even more difficult. Such activities require that measures for compliance verification be extremely intrusive to be effective. This is particularly essential given the fact that many of the materials that are necessary for lethal weaponry production, have perfectly legitimate civilian uses (dual-use items). This problem is especially salient in the realms of chemical and biological weapons, but it is by no means confined to these realms. Indeed, dual-use items are employed, almost as widely, in the development and production of missiles, and in the construction of clandestine nuclear facilities. Thus, end-user verification would have to be conducted — a highly demanding task. The region's newly independent states are bound to object that highly intrusive measures constitute unacceptable infringements upon their sovereignty.

Further, the difficulties of defining the region's boundaries for arms control purposes are substantial. Most states residing on the region's outskirts view neighbors that are located even further out on the periphery of the region, as presenting them with security threats requiring constant vigilance and armament. This would, for example, render impossible any effort to include Iraq without including Iran, or to include Egypt without including Libya, in a Middle East arms control agreement. It also means that the conclusion of such arms control agreements would remain hostage to regimes such as those that were ruling Iran, Iraq and Libya in 1990.

Finally, the absence of political relations and of direct channels of communication between Israel and most Arab states is likely to present serious obstacles to any effort to tailor and manage a regional arms control regime. Clearly, such a regime cannot be sustained if concerns about possible violations cannot be communicated rapidly, and immediately verified.

The cumulative weight of these difficulties is sufficient to discourage any optimism regarding possible implementation of arms control proposals that do not enjoy the full cooperation of the region's states. Therefore proposals in this realm must be tailored not only to improving Middle East stability, but also to addressing the security and other concerns that led the region's states to seek ballistic missiles and chemical-biological weapons in the first place. Alternative responses to these motives for weapons acquisition would have to be found if the missile and chemical-biological arms race is to be capped.

Existing obstacles to controlling Middle East arms acquisitions also justify our asking whether greater gains cannot be made by first applying confidence-building measures, i.e., by attempting to affect the likelihood that missiles and chemical-biological weapons might be used. These may include the tacit establishment of 'rules of engagement' and crisis prevention measures, with particular emphasis on efforts to reduce fears of surprise attack. Such mechanisms could be supplemented by other confidence-building measures designed to enhance regional stability.

Fortunately, policies and mechanisms adopted for these purposes have already acquired a positive track record in the Middle East. The arrangements defining the demilitarization of Sinai following the 1979 Israeli-Egyptian peace agreement constitute the best example.

By 1990, however, it was still far from clear that the requisite cooperation of the region's states in implementing arms control measures could be obtained in the absence of a comprehensive settlement of the Arab-Israel and Iraqi-Iranian conflicts, and without extensively curtailing the regional threat projected by Iraq. Parties carrying long-held grievances and claims are unlikely to surrender the option of using arms to materialize their objectives, and will therefore resist schemes designed to constrain their use of such weapons. For example, as long as the Arab-Israel conflict remains unresolved, most Arab states are likely to resist direct arms-control negotiations with Israel, fearing that such negotiations would imply or require formal recognition of the Jewish state. Needless to say, in the absence of such a solution, the parties concerned are especially unlikely to accept the intrusive verification measures — such as on-site inspections — necessary for checking compliance with whatever arms control agreements are reached.

Moreover, it appears unlikely that Arab states will agree to limit their acquisition of chemical and biological weapons without a simultaneous Israeli commitment to disarm or at least limit its perceived nuclear potential. However, since negotiations for a comprehensive peace seem unlikely to be convened in the near future — and once convened are likely to extend over a lengthy period — and since the territorial concessions that Israel would have to make in the framework of such negotiations would probably be far-reaching, the Jewish state is in turn unlikely to accept limitations on its presumed nuclear capacity at such an early stage of the peace process.

Yet it is equally clear that the application of regional arms control measures cannot await the conclusion of a comprehensive Middle East peace; by that point, mankind's most lethal weapons will proliferate in ever greater quantities to many of the region's states. Thus, as in the past, confidence-building measures are likely to prove an integral part of whatever peace talks evolve. Indeed, the dangers entailed in recent proliferation trends, particularly in Iraq, require that the discussion of arms control issues gradually be woven into the process. Otherwise, any comprehensive peace agreement that is reached might eventually fall victim to the destabilizing effects of proliferation.

★ ★ ★

The crisis in the Persian Gulf generated by Iraq's conquest of Kuwait on August 2, 1990, dramatically increased the saliency of missile and CBW proliferation in the Middle East. By early October it was still too early to assess the concrete implications for the issues addressed in this chapter. Nevertheless, a number of general ramifications of the crisis on these issues were already quite apparent.

First, the crisis sharpened the realization that the proliferation of nonconventional weapons had altered the distribution of power between regional powers and the superpowers. The magnitude of the forces that the United States had to mass in Saudi Arabia in order to withstand the Iraqi challenge provides an excellent illustration of this point.

Secondly, America's fears that Iraq might invoke the operational use of missiles and/or chemical and biological weapons against its forces in the Gulf transformed the proliferation issue in Washington's eyes from a matter primarily affecting international peace and security, to one directly touching on its own national security. To a lesser degree, the perceptions of the other major powers participating in the anti-Iraq coalition were similarly transformed.

Third, realizing the magnitude of the problems that proliferation poses, many actors in the crisis quickly altered their views regarding the relative merits of alternative arms control strategies. Thus, many in the United States and Europe — even in France and the USSR — now paid tribute to Israel's 1981 bombing of Iraq's French-supplied Osiraq reactor.

Further, a general consensus seemed to be emerging to the effect that, irrespective of the manner in which this particular crisis was resolved, a serious effort to prevent the proliferation of nonconventional arms would have to be launched in its aftermath. Indeed, the spirit manifested in forming the coalition facing Iraq — and particularly the unprecedented degree of US-Soviet cooperation involved — pointed to the possibility that these powers might continue to cooperate after the crisis, this time in a renewed effort to stem proliferation.

More far-reaching implications of the Gulf Crisis would depend on the precise manner in which it was resolved. In this context, three variables might turn out to be crucial. The first turned upon whether the missile and chemical/biological weapons infrastructure that Saddam Hussein constructed would be destroyed or remain intact. Clearly, the destruction of the most advanced weapons infrastructure in the Arab world might provide an excellent context for a fresh effort to implement policies aimed at halting the proliferation of nonconventional arms to the region.

On the other hand, one could speculate that, only if Iraq's infrastructure did indeed remain intact would the major powers be likely to cooperate in attempting to curb further nonconventional and missile development in the region. Put differently, were this infrastructure to be destroyed, the major powers might see the issue as having been resolved, and their incentives for an ongoing engagement in effective efforts to control the flow of arms would diminish accordingly.

A second important variable was whether Iraq would actually use nonconventional arms against the coalition forces. Should the major powers themselves become victims of the proliferation of nonconventional capabilities, their incentives to act forcefully and effectively to halt further proliferation in the aftermath of the crisis would increase correspondingly.

Finally, there would be far-reaching repercussions should the major powers, primarily the United States, themselves initiate the use of nonconventional weapons against Iraq. This could conceivably happen in the unlikely event that American forces found themselves unable to withstand an Iraqi ground assault. In the aftermath, it would be extremely difficult to prevent regional powers from equipping themselves with nonconventional weapons for precisely such contingencies.

Notes

1 This chapter is an expanded and updated version of a paper first presented by the author at the annual conference of the American Association for the Advancement of Science held in New Orleans from February 15-20. 1990. It is not intended to provide a detailed account of the relevant arsenals held by the Middle East states. The best surveys and analyses of the proliferation of ballistic missiles and chemical and biological weapons in the Middle East are to be found in Aharon Levran, *Surface-to-Surface Missiles: the Threat to Israel*, Memorandum no. 24 (Tel Aviv: Jaffee Center for Strategic Studies, Tel Aviv University), July 1988; and in W. Seth Carus, "Missiles in the Middle East: A New Threat to Stability," *Policy Focus* no. 6 (Washington DC: The Washington Institute for Near East Policy), June 1988, and "Chemical Weapons in the Middle East,"*Policy Focus* No. 9, December 1988. See also Carus, *The Genie Unleashed: Iraq's Chemical and Biological Weapons Production*, Policy Papers, no. 14, 1989; and his "NATO, Israel, and the Tactical Missile Challenge,"*Policy Focus* no. 4, May 1987. See also Martin S. Navias, "Ballistic Missile Proliferation in the Middle East,"*Survival* 31 (May-June 1989). For a reliable inventory of surface-to-surface launchers in the region's states see Shlomo Gazit and Zeev Eitan,*The Middle East Military Balance 1988-1989,* The Jaffee Center for Strategic Studies (Jerusalem: The Jerusalem Post and Boulder: Westview Press, 1989), p. 329, and the various country chapters in Part II of this volume.

2 *Ha'aretz*, June 7, 1990; *Ma'ariv*, June 8, 1990.

3 FBIS Daily Report: Near East and South Asia, April 18, 1989, p. 52; and August 12, 1989.

4 *Janes Defense Weekly*, December 23, 1989, p. 1384; see also chapter on "Israel: Offensive Weapons," in *Janes Strategic Weapons Systems*, 1989

5 See "The IDF Gets Ready for Chemical Warfare," *Jerusalem Post*, August 17, 1988.

6 See Levran, p. 23.

7 The warning was issued by Mr. Yossi Ben Aharon, Director General of Israel's Prime Minister's Office. See *Ha'aretz*, March 3, 1988. For other references see FBIS-NES-88-054, March 21, 1988; FBIS-NES-88-055, March 22, 1988; and FBIS-NES-056, March 23, 1988. See also Reuven Pedhatzur, "New Rules of the Game," *Ha'aretz*, June 26, 1988, and "The Return of the First Strike," *Ha'aretz*, July 14, 1988.

8 For example, see the statement made by Israel's Defense Minister Rabin on June 21, 1988. See *Ha'aretz*, June 22, 1988.

9 Regarding the launching of Israel's Ofek-1, see *Davar*, September 20, 1988; regarding the launching of Ofek-2, see *International Herald Tribune*, April 14, 1990; regarding the reported range of the alleged Israeli 1300 km range test of an Israeli ballistic missile, see *Davar*, September 17, 1989, quoting *Janes Defense Weekly*.

4. The Iraqi Armed Forces After The Gulf War

by Dov Tamari

Although a ceasefire in the Iran-Iraq War went into effect in July 1988, the conflict between the two nations had not been resolved. Given the prevailing atmosphere of instability and the ensuing absence of progress toward a settlement, Iraqi political and military thinking continued to be influenced primarily by the repercussions of the war and the fear of renewed conflict. Yet this was not the sole consideration. Iraq also renewed its traditional quest for a position of leadership among the Arab states of the Middle East, often using Israel as a catalyst.

The Iraqi leadership argued that Iran surrendered both politically and militarily in 1988 when it realized that it could not win the war, whereas Iraq, having built its forces to a point where it could pursue hostilities within Iranian territory, had indeed won the war. This conclusion was vital to the Iraqi leadership. It justified the monumental war effort and the enormous sacrifices of the Iraqi nation.

Though accepted increasingly as fact by the world, Iraq's self-proclaimed victory was relative. Given the terrible crises that Iraq had successfully overcome, such as Iran's conquest of Faw and its penetration of Iraqi territory to the outskirts of Basra, the Iraqi Army indeed ultimately achieved significant gains. However, when compared to Iraqi objectives at the outset of the war in 1980, the victory takes on a different meaning entirely. When Iraq entered the war, it took advantage of Iran's low fortunes: the Islamic revolution was not yet firmly entrenched and the Iranian Army had been weakened by the purges carried out by the new regime and by the discontinuation of American aid and support. While the Iraqi leadership did not intend to conquer Tehran, it did propose to weaken Iran militarily and politically to the point where it would be possible for Iraq to annex Khuzistan, an area rich in oil and populated mainly by Sunni Arabs, and to achieve a favorable permanent settlement of the Shatt al-Arab conflict. None of these objectives were achieved, and post-war Iran was markedly less inferior to Iraq than it was during the Khomeini pre-war era.

In retrospect the Iraqi victory, which was essentially only a cessation of hostilities, may be attributed to the failure of Iranian strategy at the highest level. Khomeini's Islamic revolution directed its extremist anti-West bias against a broad spectrum of regimes and states in the western world. The Iraqi leadership believed — correctly, as it turned out — that Iranian extremism and hostility would leave Iran isolated in the event of a war. Iran failed to enlist the support of either the United States, the Soviet Union or a lesser major power, and was left without a steady supply of major modern weapons systems. It was forced to endure a long, drawn-out war, with second-rate equipment acquired through dubious back channels, from the PRC, North Korea and others. Nor could the Khomeini regime attract major investments as the Shah had done before it.

Iraq succeeded precisely where Iran had failed. It managed to enlist the support of most of the Arab world, particularly financial aid from the oil-producing states. With the Gulf closed to Iraqi shipping, Jordan acted as a land bridge and logistics pipeline, while Egypt supplied arms and materiel. The USSR banned arms deals with Iraq in 1980, but renewed them after June 1982, when Iraq announced that it had retreated to the international border and was preparing solely to defend it. The Western European states, and France in particular, provided Iraq with an unlimited supply of modern weaponry.

Thus Iran failed in its general strategy rather than its fighting prowess, while Iraq successfully maneuvered to obtain the support it needed to ensure a steady supply of arms throughout the war and successfully challenge Iran's numerical superiority. In the two years following the cessation of hostilities, Iraq's strategy fortified its victory far beyond the new stalemate that characterized the cessation of hostilities. Yet even if Iraq had indeed won the war, as it claimed both at home and abroad, it is doubtful that it could subsequently formulate a policy divorced from its conflict with Iran, with regard to its position in the Arab world or its active participation in the conflict with Israel. On the contrary, Iraqi policy relating to both the Arab world and Israel continued to be influenced by the Iran-Iraq conflict and by the urgent need to update its late '70s pre-war strategy toward Iran. One thrust of the new strategy would be the development of a deterrent capability against Iran.

Following the ceasefire, the policy of both states was to forge new ties with both East and West in order to revitalize their economies. Iran opened its doors to investment from Japan, the USSR, Germany and other states. Yet this course of action did not yield a source of modern, advanced weaponry. Moreover, Iran's economic resources were strained by attempts to rehabilitate both the economy and the military at one and the same time.

In contrast, Iraq's political flexibility enabled it to purchase the most sophisticated weapons with almost no strings attached. It bought both Soviet weaponry and the most advanced European arms, and continued to develop nonconventional weapons, despite an American-led campaign to restrict this effort.

By 1990 Iraq was continuing to employ a strategy developed during the war, with regard to three key sectors: Iran, the Arab Middle East and Israel, and military developments.

The Iraqi leadership wished to improve relations with Iran from a position of strength, at least for a few years, in order to reduce the likelihood of renewed warfare. Iran, however, refused to go beyond a ceasefire, and Iraq, unable to threaten renewed warfare, had no leverage. A flare-up of hostilities would directly conflict with its own basic interests: it desperately needed a period of social, military and economic rehabilitation. Iraq's inability to renew the war thus left it subject to the inescapable fear that Iran would do precisely that. This fear dictated its actions, despite the fact that Iran was in a similar situation.

Policy toward the Arab Middle East and Israel was also still influenced more by the conflict with Iran than by Iraq's traditional vacillation between its Persian Gulf and Middle East orientations.

With the possible exception of preliminary coordination with Saudi Arabia, Iraq had seen no need to enlist the support of the Arab world in 1980, when it initiated the war. Soon, however, its failure to achieve a speedy victory, and its subsequent entanglement in a long, debilitating struggle compelled it to muster broad Arab support. Following the war, had it been forced to repay its debts to the Arabian Peninsula states that provided financial aid throughout the war, it would have gone bankrupt. Iraq thus felt compelled to set itself up as champion and protector of the entire Arab world against the threat of Khomeini's Islamic revolution. Although it had consistently opposed any settlement with Israel, Baghdad was also obliged to moderate its position toward Egypt which had signed a peace treaty with Israel. It championed Jordan, which was small, weak, and felt threatened by Israel, thus securing for itself a land bridge and a vital outlet to the sea to replace the Persian Gulf. And it sought hegemony on the Arabian Peninsula.

Thus Iraq emerged from the war allied tentatively with the Gulf states, Egypt and Jordan. To preserve these alliances and develop its own dominance within them, it continued to style itself as a buffer between Iran, with its revolutionary excesses, and the "moderate" Arab world. But it also began to present itself as the spearhead of the Arab struggle against Israel, and sought recognition as the dominant regional Arab power. And it sought to punish Syria — both because of the latter's support for Iran during and since the war, and because Baghdad and Damascus remained traditional rivals.

This aspiration to a dual leadership role required broad-based military power and an ability to intervene in all regional conflicts. That power exceeded conventional limits and generated a new, enhanced capacity to launch long-range operations and inflict heavy damage on the enemy. It also required financing beyond Iraq's means.

The Iraqi Army After the War

Following the ceasefire, a cutback in armed forces was clearly a necessity. Iraq assessed that it had achieved a significant breathing spell that would allow it to reduce its permanent army of one and a quarter million troops — a size it was in any case incapable of maintaining. A limited discharge of troops took place, especially veteran reservists. Priority was given to eliminating infantry formations, which numbered 45 divisions by the end of the war. According to conservative estimates, approximately 200,000 soldiers were released; other estimates place the figure closer to 500,000.

The discharge of hundreds of thousands of soldiers made the transition from a war economy to a peacetime economy more difficult, especially since there was no real peace. Jobs were needed for discharged soldiers who expected to be reabsorbed into the work force. A similar problem had confronted Egypt in the years after the Yom Kippur War in 1973. In Iraq's case, a reduction in the armed forces was imperative for budgetary and economic reasons and, perhaps most significantly, for social reasons. It was accomplished by mustering out troops — the infantry suffered the greatest cutbacks since it had increased more than fourfold during the war — and releasing funds saved as a result of the ceasefire and the consequent reduction in ammunition consumption, operating time for planes and tanks, and wear and tear of materiel.

The cutbacks required both long- and short-range military planning for force-building. The ongoing conflict with Iran required that, in the short term, the army be reorganized on a smaller scale, yet be capable of a quick response in the event of renewed hostilities. Long-range planning involved developing a military capability that would deter Iran from opening hostilities, and ensure Iraq's position as the most powerful state in the region, while at the same time enabling it to reduce its army to acceptable proportions.

In the immediate future, it would be impossible to scale down to anywhere near the scope of the 1980 army, which comprised 12 divisions. The 1,200 km border with Iran requires several divisions to blunt an expected attack, more divisions to counterattack and break up large concentrations of Iranian soldiers, and special forces to deal with crises in battle. A large, powerful air force was needed as well as an army aviation corps, which proved its effectiveness during the war.

Accordingly, the Iraqi Army maintained its wartime mechanized and armored units, with their 6,000 or so tanks, most of which functioned as counterattack reserves during the final years of the war. Perhaps the poor quality tanks seconded to the infantry would be taken out of active service. Iraq invested the greater part of its effort and resources in the Republican Guard, which continued to comprise two corps commands and nine divisions: two armored, one mechanized and six special forces. With top priority in manpower and equipment, the Republican Guard formed the Iraqi General Staff strategic reserve, designated to tip the scales in war or help resolve a crisis or a conflict beyond Iraq's borders.

With the reduction in infantry formations and discharge of large numbers of troops, new organizational solutions were called for. One possibility was to establish reserve divisions. Hitherto, Iraqi army reservists were discharged soldiers who could be called up on an individual basis, but were not organized into reserve units. Could the Iraqi Army successfully establish combat reserve formations? In 1990 Israel was still the only Middle Eastern state whose army was organized along these lines. Egyptian, Syrian, and Jordanian attempts at building combat formations had thus far proved unsuccessful, and it was uncertain whether the Iraqi Army could succeed where they had failed, despite the fact that this was the best way to exploit its manpower potential at a relatively low cost. For the time being the disbanded infantry divisions apparently retained their headquarters staffs, thus facilitating any call-up of reserves in an emergency. Any crisis that did not require immediate entry into combat would thus not constrain the restoration within weeks of the full combat strength that characterized the Iraqi Army at the close of the Iran-Iraq War. Still, the necessity to maintain a strong, permanent combat-ready military force on the one hand, and the need to significantly reduce the size of the standing army on the other, called ultimately for the establishment of a force based on long-range planning, and differing radically from the existing one.

The Iraqi Air Force of 1989-90 was a modern, high priority military force incorporating both long- and short-range force-building programs. Along with Army Aviation, it received 60-70 percent of acquisition appropriations. It possessed an advanced interceptor component, including the high quality MiG-29. This type of plane was not crucial to the war, since Iran's air force was decidedly inferior to Iraq's even without the interceptor aircraft, and in this sense the MiG-29 represented the long-range thinking of the Iraqi Air Force. The second component was an attack/interception capability using Su-24s, Su-25s and Mirage F-1s.

In 1989-90, plans called for the Iraqi Air Force to continue to acquire modern Soviet aircraft, and to obtain the Mirage 2000 from France. It had developed no less than five different mid-air refueling systems for combat aircraft, thereby enabling it to penetrate deep into Iran and attack targets at a great distance from the front, as well as to vie for supremacy in the Persian Gulf, where it had previously been at a disadvantage. Air supremacy requires early warning and intelligence aircraft, and therefore the Iraqi Air Force made efforts in this direction too.

Army Aviation, with its attack and anti-tank helicopters and observation helicopters, also received priority in light of its combat success as a fighting and troop mobility reserve. Most of Iraq's military helicopters — close to 600 — were concentrated in this force. There appeared to be no plans to reduce the size of Iraq's air arm; indeed, a modern air force with top priority in resources could compensate to a great extent for infantry cutbacks.

Throughout the war the Iraqi Navy was inferior to that of Iran, and it seemed likely to remain so. Iraq's coast was only a few dozen kilometers long, and all its ports and anchorages were located within firing range of Iran. In contrast, Iran's extended coast along the Persian Gulf gave it the advantage. In the early 1980s Iraq placed orders for four missile frigates and six missile corvettes from Italy. By mid-1990 these had not yet arrived in the Gulf. Were they to anchor in Iraqi waters, they would be under direct Iranian threat; were they to anchor in friendly Arab ports, their operational effectiveness would be limited. In any case, even with their arrival, Iraqi naval inferiority in the Gulf would be unaltered.

In view of its naval inferiority, Iraq continued cultivating ties with Jordan, which functioned as a logistics base and a channel for goods and materiel. Iraqi oil also continued to be rerouted through the Saudi pipeline to the Red Sea, and via Turkey to the Mediterranean. Plans for an additional pipeline via Jordan to the Red Sea were also underway.

The conclusion of the Gulf War and the time interval since then allow for a retrospective evaluation of the effectiveness of the Iraqi missile and chemical weapons campaign against Iran. For one, it now seems clear that the use of surface-to-surface missiles against military objectives did not influence the operational course of the war. The number of military casualties was relatively small in comparison to those caused by artillery or air attacks.

Even before Iraq had entered the Gulf War, it possessed short- and medium-range Soviet FROG-7 rockets and Scud B surface-to-surface missiles of the types sold to the Middle Eastern Arab states. These were equipped with explosive warheads that carried the impact of a medium-size iron bomb dropped from an aircraft. During the course of the war Iraq upgraded its Scud missiles, achieving a range of almost 600 km. Its chemical arsenal could be used with artillery shells or dispersed by attack aircraft. The long war with Iran accelerated the creation and development of nonconventional weapons in decidedly new directions. Only the development of nuclear weapons, commenced before the war in the 1970s, was curtailed as a result of the Israeli destruction in 1981 of Iraq's Osiraq nuclear reactor.

Iraq used missiles even in the early stages of the war. During 1980-1981 dozens of FROG-7 rockets were fired at close military targets; Scud B missiles were used from 1982 onward. The Iraqi Army began to use chemical weapons during the second half of 1982 when it withdrew from most of the areas it had conquered in

Iran and adopted a defensive strategy within the international border between the two countries. Extensive efforts were made during the course of the war to develop and acquire surface-to-surface missiles and chemical agents and delivery systems.

Notably, during the war Iraq did not acquire the ability to fire chemical warheads with any type of surface-to-surface missile. Missiles were primarily used against civilians in major cities located within range. Casualty counts and property damage were relatively low, but impact on morale was significant. In 1988, for example, missile attacks on Tehran caused more than one million residents to flee the city. Yet surface-to-surface missile attacks on civilians were neither the most important nor the only factor affecting morale. Other contributing factors were the bombardment of the cities, the use of chemical weapons at the front against soldiers and civilians alike, and the fear that Iraq had the capability to attack major cities with surface-to-surface missiles armed with chemical warheads.

Iraqi use of artillery and combat aircraft at the front, and air attacks against civilians deep in Iranian territory, had greater impact than the use of missiles. In chemical warfare, aerial bombardment and artillery are a more effective means of spreading chemical agents than missile warheads even when the warhead is specifically designed for this purpose. The principal advantage of a missile, and the one for which it was intended, is the firing of a nuclear warhead. Furthermore, a missile can reach targets that a plane has difficulty in reaching. The Iraqi use of surface-to-surface missiles and chemical agents led to a significant lowering of morale among the Iranian population, but it was not the principal or only factor that caused Iran to agree to a ceasefire in 1988. Rather, the inability to conquer Iraqi territory, the progressive weakening of the Iranian state, society and economy, and the recognition that the Iraqi Army was now strong enough to pursue an offensive and penetrate deep into Iranian territory, were the main reasons behind Iran's capitulation. Iran also used surface-to-surface missiles and chemical agents, but its capability in these areas was significantly inferior to that of Iraq both in quality and quantity. It could not withstand Iraqi attacks on its populace and this sense of helplessness contributed to the low morale in the major cities.

The disparity between the actual results and the impact on morale of Iraqi chemical attacks is reflected in the following statistic: of a total of more than one million casualties on both sides, chemical agents were responsible for only 45,000. Obviously, then, this figure is low in contrast to the number of casualties caused by other types of weapons.

If Iraq's use of surface-to-surface missiles was effective but not decisive, its air attacks deep within Iranian territory reflected a more significant capability. By midway through the war the Iranian Air Force had been so decimated that Iraqi bombardment of both military and civilian targets was accomplished without a struggle for air supremacy. In this sense Iraq's missiles served no unique function but, rather, reinforced Iraqi bombing capabilities both at the front and in the rear. Moreover, the cost-effectiveness of an aircraft vis-a-vis that of a surface-to-surface missile works out in favor of the aircraft. Iraq's Scud missiles cost approximately $500,000 each; they could be used only once, and were generally inaccurate, especially against military targets. Thus as long as air supremacy was maintained, the overall contribution of the missile was not significant.

To attain a genuine strategic advantage through the deployment of nonconventional weaponry and missile delivery systems, Iraq sought even before the Gulf War to acquire nuclear weapons. These would enable it to deter Iran and achieve hegemony in the Gulf on the one hand, and to balance what Iraq perceived as Israel's superiority in nonconventional weaponry on the other. After Iraq's Osiraq nuclear reactor was destroyed in 1981 by the Israel Air Force, Baghdad realized that it must protect its vital nonconventional installations by developing a deterrent capability against Israel, which it regarded as the principal threat to these installations. It found the answer in long-range surface-to-surface missiles with standard and/or, eventually, chemical or biological warheads. These missiles were all intended to threaten Israel's civilian population; their impact on possible conflicts between Israel and, say, Syria or Jordan, would be marginal.

By 1990 Iraq had developed a weapons program in several key areas of advanced weaponry, most notably long- and medium-range surface-to-surface missiles, a nascent nuclear and advanced chemical warfare program, and the provision of modern tactical weaponry for air and ground forces.

Iraq's international position enabled it to advance in these directions. By mid-1990 it was not subject to effective superpower constraints: Soviet pressure was slight and US pressure relatively ineffective. Nor was Iraq making any overtures to the United States that were liable to reduce its maneuverability in developing nonconventional weaponry. As long as Iraq could command the required resources, and European and relatively developed third world states such as Argentina refused to police effectively their firms that aided in arms developments of all types, there was no reason for Iraq to slow down its development. Further, Iraq sought to reduce its reliance even on third world know-how by developing its own military R&D center, near Mosul in northern Iraq.

To sum up, in 1989-90 the Iraqi Army was in transition, from an army at war to a post war army with the threat of war still hanging over it. Several years of quiet were required for Iraq simultaneously to build both its economy and an army of great deterrent capability. This was the main reason behind Iraq's interest in improving relations with Iran.

The expansion and development of Iraqi military power was intended to deter both Iran and Israel, and to cow the weaker Arab states near Iraq's borders. Iraq's new military capability would be respected for its proven ability to stop the Iranian-style Islamic revolution and for its unique capability to challenge what it perceived to be Israel's superiority in the area of nonconventional weaponry. Iraq's ability to deter Iran would enable it to deter Israel as well. In this strategy, Iraq in effect presented an antithesis to Syria's version of strategic parity. President Assad argued that Syria could eventually stand alone against Israel; Saddam Hussein sought to show that any Arab attempt to challenge Israel, either politically or militarily, would be unsuccessful without Iraqi participation.

From a military strategic standpoint, Iraq's invasion of Kuwait appeared to reflect two corollaries of the Iran-Iraq War that Saddam Hussein had recognized — but that outside observers and analysts had underestimated. The first regarded access to the Gulf. Both the initial failure in 1980-81 to capture Khuzistan, and the ongoing Iranian threat to Iraqi shipping and naval freedom of maneuver embodied in the 1988 ceasefire, left Saddam in need of alternative unfettered access to the Gulf, if he were to advance his scheme to achieve hegemony in the region. The invasion of Kuwait satisfied this aim.

The second corollary involved finances. In order to fuel his ambitious force-building and weapons development plans, Saddam required more than the mere forgiving of wartime loans by the Saudis and Kuwaitis. Only oil — the combined sales of Iraq's and Kuwait's oil, and at inflated prices — could satisfy his needs. Hence the emphasis in Iraqi pre-war demands on Kuwait on the oil pricing issue, and the right of access to the Rumaillah field. And hence, ultimately, the conquest of Kuwait.

From an international standpoint, the Iraqi invasion triggered a long-delayed reaction, by the United States and Western Europe, to Iraq's ambitious missile and nonconventional weapons development programs. In a military strategic sense, the most significant aspect of the ensuing embargo on Iraq was the constraints it placed on the import of strategic raw materials and expertise; this was also the aspect most likely to be perpetuated in any post-crisis arrangements designed to reduce Iraq's regional threat profile.

Perhaps the most striking strategic decision made by Iraq in the early days of the crisis was its one-sided rapprochement with Iran, in which it abruptly conceded virtually all of Tehran's demands for a post-war peace treaty. This appeared to reflect both an assessment that the annexation of Kuwait provided a satisfactory alternative in fulfilling Iraq's strategic needs in oil and access to the Gulf, and the renewal of Iraqi fears lest Iran join the anti-Iraqi coalition and, in some way, renew its war with Iraq.

Turning to the military sphere, the actual invasion of Kuwait offers little by way of lessons or indications of Iraq's fighting strengths and weaknesses. Essentially it reinforced the assessment that had crystallized in the waning days of the war with Iran, that against a weak enemy Iraq could carry out a successful short-term, and short distance, mobile armored and airborne attack. It also added credence to the impression that the Republican Guard was the primary operational arm of the ground forces.

The invasion offered a convincing explanation for Saddam's hesitancy, during the preceding two years, to demobilize his huge army in some significant way. Further, having maintained divisional frameworks and staff for the units mustered out, he was able to call up 15 divisions fairly quickly once it became clear that the invasion of Kuwait had run into unexpected opposition. Not that Saddam needed even two-thirds of his 1988 army to capture Kuwait; rather, it was the necessity of preparing for unexpected opposition or complications following that conquest, that dictated his superficial demobilization effort.

Finally, to complete this survey of early and tentative lessons of the crisis with regard to the Iraqi military, one cannot ignore the reemergence (as in the latter half of the Iran-Iraq War) of missile and nonconventional capabilities as elements of key psychological impact on public attitudes toward Iraq. At the same time, and to a far greater extent than in the case of Iran during the '80s, the forces aligned against Iraq in the Gulf (and Israel), could essentially downgrade the strategic military saliency of the Iraqi missile and chemical warfare threats in deciding the outcome of a conflict. Rather, the main potentially strong card Iraq could play would be its experience in waging a defensive war, using its mobile armored reserves to best advantage. Yet, even if fighting were avoided, the size of Iraq's armed forces would weigh increasingly heavily on the Iraqi economy — with no one but the beleaguered Iraqi people to pay the bill.

5. The Influence of the Peripheral Arab States on Arab-Israeli Wars

by Dov Tamari

Israel and its Arab neighbors have fought since 1948. There have been all-out confrontations, such as Israel's War of Independence in the years 1947-1949, the Six-Day War in 1967 and the Yom Kippur War in 1973. Other conflicts have been limited in scope, such as the Sinai Campaign in 1956, the War of Attrition in 1969-1970 and the 1982 Lebanese War. In many of these wars, military involvement by the peripheral states has been instrumental in promoting Arab unity. From Morocco in the west to Iraq and Kuwait in the east, Arab states have generally responded to the call to arms against Israel. Thus in the 1948 War Egypt, TransJordan, Syria and Lebanon were the chief antagonists, but they were supported by volunteer detachments sent by the peripheral states of Iraq and Saudi Arabia. In the 1967 War Egypt, Jordan and Syria were totally involved in the conflict, while Iraq, Saudi Arabia and Kuwait furnished expeditionary forces.

In the 1973 War, Syria and Egypt were Israel's principal adversaries, while Algeria, Iraq, Jordan, Libya, Morocco, and Saudi Arabia dispatched auxiliary troops before, during and after the war, and Sudanese soldiers reinforced the Egyptian Army. Finally, Libyan soldiers appeared in Lebanon during the summer of 1982 following the first stage of the war there.

In addition to the Arab states, Communist Bloc countries were also drawn into the conflicts. Both Soviet and North Korean pilots flew with the Egyptian Air Force. The Soviets operated weapons systems for Egyptian air defense in the War of Attrition from 1969-1970. And Cuban troops were dispatched to Syria and deployed along the Golan border after the Yom Kippur War.

The military involvement of the peripheral Arab states during past decades fostered the prevailing concept of "Israel versus the Arab world." Conceived in 1948, this concept profoundly influenced the State of Israel's approach to defense, the development of the Israel Defense Forces (IDF), and the conduct of war. No less impressive was its effect on the Arab states with regard to military matters. Gamal Abd al-Nasser considered Arab military and political solidarity as the key to winning the Arab-Israel conflict.

This chapter seeks to analyze the significance of military involvement in Arab-Israel conflicts by peripheral Arab states. To do so, we shall first briefly survey past manifestations of peripheral state involvement. Considerable attention will be devoted to Iraqi involvement, since it has always been the most substantial of all the peripheral states, and will, apparently, continue to be so in the future.

First a word on the varieties of peripheral involvement.

Looking back over past Arab-Israel wars, peripheral involvement may be divided into the following categories:

— Dispatching air and ground forces to the theater of operations before, during and after the war. These troops either join the ranks of the Arab armies directly involved or act as independent combat formations, such as the Iraqi Army in 1948-1949.
— Deploying small contingents of highly trained soldiers without heavy equipment. Such troops are used to man local military units and equipment, such as the Cuban tank crews in Syria in 1973.
— Supply of arms and military equipment to reinforce the army of an Arab confrontation state or to replenish its arsenal during or after the war.
— Future involvement might entail deployment of long range weapons — missiles or aircraft — from bases in the home territory of the peripheral state, to replace or augment its military presence on the battlefield.

Israel's War of Independence, 1947-1949 (The 1948 War)

Iraq's involvement in the War of Independence began in the summer of 1946, as the nascent Arab League contemplated military action against the future Jewish state. The League appointed senior Iraqi officers to plan an offensive in anticipation of British withdrawal. Iraq's participation in the war was prompted by its own self-interest. First and foremost, it sought to maintain a leadership position within the Arab world. In addition, it hoped to gain control of the pipeline carrying Iraqi oil from Kirkuk to Haifa, affording it easy access to the Mediterranean.

Iraqi military involvement may be divided into three stages:

— From December 1947 to May 1948 Iraq sent some 800

volunteer troops and officers to fight against the Jewish *Yishuv* in Palestine.

— An Iraqi military force comprising two mixed brigades, with some air support, invaded Israel from northern TransJordan in May 1948, moving toward Haifa along the Iraq Petroleum Company pipeline. During this stage, Iraqi expeditionary forces attacking the IDF were repulsed in two decisive battles and pushed east of the Jordan River.

— From June 1948 Iraq increased its troop strength in Palestine to four brigades, two Iraqi-Palestinian mixed volunteer battalions, and two air squadrons.

All told, Iraq dispatched approximately one-third of its entire fighting force. Its army fought in Beit Shean, the Jezreel Valley, and in western Samaria. The fighting was primarily defensive in nature, combined with counterattacks against the IDF.

There is no doubt that the borders of central Israel delineated in the armistice agreements of 1949 were determined to a great extent by Iraq's military presence. During the course of the war, Iraq rejected UN proposals for a ceasefire that were accepted by Israel and the Arab armies. In keeping with this rejectionist stance, it also repudiated the armistice agreements, and consequently withdrew its troops.

In 1948 *Saudi Arabia* furnished three infantry battalions for the war against Israel. They fought alongside the Egyptian Army in the southern part of the country. One company actually advanced to within several kilometers south of Jerusalem, taking part in the battles there. Saudi units suffered heavy losses in the summer of 1948, and in October of that year some 70 Saudi troops were killed in the IDF's campaign to break through to the Negev.

The Sinai Campaign, 1956

By 1952, *Jordan* had already sought Iraqi military support for its ongoing hostilities with Israel. The request was reiterated in June 1956, in light of the worsening military situation on Israel's borders with Egypt and Jordan. Jordan and *Iraq* formed a joint high commission on defense along with a military council and headquarters. An Iraqi division, about one-third of Iraq's ground forces, was organized as an expeditionary force, deployed between Habbaniyah and H-3 near the Jordan border. These agreements and preparations prompted Israel to declare in September 1956 that the introduction of Iraqi forces into Jordan would be regarded as a casus belli and would compel Israel to send troops into Jordan's West Bank. In September and October, several extensive military confrontations occurred between Israel and Jordan. Britain warned Israel that a continuation of hostilities was liable to oblige it to fulfill its defense commitment to Jordan. Britain also cautioned Israel to refrain from any military response in the event that an Iraqi division entered Jordan.

Military and political cooperation between Jordan, Iraq and Britain led to another Israeli declaration on October 15, stating that any violation of the status quo would lead to a military response on the part of Israel. Jordanian parliamentary elections, ending on October 20, culminated in a resounding victory for supporters of Egypt's Nasser, and Egypt announced that it would extend military assistance to Jordan. Meanwhile, Jordanian-Iraqi relations cooled. In the event, when Israel attacked Egypt on October 29, neither Jordan nor any other Arab state joined the conflict.

The Six-Day War, 1967

In mid-May 1967, as the situation deteriorated between Egypt and Israel, *Iraq* moved to participate in military and political steps taken against Israel. On May 19 the army was placed on a high state of alert, and an Iraqi delegation was dispatched to Damascus to coordinate military assistance, consisting primarily of air support. Armored forces of brigade strength advanced toward the Iraqi-Jordanian-Syrian border junction.

Concurrently Iraq, while inviting its non-Arab neighbors, Iran and Turkey, to join the pan-Arab effort, attacked King Hussein and his government for remaining aloof. When the Joint Arab Military Command was established and the Egyptian General Abd al-Moneim Riyad set up headquarters in Amman, Iraq sent military assistance to Jordan rather than Syria, and signed a defense pact with Egypt.

In early June Iraq flew an infantry battalion into Egypt, and on June 4, the day before hostilities commenced, Iraqi expeditionary forces of division strength began moving into Jordan. Iraqi troops in Jordan, with their headquarters in Amman, comprised approximately one-fourth of the entire Iraqi military force. As hostilities commenced, an Iraqi advance motorized infantry brigade en route to the Jordan Valley was attacked by the Israel Air Force (IAF). Its vanguard crossed to the West Bank of the Jordan River but did not encounter IDF troops advancing from the west. After June 8, with all Jordanian forces withdrawn from the West Bank, the Iraqi division was integrated into the defense of the East Bank.

As for the war in the air, a squadron of Iraqi combat aircraft was deployed at H-3 near the Iraqi-Jordanian border on the eve of battle. Iraqi planes twice attacked IDF forces advancing in the northern sector of the West Bank. An Iraqi bomber attacked the Israeli coastal city of Netanya and was downed. Other combat aircraft helped defend H-3 against Israeli attack.

As the war ended, Iraq rejected a ceasefire, despite urgings from Jordan and the Egyptian commander of the Joint Arab Military Command. During 1968 the Iraqi division remained in northern Jordan and took part in a number of incidents involving Israeli settlements across the Jordan River. The IAF responded in December by attacking this force. In September 1970, the "Black September" confrontation between the Kingdom of Jordan and the Palestinian terrorist organizations reached its peak, and fighting erupted between them. Syria attacked Jordan and was repulsed. Iraqi forces stationed in Jordan remained uninvolved. The crisis culminated in a decision by Baghdad to pull its troops out of Jordan. The withdrawal was completed by the beginning of 1971.

The Six-Day War was not initiated by any of the belligerent parties. Rather, it was the denouement to a progressively deteriorating situation. Iraq had prepared for war with no definite goal in mind and with no systematic plan of action. Some of the Iraqi forces that reached the war zone in air force contingents actually took part in the hostilities. However they were too few and too late to have any impact on either the specific battles or the course of the war. At the time, a significant part of the Iraqi Army was tied up in the Kurdish provinces in the northern sector of the country. Despite this handicap, Iraq dispatched a significant military force.

With tension mounting toward the end of May 1967, *Saudi Arabia* first sent ammunition to the Jordanian army. The shipment arrived on June 5, the day war broke out. On June 6, the first Saudi battalion entered Jordan, and the Saudi contingent during and after the war reached brigade strength. The Saudi force consisted of infantry, reinforced by artillery, tanks and other support units and services. Saudi troops did not cross the Jordan River to the West Bank, nor did they participate in any of the fighting. The brigade was deployed in southern Jordan, and was subsequently charged with the defense of the city of Karak. During the course of 1970 IDF forces clashed with Saudi units in several marginal incidents in southern Jordan. The brigade was finally withdrawn from Jordan ten years after the war as part of an effort by Riyadh to reorganize its armed forces. *Kuwait* sent a well trained armored battalion, equipped with British Centurions, to help in the war effort. It operated on the Egyptian front, in the Sinai, where some of the tanks were disabled or abandoned and fell into IDF hands.

The Yom Kippur War, 1973

Iraq was not directly involved in the secret military preparations for war in 1973, but it was aware of Egyptian and Syrian intentions and furnished Egypt with a squadron of antiquated Hunter fighter planes in the spring of that year. In any case, prior to October 1973 no real preparations for war with Israel were carried out. Iraq and its neighbor, Iran, were at loggerheads over the issue of three small islands in the Persian Gulf under Iranian control since 1971. This dispute precipitated the severing of relations between the two countries. Tensions also continued in the Kurdish provinces, despite Iraqi acquiescence in 1970 to demands for autonomy scheduled to go into effect by 1974. The main body of Iraqi infantry was thus deployed in the Kurdish district, and most of the mechanized armored detachments were positioned along the Iranian border.

The outbreak of hostilities caught both Iraq and Israel unaware. From October 6, 1973 onward, Iraq's political and military leadership set in motion a war machine surpassing that of any other peripheral Arab state in a Middle East war. The Iraqi Revolutionary Council and the political leadership of the Ba'ath Party convened on October 6 and decided to ready a military force for dispatch to Syria. By nightfall Iraqi forces stood armed and ready, and the first mechanized brigade began moving toward the Syrian border.

As a preventive measure, Iraq notified Iran of its willingness to renew relations and open negotiations aimed at settling any disagreements between them. Iran reciprocated by using its influence to discourage renewed hostilities by the Kurds in northern Iraq. Baghdad also asked the Soviet Union to exert its influence on Iran to maintain quiet on the borders and in the Kurdish provinces.

Syria apparently actually turned to Iraq for military support only on October 8, when the Syrian offensive on the Golan Heights had ground to a standstill and there was little likelihood that Damascus would achieve its war goals. Iraq dispatched two armored divisions, an infantry brigade, a mountain infantry brigade and a commando brigade — an estimated 30-40,000 troops. The expeditionary force comprised 500-700 tanks, some 700 armored troop vehicles, 12 artillery battalions and transport units, and logistics and other support units. This comprised almost three-quarters of Iraq's armored force and one-fifth of its infantry — all told, about one-third of its ground forces. In addition, four fighter squadrons were deployed at Syrian airfields, one squadron, sent in the spring of 1973, operated from Egypt, and additional squadrons provided air cover for the troops advancing toward Syria.

All Iraqi forces in Syria were placed under Syrian command. The Iraqi vanguard arrived in Damascus on October 9, and the rearguard on October 24, one day after the ceasefire. They had traversed a distance of 1,200-1,500 km, encountering no opposition from the Israel Air Force, which had suffered heavy losses during the first week of the war against Egypt and Syria, but nevertheless retained a high combat profile. A first armored brigade entered the war against the IDF on October 12, and was subsequently joined by two additional brigades. Toward the end of the war, additional forces engaged in insignificant skirmishes with the IDF. The Iraqi Sixth Armored Division was prepared for an offensive on October 23-24, but this was canceled when Syria agreed to a ceasefire. Iraqi expeditionary forces suffered fairly heavy casualties, with approximately 800 dead, 111 tanks and armored troop vehicles disabled or destroyed, an additional 250 vehicles of various types disabled or destroyed, and 26 combat aircraft downed.

The large Iraqi force that managed to reach the front had very little influence on the course of the war and its aftermath. By the time it arrived, the Syrian Army was already on the defensive, and the IDF had overrun most of its frontline fortifications and begun its march toward Damascus. Iraqi intervention did stop the IDF advance along the Der'a-Damascus road, the main artery connecting southwest Syria with the capital. Yet this tactical gain held little significance; the Iraqi Third Armored Division Command failed to wage a war at the divisional echelon, committing its forces sporadically.

All told, the arriving Iraqi expeditionary force failed to bolster the Syrian Army, which was on the verge of collapse, and this enabled the IDF to divert its main effort to the Egyptian front. The Egyptian Army, compelled thereby to move its armored reserves east of the Suez Canal, had to launch its second-stage attack from there. This effort ended in complete failure and paved the way for the IDF to begin crossing the canal, a decisive move which gave Israel the advantage on the Egyptian front and precipitated the end of the war.

On the evening of October 23 Syria agreed to a ceasefire and Iraq, true to a tradition begun in 1949, rejected it. Iraq instructed its forces to return home, despite the fact that the Syrian government regarded an Iraqi military presence within its borders as vital to its interests during the interim between the ceasefire and a separation-of-forces agreement. The withdrawal process lasted until the middle of November.

Other peripheral forces participated in the 1973 War as well. *Saudi Arabia* furnished Syria with an infantry brigade, a paratroop battalion and an armored battalion equipped with artillery and logistic units. Apparently a small number of Saudi forces clashed with the IDF toward the close of the war, on October 21. Concurrently, Saudi Arabia reinforced its brigade, which was permanently stationed in Jordan, providing anti-aircraft batteries for its protection. Saudi forces remained in Syria until 1977, often participating in maneuvers with the Syrian Army.

Jordan supplied Syria with two armored brigades, one of which took part in the actual fighting. They arrived in Syria following IDF penetration deep into Syrian territory and were able to join the Syrians only in the defensive phase of the war. They lost men and armored vehicles, and their influence was negligible.

Months before the war began, *Morocco* sent a small armored brigade to Syria. In the course of the war it encountered IDF attack forces, and one of its battalions was destroyed. *Libya* dispatched approximately 100 tanks with crews to the Egyptian front. They arrived in Cairo on October 17. The Egyptians preferred not to use the tank crews, but used the tanks to replace losses suffered at the front. A number of Libyan Mirages were sent as well, and flew under the command of the Egyptian Air Force. *Algeria* furnished less than 100 tanks to Egypt along with approximately 2,000 troops. Finally *Cuba*, as noted, sent Syria a force of brigade strength to man Syrian tanks following the war.

The Lebanon War, 1982

The outbreak of the Lebanon War in 1982 found *Iraq* immersed in one of the most difficult phases of its war with Iran. Confronted with IDF penetration into Lebanon and the spread of the war northward against Syrian and Palestinian forces, Iraq proposed a ceasefire on the Iranian front in order to free its armed forces for the war against Israel. The declaration proved to be merely a political ploy in Iraq's ongoing struggle with Iran; all the evidence indicates that Baghdad had no intention of sending troops into Lebanon, particularly insofar as its relations with Syria at that point were at an all-time low.

Libya, along with other North African states, sent resident Palestinians to fight in Lebanon after the outbreak of hostilities. Libya was the only state to send a military force, albeit a small one. It consisted of one or two commando battalions, a small artillery unit and an anti-aircraft unit. Deployed in northern Lebanon and in the Biq'a under Syrian control, they did not encounter IDF forces.

Shipment of Arms and Materiel from Peripheral Arab States

In nearly all the wars against Israel, the peripheral states supplied arms and materiel to the confrontation states surrounding Israel. The largest shipments were sent during and after the Yom Kippur War in 1973. *Libya* furnished Egypt with ten Mirage fighters and about 100 T-54/55 tanks. *Algeria* contributed about 100 tanks and several dozen combat aircraft. *Morocco* sent 50-60 tanks to Egypt and a similar quantity to Syria even before the war began. *Saudi Arabia* gave Egypt some ten helicopters and one transport plane. *Kuwait* provided Syria with dozens of tanks.

All this materiel had little if any influence on the course of the war, and did little to replenish depleted supplies. Egypt and Syria were resupplied by the Soviet Union and other Eastern European states, including Yugoslavia. Israel was resupplied by the United States. The Arab contribution was minimal.

In 1982, following the initial battles in Lebanon, *Libya* gave Syria a number of MiG-23s and several SA-6 and SA-9 missile batteries. These were largely a symbolic gesture, as the Syrian Air Force had suffered tremendous losses: 90 of its most sophisticated aircraft were downed in aerial combat, and its air defense system in the Biq'a was destroyed.

Thus we may tentatively conclude that, since 1947, provision of materiel by the peripheral Arab states has been negligible. This statement bears some thought, particularly in light of the arms buildup in the peripheral Arab states. In particular, Libya has the largest military stockpile in the region, many times greater than quantities needed by the Libyan Army in the present or the foreseeable future. Since 1973, Saudi Arabia has had a stockpile on a par with that of Libya. It has been suggested in the past that the purpose of Libya's arms stockpile was to facilitate the speedy transfer of arms to Middle East confrontation states — either in accordance with the political and military needs of the USSR, their original supplier, yet without direct Soviet involvement, or, more convincingly, to assure Libya itself a powerful influence over the belligerent states before, during and after a war. By 1990 it was apparent that the Libyan stockpile, as well as that of the Saudis, was not intended as a tool of either great power or local needs within the framework of an Arab-Israel war.

This behavior is in complete contrast to the monetary aid lavished by the peripheral Arab states on the confrontation states. Arab economic assistance, both past and present, to Egypt, Iraq, Syria and Jordan has been vital to their military capabilities. Egypt in 1973 is a case in point: Sadat acknowledged a number of times that directly preceding the war, Egypt's economy had hit rock bottom. It was impossible to finance the huge outlays required for the building and maintenance of its 800,000 man force. Leaders of the Arab oil-producing states warned him that if he did not go to war, they would cut off their aid. In this sense, Arab economic pressure and incentives were one of the causes underlying Sadat's decision to take up arms in 1973. Yet if monetary aid given by the peripheral states has been of vital importance to the military capability of the Arab confrontation states, and to Iraq in its war with Iran, direct military support has been negligible. It is likely to remain so in the future.

The Significance of Expeditionary Force Involvement

Nearly all of the peripheral Arab states have waged war against Israel at one time or another. With the possible exception of Iraq, however, their military support has had little or no impact on the course of battle.

In examining all the instances of peripheral state participation, there appears to be no correlation between the degree of extremism espoused by a regime and the level of its military involvement. *Libya*, an extremist state particularly in regard to Israel, was not significantly more involved than so-called moderates like *Morocco* and *Saudi Arabia*. Politics and ideology seem not to have played a decisive role. Save for Israel's War of Independence, the limited duration of most of the wars precluded effective military participation on the part of the peripheral states. In future, Egypt's absence from the battle arena should have a deterrent influence on potential North African military intervention.

Unfailing in its extensive military support, Iraq has been unique among the Arab states. Fully one-fourth of Iraq's entire ground forces participated in all of the wars except the Sinai Campaign in 1956 and the Lebanese War in 1982. During the Yom Kippur War in 1973, nearly half the Iraqi Air Force took part in the conflict or provided air cover for troop movement to the front. Nevertheless, save for the War of Independence, Iraq had little impact on the outcome of the conflicts; its forces were too few and arrived too late. Interestingly, the IDF never retaliated directly against Iraq for this belligerency, and Iraqi forces never suffered heavy casualties. From October 7 to October 24, 1973, Iraqi troops traversed some 1,200 km of open, unprotected desert without incident.

Iraq allowed no impediment to stand in the way of its military involvement in the Arab-Israel conflict. Political crises, strained relations with neighboring states such as Iran, and tensions in the Kurdish provinces had little deterrent effect. Nor did regime changes — from a monarchy in the '40s and '50s to a revolutionary-military regime beginning in 1958, and a single-party Ba'ath regime since 1968 — affect Iraqi ardor to participate. Further, more than any other Arab belligerents, Iraq consistently rejected any proposed truce, however fragile, including the armistice agreements of 1949, the ceasefire of June 1967, UN Resolutions 242 and 338, and the ceasefire of October 1973.

Given the size of its fighting force and the eagerness of its leaders to confront Israel, why did Iraq have such a minor effect on the course of Arab-Israel wars? Apparently, there were two underlying causes: the state of Iraqi preparedness for war with Israel, and IDF combat doctrine in past conflicts.

Iraqi Preparedness

War with Israel was never the sole raison d'etre of the Iraqi Army, nor did it profoundly influence its structure, organization or performance. Since the 1940s, Iraqi regimes were faced with the dilemma of whether to assign priority to Persian Gulf issues or to those of the Middle East as a whole. In its indecision, Iraq seesawed back and forth between the two spheres. When one predominated, the other receded into the background.

With its natural sphere of operations in the Persian Gulf region, Iraq's army was designed chiefly to safeguard Iraqi interests close to home, to deal with neighboring Iran and Turkey, and to contend with the ongoing Kurdish problem. In contemplating hostilities with Israel, the Iraqi Army presumably prepared contingency plans for sending an expeditionary force to Syria and/or Jordan. Yet these could not guarantee effective performance unless accompanied by a constant state of preparedness, reflected in military and political thinking at the highest echelon and by a threat assessment that regarded war with Israel as a primary objective, and was translated into specific training exercises and maneuvers. Given the absence of these components, Iraq could never fully exploit the resources necessary to overcome the additional handicap of geographical distance. As for removing that handicap — Arab unity has never reached the point where Jordan and Syria would consent to large-scale Iraqi forces permanently stationed on their home ground. Nor did Iraq itself ever take definitive action to facilitate the deployment of its forces near Israel's borders on a permanent basis.

Iraq's initiation of hostilities against Iran in 1980 precipitated a shift toward a Persian Gulf military orientation which prevailed throughout the 1980s. At the same time three key developments took place that affected Baghdad's future ability to intervene in an Arab-Israel war. For one, Iraq developed medium-range ballistic missiles capable of reaching Israel from Iraqi soil, thereby rendering intervention possible without the deployment of Iraqi troops on Syrian or Jordanian soil.

Iraq also forged close strategic links with Jordan. During the war, these took the form of Iraqi reliance on Jordanian roads and the Red Sea port of Aqaba for resupply. Following the July 1988 ceasefire, Iraq sent ground forces commanders and its own aircraft to reconnoiter the Jordan-West Bank border, and the two countries formed a joint air squadron based on Iraqi soil. One may assess that King Hussein accepted these expressions of cooperation largely out of economic necessity and his need for a strong military ally to shield him from the Syrian and/or Israeli threats that he perceived. Nevertheless, his acquiescence reflected a certain readiness to discuss an even larger Iraqi military presence, even if by mid-1990 King Hussein openly acknowledged constraints (Israel's "red lines") upon his freedom to again accept an Iraqi force on his territory.

Finally, the Gulf War expanded the enmity between Iraq and Syria — the lone Arab state that actively supported Iran. In particular, Syria 'stabbed Iraq in the back' when it closed the Iraqi oil pipeline located within its borders and permitted Iranian fighter planes to use its airstrips. It came as no surprise, therefore, when Iraq, catching Syria off-guard in 1989, dispatched military equipment via Jordan to Lebanese Christian leader Michel Aoun. Under the circumstances, for Syria to accept an Iraqi expeditionary force would require a radical shift in position by Saddam or President Assad, or a change in leadership, or some other equally traumatic development.

By mid-1990 there were three basic possibilities for future Iraqi military involvement in an Arab-Israel conflict: a 'traditional' expeditionary force; medium range missiles with conventional, chemical or bacteriological warheads; and bombing by aircraft that have the capability to reach Israel. A combination of all three was also possible.

Expeditionary force. The Iran-Iraq War left Iraq with a very large army chiefly made up of infantry, reinforced by a considerable number of armored and mechanized divisions. The most prominent body was the elite Republican Guard, nine divisions strong, consisting of armored, mechanized and commando units. The Republican Guard reached its peak in the final years of the war. It was responsible for the major counterattacks and, consequently, enjoyed first priority in arms and manpower. It was the strategic reserve of the Iraqi General Staff, the regime and the entire nation. Certainly it was the Iraqi military formation most qualified to confront Israel in the event of war. Such a move, however, would clearly weaken defenses along the Iran-Iraq and possibly other borders. Moreover, should such an Iraqi force once again engage in hostilities against Israel without undergoing an extended program of preparation for an offensive war, it was almost certain that its impact would in no way correspond with its size.

Eventually, of course, significant Iraqi armed forces could be permanently stationed in a country bordering on Israel. However, as we have seen, under prevailing circumstances in 1989-90, neither Jordan nor Syria looked upon this move with equanimity. Even under ideal circumstances, it is doubtful whether Jordan or Syria would want to see Iraqi armed forces of greater than division strength permanently stationed within their borders either before or after a war.

Long-range missiles. Iraqi use of long range missiles with conventional or chemical/bacteriological warheads could not greatly influence the military course of a war. But directed at a civilian population, they could cause casualties and considerable psychological trauma. Yet Iraq had to consider Israel's greater destructive capacity with regard to civilian population and other sensitive targets before embarking upon such an enterprise. Iraq regarded its missile capability primarily as an effective deterrent against Israel or, if necessary, a devastating weapon against its archenemy, Iran. Thus if an Arab-Israel war broke out, an Iraqi commitment to a policy of missile and/or nonconventional warfare could not be regarded as a foregone conclusion. Moreover, Iraq after the Gulf War retained considerable sensitivity to the issue of unnecessary losses caused by war conducted far from its borders.

In summary, Iraq in 1989-90 did not appear to be formulating organized, long-term plans for war against Israel. In the event of an unforeseen crisis between Israel and its neighbors, Iraqi military might, tested in battle, could suddenly be redirected westward. Yet Iraq had not effected a political rapprochement with Syria that could facilitate joint maneuvers, as a preliminary to armed conflict with Israel. Even the physical and moral support that Iraq gave Jordan was no indication that it was contemplating an offensive against Israel. Finally, the prospect of integrating

Iraqi troops into the Jordanian or Syrian army appeared to be an unlikely scenario.

By mid-1990, the degree of Iraqi preoccupation with the possibility of war with Israel would still be determined first and foremost by the course of the Iran-Iraq conflict, or some other conflagration along Iraq's border. As long as there was no significant change in the status quo, Iraq's involvement in the Middle East conflict would probably remain commensurate with its past record. Should war break out, that involvement would probably resemble past conflicts. But future expeditionary forces would be larger and better equipped, with more battlefield experience; and the use of missiles could not be ruled out entirely.

Arab Expeditionary Forces and IDF Capabilities

In the past, the IDF generally fought against peripheral forces only after they had reached the war zone. This was the case in 1948 and again in 1967, when the Iraqi advance brigade was attacked from the air only a few dozen kilometers from the Jordan River.

In 1973, the IDF did not intercept any of the expeditionary forces furnished by peripheral states before they reached the front. With the exception of two isolated and unsuccessful IDF attacks, even the Iraqi force was allowed to proceed. The reason for this IDF inaction was that, on the whole, intervention was unnecessary. Interception delays the arrival of hostile troops and may forestall their participation in a war that could be prolonged by their presence. But past wars were fast-paced affairs with fighting directed deep into enemy territory. This strategy precipitated demands for a ceasefire after only a few days of hostilities, before an expeditionary force could even become involved. Moreover, with the exception of Iraqi troops, auxiliary forces were never perceived by the IDF as a serious threat.

That the IDF relaxed its vigilance toward the Iraqi expeditionary force in 1973 was a mistake. This negligence may be attributed to the partial and temporary disequilibrium produced by the early stages of the war, particularly in the General Staff and the Air Force. Apparently, the lesson was well-learned, and by 1990 it was difficult to envisage the movement of Arab expeditionary forces from the periphery without the IDF seeking to intercept them far from Israel's borders. This policy predicated a continued reliance on a combat doctrine that advocated short wars fought on enemy territory, even if the enemy was first to attack. Any shift toward a combat doctrine that did not include an offensive into enemy territory, would reduce the IDF's capacity to intercept expeditionary forces.

This ongoing reliance on IDF interception of expeditionary forces drew upon the IDF capacity, particularly since 1967, to exact a heavy toll on enemy targets far from Israel. Some telling examples were the attacks on army camps, bridges and electrical installations in Upper Egypt in 1968-1969, the rescue of the hostages at Entebbe along with the destruction of Uganda's entire fleet of MiG-21s in 1976, the destruction of Iraq's Osiraq nuclear reactor in 1981, and the bombing of terrorist camps in Tunis in 1986. Thus no peripheral state could engage in hostilities with Israel without taking into account the IDF's long-range interception capacity, as well as the retaliatory attack that might follow.

Some of Israel's tactics have changed over the years. In the past Israel maintained military pressure on the peripheral states by means of substantial aid to opposition forces. For example, Israel supported the Kurdish minority in Iraq in its war for autonomy in 1965-1966. Moreover, Israel helped Iran during the reign of the Shah and furnished arms to Khomeini's forces in the war with Iraq. The principal aim of this aid was essentially political: to end Israel's regional isolation through ties with states and peoples that border on the peripheral Arab states. But it also enabled Israel to maintain indirect military pressure on peripheral states like Iraq.

In retrospect, it is difficult to see that extensive benefits derived from the secondary objective of this aid. For example, the Kurdish insurgency failed to discourage large-scale Iraqi military participation in 1967 or in 1973, although it is virtually impossible to determine whether the Arab military force facing Israel in 1967 or 1973 would have been bigger without this Israeli aid. In any case, looking beyond 1989, assistance of this nature was not anticipated. The regional climate had changed, and it seemed unlikely that this type of aid would enhance Israel's position.

★ ★ ★

Iraq's invasion of Kuwait reflected its ongoing military preoccupation with its proximate environment, rather than the relatively distant Israeli theater. Nevertheless, the ensuing inter-Arab and international reaction soon caused Saddam Hussein to suggest, by open threat and subtle innuendo, the possibility that he would attack Israel as a means of refocusing the conflict in a manner that might oblige neutral and even hostile Arab states to rally to his side.

Seen in the light of the history of Iraq's interventions against Israel, Saddam's options were highly constrained. Of the two traditional host states, Syria was openly hostile, while Jordan, however helpful to Iraq, nevertheless struggled to maintain the status of a neutral buffer, at least in a military strategic sense. Iraq's key strike force, the Republican Guard, was pinned down to the Kuwait-Saudi Arabia front. There remained the possibility of a preemptive Iraqi attack on Israel by missiles and/or aircraft.

Israel hastened (Defense Minister Arens, on August 7, 1990) to warn Iraq that entry of its troops into Jordan would constitute a casus belli. Here Israel was proving mindful of past lessons, particularly that of 1973, when it allowed the Iraqi expeditionary force to reach Syria unhindered. It was also invoking the fresh experience of Kuwait, which had negotiated unsuccessfully with Saddam in late July under the threat of an Iraqi invasion force poised on its borders.

6. The Syrian-Israeli Balance of Forces and Strategic Parity

by Dov Tamari

Since the Yom Kippur War in 1973, Syria was the only one of the three functioning Arab states bordering Israel that did not lower its belligerent profile. Quite the contrary, Syrian forces confronted IDF troops in Lebanon between 1977 and 1981. In 1982, they engaged IDF forces that invaded Lebanon and attacked their positions in the Biq'a and the Beirut region.

The concept "strategic parity" first appeared in Syria in the late 1970s in describing a long-term process. This chapter assesses that concept and its influence on Syrian force-building over a 12-year period, ultimately drawing a military balance between Syria and Israel. It asks whether the concept of strategic parity comprises a grand strategy in the struggle with Israel. How far has this Syrian concept developed in the last decade? Does strategic parity lead inevitably to a Syrian-initiated war against Israel, and what could such a war accomplish? Finally, how did the Syrian-Israeli military balance stand by early 1990? Answers to these questions seem particularly relevant in 1990, in view of the apparent reduction in Soviet backing for a Syrian military option, and the possibility that this and additional constraints may bring about a Syrian reevaluation of its strategic position.

The Concept of Strategic Parity

The Yom Kippur War sowed the conceptual seed in Syria of the need to achieve strategic parity with Israel. Syria regarded its surprise attack on Israel and its ability to breach Israel's lines of defense on the Golan Heights as more than a trifling accomplishment. While initial Syrian gains were quickly neutralized by the IDF counterattack deep into Syrian defense lines, the war, in Syria's perception, nevertheless differed completely from the 1967 confrontation, when Syrian forces on the Golan Heights enjoyed a clear topographical advantage and were nevertheless routed by a secondary Israeli effort.

The ceasefire of May 1974 left the military situation on the Syrian-Israeli border essentially similar to that of pre-October

1973. In parallel, Syria was bitterly disappointed by Egyptian strategic decisions between 1973 and 1976, focusing as they did on military arrangements in the Sinai and a realignment with the US as the key superpower actor in the Middle East.

The Syrian leadership evidently decided that even though Syrian strength was inferior to Israel's, it was manifestly possible to achieve parity and even gain the advantage. At this juncture Syrian thinking was still predicated on Arab unity and reliance on Egypt as a prime mover in the Arab world.

Anwar Sadat's visit to Jerusalem in 1977 and the peace treaty signed in 1979 confronted Syria with a totally new situation. Egypt, hitherto the vanguard of the struggle against Israel, had walked away from the confrontation. Jordan could never fill Egypt's role. And as Syria's efforts to recruit Iraq at the Baghdad Conference of 1978 proved fruitless, the chances of a Syrian-Iraqi axis that could attract other Arab actors were also reduced sharply.

Syria's most serious problem for the moment was defense. The IDF, no longer deployed in the Sinai, could easily reinforce its troops facing Syria and achieve a decisive qualitative and quantitative advantage. We recall that Syria permanently stationed troops in Lebanon beginning in 1976, thereby weakening its own defenses on the Syrian-Israeli border and opening a secondary front for Israel to attack via Lebanon — a challenge for which the Syrian Army found no appropriate solution.

Against this backdrop, the concept of strategic parity that first appeared in 1978 was primarily aimed at enabling Syria independently to withstand an Israeli attack and defend itself, without the aid of an additional Arab army. But did this imply that Syria would enter a conflagration with Israel out of choice, or out of necessity? A survey of Syrian statements from 1978 indeed points to a new Syrian approach to the situation, but does not necessarily imply that Syria would deliberately stand alone.

A number of underlying principles of strategic parity were outlined:

First, Syrian Minister of Information Ahmed Iskandar was quoted by the Kuwaiti *Al-Rai al-Aam* on February 14, 1978 as saying, "The balance of forces was upset in favor of the Zionist enemy after Sadat's steps and moves to isolate Egypt from the Arab nation. Syria, on the other hand, works toward building a defense potential that is aimed at strategic parity with the Zionist enemy, while acknowledging that even if it is the only one left...it would still remain firm.... Actually we believe that our stand not only benefits the citizens of Syria but meets the expectations of the Arab masses wherever they may be." In other words, parity is essentially defensive and is part of an overall Arab drive that Egypt has chosen to abandon.

In order for Syria to defend itself against Israel, it must strengthen its staying power. According to Iskandar, during the 1973 Yom Kippur War Syria withstood the bombing of its civilian infrastructure — electricity, transportation, ports and water — and sustained heavy losses and damages, but its stamina was undeterred. In future, it must strengthen its staying power yet further.

But as Bassam al-Asali wrote in *Tishrin* on March 5, 1979, a third basic goal of Syria is to "liberate occupied land." According to the Syrian perception, all of Israel is considered "occupied," but priority is given to the Golan Heights conquered by Israel in 1967. The land will be liberated by "adopting a combat doctrine that is essentially aggressive and is capable of upsetting the current balance of forces." This concept offered no definition of the stages or prerequisites necessary for achieving the ultimate objective and putting the plan of attack into practice. Defense was perceived as the goal at hand and attack as the ultimate vision.

Finally, laying the groundwork for strategic parity entailed boosting the morale of the army and of society-at-large, preparing and restructuring the economic front in order to derive maximum benefit from Syrian resources, and bolstering the diplomatic and home fronts.

Diplomatic preparedness was described in various journals as a planned political process based on a number of principles: isolating Israel from its allies, attaining international legitimization for Syria's ultimate use of force, acquiring worldwide sympathy, and creating appropriate strategic alliances — first and foremost with the USSR. On the internal front, the economy should be kept vital during preparations for war, and made capable of functioning throughout the duration of war, to provide necessary supplies for the population.

It would therefore appear that strategic parity was primarily intended to protect Syria against Israeli attack. The idea of Syria standing alone was not a principle but a necessity. It was based on the assumption that Syria would require the support of a superpower, and that its steadfastness would eventually be rewarded by the military solidarity of additional Arab states. Indeed, reliance on Arab aid has been a cornerstone of Syrian policy. Its coffers have been filled by large amounts of aid from the oil-rich Arab states ever since strategic parity was conceived — one billion dollars by 1989. Strategic parity, then, also aimed at providing a framework for a variety of concepts and operations in implementing the doctrines of Syrian national security, bolstering the armed forces, strengthening the society and the regime, and improving the economy and cementing political ties with the USSR and other Arab countries, with the exception of Egypt.

Force-Building

During the Yom Kippur War, the Syrian armed forces suffered significant losses in weapons systems and materiel. Human losses, though not insignificant, were not critical: some 4,000 soldiers killed and another 10,000 injured. But the Syrian Air Force lost 135 combat aircraft, some 1100 tanks were destroyed or disabled — many of them captured by the IDF — and 250 artillery pieces were put out of commission.

After the war, a rehabilitation effort got underway that assimilated the lessons learned from the war. In particular, air defense was upgraded: new SAM batteries, including the mobile SA-6, were acquired, with total deployment rising from 36 in 1973 to about 70 in 1978. During the same period the Syrian Air Force was equipped with the latest MiG-23 and MiG-25 combat aircraft and, for the first time, anti-tank helicopters. The regular army was enlarged from 185,000 in 1973 to more than 290,000 in 1978. Armor increased from about 1650 tanks before the war to 2650 in 1978 — this, after replacing tanks lost in the war; APCs and artillery from 1000 in pre-war 1973 to 1650 in 1978, and from 1200 to 2200, respectively. Infantry divisions were converted to mechanized divisions, and a third armored division was added.

In addition to this enhancement of forces and arms, the entire front with Israel was fortified from the Jordan border in the south to Mt. Hermon in the north. The line of fortifications that was overrun in 1973 was widened and deepened. A series of artificial obstacles was added, as well as deeper defense alignments and fortified positions for mechanized formations, based on infantry and anti-tank defenses, tanks and APCs that take up prepared positions. Tanks were concentrated in an armored reserve force from the brigade echelon to the general staff echelon, to respond to the contingency of an enemy breakthrough. For the first time, the Syrian Army, totalling 5-6 divisions, posed a real challenge to IDF mobility and maneuverability.

Syria's force-building efforts gave it a viable defensive potential. Its political and military leaders felt assured of its effectiveness. In 1981, when Israel intervened in the Lebanese Christians' conflict with Palestinian and Muslim forces and the IAF downed two Syrian helicopters in the Zahleh sector of the Biq'a, Syria responded by deploying surface-to-air missiles along the Syrian-Lebanese border and in the Biq'a. Israel refrained from reacting to what was clearly a marked change in the Lebanese military situation. The Syrian move and the IDF's avoidance of a response gave Syria additional confidence in its defensive potential.

Attaining strategic parity generated further intensification of the Syrian-Israeli arms race. The Syrians were aware that between 1974 and 1979, in parallel with Syria's own enhancement program, the IDF doubled its combat aircraft force and enhanced its qualitative capabilities, and doubled its armored divisions and total tank contingent. A new increase was now needed by the Syrian Armed Forces, and a new stage in the arms race began. It lasted until summer 1982, when the Syrian Army in Lebanon was forced to defend itself against a massive IDF attack.

From 1978 to 1982 manpower increased from 290,000 to about 313,000; combat aircraft from 480 to 600; the helicopter force rose from 100 in 1978 to 165 in 1982, 45 of which were anti-tank helicopters; and SAM batteries reached nearly 110, compared with 70 in 1978. In the army, an armored division was added at the expense of a mechanized one; tanks were increased from 2200 to 3600, and the new high quality T-72 made its appearance. APCs rose from 1650 to 2700. For the first time, the Syrians obtained Scud SS missiles with a range that covered many sensitive targets in Israel.

Concurrently, Syria stationed a considerable part of its six division-strong army in Lebanon. Its military presence there was not aimed against Israel. Rather, it was dispatched because of the civil war and in view of the danger perceived to Syria's permanent interests in Lebanon — one of which was a say in political developments there. The Syrians were quick to see that, notwithstanding the massive deployment of their army, Lebanese problems did not lend themselves to easy solutions. The Syrian Army soon took on the attributes of a permanent force in Lebanon.

The Syrians had to contend with the possibility that their stay in Lebanon, perpetuated by deteriorating central rule there, coupled with the Israeli struggle against the PLO's "state within a state" in Lebanon, might open up an additional front between Syria and Israel. This danger found graphic expression in 1978, when a large IDF force invaded Southern Lebanon up to the Litani River. But at the time, Syrian and Israeli forces did not clash.

Thus basic Syrian defense requirements, the permanent presence in Lebanon, and the enhancement of Syria's armed forces, all contributed to a decision to develop a defensive alignment in the Biq'a aimed at protecting Syria against a move by the IDF to outflank Syria's main line of defense on the Golan Heights.

If we compare the scope of Syrian force-building following the Yom Kippur War from 1974 to 1978, with the force-building effort generated by the policy of strategic parity, it emerges that the former effort was greater than the latter. This may be explained by a prevailing phenomenon in the Middle East: every war brings in its wake, for victor and vanquished alike, a new arms race that is much more intensive than the preceding one. Such an arms race exceeds in scope any force-building effort that derives from the adoption or alteration of a national security doctrine.

Notably, Syrian efforts to achieve a defensive potential were accompanied by a complete relaxation on the Golan Heights front — in sharp contrast with the flammable situation before 1973. Syrian policy apparently held that as long as Syria did not have a viable defensive capability and had not achieved strategic parity, there was no point in tangling with the IDF. The only exceptions were dogfights over Lebanon when the IDF attempted to enforce a policy of free access to Lebanese air space with flights close to Syria's western border; a number of Syrian interception attempts led to the downing of Syrian aircraft by the IAF.

Strategic Parity and the Soviet Union

Strategic parity as a policy was not the result of prior coordination between Syria and the Soviet Union. However it was clear to Syria that it required the comprehensive military and political backing of a superpower. This was particularly critical if it wanted to develop the potential to defend itself independently against the powerful Israeli army or, alternatively, even initiate war against Israel. Although Syria had acquired advanced Soviet weaponry by the early '60s, it did not then rely exclusively on Soviet political and military aid. Even after its army was crushed in 1967 and it commenced intensified weapons acquisitions from Moscow, Damascus avoided formulating a policy of constant reliance on Soviet aid. Syrian President Hafez al-Assad, who came to power at the beginning of the '70s, sought for two years to pursue a policy aimed at diversifying weapons sources and abstaining from complete Soviet reliance. This contrasted with the Egyptian policy of the time, of acquiring nearly all weaponry from the Soviet Union, with little attempt to diversify. Soviet-Syrian diplomatic relations, as well as Assad's personal relationship with the Soviet leadership, were not exemplary, and the Soviets feared a further cooling off. After all, Moscow had backed Assad's opponents in their struggle for power in the year 1969-1970.

Assad's 1972 visit to Moscow ushered in a new era. An agreement was signed for the intensive supply of Soviet weapons systems to Syria. For a year and a quarter, until the Yom Kippur War, the Syrian Army absorbed new acquisitions from the USSR, and consequently entered the war well equipped. During the course of the war, and in its aftermath, the Soviets replenished all Syrian losses, usually with superior new systems. From that time on, Syria was one of the world's biggest consumers of Soviet weaponry. Certain arms, principal weapons systems in particular, appeared in Syria two or three years after they were first introduced in the USSR, and sometimes before they were sent to Warsaw Pact states.

While strategic parity meant another escalation in the supply of all types of weapons, Syria did not consider this adequate, as it perceived that the US-Israel relationship still gave Israel an edge. The entry of Egypt into the American sphere of influence further heightened Israel's advantages and superiority over Syria. Prior to 1980, Assad had shied away from a binding political and military pact with the USSR, out of domestic considerations and concern for his position in the Arab world, and had therefore rejected Soviet offers to establish a friendship and cooperation pact.

In 1980 Assad did an about-face. Domestically, both his personal position of power and that of the regime were deteriorating. Disquiet and riots were spreading. An agreement with the USSR looked like a promising way to shore up his stature. Beyond Syria's borders, there was a need to find an external deterrent against Israeli attack and to provide backing for initiatives in Lebanon that Syria was hesitant to undertake for fear of Israeli response. Moreover, Syria remained extremely isolated in the Arab world: Egypt had formalized the peace process; Iraq was preoccupied with Iran, and preparations for war were in full swing; Jordan supported Muslim Brotherhood elements that were chiefly responsible for the riots in Syria in 1980; and Israel was enjoying a growing political and military relationship with the US. The quest for strategic parity, Syria's domestic situation, its position in the Middle East and Lebanon, and its sense of vulnerability in the event of an Israeli attack, caused Damascus to seek compensation in the form of a new relationship with the USSR.

For its part, global and regional interests and a desire to protect its vast investment in Syria gave Moscow sufficient cause to sign a friendship and cooperation agreement. Yet the accord evidently fell far short of Syrian wishes. It was not a binding defense pact, and there were no unequivocal Soviet military undertakings and no clear promise of Soviet intervention if Syria became embroiled in war. Indeed, it was difficult to find any real change from the prior military and political configuration of Syrian-Soviet relations. Syria judged the friendship and cooperation agreement to be far inferior to the framework of American-Israeli strategic cooperation.

True, the new pact did comprise a clear Soviet pledge to support Syria in extreme cases. But undertakings of this kind had preceded the treaty. Thus the USSR conceivably would intervene militarily to defend Syria in the event of a military threat to its sovereignty or the survival of its regime. Intervention would take the form of a naval deployment near Syria, and resupply of losses in aircraft, air defense systems and intelligence early warning and EW systems. In the most drastic scenario, a Soviet deterrent force might be transported by air and sealift.

If we examine Syria's military crises since the 1973 Yom Kippur War, it appears that Soviet aid, including limited direct and indirect involvement, reached a peak during that war and the ensuing war of attrition from February until the end of May 1974. This predates by far the signing of the agreement in 1980. But actual fighting was then taking place on Syrian territory.

Other instances of peak military activity, such as the entry of Syrian troops into Lebanon in 1976, the missile crisis in the

Lebanese Biq'a in April 1981, and the Lebanon War in 1982, all reflected a Syrian readiness to take crucial steps without prior consultation with the Soviets. For its part, even while providing political and propaganda support for Syria, the USSR took no meaningful military steps as long as Syria was not in any sort of existential danger. Thus neither strategic parity on the one hand, nor the Syrian-Soviet friendship pact on the other, appeared to provide Syria with more Soviet aid and backing than it had enjoyed prior to 1973. Syria never once attempted to find a substitute for the USSR, as such a move would have forced it to drastically alter its policy. However by 1985 an approach to strategic parity began surfacing in Syria that advocated a reduced reliance on the Soviets. This trend gained impetus progressively, as the Soviet Union became increasingly engrossed in its own internal affairs and in developments in the Eastern Bloc, and as Syria was called upon to pay full price for Soviet arms that it used to receive on special terms.

In an interview with *The Washington Post* in September 1987, President Assad raised a number of important points regarding strategic parity and Soviet-Syrian relations. He claimed that Syria would continue to strive toward military strategic parity with Israel in spite of the ongoing calm on the Golan, and notwithstanding Soviet efforts to reduce the level of enmity between Syria and Israel. Assad assessed that as long as Israel felt that it had the upper hand, it would never agree to a 'just peace.' As for the new thinking in Soviet policy, it could not possibly modify Syria's declared ambition to achieve military equality with Israel.

Strategic Parity, the Arab States, and the Lebanon War

Egypt's isolation in the Arab world following the signing of the peace accords facilitated Syria's task of recruiting Arab financial support for its force-building program. Less successful was Syria's attempt to forge an eastern military front to supplant Egypt's contribution to an Arab war effort with Israel. The Baghdad Summit of November 1978 ended non-committally, and Jordan did not wish to join a front headed by Syria. The Iraq-Iran War, which began in late 1980, exacerbated tensions between Iraq and Syria. Thus from the outset strategic parity did not obtain sufficient Arab backing. Syria remained isolated, supported only by Libya, whose backing was minimal.

The Lebanon War of 1982 proved detrimental to Syria's defensive capability and its strategic parity concept. Israel launched the war in Lebanon against Palestinian concentrations in the south; lack of restraint in its decisionmaking process led it to expand the campaign to eliminate the political and military presence of Palestinian groups elsewhere in Lebanon, and even to attack Syrian troops in the Shouf Mountains and the Biq'a. By taking the initiative the IDF had sufficient time to mobilize forces so as to neutralize any possible counterattack by the Syrian Army on the Golan Heights front.

When Israel turned upon it, the Syrian surface-to-air missile alignment in the Biq'a, an integral part of the Syrian air defense network, was destroyed within hours, along with 90 Syrian combat aircraft; 10 anti-tank helicopters were downed in the first week of fighting. In land battles, a Syrian armored division that defended the Biq'a suffered serious losses and withdrew. IDF forces reached within tank gun range of the Beirut-Damascus road. The army, which Syria claimed to have stationed in Lebanon to protect that country from attack, did not fulfill its mission. Although the Syrian Army and leadership regarded the land battles as successful in light of circumstances and in view of the IDF's superior forces, there was no way to excuse the dismal showing of the air force and air defense forces, both pivotal elements in any successful defense. The overall Syrian order-of-battle, which had nearly doubled since 1974, was still incapable of simultaneously defending two fronts when the IDF was not otherwise involved in attacking or defending along its Egyptian and/or Jordanian fronts.

The fact that not one Arab state came to its aid when it was directly attacked by Israel, added insult to Syria's injury. Libya's weapons contribution was negligible. Syria's experience once again proved that the primary goal of strategic parity should be defense. If the main problem had been centered until 1982 on a single front, the Golan Heights, then after 1982 an adequate defensive response would be necessary on the Lebanese front as well. Syrian leaders and the military recognized that a successful defensive posture would have to take into consideration a surprise strike by Israel in the manner of 1967 or 1982. This deduction in turn generated drastic changes in permanent deployment and in the structure of the senior staff echelon after 1982.

Yet neither these dramatic events nor Syria's disappointments could alter its basic perception. It could not turn to the Arab world because there was no help forthcoming: Egypt persevered in the peace process; Iraq was in a critical phase of its war with Iran; and the remaining Arab states were neither capable nor sufficiently motivated to provide any real support — even traditional Saudi aid was reduced by plummeting oil revenues.

Considering these pressing circumstances, the new force-building effort was more impressive than ever. Emphasis was placed not on weapons systems, but on an effective force reorganization to facilitate simultaneously combat on two fronts. From 1982 to 1986, armed forces manpower grew from 313,000 to about 400,000 soldiers. Three new divisions, two armored and one mechanized, were established. By 1990 land forces had been brought to 11 divisions as opposed to six in 1982. Two headquarters were set up, one for the Golan Heights and one for the Lebanese front, so that General Staff Headquarters would not have to cope with the impossible task of controlling 11 fighting divisions. Commando forces were increased and subordinated to a divisional framework and an additional seven independent brigade-size formations. The expansion of ground forces enabled the development of a general staff strategic reserve that could be committed to either of the fronts at a critical juncture. The additional field command at the corps echelon that was required to fulfill such an objective was lacking by 1990, but was expected to make its appearance eventually. Along the Golan Heights and in the Biq'a fortifications were reinforced; by 1990 they were considered to be the strongest in the world.

A special effort was invested in force-building in the air force. Some 70 percent of total expenditures for arms acquisition was devoted to acquiring advanced aircraft such as the MiG-29 and the Su-24, attack/anti-tank helicopters, surface-to-air missiles and C^3I and EW systems.

Air defense, once based almost exclusively on obsolete missiles like the SA-2, SA-3 and mobile SA-6 batteries, took on a new dimension. New Soviet supplies included long-range SA-5 batteries with a wide, deep parameter of coverage, and SP missile batteries of the SA-7, SA-8, SA-9, SA-13, SA-14 and SA-16 class. This expanse of surface-to-air missile coverage — from SA-5s with a range of 100 km or more down to short-range shoulder-launched missiles — was intended to cover the entire combat arena, while holding Syrian losses to a minimum.

The range of Syria's surface-to-surface missiles — FROG, Scud and SS-21 — had little direct defensive significance. Rather, they played a deterrent role vis-a-vis Israel, and were intended to balance what Syria perceived as a nonconventional potential equal to none in the region. When employed, the missiles were designated to be part of a joint, comprehensive attack on Israel. Thus the Syrian force-building effort after 1982 continued along the lines prescribed by the doctrine of strategic parity, but gained a new dimension in light of the lessons of the Lebanon War. The idea of war on two fronts — the Golan Heights and Lebanon — had now become a distinct possibility.

Here we encounter the question, whether the concept of strategic parity altered the normal course of force-building. In point of fact, since the 1967 Six-Day War, there has been no 'normal' force-building either in Israel or among its neighbors, Egypt, Syria, Jordan or even distant Iraq. It was the wars themselves and their outcomes that dictated patterns of expansion, such as that of the IDF from 1974 to 1980, or the Egyptian Army from 1968 to 1973. Syria's force-building program was also determined by extraneous events: the 1973 Yom Kippur War followed by Egypt's move in 1974 toward a political settlement, the Egypt-Israel rapprochement of 1977 and the doctrine of strategic parity that came in its wake; and the 1982 Lebanon War. The periods of most intense force expansion occurred in the aftermaths of the 1973 and 1982 wars.

The Economic Crisis and its Ramifications

As a result of wartime losses and as a consequence of its doctrine of strategic parity, Syrian efforts at military expansion beginning in 1973 required heavy budgetary outlays. The defense spending allotment in the Syrian budget, for example, was $2.5 billion in 1982 and $3.2 billion in 1984 (the latter reflecting Lebanon War-induced expenses).

Syria moved in two directions to expand its military: striking power and staying power. In 1973, the offensive strike capability had proven inadequate, while Syrian staying power had proven itself. By 1982, with the failure of Syrian defenses, there was a new incentive to enhance stamina as well as developing an attack capability. All told, by 1990 Syria had spent 20 years trying to develop these two cardinal capabilities. For a country on the scale of Syria an undertaking of these dimensions is nearly impossible to sustain over a long period of time. With worsening economic conditions in 1984 and in 1986 a crisis was reached, and the armed forces and force-building programs were among the earliest casualties.

The army was forced to cut expenses. Training was cut back by over 50 percent in 1987. Combat units in most formations were frozen and their activities cut to a minimum. The economic crisis not only affected training, which can be compensated for over time, but it also hit the salaries of NCOs and officers, and the pinch was felt throughout the ranks. This, in turn, influenced the regime's ability to take new political and military initiatives.

In 1988 the economy, particularly the agriculture and oil sectors, showed signs of recovery. The scope and frequency of training increased, but did not reach their previous level. Units at the fronts renewed many activities, and some mothballed weaponry was reissued. Still, the wealthy Arab states continued gradually to cut back their financial aid, and the USSR insisted on full payment for its military equipment. Unless there were a war, which could change the entire picture, it was unlikely that the Syrian Army would be able to sustain the force-building rate that it had in the past. Indeed, force-building could conceivably come to a full stop.

Strategic Parity and an Offensive Against Israel

Inherent in the concept of strategic parity from the very outset was the goal of eventually developing a capability to attack Israel in order to challenge its extended occupation of Syrian territory on the Golan Heights.

The offensive approach, having proven itself in 1973, remained a constant component of Syrian doctrine. Yet more burning issues had since pushed to the forefront. The first priority was the development of a defensive capability. Next on the agenda was the need for a military presence in Lebanon to safeguard Syria's short- and long-term interest and to protect its western flank against possible Israeli attack.

Following the war in Lebanon and throughout the 1980s, Syria's force-building program — particularly the doubling of its divisions and establishment of two corps headquarters — gave the regime reason to believe that it had achieved a suitable defensive capability. Yet this did not imply a direct path to an offensive capability. In order to initiate a war, several prerequisites had to be met.

A discussion of prerequisites for an offensive initiative requires extreme caution lest it leave the impression that once the list is completed, war is inevitable. For one, there are several contradictory preconditions, and frequently it is difficult to sort out their relationship. It is also virtually impossible to distinguish between necessary and merely desirable conditions. We recall for example the inaccuracy of Israel's 1972-1973 appraisal of conditions that it thought were prerequisites for Egypt to go to war.

With regard to Syria and strategic parity, Damascus' list of prerequisites appears to be as follows: First, there must be a national goal that justifies going to war, despite the risks it engenders. The first and foremost goal is the return of Syrian territory on the Golan Heights conquered by Israel in 1967. Secondly, Syria requires a defensive capability that will prevent a military defeat in the event of war with Israel. By 1990 Syria evidently was convinced that it had reached such a defensive capability, even though it remained vulnerable on several accounts, particularly with regard to Israel's superior air power.

Third, sufficient military might is required for a preemptive strike. Obviously it is not easy to measure this strength, but by 1990 Syria appeared to possess an offensive capability that depended on the circumstances in which war was initiated. This points to the importance of the fourth and fifth prerequisites: superpower political and military backing, and a united Arab front or joint effort with another strong Arab state analogous to 1973. By 1990 Syria had new reasons to doubt whether the Soviet Union would back it in the event it initiated warfare; and there was no such Arab front. Egypt had removed itself from the cycle of war and Jordan did not see itself as part of an attack coalition. Iraq had the largest and strongest army in the Middle East, but because of its longstanding enmity toward Syria, it would not wish to be dragged into a war in which Syria led the coalition and took the initiatives. Iraq would perhaps be prepared to set up its own front against Israel, but only in accord with its own interests and with Syria as a junior partner.

As a sixth prerequisite, Syria would need to rely on a global climate conducive to confrontation in the Middle East, i.e., an atmosphere of superpower tension. Yet in 1990 the direct opposite trend was evident. The superpower component relates also to a seventh prerequisite: the possibility of generating a prolonged political process to exploit, to Syria's advantage, either battlefield victories or the impact of the war itself. Prior to the 1973 war Syria had not recognized the need for a political process. Having joined forces with Egypt to launch the war, it was determined to recapture the Golan Heights, in part or in full, and to hang onto its achievements by dint of military force alone. This explains why Syria gained no further ground politically after forfeiting its initial military gains at the outset of the war. Egypt, on the other hand, emerged with more impressive achievements because it adroitly exploited both Soviet aid and the US political initiative during the course of the war itself. In this sense, recent signs of a possible readiness on the part of President Assad to discuss a settlement with Israel, do not necessarily preclude an offensive initiative on his part. On the contrary, they could dovetail with it.

An eighth prerequisite for a Syrian offensive is that Israel's political and military fortunes be at a low ebb. By 1990 Israel was indeed experiencing political difficulties, but it was doubtful whether its military capability had been reduced. And finally, Syria would have to assess that maintaining the present situation was worse than war. There were no clear indications that either the president or the regime had reached this conclusion by mid-1990.

Before the Lebanon War in 1982, and during the immediate aftermath, it was commonly held that Syria would take pains to avoid jeopardizing its presence and influence in Lebanon by initiating a war against Israel. By mid-1990, in view of Israel's failure to influence developments in Lebanon in the period following 1982 and until the IDF evacuation in 1985, Syria did not seem bothered by this possibility. The evacuation was undertaken without direct Syrian pressure. Nor did Syria assess, in the aftermath, that Israel would repeat its Lebanese adventure. Still, it had to contend with the fear that Israel would use Lebanese territory for a strike against Syria itself.

To conclude this assessment of Syria's offensive calculations, the Syrian regime has demonstrated patience and restraint on the one hand, persistence and stubbornness on the other. In March 1987 Assad stated that Syria confronted economic difficulties, yet these were merely temporary impediments. In August of 1987, he declared that Syria was firm in its determination to reach strategic parity with Israel, but that this was a long process requiring stamina, patience and forbearance. In a March 1988 speech, Assad claimed that it was clear to him and the ruling regime that strategic parity could not be reached overnight. It would require time and effort, but Syria had already come a long way toward achieving it. In August 1988 he added that there could be no turning away from the goal of strategic parity between an isolated Syria and Israel, because it was incumbent upon Syria to uphold the Arab nationalist struggle against Zionism. If victory did not seem immediately at hand, this did not mean defeat. In even more recent statements, possibly provoked by Saddam Hussein's presentation of Iraq's chemical-warfare capabilities as constituting a kind of strategic parity with Israel, Assad, too, made guarded assertions of this nature.

Scenarios for a Syrian Offensive Against Israel

If and when Syria decides that it has the capability to launch a war against Israel, it could choose between several possible courses of action.

Remembering its joint success with Egypt in 1973, Syria is likely to open with a surprise attack on the Golan Heights. The permanent, unalterable state of affairs is that regular IDF forces there will always be numerically inferior to Syrian regular forces, whose deployment facilitates a surprise attack. Hence Syria has an incentive to undertake this step. Would Israel and the IDF be taken by surprise? The answer is not clear. If Israel mobilized enough reserve troops in time, a Syrian preemptive strike would have little chance of registering any achievement.

While a war against Israel would be designed essentially to liberate the Golan Heights, a secondary offensive from Lebanon could help attain that objective. Even in the event of war, the sizable Syrian forces permanently stationed in the Biq'a would not be redeployed in the Golan for fear that an Israeli counterattack would be delivered via Lebanon.

Syria could reduce the scope of its combat objectives by attacking, capturing and securing only the most accessible parts of the Golan Heights. Its ability to defend the captured territory after instigating the attack would determine the true military merit of the action.

Under all of its offensive options, Syria could attack the IDF rear-echelon infrastructure with surface-to-surface missiles mounted with chemical warheads; this would confuse and delay the call-up and deployment of reserve units. This option is a realistic one, yet it is doubtful whether it would significantly change the balance of forces, since IDF military installations and forces are well protected against this kind of attack.

Syria is also capable of wreaking havoc by deploying missiles, combat aircraft and chemical warfare agents against the Israeli civilian population in an effort to erode Israel's endurance and force it to consider far-reaching concessions. This option presumably reflects a Syrian line of thought predicated on the theory that Israel is extremely sensitive to losses. Yet Israel's own capacity for striking the Syrian civilian population is ten times greater than Syria's, and one may doubt whether the regime in Damascus could depend on the Syrian civilian population's readiness to make such sacrifices.

As for Israel, there is a longstanding myth regarding its sensitivity to losses. True, it has on occasion made unusually far-reaching efforts with adversaries to effect the return of POWs and even the bodies of fallen soldiers. IDF military operations are also undoubtedly planned with the goal of minimizing casualties. Yet there is no clear proof that national morale is lowered in the wake of losses, nor is there evidence that Israeli governments have avoided specific military options because of the casualties they might incur. The War of Independence was conducted with no thought of losses. Israeli cross-border retaliatory attacks have often generated more casualties among IDF soldiers than the number of civilians and soldiers killed by the Arab terrorist acts that instigated them. During the stormy period between Israel and its neighbors from 1967 to 1973, political and practical military considerations took precedence to a degree over concern for losses, say, in the War of Attrition with Egypt. Nor were the war in Lebanon and the military operations that followed guided by a supreme need to prevent casualties. Certainly were Israel to be the victim of a premeditated Syrian chemical attack on its civilian population, any lingering doubts in Israel about the legitimacy of its war aims would quickly be dissipated. It is therefore difficult to conceive of Syria using Israel's concern about possible losses as a consideration for instigating war, unless Syria were absolutely convinced of its veracity. In instigating a war against Israel with the objective of capturing territory and causing civilian casualties,

Syria is thus liable to wind up emptyhanded.

Nor do any of the options mentioned above offer Syria the hope of registering a decisive victory. It could of course hope for partial gains — yet these could be neutralized by an IDF counterattack deep within Syrian territory. If the counterattack were not decisive, the conflict would develop into a stalemate, particularly were Iraqi or Jordanian troops to reinforce Syria during the course of the war. Even in the event of such a draw, in the absence of a Syrian political initiative to exploit the gains of the war it is difficult to visualize any real Syrian success in loosening Israel's grip on the Golan Heights. Yet under circumstances prevailing in 1989 and early 1990 Syria could not count on support from either Iraq or Jordan, nor could it rely on superpower backing during the course of a war it had initiated.

All of the preceding scenarios would be subject to change were the Syrian leadership to conclude that the present situation was worse than an unsuccessful war. This would involve considerations and decisions of a highly subjective nature. To the extent that we can rely upon past experience, Assad's decisionmaking process has been handled along absolute pragmatic lines, although he has erred at times in his judgments.

In any event, by mid-1990 Syria and its armed forces were actively preparing an offensive war military option against Israel — while at the same time maintaining a defensive capability. Indeed, from company training and maneuvers to general command headquarters exercises, the army has been readying itself for years toward this end. The offensive mode dominates the army's day-to-day agenda. The structure, organization and ordnance of tactical forces unequivocally points to routine preparations for attack.

Two processes thus apparently exist side by side. The first is a continuous buildup for a Syrian offensive; the second — political and economic developments in Syria itself, in the Middle East and throughout the world that are not advancing Syria toward its coveted goal: the strategic parity that would enable it to initiate a war. These two trends do not contradict one another. In 1989-90, while the general drift of Syria's intentions had not essentially changed, it was not on the brink of war. In the long run, Syria had no intention of giving up the Golan Heights, while there seemed to be little inclination in Israel to discuss the future of the Golan Heights with it. Such intransigent positions on both sides could eventually lead to war. Yet the timing, the opportunity and the circumstances remained obscure.

★ ★ ★

Both Iraq's invasion of Kuwait, and the subsequent inter-Arab and international reaction, in effect constituted new constraints upon any conceivable near-term Syrian planning for war with Israel. Not only were no primary Arab partners available to establish an eastern front, but Syria itself was quickly persuaded to assign priority to the Iraqi threat, and sent troops of its own to Saudi Arabia to confront Iraq. Moreover the primacy of American leadership in the Gulf Crisis, and the dimensions of US-Soviet cooperation, seemed to guarantee that, at a minimum, no new Soviet support for Syrian war aims was in the offing. Most significantly, President Assad had taken a major step toward moving Syria away from both its inter-Arab and international isolation and its crumbling alliance with the Soviet Union, and realigning it with a pro-western bloc of Arab states.

The international dimension of the Gulf Crisis, Syria's decision to participate actively on the side of the anti-Iraq coalition of Arab and western powers, and the fact of PLO and Jordanian acquiescence in Saddam Hussein's aggression, bespoke the prospect of an energetic attempt by the US and its Arab partners to advance a Syrian-Israeli peace process in the post-crisis environment, perhaps at the expense of a Palestinian process. By addressing both Syria's claim on the Golan and its concerns in Lebanon, such a political process could conceivably go a long way toward alleviating two of Syria's key military strategic problems, thereby mitigating the need for an ongoing force-building program that has already strained the country's objective capabilities.

The prospect of such a process had not been entirely without foundation in the pre-crisis period. During the first half of 1990 Assad, having taken note of the growing Iraqi threat and taken stock of Syria's overall poor economic and strategic situation, had effected a rapprochement with Egypt. There were even hints of Syria-Israel communications about a peace process.

By October there were far too many variables at play to assess Syria's chances of reaping political benefits from the Gulf Crisis. Certainly, Syria's success in removing General Aoun in Lebanon appeared to reflect an enhanced freedom of maneuver in that arena. And President Assad had clearly taken a major step toward associating Syria with a political, in addition to a military option toward Israel. One key test of the permanency of any major Syrian realignment would be the prospect of Syrian arms acquisitions, however symbolic in scope at the outset, from the US. This could also be a serious harbinger of change in US attitudes toward Israel.

7. The Israeli-Palestinian Conflict and the Peace Process

by Joseph Alpher

The year 1989 corresponded roughly with the second year of the *intifada* — the Palestinian uprising in the Israeli-administered territories of the West Bank and Gaza. While the uprising itself continued to display many of the features and characteristics of the previous year, 1989 marked the initiation of a new Israeli-Palestinian political process. The process was generated by the uprising, and developed around an Israeli initiative to develop terms for an interim settlement.

The Israeli initiative and the Palestinian uprising both survived the calendar year; neither registered remarkable progress toward a resolution of the Palestinian issue. What constrained the peace process in particular was the reticence of the three parties primarily involved — Israel, the PLO and the United States, each for different reasons — to make significant concessions or take dramatic initiatives. Even Egypt's rather remarkable innovative role in the process could not compensate for this.

The Israeli government of national unity barely survived the calendar year — brought down, for the first time in Israeli history, by the peace process. The Palestinian issue, and within it the question of how to deal with the Palestinian national leadership, the PLO, had become increasingly central to Israeli politics.

At the heart of the matter, what may have appeared to outsiders to be tactical concessions by Israelis and Palestinians were seen by these actors themselves as being of a strategic nature. The possible participation in peace talks of non-West Bank and Gazan Palestinians; the question of even an indirect role for the PLO in the process; these and other seemingly procedural issues tended frequently to obfuscate to outside observers the essence of the struggle. This pitted Israeli readiness — in varying degrees, depending on political orientation — to begin a long peace process in the Territories alone, without acknowledging a Palestinian right to sovereignty, against the PLO demand, supported almost universally by the Palestinians, that in one way or another, ultimate sovereign status for all Palestinians be assured at an early stage of the process.

Perhaps the most significant ramification of the process during 1989 and early 1990 was a dramatic erosion in US public support for Israel. By mid-1990 a survey sponsored by the Anti-Defamation League of B'nai B'rith indicated that more Americans supported the Palestinian camp than Israel.

The Israeli Initiative

Throughout the spring of 1989 two interlocking developments combined to generate a new Israeli government proposal for a peace process on the Palestinian issue. One was the ongoing pressure generated by the *intifada.* Despite the self-imposed physical deprivation of the Palestinian population (a 30-40 percent drop in standard of living, generated by continuing strikes and boycotts), and against a controlled effort by Israel to subdue the uprising, it was clear to the Israelis that, unless they were to transgress both their self-imposed moral constraints and their externally-generated political constraints, they could, at best, contain the uprising and limit its scope.

A second key factor was the advent of a new administration in Washington that sought to exploit its dialogue with the PLO, and its influence over Israel, to generate momentum for a peace process. Secretary of State James Baker called upon Israel as early as February to produce new and effective ideas toward that end. A March visit to Washington by Foreign Minister Arens was exploited to transmit a clear message to Jerusalem that Washington expected it to do something on the political plane to end the *intifada.* At the same time, it became apparent that the Bush administration would neither advance a plan of its own nor offer the Israelis and Palestinians far-reaching guarantees to entice them into a process.

These developments combined to produce a growing recognition on the part of the Likud bloc in the Israeli government that the absence of a political program for ending the *intifada* had become counterproductive (the Labor contingent in the renewed government of national unity had long held to this view) — at least as the foundation for a political position vis-a-vis the United States. As the Likud and Labor contingents in the new Israeli government developed their ideas on a peace process in the early months of 1989, two key elements were prominent. Both Likud and Labor continued to maintain the Israeli mainstream political rejection of dialogue with the PLO and of the establishment of a Palestinian state. Beyond this, what innovations and concessions they offered reflected primarily an Israeli readiness to talk with local Palestinians who were known supporters of the PLO, and a recognition of the need to improve Israel's image in the world, and primarily in the United States.

The substance of what came to be known as the Shamir Plan evolved out of a plan presented in late January by Defense Minister Rabin (Labor). Rabin's initial formulation envisaged a three to six month period of quiet in the Territories, followed by free elections; Israel would then negotiate with the elected Palestinians — regardless of their affiliation — and offer them comprehensive autonomy; after the autonomy stage Israel would propose a federative structure involving itself and Jordan.

Rabin emphasized that his plan rejected the notions of a Palestinian state or of direct negotiations with the PLO. Rather, it was conceived in accordance with the principle that the 1.5 million Palestinians in the West Bank and Gaza should negotiate their future for themselves. Accordingly, he accompanied his initiative with a broad effort at dialogue with local Palestinian leaders, including even Islamic fundamentalist extremists from Gaza. He also ordered the release from administrative detention of the most prominent of the local Palestinian nationalists, Faisal al-Husseini.

In April 1989 Prime Minister Shamir unveiled the outlines of his plan in Washington, and on May 14 it was approved in final form by the Israeli government. The Israeli plan comprised four steps, to "be dealt with simultaneously:" a mechanism for carrying out the Palestinian autonomy provisions of the Camp David Accords; a provision for enhancing relations between Israel and Egypt; a call for rehabilitation of the Palestinian refugees in camps in the West Bank and Gaza; and expansion of the peace process to include all Arab states still at war with Israel. (See complete plan in appendix.)

Of these four elements, the plan went into detail only regarding the autonomy phase, and then only after setting forth the twin premises of Israeli rejection of the establishment of a Palestinian state in the Territories and Israeli refusal to negotiate with the PLO. It proposed that the residents of the Territories freely elect representatives to negotiate a five year transition period of autonomy. After three years of autonomy, a permanent political solution would be negotiated, with the new self-governing authority constituting the Palestinian delegation in these negotiations. At that time any and all proposals could be tabled for discussion. This final stage would also include "arrangements for peace and borders between Israel and Jordan."

The Israeli proposal essentially began with the Camp David autonomy idea agreed upon in 1978 between Israel, Egypt and the United States, with two key changes: the process was now to be negotiated directly with the Palestinians; and elections would be the means of selecting the Palestinian delegation. It referred only to Palestinians in the West Bank and Gaza — not members of the exile community, nor even residents of East Jerusalem. Its great advantage from the Israeli domestic standpoint was its acceptability to both Labor leaders Rabin and Shimon Peres and to the Likud. Prime Minister Shamir argued that the proposal accommodated the Likud position on the Territories — i.e., they must never be delivered to non-Israeli rule — in that Israel would be free, in the second stage negotiations, to reject proposals for Arab sovereignty, thereby perpetuating autonomy. Rabin and Peres, who continued to seek heavy Jordanian involvement in a final settlement (a traditional Labor position regarding the Palestinian issue), and rejected the concepts of a major PLO role or a totally sovereign Palestinian state as unacceptable politically from the Israeli domestic standpoint, argued that they would be free to proffer their "territories for peace" formula when, three years after the beginning of autonomy, final stage negotiations began.

Meanwhile, both the Likud and Labor leaderships recognized that the key to maintaining a consensus over the proposal lay in avoiding the necessity of dealing with details that might reveal their differences. Presumably, they had produced the plan on the assumption that it would be possible to persuade local Palestinian leaders to run in elections without the direct involvement of the PLO. Yet, because Shamir and Rabin disagreed over even "local" issues such as the right of East Jerusalem Palestinians to vote (Shamir was opposed, Rabin in favor), they sought to avoid tackling these questions at least until the Arab side had agreed on the principles they had put forth.

Initial Reactions

Herein lay the first difficulty. Most local Palestinian leaders hastened — in a statement signed by 80 of them and published on April 27, 1989 — to reject the very idea of elections held without PLO involvement, and prior to some form of IDF withdrawal from polling areas. The PLO was more explicit. Following the unveiling of the Israeli plan, Bassam Abu-Sharif, who regularly "tested" new ideas for Arafat, published an initial PLO response in *The Washington Post*. It insisted on at least partial IDF withdrawal prior to elections, international monitoring of the electoral process, and ultimately an international conference based on "the Palestinian right to self-determination." It made clear that East Jerusalem Arabs must participate in the initial stage, and the PLO in the final stage. But it did not totally reject the Israeli plan.

The Shamir-Rabin team would indeed prove flexible on some of these questions, such as monitoring and partial withdrawal. Yet the agreement to their plan on the part of "the Arab side" could not, from their standpoint, come from the PLO. This focused the spotlight on the United States, where Secretary of State Baker's Middle East team, led by Policy Planning chief Dennis Ross, began playing an active role in April and May in seeking clarifications regarding the Israeli plan and the PLO attitude. Ross led a visit to the region in mid-May in which the Israeli government was asked to prepare responses to its queries.

Thus while Israel argued that its plan had placed the ball in the Arab court, it directed its remarks to the Arab states and the United States rather than to the PLO; at the same time the US focused its efforts on extracting a green light for the Israeli initiative from the Tunis-based PLO leadership; finally, the local Palestinian leadership essentially deferred to the PLO, refusing to play the role Israel had designated for it.

The backdrop to the new US role was the American position regarding the process, as it evolved in April and May. On the one hand, President Bush and Secretary Baker publicly praised the Israeli initiative; on the other, they pressed for a "fleshing out" of the proposal, and outlined positions that were clearly incompatible with the Likud half of the government. In effect, Washington had seized upon a fairly minimalistic Israeli initiative that had been produced at its behest, and declared it "the only game in town," with the clear aim of developing it into a formula for progress — but only by mediating, not by offering a commitment of its own.

This process came to a head in Secretary Baker's speech to the AIPAC convention in Washington on May 22 — the sole detailed high-level enunciation of American policy on the Palestinian issue that was made throughout 1989. Baker offered a carefully balanced prescription of the many policy changes the US sought from both the Arab and the Israeli sides. In particular he elaborated US positions that conflicted with those of the Likud. Negotiations, he argued, would for Israel have to "involve territorial withdrawal and the emergence of a new political reality;" Israel must abandon "the unrealistic vision of a greater Israel. . . . Foreswear annexation. Stop settlement activity. . . . Reach out to the Palestinians as neighbors who deserve political rights." In a variety of references to the Palestinians' rights and status, Baker appeared to be describing an entity that approximated that which the PLO sought. In ascribing PLO positions to "Palestinians," he appeared to be equating the two and indirectly recognizing the PLO's role in a settlement.

Baker's speech was greeted angrily by Shamir, who called its innovations "useless" — they obviously went beyond his own vision of the plan that bore his name — and stonily by Rabin, who probably found Baker's approach broadly acceptable, but complained that it was counterproductive to dwell at this stage on issues upon which Likud and Labor were divided.

One of Baker's principal target audiences was probably the Arab summit which met shortly thereafter in Casablanca. There, in return for Arab readiness to avoid pressuring Syria over its role in Lebanon, Damascus was persuaded to endorse the PLO position on a settlement and to allow Egypt to return to the Arab League fold despite its peace with Israel. While these measures hardly added up to an Arab endorsement of either the Israeli or the American positions, they also could not be considered a rejection; indeed, the Arab world had implicitly given its support to the notion of a negotiated compromise Palestinian settlement with Israel.

Within Israel, most of the parties to the left of Labor, along with Labor's doves, gave their reluctant blessing to the Shamir initiative, noting that its eventual success would depend on Israel's readiness to satisfy at least some of the PLO's minimal conditions. On the Right, including within the Likud, Shamir encountered immediate and strident opposition. His plan was castigated as the "beginning of the end:" an initial set of concessions that would inevitably lead to a vicious circle of US and internal Israeli pressures for more, until Israel was forced to give up the Territories. Certainly the Right must have been upset by Finance Minister Peres' remark that the plan represented a "radical change in Shamir," and should therefore be supported. A coalition of forces within the Likud soon tried to place clear constraints on Shamir's freedom of maneuver. Ministers David Levi, Yitzhak Modai and Ariel Sharon forced Shamir to convene the Likud Central Committee, on July 5, 1989, to discuss their objections. These consisted of four demands: that East Jerusalem Arabs not be allowed to participate in autonomy elections; that Arab terrorism and violence cease before any negotiations begin; that no foreign sovereignty be applied anywhere within the bounds of the Land of Israel; and that no negotiations be held with the PLO.

After considerable political maneuvering, Shamir largely adopted these four principles in his policy speech to the Likud caucus. Indeed, it was clear that in terms of his personal views regarding his peace initiative, he was merely rendering explicit those constraints that in any case had determined his position all along, but which had been omitted from the Israeli plan in deference to the need to maintain a consensus with Labor. Hence Shamir hastened to clarify, after the caucus, that his acceptance of these constraints had in no way altered the Likud-Labor consensus over the peace plan. This flexibility on Shamir's part would at least allow the process to continue for a few more months. But the prime minister's ambivalence was also to prove increasingly a strain upon the minimal coalition consensus needed to maintain the Israeli peace initiative.

In summing up the overall ramifications of the introduction of the Israeli plan, one cannot ignore the interaction between internal Israeli reactions and those of the Palestinians and the US. By the end of May 1989 there appeared to be a distinct possibility that the demands upon Israel to elucidate key aspects of the plan in order to make it acceptable to the Palestinians — or even to the United States — could cause not only friction in US-Israeli relations, but an Israeli government crisis as well, insofar as Labor would be forthcoming with concessions while the Likud would not. In view of the positions delineated by Secretary of State Baker, and assuming an acceptable Palestinian response were forthcoming, it seemed inevitable that Washington would, within a few months, be asking for these concessions in order to maintain the momentum of the process — unless Palestinian objections to the plan rendered it a dead letter.

The United States sought to elicit a Palestinian response primarily by contacting the West Bank and Gazan leadership and via the direct channel opened up in Tunis in December 1988, but also, and increasingly, through Egyptian good offices. It found that Palestinian objections centered on what the Israeli proposal clearly did *not* contain: it focused strictly on the residents of Judea, Samaria and Gaza, avoiding mention of the Palestinian diaspora or the PLO; it offered no Israeli commitment as to the nature of a final settlement once the 3-5 year autonomy transition period was over; and it did not include the East Jerusalem Arabs among those who could vote and be elected in the autonomy negotiations. This was the mainstream PLO response. Outright rejection of the plan commenced within the PLO among Fatah hardliners like Farouq Kaddoumi, and included George Habbash and the PFLP. The DFLP, too, appeared to be divided, with movement leader Naif Hawatimah in opposition and Yasir Abd-Rabo (designated by Arafat to head the PLO delegation in talks with the US) leading a group of supporters. Beyond the PLO, the plan was opposed by Abu Musa's Fatah Rebels, Abu Nidal, the PFLP-GC and other pro-Syrian groups centered in Lebanon and Syria and supported increasingly by Iran, and by the *Hamas* Islamic fundamentalist movement centered in the Gaza Strip.

Hence PLO leader Arafat was also subject to conflicting pressures. These caused him to walk a political tightrope in responding to American and Egyptian demands for greater flexibility. In general, by summer 1989 the entire cumbersome process appears to have caused Arafat to call a halt to the flexibility and escalating moderation that he and the mainstream PLO had evinced for more than a year. This had culminated in the PNC affirmation of a two-state solution at Algiers in November 1988, the subsequent initiation of a US-PLO dialogue, Arafat's declaration in the spring of 1989 that the controversial Palestinian Covenant (which rejects not only Israel's existence, but even the existence of a Jewish people) was "caduque" — variously translated as "null and void," "obsolete," or "superseded" — and a plan unveiled by Arafat on July 27 that claimed to be modeled on the peace settlement in Namibia.

To break the summer deadlock, President Mubarak of Egypt

weighed in with his own plan. By now Egypt, with increasingly comprehensive inter-Arab and superpower backing, had assumed the role of official presenter of the PLO viewpoint to Israel. This circumvented, to the satisfaction of all parties, Israel's objections to being addressed directly by the PLO, and allowed Jerusalem to ignore its own inability to elicit independent responses from the West Bank and Gazan leadership to whom it had sought to address its initiative. Rather than describing a comprehensive peace, Mubarak sought, in messages passed to the parties to the conflict between June and September, to lay down a set of ten compromise principles aimed at facilitating the Israeli election plan. Once accepted by all, they were intended to enable the parties to begin active negotiations over implementation of the Israeli plan. The ten points went through a number of permutations, as they were transformed from what was essentially a gimmick suggested by Peres as a detour around Likud objections, to an Egyptian initiative designed to place Cairo firmly at the center of the process. According to their final formulation, embodied in a note from Egyptian Ambassador Bassiouny to the Israeli government on September 15, they stipulated:

1. An Israeli commitment to accept any and all results which derive from these elections.
2. Complete freedom in the election campaigning.
3. Participation of the residents of [East Jerusalem] in the elections.
4. The placement of international observers to supervise the elections.
5. Prohibition of the entry of Israelis into the West Bank and Gaza on election day.
6. The withdrawal of Israeli forces from the polling centers.
7. The granting of complete immunity to the representatives ...elected.
8. An Israeli commitment to commence discussions concerning the final status of the occupied land upon a specified date.
9. The freezing of all settlement activity.
10. Israeli acceptance of the four principles of American policy in the Middle East: the solution [to] be founded upon Security Council Resolutions 242 and 338; land in exchange for peace; protection of the security of all

states of the region; and affirmation of the political rights of the Palestinians.

Mubarak's ten points sought to bridge two key gaps between Israel and the Palestinians. First, the territories for peace principle — roughly equivalent in the eyes of the PLO mainstream to its demand for an ultimate stage of Palestinian sovereignty — was enshrined in resolutions 242 and 338, both of which Israel had long since accepted (although the Likud did so without applying "territories for peace" specifically to Judea, Samaria and Gaza). Secondly, the Egyptian plan assumed that the Palestinian delegation would be composed of residents of the Territories and East Jerusalem, it being understood (in verbal clarifications) that this could include two Palestinians who had been exiled by Israel from the Territories. In this way, a key PLO demand — that the Palestinian diaspora be represented in the process from the beginning — would be met, yet in a way that did not explicitly contradict Israel's refusal to involve the diaspora in negotiations, since legally the additional Palestinians could be considered residents of the Territories.

The Egyptian plan was broadly endorsed by the United States. By mid-September the official PLO position on the plan remained ambiguous, but Cairo and Washington appeared confident that they could elicit a favorable response from Arafat if Israel were to concur. In Israel the plan aroused controversy: it was accepted on a limited basis by Rabin and Peres, who specified that they had no objection to meeting in Cairo to discuss autonomy elections with a Palestinian delegation that adopted the ten points as its opening position, while Israel adhered to its own four-point plan. The Likud, however, objected, claiming that the Egyptian plan opened the way for PLO representation in the process, which both Likud and Labor had opposed. Accordingly the Israeli Inner Cabinet, in which the Likud and Labor had equal representation, failed in early October to endorse the plan.

The tie vote in the Cabinet generated considerable tension within the Likud-Labor coalition. It also revealed the first clear signs of a difference of tactics within the Labor Party, between Rabin and Peres. Rabin, on the one hand, held to a view that only a broad coalition could move Israel into genuine negotiations over a Palestinian settlement; Labor would be foolhardy to leave the government, try to set up an alternative narrow-based coalition, or precipitate elections, unless it could appear as the champion of a peace process that was in place and on track. Peres, on the other hand, began actively to pursue negotiations with several small ultra-orthodox and leftist parties with a view to forming an alternative coalition if and when the government reached a stalemate — even if this occurred before a peace process began.

At the heart of the ongoing tension over the process was a six-sided paradigm: The Likud refused to countenance any PLO role in the process or mention of a territories-for-peace stage, insisting that the process should involve Israel and the "local" Palestinians (i.e., residents of Judea, Samaria, and Gaza) in autonomy arrangements alone. Labor would accept some form of symbolic representation of the Palestinian diaspora, as well as East Jerusalem Palestinians, in the Palestinian delegation, and was prepared to countenance some form of discussion of the ultimate, post-autonomy territories-for-peace issue. The PLO, itself hardly a monolithic body, refused to sanction any process in which it did not participate. The "local" Palestinians, whatever their true sentiments — it was not beyond reason that, as the ones who had initiated, executed and ultimately suffered in the *intifada*, they might indeed have liked to negotiate a settlement for themselves — were adamant in refusing to enter a process without the PLO. Egypt utilized its contacts with both Israel and the PLO, and its enhanced inter-Arab status, to pressure a reluctant Arafat into making the concessions required to enter the American-sponsored process. And the United States attempted to persuade the PLO in Tunis, primarily through Egyptian good offices, of the merits of the Israeli plan. Washington searched for a formula that would satisfy all parties sufficiently so as to move them into the first crucial stage of a peace process — where, it hoped, a "peace dynamic" would develop that would commit all the parties to modifying their views.

Notably, Israel's relations with the United States showed growing signs of strain during 1989. Administration and congressional anger at instances of independent Israeli initiative that directly affected US interests, such as the abduction of the extremist Shi'ite leader, Sheikh Obeid, from Southern Lebanon in July and the revelations in November regarding Israeli-South African collaboration in weapons development, seemed to dovetail with the perception of Israeli intransigence over the Palestinian issue and brutality in dealing with the uprising. An added factor was the new policy and aid priorities generated by the emergence of fledgling democratic regimes in Eastern Europe and Central America.

Taken together, these developments seemed to be eroding away at Israel's image as both a democracy and a strategic ally, thereby possibly presaging some diminution in the two countries' close relationship during the early '90s, in the form of cuts in aid or collaboration. One indication of things to come may have been Washington's persistence in pursuing its dialogue with the PLO, even when the Israelis produced occasional evidence that Arafat and his close supporters were still directing terrorist attacks against Israelis inside the country, and from Egypt and Lebanon.

Superficially, this may be seen to have been balanced by the USSR's readiness to permit mass immigration of Jews to Israel, and to admonish Arab leaders who protested on the necessity of dealing with Israel realistically. Yet Moscow was essentially a passive actor in the process throughout the year. In view of its preoccupation with internal and Eastern Bloc events, it did little more than exercise diplomatic pressure on Syria and the PLO to abandon armed conflict as a means of solving their problem with Israel — itself a significant act. While indicating a strong desire to participate in the process, and verbally supporting Baker's efforts, it was prepared to offer Israel (and the US) the one essential concession thought to be necessary for its entry — restoration of diplomatic relations with Israel. (Its readiness to allow hundreds of thousands of Soviet Jews to emigrate to Israel turned out to be much more vexing to the Arabs, insofar as it had far-reaching strategic significance for Israel's viability, and was perceived by the Arabs as strengthening an Israeli desire to expand territorially.)

Two additional actors, Jordan and Syria, require mention. Jordan grew increasingly frightened throughout 1989 of the intention it attributed to the Shamir government, or at least its Likud component, to replace the Hashemite monarchy with Palestinian rule ("Jordan is Palestine"), thereby at a stroke 'solving' the problem of the Palestinian quest for a sovereign state. It viewed the Shamir peace initiative, like the mass immigration of Soviet Jewry, as mere phases in this conspiracy. Hence whereas King Hussein was reportedly prepared to offer Jerusalem (in April 1989 in a visit to Washington) security collaboration within the framework of the creation of a Palestinian state, he rejected US requests to support the peace process that Washington sought to create around the Shamir initiative, thereby further isolating

Amman from the moderate Arab bloc.

The possibility of a moderation in the views of Syrian President Assad toward Israel was broached in early 1990 by former US President Jimmy Carter and others who spoke with the Syrian leader. It seemed logical that the reduction in Soviet backing for his regime, along with his inter-Arab isolation, ongoing hostility with a powerful Iraq, and economic ills, had given Assad cause to reexamine his position. Yet Syria had yet to make a concrete gesture toward Israel that might reflect a genuine readiness to step down from a war footing and coexist with the Jewish state; for the most part, Assad maintained his usual belligerent language. At best, he seemed to be reevaluating his position carefully, hinting at a readiness to join a political peace process under certain conditions. Meanwhile, any 'thaw' in his regional isolation would begin with Egypt, not Israel or even the PLO, which he continued to accuse of selling out on the Palestinian issue.

But whereas, by early 1990, the direct relationship between events in Eastern Europe and the Soviet Union, or even in Syria, and the future of the peace process was difficult to assess, it did seem quite possible that progress by Israel toward a Palestinian settlement could soon become vital to the maintenance of its alliance with the United States.

The Baker Plan

Here, in autumn 1989, Secretary of State Baker — prodded by a request from Arens to present his clarifications in writing — reluctantly stepped in with a five-point formula of his own to facilitate the Likud's agreement to commence negotiations in Cairo:

1. The United States understands that because Egypt and Israel have been working hard on the peace process, there is agreement that an Israeli delegation should conduct a dialogue with a Palestinian delegation in Cairo.
2. The United States understands that Egypt cannot serve as a substitute for the Palestinians and that Egypt will consult with Palestinians on all aspects of the dialogue. Egypt will also consult with Israel and the US.
3. The United States understands that Israel will attend the dialogue only after a satisfactory list of Palestinians has

been worked out. Israel will also consult with Egypt and the United States.

4. The United States understands that the Government of Israel will come to the dialogue on the basis of the Government of Israel's May 14th initiative. The United States further understands that Palestinians will come to the dialogue prepared to discuss elections and negotiations in accordance with Israel's initiative. The United States understands, therefore, that Palestinians would be free to raise issues that relate to their opinions on how to make elections and negotiations succeed.
5. In order to facilitate this process, the United States proposes that the foreign ministers of Israel, Egypt and the United States meet in Washington within two weeks.

This attempt to frame an acceptable summary of the main parties' positions also failed to satisfy the Likud on the key issues of preventing "outsider" Palestinian participation and restricting negotiations to the modalities of elections. This contributed to a growing assessment in Washington that Shamir was intent on preventing his plan from being implemented according to any but the most narrow of premises. Whether this was due to pressure from Shamir's own hardliners, or because from the outset he had never intended for his plan to gather any more momentum than that needed to placate the American administration and keep his coalition government together, was of secondary relevancy. The result was a period of US-Israeli tension, beginning in the second half of October: on October 17 Shamir declared that Israel would "stand firm and not give in" to American pressure over the issue, even "if we must face a clash . . . in which case our relations will change." Likud-Labor tensions reached a point where most of the Labor MKs walked out of a Knesset vote of no-confidence on October 23 rather than support the government.

Clearly, the peace process, the future of the Israeli government, and the state of Israeli-American relations all hung in the balance. Were Shamir and Arens to maintain a position unacceptable to Washington, a crisis in relations could develop. Still, a great deal obviously would depend on the PLO response (via Egypt), and on the degree of priority that the US in general, and Secretary Baker in particular, assigned to the Palestinian issue. In view of the momentum of dramatic events in Eastern Europe this was difficult to determine.

By early November a way out of the crisis appeared to be developing. Baker agreed to a few cosmetic changes in the five points, which were seen by Shamir and Arens as face-saving concessions, albeit insufficient in and of themselves, in the direction they sought (indeed, one of the changes was apparently a concession by Baker to the PLO rather than to Israel). It was also tacitly agreed that both Israel and the PLO would seek to resolve their remaining reservations in the form of unilateral US assurances to them. This enabled the Israeli Inner Cabinet, on November 5, to approve the Baker Plan, along with a list of requested "assurances" that were "assumed" to be forthcoming, by a 9 to 3 vote. Only the three Likud hardliners — ministers Sharon, Modai and Levi — voted against the proposal.

The assurances, like the alterations to the Five Point Plan that preceded them, by now appeared to many to be an exercise in the diplomatic art of splitting hairs. They were essentially throwbacks to Likud demands to exercise a veto over "outsider" and East Jerusalem Palestinians in the Palestinian delegation to the Cairo meeting, and over the discussion in Cairo of issues (territories-for-peace) not directly related to the autonomy elections issue, coupled with a rephrasing of the hoped-for American promise that Israel would not be urged to negotiate with the PLO at some later stage.

On a more critical plane, the relevancy to the process of these assurances was assessed very differently by Baker, who refused to treat them as a condition for moving the process forward, and by Shamir, for whom they appeared to provide another brake upon a process that was placing growing constraints upon his political freedom of maneuver. Shamir could now expect to confront a vigorous campaign within his own party, spearheaded by Sharon, Levi and Modai, to negate what they saw as new policy compromises on his part. The three ministers continued to insist that the inevitable outcome of any deliberations based on the Mubarak and Baker plans would be Israeli negotiations with the PLO over the establishment of a Palestinian state — in complete contradiction to Likud policies. In parallel Rabin and Peres, each with a slightly different party political agenda within Labor, would now seek, in contacts with Washington and Cairo, to refine the modalities of the Baker Plan so as to present Shamir with a formulation that he could not refuse without abandoning the peace plan that bore his name.

As for the Arab side to the process, in early November it was reported from Cairo that the PLO intended to seek its own, parallel set of assurances from the US as a condition for entering the process. These would guarantee that the agenda for the Cairo autonomy elections negotiations include the Mubarak ten points; that Palestinians from East Jerusalem and from outside the Territories could participate; that "the Palestinians" would form the Palestinian delegation; that the PLO would be the dominant Palestinian actor during all stages of the process; that the two superpowers would provide auspices for the negotiations; and that the autonomy plan would be viewed as a stage toward a comprehensive settlement, achieved within the framework of an international conference.

Clearly, alongside the obvious progress that had been achieved, the prospect of two parallel (and possibly contradictory) sets of American assurances, to Israel and the PLO, suggested that either a great deal of constructive ambiguity would be required by State Department specialists to keep both sides in the process, or that this new plateau of progress, such as it was, would soon dissipate.

From mid-November 1989 into January 1990, the Middle East peace process focused upon efforts, centered in Cairo and Washington, to square the Israeli and Arab responses to Secretary of State Baker's Five Point Plan in a way that would allow both Shamir and Arafat (the latter via Egypt) to give the green light to the tripartite foreign ministers meeting that had been designated by the Baker Plan to commence the process. Egypt was soon able to bring the PLO to a parallel status with that of Israel, i.e., agreeing to the Plan, but harboring certain "assumptions" that in effect constituted its well known reservations.

Baker, faced with the two sides' contradictory reservations, in effect refused to grant most of their requests for reassurances. To Jerusalem he reportedly was willing to promise only that Israel would not be pressured to deal directly with the PLO "at this stage." The US continued to insist that the Palestinian delegation should include one or two persons with an East Jerusalem home or business address, and one or two repatriated exiles from among those previously expelled by Israel from the Territories, and that the Palestinian delegation's opening statement could relate to the broader, long term peace process. In parallel, Baker also reportedly assured the PLO of the United States' commitment to a territories for peace solution and to a final settlement in which the

Palestinians realized their legitimate political rights; its opposition to annexation and continued occupation by Israel; and its readiness that, within the framework of their dialogue with Israel, the Palestinians table their demand for an independent state. He also noted that the PLO's future direct participation in the process would be a function of its behavior during the present stage. The first concrete step would be the long awaited meeting of the American, Egyptian and Israeli foreign ministers, to prepare the Cairo conference of Palestinians and Israelis. In response to an admonition from Shamir that he was not trying hard enough, Baker indicated that, given the press of momentous world events, he was close to a decision to abandon his efforts on behalf of Israel and the Palestinians. This was accompanied by hints that the administration might not oppose a move to cut aid to Israel, albeit symbolically.

Within little more than a month — by early February 1990 — the setting appeared to have been laid for a showdown among the various protagonists over the key remaining issues of contention in the process. The PLO, Egypt, and Israel's Labor Party leadership had signaled to Baker their acceptance of a compromise according to which the Palestinian delegation to Cairo would be announced by the Egyptians, and would include two exiles (who would be allowed to take up residency in the Territories again) and two residents of the West Bank who also maintained homes or offices in East Jerusalem. Baker traveled to Moscow (on summit and global arms control business), where he obtained Soviet agreement to the prospective process.

Shamir's position on this proposal now awaited another Likud caucus, again held at the initiative of Sharon, Levi and Modai, where the hardliners attempted to force upon Shamir a platform that would have obliged him to abandon his plan, and probably to resign as well. This was held on February 12, and resulted in a serious split within the Likud, with Sharon tendering his resignation from his ministerial post, and Levi and Modai becoming even more disaffected, in response to Shamir's perceived readiness to compromise.

Still the process faltered: Shamir appeared to have emerged from his party infighting no more ready to compromise on the key remaining issues than he was before Sharon's resignation. Indeed, Shamir's efforts to restore party unity even at the expense of progress in the peace process seemed to strengthen Labor Party suspicions that he had been using his proposal all along to buy time. Nor did Arafat appear to enjoy much more room for maneuver; by February key figures in the PLO were backtracking publicly on their previous acceptance of the principle that Egypt, rather than the PLO, would announce the composition of the Palestinian delegation.

By mid-February 1990 the parties seemed to have exercised the diplomatic process — and American and Egyptian good offices — to their limits. Yet they remained in the prenegotiation stage, and were still dealing with a superficial agenda of issues. Indeed, in some ways they were backtracking. The PLO was evincing growing signs of impatience with US and Egyptian efforts; key leaders like Abu Iyad were indirectly threatening to return to a declared policy of terrorism. Shamir, apparently hoping to perpetuate the status quo on the assumption that Israel's position could only improve — was finding new reasons to delay the process: internal Likud opposition; growing Israeli success in containing the *intifada* and Israeli and world public indifference to the Palestinian cause; the prospect that mass immigration of Soviet Jews to Israel would weaken the demographic argument for territorial concessions by Jerusalem; the prospect that US congressional elections would cause the administration to avoid pressuring Israel; even the advent of *Ramadan* in late March. And in Washington, Secretary Baker was sufficiently preoccupied with events in Eastern Europe, and wary of the political dangers of pressuring Israel, to consider relegating the Middle East peace process to the back burner.

Before describing the denouement of the process — and with it, the collapse of the Israeli government — mention must be made of the *aliyah* (Jewish immigration) issue as a factor that increasingly affected the peace process. Large numbers of Jews from the Soviet Union began arriving in Israel in late 1989. Initially Israeli officials were unable to estimate the probable extent of this new migration. But when Prime Minister Shamir stated in January 1990 that "we need a large Israel for a large Jewish people," the statement generated a wave of criticism in the US, the USSR, and particularly among the Arab states and the PLO, all of whom expressed fear that mass *aliyah* would somehow be used by Israel to perpetuate its control over the Territories.

In the Arab world, Jordan in particular was outspoken, claiming that the mass immigration was part of Israel's "Jordan-is-Palestine" plot. On a broader scale, Arab reaction and pressures on the US and USSR appeared to reflect a deepseated (and unfounded) apprehension that Israel was incapable of absorbing masses of immigrants without grabbing new territory, as well as a grudging and angry admission — interesting in and of itself — that the addition of hundreds of thousands of highly skilled Jews to Israel's population would somehow bring Israel to a kind of unbeatable critical mass that would guarantee its long-term survival. These attitudes would likely influence Arab perceptions of the peace process in the future.

In the event, that process ground to a halt with the advent of the "Baker Question." Directed by Secretary of State Baker to the Israeli government in early March 1990, the question was understood to be acceptable to Egypt and the PLO, and to reflect an understanding that, while the PLO might declare that the Palestinian delegation had been appointed by it, the delegation itself would not do so. The question read: "Will the Government of Israel be ready to agree to sit with Palestinians on a name- by-name basis who are residents of the West Bank and Gaza?" It was followed by an explanatory sentence: "There will be individuals in the list once it is agreed upon that will fit the categories of deportees and dual addressees — meaning people who are residents of the Territories and have an apartment or office in East Jerusalem." Washington asked Israel to respond formally in the affirmative, as a condition for convening a meeting of the foreign ministers of Israel, Egypt and the United States, in Washington, to prepare the Cairo meeting.

Baker backed up his new initiative with pressure upon Israel: hints of an aid cut, a refusal to guarantee loans for immigrant absorption, and verbal appeals for an end to footdragging. President Bush contributed a statement of opposition to Israeli settlement activity, not only in the Territories but in East Jerusalem as well.

These developments found Shamir with a Likud contingent in the government that was now almost universally united behind him. Yet when the showdown came over the future of the government, he voted with his hardliners, rather than with the younger generation of Likud pragmatists, to reject the Baker Question and allow the government to fall.

Meanwhile in the Labor Party, the ongoing tensions between Finance Minister Peres, who was pressing to accelerate a governmental showdown and have a try at forming a Labor-led government, and Defense Minister Rabin, were essentially resolved by March. Rabin, having long held out for preserving the unity government as long as possible so as to advance the peace process on the basis of consensus, appeared to conclude sometime in February that there was nothing left to negotiate: either the Likud could accept the Baker Question, or Labor would have no rationale for remaining in the government. Hence Labor moved into the decisive days of March behind a united Peres-Rabin leadership front.

The government fell on March 15, 1990. While the act itself took place midst a swirl of Byzantine party maneuvering, the reasons, and ramifications, were profound. For one, this was the first time an Israeli government had fallen over the Arab-Israel peace issue, and the event clearly reflected the new primacy of the Palestinian issue in Israeli politics and Israeli public debate. Whatever happened now, the Likud leadership would plainly reject any but the narrowest interpretation of its peace initiative — one that, however consistent, would likely be unacceptable to Palestinian Arabs, unless some new major event altered their calculations.

Then too, Labor's prospects for forming a government were to prove illusory. Moreover, given the delicate nature of Israeli-American relations, a prolonged government crisis at this juncture would add to the considerable erosion of Israel's image in American eyes that had been caused by the *intifada*.

Finally, the crisis reflected the success of Secretary Baker and President Mubarak of Egypt in persuading the PLO to endorse a process acceptable to a large Israeli public. Yet the demise of the national unity government did not necessarily spell success for that process. Even if no stable government could be formed in Israel, and new elections were held, there was no guarantee of change in the broad pattern of Israeli public opinion. Moreover, even if the parties did inaugurate a peace process by holding a meeting in Cairo between Israelis and Palestinians, the sides were likely to remain divided over all the substantive issues that had doomed the Camp David autonomy talks — the nature of autonomy, Israeli security requirements, Jerusalem. Beyond Cairo, they were certainly still at odds over the heavier strategic questions: the acceptability to Israel of a Palestinian state, Palestinian acceptance of Israel's existence and role in the region, the role of the PLO, and the overall architecture of an Arab-Israel peace process.

★ ★ ★

The Iraqi invasion of Kuwait on August 2, 1990, put a new perspective on these and additional aspects of the peace process. The Palestinians' broad support for Iraqi leader Saddam Hussein weakened their short-term prospects for renewing the process from a position of strength. The weakness and vacillation displayed by Jordan's King Hussein raised doubts as to his potential role. But the advent of a far-reaching American-Arab alliance against Iraq bespoke the prospect of renewed pressure on Israel — though probably not before the Gulf Crisis was over — to produce workable positions on the process. And Syria's adherence to that alliance offered the intriguing possibility that Damascus might pursue, in coordination with Washington, policies designed to integrate in into the process.

Appendix

The Israeli Government Peace Initiative

[Source: *The Jerusalem Post*, Monday May 15, 1989; minor grammatical corrections introduced]

The Government's Resolution:

It is decided to approve the attached peace initiative of the Government of Israel.

A Peace Initiative by the Government of Israel

General

1. This document presents the principles of a political initiative of the Government of Israel which deals with the continuation of the peace process; the termination of the state of war with the Arab states; a solution for the Arabs of Judea, Samaria and the Gaza district; peace with Jordan; and a resolution of the problem of the residents of the refugee camps in Judea, Samaria and the Gaza district.

2. The document includes
   a) The principles upon which the initiative is based.
   b) Details of the processes for its implementation.
   c) Reference to the subject of the elections under consideration. Further details relating to the elections as well as other subjects of the initiative will be dealt with separately.

Basic Premises

3. The initiative is founded upon the assumption that there is a national consensus for it on the basis of the basic guidelines of the Government of Israel, including the following points:
   a) Israel yearns for peace and the continuation of the political process by means of direct negotiations based on the principles of the Camp David Accords.
   b) Israel opposes the establishment of an additional Palestinian state in the Gaza district and in the area between Israel and Jordan.

c) Israel will not conduct negotiations with the PLO.

d) There will be no change in the status of Judea, Samaria and Gaza other than in accordance with the basic guidelines of the Government.

Subjects to be Dealt with in the Peace Process

4. a) Israel views as important that the peace between Israel and Egypt, based on the Camp David Accords, serve as a cornerstone for enlarging the circle of peace in the region, and calls for a common endeavor for the strengthening of the peace and its extension, through continued consultation.

b) Israel calls for the establishment of peaceful relations between it and those Arab states which still maintain a state of war with it, for the purpose of promoting a comprehensive settlement for the Arab-Israel conflict, including recognition, direct negotiations, ending the boycott, diplomatic relations, cessation of hostile activity in international institutions or forums, and regional and bilateral cooperation.

c) Israel calls for an international endeavor to resolve the problem of the residents of the Arab refugee camps in Judea, Samaria and the Gaza District in order to improve their living conditions and to rehabilitate them. Israel is prepared to be a partner in this endeavor.

d) In order to advance the political negotiation process leading to peace, Israel proposes free and democratic elections among the Palestinian Arab inhabitants of Judea, Samaria and the Gaza District in an atmosphere devoid of violence, threats, and terror. In these elections a representation will be chosen to conduct negotiations for a transitional period of self-rule. This period will constitute a test for coexistence and cooperation. At a later stage, negotiations will be conducted for a permanent solution during which all the proposed options for an agreed settlement will be examined and peace between Israel and Jordan will be achieved.

e) All the above-mentioned steps should be dealt with simultaneously.

f) The details of what has been mentioned in (d) above will be given below.

The Principles constituting the Initiative

Stages:

5. The initiative is based on two stages
   a) Stage A - A transitional period for an interim agreement.
   b) Stage B - Permanent Solution.
6. The interlock between the Stages is a timetable on which the Plan is built: the peace process delineated by the initiative is based on Resolutions 242 and 338 upon which the Camp David Accords are founded.

Timetable:

7. The transitional period will continue for 5 years.
8. As soon as possible, but not later than the third year after the beginning of the transitional period, negotiations for achieving a permanent solution will begin.

Parties Participating in the Negotiations in Both Stages:

9. The Parties participating in the negotiations for the First Stage (the interim agreement) shall include Israel and the elected representation of the Palestinian Arab inhabitants of Judea, Samaria and the Gaza district. Jordan and Egypt will be invited to participate in these negotiations if they so desire.
10. The Parties participating in the negotiations for the Second Stage (Permanent Solution) shall include Israel and the elected representation of the Palestinian Arab inhabitants of Judea, Samaria and the Gaza District as well as Jordan; furthermore, Egypt may participate in these negotiations. In negotiations between Israel and Jordan, in which the elected representation of the Palestinian Arab inhabitants of Judea, Samaria and the Gaza district will participate, the peace treaty between Israel and Jordan will be concluded.

Substance of Transitional Period:

11. During the transitional period the Palestinian Arab inhabitants of Judea, Samaria and the Gaza district will be accorded self-rule by means of which they will, themselves, conduct their affairs of daily life. Israel will continue to be responsible for security, foreign affairs and all matters concerning Israeli citizens in Judea, Samaria and the Gaza district. Topics involving the implementation of the plan for self-rule

will be considered and decided within the framework of the negotiations for an interim agreement.

Substance of Permanent Solution:

12. In the negotiations for a permanent solution every party shall be entitled to present for discussion all the subjects it may wish to raise.
13. The aim of the negotiations should be:
    a) The achievement of a permanent solution acceptable to the negotiating parties.
    b) The arrangements for peace and borders between Israel and Jordan.

Details of the Process for the Implementation of the Initiative

14. First and foremost, dialogue and basic agreement by the Palestinian Arab inhabitants of Judea, Samaria and the Gaza District, as well as Egypt and Jordan if they wish to take part, as above-mentioned, in the negotiations, on the principles constituting the initiative.

15. a) Immediately afterwards will follow the stage of preparations and implementation of the election process in which a representation of the Palestinian Arab inhabitants of Judea, Samaria and Gaza will be elected. This representation:
    I) Shall be a partner to the conduct of negotiations for the transitional period (Interim Agreement).
    II) Shall constitute the self-governing authority in the course of the transitional period.
    III) Shall be the central Palestinian component, subject to agreement after three years, in the negotiations for the permanent solution.

    b) In the period of the preparation and implementation there shall be a calming of the violence in Judea, Samaria and the Gaza District.
16. As to the substance of the elections, it is recommended that a proposal of regional elections be adopted, the details of which shall be determined in further discussions.
17. Every Palestinian Arab residing in Judea, Samaria and the Gaza district, who shall be elected by the inhabitants to represent them — after having submitted his candidacy in accordance with the detailed document which shall deter-

mine the subject of the elections — may be a legitimate participant in the conduct of negotiations with Israel.

18. The elections shall be free, democratic and secret.
19. Immediately after the election of the Palestinian representation, negotiations shall be conducted with it on an interim agreement for a transitional period which shall continue for five years, as mentioned above. In these negotiations the parties shall determine all the subjects relating to the substance of self-rule and the arrangements necessary for its implementation.
20. As soon as possible, but not later than the third year after the establishment of the self-rule, negotiations for a permanent solution shall begin. During the whole period of these negotiations until the signing of the agreement for a permanent solution, the self-rule shall continue in effect as determined in the negotiations for an interim agreement.

8. The Second Year of the Intifada

by Aryeh Shalev

This chapter, updated to the end of March 1990, compares the second year of the *intifada* (December 9, 1988 to December 9, 1989) with the first (December 9, 1987 to December 9, 1988). In cases deemed significant, it also integrates data from the last month of 1989 and the first three months of 1990. Three main topics will be examined: violent aspects of the uprising, civil disobedience, and ramifications for the parties involved.

In certain respects, the Palestinians registered fewer gains in 1989, particularly in the second half of the year, than in 1988. In others, 1989 was a more advantageous year for them. But it must be stressed from the outset that the overall picture is complex and multi-dimensional: in each of the two areas of primary struggle (violent acts and civil disobedience) there were positive and negative developments.

Violent Aspects

Reduction in Intensity

There was no letup in the frequency of hostile acts directed against Israel in the second year of the *intifada* and the first quarter of the third year, but the incidents did become less violent, particularly toward the end of the period under review. By early 1989 it seemed possible that the *intifada* had arrived at the proverbial crossroads, and it was questionable whether the Palestinians would succeed in finding a formula that would give new impetus to the struggle.

A decrease in the intensity of violence could be attributed to a number of factors: a marked improvement in the tactics of security forces, the introduction of passive defense safeguards for buses and automobiles (mainly protective plastic coatings and wire mesh for vehicle windows), the deploying of special forces to pinpoint and deal with the masked youth commandos of the uprising, the refining of orders to open fire at youths throwing petrol bombs, and the improved effectiveness of the General Security Service. In contrast, the Palestinians continued to employ essentially the same methods as in the first year.

The IDF and security forces scored a number of successes and restored something of their deterrent image insofar as the Palestinian general public was concerned. But they had no serious effect on the youth. Thus, mass demonstrations no longer attracted thousands of participants, and violent activity was perpetrated in the main only by small groups of youths. Moreover, on the occasion of rioting (following a rumor of the death of one or more young Palestinians), crowds of dozens or even hundreds of participants usually dispersed at the mere approach of two or three military vehicles.

Consequently, during the latter half of 1989 and the beginning of 1990, the military command at diverse echelons, the regular soldiers serving in the Territories, and the reservists, all began to feel more confident. The sense of lack of control that characterized the early stages of the uprising was replaced by one of relative control. Hence the IDF was able to make a sizeable cut (approximately a third) in forces stationed in Judea, Samaria and the Gaza Strip and to lighten the burden on reserve troops. Nevertheless, the soldiers who were still constantly coping, relatively ineffectively, with stone-throwing children continued to experience considerable frustration. The stone continued to be both the weapon and the symbol of the *intifada*.

Palestinians Killed and Wounded

Toward the end of 1989, the IDF began a concerted effort to cut down on violent acts perpetrated by the rioters while at the same time taking precautions to keep the number of Palestinian deaths to a minimum. The figures bear this out. From the beginning of November 1989 there was a significant decline in Palestinians killed by security forces (according to the statistics of the IDF Spokesman). In each of the first three months of 1990 the figure was lower than 10 (see Table 1). There was also a decrease in the number of Israelis killed. But on the other hand there was an increase in Palestinians wounded, and no decline in wounded Israelis (soldiers and civilians). All in all, there was little in this essentially positive trend to balance the total annual figures for the second year of the uprising, which showed more Palestinians killed than in the first year (see Table 2).

Data on the numbers of killed and wounded residents of the Territories are published by two Israeli sources: the IDF Spokesman and *BTselem* (Israeli Information Center for Human Rights in

Table 1

Numbers of Palestinians killed by security forces from September 1989 to February 1990,* IDF Spokesman figures

Month	Judea-Samaria	Gaza	Total
1989			
September	19	7	26
October	17	6	23
November	11	2	13
December	11	4	15
1990			
January	4	3	7
February	3	3	6

*In this and following tables, figures are tabulated from the 9th of a particular month to the 8th of the following one.

the Territories). According to IDF figures, the number of Palestinians killed by security forces grew in the second year by 36 over the first year (248 in the first year, 284 in the second). *BTselem* gives identical figures (293 killed) for both years. The total number killed by security forces in two years is 532 according to the IDF Spokesman and 586 according to *BTselem*, a discrepancy of 54. Moreover, if Palestinians killed by Israeli civilians in the Territories (25 according to *Btselem*) are included in the count, then the number of residents killed by Israelis (security forces and civilians) was 611 over the two years according to *BTselem*, and 557 according to IDF figures.

The IDF Spokesman's figures show an increase in the number of residents of the Territories wounded by the security forces. These figures, which the Spokesman himself defined as an estimate, show a 42 percent increase in 1989 (5,391) compared with 1988 (3,852). This is due to increasingly widespread use of the plastic bullet by the IDF. The total wounded in two years of the uprising is 9,243, or an average of 12 per day. Peak months (over 500 wounded) were September 1988 (537), March 1989 (523), April 1989 (640), May

Table 2a

Numbers of Palestinians killed by security forces, from December 1987 to February 1990, IDF Spokesman and BTselem figures

December 1987-November 1988

Month	Judea-Samaria	Gaza	Total	Judea-Samaria	Gaza	Total
	(IDF figures)			(BTselem figures)		
1987						
December	9	17	26	8	14	22
1988						
January	10	9	19	4	13	17
February	22	3	25	27	5	32
March	33	6	39	37	5	42
April	19	16	35	26	18	44
May	8	3	11	13	4	17
June	8	2	10	9	4	13
July	17	3	20	20	4	24
August	8	10	18	16	11	27
September	12	6	18	8	8	16
October	14	3	17	21	3	24
November	5	5	10	10	5	15
TOTAL FIRST YEAR	165	83	248	199	94	293

1989 (568) and January 1990 (559). There was no reduction in the figures for the first two months of 1990 (see Table 3). The United Nations Relief Works Agency (UNRWA) claims that there were actually many more wounded. The annual report of *BTselem* for 1989 puts the UNRWA figure at 37,439 wounded in the Territories.

The ratio of dead to wounded in the Territories also showed significant fluctuations; in any case it was particularly high in the Gaza Strip, according to statistics from the IDF Spokesman: for instance in November 1989 it was 1:114, and in January 1990 it was 1:125. The number of wounded continued rising in Judea and

Table 2b

December 1988-November 1989

Month	Judea-Samaria	Gaza	Total	Judea-Samaria	Gaza	Total
	(IDF figures)			(BTselem figures)		
1988						
December	17	9	26	21	8	29
1989						
January	18	9	27	13	6	19
February	5	3	8	11	6	17
March	14	9	23	11	13	24
April	19	13	32	20	11	31
May	19	19	38	15	18	33
June	10	10	20	9	10	19
July	10	11	21	19	12	31
August	14	13	27	14	13	27
September	19	7	26	16	7	23
October	17	6	23	20	10	30
November	11	2	13	12	1	13
TOTAL SECOND YEAR	173	111	284	181	115	296

Samaria as well (see Table 3). Although the ratio of killed to wounded in this area was also steep, it was still lower than in the Gaza Strip. In November 1989 it was 1:18 and in January 1990 it was 1:46.

Israelis Killed and Wounded

The number of Israelis killed remained low in both years, while there was an overall increase, approximately 9 percent, in the number of wounded. In Judea and Samaria there was no marked change in the number of soldiers wounded in 1988 (490) compared with 1989 (489). It was in the Gaza Strip that the number was significantly higher: 426 in 1989 as opposed to 254 in 1988. There was only a slight drop in the number of Israeli civilians wounded

Table 2c

December 1989-February 1990

Month	Judea-Samaria	Gaza	Total	Judea-Samaria	Gaza	Total
	(IDF figures)			(BTselem figures)		
1989						
December	11	4	15	-	-	21
1990						
January	4	3	7	9	2	11
February	3	3	6	3	6	9
TOTAL 3 MONTHS THIRD YEAR	18	10	28	?	?	41

Notes:

a. Peak months of Palestinians killed (over 30 per month): March and April 1988.

b. Minimum killed (less than 10 per month): June, November 1988, and January-February 1990.

in both areas, but as a result of passive defense safeguards in vehicles most of those involved in 1989 were lightly injured.

According to the IDF Spokesman's statistics, 11 Israeli civilians and 9 soldiers were killed in the first two years of the *intifada*. In the same period, 803 civilians and 1,635 soldiers (2,438 all told) were injured. There was a slight drop in the number of killed, 9 in 1989 compared with 11 in 1988, and a small decrease in the number of wounded civilians, 359 in 1989, compared with 414 in 1988, and a significant increase in the number of soldiers wounded, 915 in 1989 compared with 744 in 1988. There were far fewer Israelis killed (20) than Palestinians — 557 according to IDF figures, or 611 according to *BTselem*. The number of Israeli wounded, 2,432, reached more than a quarter (26 percent) of the Palestinian figure, 9,243.

The relatively high number of wounded Israelis may be attri-

Table 3

Judea, Samaria, Gaza: Numbers of Palestinians wounded by security forces, IDF Spokesman figures

Wounded during peak months 1988-1989

Month	Judea-Samaria	Gaza	Total
1988			
September	402	135	537
1989			
March	385	138	523
April	282	358	640
May	392	176	568
August	300	193	493

Wounded from September 1989 to end of February 1990*

Month	Judea-Samaria	Gaza	Total
1989			
September	286	160	446
October	203	74	277
November	198	228	426
December	251	234	485
1990			
January	185	374	559
February	193	124	317

*During two months of the *intifada* there were less than 225 wounded per month: December 1987 (214); January 1988 (225).

buted to the use of the stone as the principal weapon of the uprising. It is one sign of the pressure that the *intifada* has succeeded in applying on Israel. Peak months for wounded

Table 4

Israelis wounded in the Territories during peak months of 1989, IDF Spokesman figures

Month	Soldiers Wounded			Civilians Wounded		
	Judea-Samaria	Gaza	Total	Judea-Samaria	Gaza	Total
March	54	37	91	45	2	47
April	48	53	101	44	2	46
May	63	29	92	45	3	48
August	42	51	93	27	2	29
September	45	47	92	42	5	47

Table 5

Israelis wounded in the Territories from November 1989 to February 1990, IDF Spokesman figures

Month	IDF Wounded			Civilians Wounded		
	Judea-Samaria	Gaza	Total	Judea-Samaria	Gaza	Total
1989						
November	24	36	60	14	1	15
December	43	37	80	0	0	0
1990						
January	34	18	52	31	1	32
February	42	30	72	30	0	30

soldiers were all recorded in 1989, whereas the highest month for civilian casualties was March 1988, with 55 wounded. The majority of the civilians injured each month were in Judea and Samaria, where the Jewish population is far larger and more dispersed than in the Gaza Strip, and generates far more Israeli traffic on roads that pass through or near Arab population concentrations. In contrast, during most months there were nearly as many wounded soldiers in the Gaza Strip as in Judea and Samaria, and in some months there were even more (see Table 4).

Over the four-month period beginning in November 1989 there was a sharp decline in Israeli civilians wounded in the Gaza Strip (one or none per month), whereas in Judea and Samaria, with the exception of December, the numbers grew steadily, reaching 31 per month (see Table 5).

Intra-Palestinian Settling of Accounts

One phenomenon that gained momentum in the second year of the *intifada* was the killing of Palestinians by Palestinians. The victims were those suspected by their fellow Palestinians of cooperating with the authorities or transgressing traditional customs; in some instances, killings took place against a backdrop of internal struggle. According to the IDF Spokesman's figures, in the second year, 138 Palestinians were killed by Palestinians, compared with 18 in the first year. Not only is this a marked increase in the number of internal slayings, but it represents a growing percentage (33% in 1989, opposed to 7% in 1988) of all Palestinians killed. According to the IDF Spokesman, by March 21, 1990, 200 Arabs had been killed by other Arabs.

These slayings were carried out with extreme brutality. The entire phenomenon tended to intensify the demonization of Palestinians and the perception of unchecked anarchy in Israeli eyes. It is virtually certain that the vast majority of those killed had no links to the Israeli security forces. Indeed, despite possible impressions and rumors among the Palestinian population, no more than 40 percent had any ties at all to Israel.

The growth of this phenomenon of lynching reflected upon an evolution in the sources of real control among the Palestinian population. In the first year, a policy dictated by the external PLO leadership had "persuaded" offenders to mend their ways. But in the second year the influence of the PLO Central Committee waned, and the local leadership became more powerful. Within that leadership, control shifted from the recognized internal *intifada* leadership to the grassroots popular committees. The internal leadership and the PLO in Tunisia appealed in broadcasts and pamphlets to call a halt to the internal bloodshed, but the orders were ignored and the brutality continued. Decisions to carry out local lynchings were clearly taken at the lower echelons, at the expense of the recognized leadership's operational role and control over local committees. The popular committees were on their way to developing enough clout to guarantee themselves a possible role at the top of the leadership pyramid.

Scope of Violent Activities

We have noted that the reduction in the intensity of violence was not accompanied by a quantitative drop in incidents. Indeed, low-level incidents proliferated in the second half of 1989, particularly toward the end of the year and the first months of 1990. Typically, these acts were perpetrated by small bands of stone-throwing youths, aged 8 to 18. Conceivably, this proliferation was a deliberate reaction on the part of the Palestinians, who were aware that the violence had subsided and were anxious to reverse the trend.

Table 6

Summary of comparative data for 1988-89 in Judea-Samaria, IDF Spokesman figures

Incidents	1988	1989	Change %
Arson	304	307	+ 1
Petrol bombs	994	557	- 44
Other disturbances	15,813	32,932	+108
Palestinians exiled	21	16	- 24
Palestinians killed	173	167	- 3
Palestinians wounded	2,812	3,298	+ 17
IDF soldiers wounded	490	489	0
Israeli civilians wounded	377	332	- 12.5
Buildings sealed	105	56	- 47
Houses demolished	37	32	- 15

Table 7

Summary of comparative data for 1988-89 in Gaza Strip, IDF Spokesman figures

Incidents	1988	1989	Change %
Arson	56	51	- 9
Petrol bombs	352	171	- 51
Other disturbances	4489	7479	+ 67
Palestinians exiled	11	10	- 9
Palestinians killed	75	106	+ 32
Palestinians wounded	1040	2093	+101
IDF soldiers wounded	254	426	+ 67
Israeli civilians wounded	37	27	- 27
Buildings sealed	12	35	+192
Houses demolished	42	46	+ 10

The only available figures for the number of violent activities carried out were provided by the IDF Spokesman. A comprehensive comparison of the full range of violent acts for the years 1988 and 1989 (see Tables 6 and 7) is problematic and fraught with inconsistencies. Many of the disturbances perpetrated in 1988, particularly in the first half of the year, were large in scale, with hundreds or even thousands of Palestinians taking part. Consequently, each one of them may be equivalent to a number of small incidents. In the following year, 1989, there were fewer participants; yet each incident, however small, merited its own report. Taking into account these limitations, violent acts increased by a factor of 1.9 in the second year: 58 percent in the Gaza Strip and 98 percent in Judea and Samaria.

In light of the difficulty of comparing the number of violent incidents in the two years, and considering the fact that they were of a fairly uniform nature throughout 1989, a comparative analysis of that year seems more instructive (see Table 8). With the exception of June, which registered a low of 2,787 incidents, all

Table 8

Peak months of violent incidents in Judea-Samaria and Gaza during 1989

	Judea-Samaria				Gaza				Total Judea-Samaria & Gaza
	Arson	Petrol Bombs	Other Disturbances	Sub-Total	Arson	Petrol Bombs	Other Disturbances	Sub-Total	
Apr	26	55	2717	2798	11	17	1010	1038	3836
Aug	30	47	3293	3370	1	20	729	750	4120
Sep	36	49	3810	3895	2	17	761	790	4685
Oct	23	48	3442	3513	0	7	422	429	3942
Nov	8	37	3025	3070	2	13	768	783	3853

Table 9

Violent incidents in Judea-Samaria and Gaza from December 1989 through February 1990

	Judea-Samaria				Gaza				Total Judea-Samaria & Gaza
	Arson	Petrol Bombs	Other Disturbances	Sub-Total	Arson	Petrol Bombs	Other Disturbances	Sub-Total	
1989									
Dec	23	47	4084	4154	3	7	1009	1019	5173
1990									
Jan	28	36	5115	5179	4	2	717	723	5902
Feb	24	47	7285	7356	2	2	1455	1459	8815

Table 10

Petrol bombs from October 1989 through February 1990, IDF Spokesman figures

Month	Judea-Samaria	Gaza	Total
1989			
October	48	7	55
November	37	13	50
December	47	7	54
1990			
January	36	2	38
February	74	7	81

other months in 1989 registered between 3,000 and 4,685 incidents, including cases of petrol bombing and arson.

The picture reveals an upward swing in incidents during the course of 1989. A comparison of the number of violent acts in the first half of the year (19,126) and the second half (22,371) points to a 17 percent rise. Peak months were August and September.

In December 1989 and the first two months of 1990, not only was there a steep increase in incidents, but there were more in that three-month period than at any equivalent time since the onset of the *intifada*. February 1990 in particular stands out (see Table 9).

It is instructive to compare instances involving petrol bombs and arson in 1988 and 1989. The data indicates a marked 46 percent decrease in the number of petrol bombs thrown: 1,346 in 1988, 728 in 1989. This reduction is probably due to changes in IDF open-fire orders, with permission being given to fire on anyone throwing a petrol bomb. Conversely, no change was noted in the number of arson incidents: 360 in 1988 and 358 in 1989.

From October 1989 until March 1990, far fewer petrol bombs were thrown in the Gaza Strip, whereas the figure for Judea and Samaria remained high, even doubling in the month of February. This is illustrated in Table 10, based on figures of the IDF Spokesman.

Terrorist Activity

The entire course of the *intifada* in the Territories has been characterized as a people's struggle that avoids reliance on use of firearms by activists in crowds or demonstrations. Nevertheless, terrorist activity in the Territories continued unabated throughout the first two years of the uprising. According to the IDF Spokesman's statistics, there was a sevenfold increase in the number of shootings, from 10 in 1988 to 71 in 1989; incidents of grenade throwing went down by 64 percent, from 34 in 1988 to 12 in 1989; and there was a 25 percent decrease in the number of explosive devices set: 80 in 1988 compared to 60 in 1989. A more careful inspection of figures for explosive devices shows that in the Gaza Strip there were four times fewer: 62 in 1988 and 16 in 1989, while in Judea and Samaria there was a 2.6-fold increase, from 18 to 50.

Scope of Incidents in the Jerusalem Area

According to figures provided by the Israel Police Department for 1989 (see Table 11), there was an overall 56 percent increase in *intifada*-related violent incidents (not including use of firearms) in the Jerusalem area from 1988 to 1989. The changing pattern of the *intifada* in Jerusalem, as in the Territories, may account for the higher figures. In 1988, especially during the early months, large-scale disturbances took place, and a single police report actually related to many single events. In 1989, in contrast, violent acts were primarily executed by small, tough groups, with one report per incident. One statistic is clear: in 1989 there were three times as many cases of arson, most of them affecting Israeli cars, many of them in West Jerusalem. The police were unsuccessful in developing an appropriate operational response.

Violent Incidents Within the Green Line (Excluding Jerusalem)

As the uprising moved through its second year and into a third, Israeli Arabs were increasingly caught between their status as citizens of Israel on the one hand and their allegiance to the Palestinian cause on the other. While the key political figures in the Arab sector pointedly abstained from escalating relations with the Jewish majority to breaking point, the *intifada* clearly height-

Table 11

Incidents in Greater Jerusalem in 1988-89 attributed to the intifada, Israel Police figures

Incidents	1988	1989	Change %
Arson	73	211	+189
Petrol bombs	122	132	+ 8
Property damage	5	32	+540
Roadblocks	723	1000	+ 56
Stone throwing	1803	3040	+ 68
Tire burning	290	345	+ 19
Total	3016	4760	+ 58

Table 12

Incidents in Israel (excluding Jerusalem) in 1988-89, Israel Police figures

Incidents	1988	1989	Change %
Arson	31	188	+501
Petrol bombs	54	44	- 19
Other disturbances	512	878	+ 71

ened the identity crisis of the Israeli Arab, and there was a serious deterioration in the feeling of loyalty to the State on the part of the silent majority.

Accordingly, the *intifada* produced a sharp increase in the number of disturbances in Israel (see Table 12), with Arab youth displaying a willingness to demonstrate and express hostility through illegal means. In the pre-*intifada* past, disturbances had been carried out by individuals on an ad hoc basis. From the outset of the uprising, however, the local groups organized, expanded, and initiated disruptions, with some eventually moving on to terrorist activity. For the most part, a minority of young, 15 to 24-year old youths were involved in incidents and terrorism. In 1989 there was a marked increase in these violent incidents: by 71 percent in riots/disturbances, and by 501 percent in arson. As in the Territories, only the use of the petrol bomb as a weapon decreased, by 19 percent.

Effects of Deportations and House Demolitions

In the *Middle East Military Balance 1988-1989* we examined Israel's reliance during 1988 on two punitive measures that have been used for years by the authorities: deportation of uprising leaders and demolition of the homes of those engaged in violence. We asked how these punishments, long regarded by the Palestinian population as the harshest invoked, affected the course of the *intifada*. We found that, statistically, neither measure had a moderating or deterrent influence on Palestinian violence, in the sense that in the month following large-scale use of deportations/demolitions, there was no decrease in the scope of *intifada* violence.

In 1989, fewer deportations took place. According to the IDF Spokesman and *BTselem* figures, 26 residents of the Territories (16 from Judea and Samaria and 10 from the Gaza Strip) were

Table 13

Numbers of Palestinians exiled in 1989 compared with number of violent incidents during the same and following months

Month	No. of Palestinians Exiled			No. of Violent Incidents		
	Judea-Samaria	Gaza	Total	Same Month	Month After	Change
Jan.	7	6	13	2468	2852	+384
June	4	4	8	2762	3019	+257
Sept.	5	0	5	4675	3942	-733

Table 14

Numbers of houses demolished in 1989 compared with number of violent incidents during same and following months

Month	No. of Houses Demolished			No. of Violent Incidents		
	Judea-Samaria	Gaza	Total	Same Month	Month After	Change
Jan.	15	0	15	2468	2852	+384
March	15	12	27	3698	4088	+390
May	15	0	12	3519	2762	-757
June	12	11	23	2762	3019	+257

deported, compared with 32 in 1988. Table 13 summarizes the data for analyzing the effect of deportations in 1989.

Following two out of the three months of 1989 in which deportations were carried out, violent activity continued unchanged, along the 1988 pattern. However, there was a marked decrease in violence after the September deportations. This may be due to the essentially unrelated fact that September was a peak month for incidents (4,675). In any case, the overall low numbers of deportees in both years, and the reduction in 1989, may indicate that the security establishment realized that there was no positive deterrent achieved by deportations.

As for the demolition or sealing of houses by the IDF, according to the IDF Spokesman's figures, the number of houses demolished in Judea and Samaria dropped by 53 percent (from 105 in 1988 to 56 in 1989), with a slight reduction in the number of houses sealed (from 37 down to 32). In contrast, in the Gaza Strip there was a slight increase in houses demolished (from 42 in 1988 to 46 in 1989), and a large increase (2.9-fold) in the number of houses sealed (from 12 to 35).

Did sealing and demolishing of homes cause a decline in the scope of violence in 1989? In order to evaluate the effect of demolitions, Table 14 illustrates the number of houses that were destroyed in peak months of 1989 in juxtaposition with the number of violent incidents for the following month.

These figures, albeit incomplete, show that there was no correlation between house demolitions and a reduction in violence. Quite the contrary, increases were noted for all subsequent months except June 1989.

Civil Disobedience and Consolidation of the Uprising

Palestinian reliance on civil disobedience in the *intifada*, and Israeli countermeasures, have produced a mixed record of Palestinian successes, failures, and inconclusive results, with successful campaigns succeeding in consolidating the uprising. In general, civil disobedience against Israeli rule did not spread in the second year of the *intifada* and the first few months of the third year.

Palestinian civil disobedience has been hampered by a number of constraints. For one, in the absence of alternative sources of employment, it has been necessary for large numbers of Arab laborers from the Territories to continue working in Israel. Despite their awareness that they are 'building' Israel, they cannot use work stoppages as a weapon. Then too, despite the readiness of youth to take chances and risk danger in order to maintain the violence, the populace as a whole was unwilling to risk the reprisals that would result from all-out hostility against the civil authority. Finally, the population was unwilling to forego civil authority-controlled services such as travel permits to and from Jordan, and reunification of families.

A refusal to pay taxes typified the *intifada* from its inception. During the second year of the uprising, strongarm tactics were used by the popular committees to obstruct the payment of taxes and VAT. Merchants' invoices, documents and receipt books were confiscated by the committees. Ramallah and Hebron accountants were the objects of harassment and threats. But Beit Sahur was the only city where all the residents, including merchants and self-employed professionals, united in their refusal to pay taxes. The revolt, begun in February 1989, was orchestrated by the PFLP, which dominated the town. As this was the only place in the Territories to take such a step, Israeli authorities feared that if Beit Sahur succeeded in its revolt, there would be far-ranging attempts at emulation throughout Judea, Samaria and the Gaza Strip.

The first Israeli response came in the form of a lien on property of the assessed who had not paid taxes. When this failed to achieve results, a campaign was launched from September 20 to October 31, 1989 to pressure the residents into paying. Household appliances, equipment, automobiles and bank accounts were attached, and offenders were arrested and brought to trial. During the course of the operation, durable goods of 209 tax evaders were confiscated, along with 40 vehicles and 30 bank accounts; 44 people were arrested and tried. Following the operation, an estimated NIS 3 million worth of confiscated goods were sold. All told, 403 out of some 600 registered taxpayers were involved in sanctions.

When the dust had settled, there was no decisive winner. The civil administration had not succeeded in forcing the residents of Beit Sahur to pay taxes, yet the authorities' reaction appeared to provide a deterrent against emulation by merchants and well-to-do residents of other cities. Thus a call by the Unified Command for a widening of the tax revolt in 1989, beginning with the Ramallah district, never materialized.

As a means of preventing undesirables and criminal elements from entering Israel, and as a symbolic way of asserting its authority, the civil administration in 1989 instituted the use of computerized entry permits to Israel for residents of the Gaza Strip who worked there. At first, the popular committees retaliated by pressuring permit holders to hand over their cards, but did not destroy them. Later the residents, who regarded the cards as their only source of sustenance, fought to reclaim them, and the committees were forced to give in and return them. Demand for the permits even increased substantially. The number of cards distributed, 105,000, was much larger than the number of Gaza residents who work in Israel, 60,000, since the cards also served as entry permits for purposes other than employment. In this instance the struggle by the local committees and the *intifada* leadership had failed. For a large part of the Gazan population the need to work in Israel was absolutely imperative. Interestingly, the experiment was not repeated in the West Bank. There, a smaller proportion of the population is dependent on work in Israel, and a multiplicity of transportation links with Israel makes supervision far more complex.

In the second year, the *intifada* leadership launched a concerted effort to gain a foothold in the Israeli-monitored civil administration of Judea and Samaria. The intent was to influence these bureaucracies from within and exploit them for the leadership's own ends. Thus, in the course of 1989 Palestinian clerks in the civil administration offices of the various districts were coerced into carrying out the dictates of the *intifada*, and PLO activists persuaded municipal authorities (city halls and local councils) through monetary bribes and/or pressure to work for the uprising. In return PLO financial support of 1.5 million dinars was pledged to civil administration employees whom Jordan ceased to support in July 1988 (it is not clear whether the money was actually dispersed). There were also fewer physical attacks against clerks of the civil administration and mayors during the second year. Unified National Command pamphlets ceased calling for the resignations of city council members and civil administration clerks.

In parallel, Palestinian 'self-rule' grew during the second year in two areas: health care and education. There was a decline to 40-50 percent of capacity in the use of emergency rooms, out-patient clinics, wards and maternity facilities in government hospitals. The population increasingly turned to private hospitals — Al-Ahalli in the Gaza Strip, Itichad in Nablus and Al-Mukassad in Jerusalem, where complicated surgery was performed — which have flourished during the *intifada* along with private health care facilities in the villages. These services were provided free to those unable to pay. As there is an oversupply of doctors in the Territories, there was no movement of doctors from the civil administration hospitals to the alternative institutions. (In any event, even civil administration facilities are run exclusively by a staff of Palestinians.)

Turning to education, notwithstanding the closure of campuses and buildings by Israeli authorities, university studies continued to take place in the second year of the *intifada*. Small classes were improvised at alternative sites, and in many cases graduation certificates were awarded.

There were numerous additional examples of Palestinian success in advancing self-rule. For one, there was increased dominance within "national institutions" that operated legally. These included labor unions, professional unions, and charitable funds that underwent personnel changes in tune with PLO demands. Related changes were made in the make-up of the Higher Education Council, and in the appointment of an advisory board to the directors of Itichad Hospital in Nablus. Efforts were made by the PLO to control the Federation of Agricultural Marketing Societies by manipulating its access to finances, and to organize the marketing of olive oil from Judea and Samaria — all in keeping with its goal of dominating the agricultural sector.

New 'supreme councils' were also established and superimposed on existing institutions in Judea and Samaria. Thus a "Supreme Womens Council" was set up in December 1988, followed by a "Supreme Students Council" in June 1989 and a "Palestinian Federation of Business and Industry" — created through the unification of eight chambers of commerce in Judea and Samaria. Steps were taken to establish a "Supreme Workers Council" in November and December 1989. Finally, from the beginning of February 1989, the Palestinian boycott of Israeli products in Judea and Samaria was intensified.

In many other walks of life in the Territories, life simply slowed down during 1989. At the municipalities, for example, the work day was shortened to end at noon; cash flow from municipal taxes was reduced; collection of revenues, primarily from water and electricity, plunged by as much as 50 percent; savings were reduced, leaving less money available for investment; the Jordanian dinar dropped in value vis-a-vis the Israeli shekel; the mayor's influence on municipal life waned, and council meetings became rare events. By the same token, civil and criminal court functioning was substantially reduced in Judea and Samaria as a consequence of reduced economic activity and difficulties in enforcement due to widespread resignations of policemen.

The number of crossings to and from Jordan over the first two years of the *intifada* dropped by some 50 percent. Thus, for example, in October 1987, 52,558 people crossed the two bridges, while in October 1988, the number was 35,535, and in October 1989, only 34,210.

There was also a drastic decline in the flow of cash funds across the bridges due to the limitations placed by Israel on sums that could be repatriated (200 dinars per person). The October figures for three years show the effect of this ruling. In October 1987, incoming funds totalled 3.3 million dinars and $12 million; in October 1988 this dropped to 1,958,000 dinars and $400,000; and in October 1989, the figures were 262,700 dinars and $7,700.

The Uprising's Effect on Palestinians

To summarize the course of the non-violent aspects of the *intifada*, the first 27 months unquestionably imposed hardships on the civilian life of the Palestinians, but no breaking point seemed to be in sight. In fact, there were signs of further radicalization. This was most evident in the Beit Sahur confrontation: the civil administration used potent means to induce the rebellious merchants to pay taxes, but not one of them capitulated. Yet for the most part, the parameters of the civil rebellion did not expand. Despite calls by the uprising leadership to withhold municipal taxes, the tax revolt did not spread to other cities, and the populace as a whole remained wary of total civil rebellion. Still, it was prepared to continue the uprising and incur the inevitable losses as long as there was no progress in the political arena.

The Palestinians and the PLO both recognized in the first year of the uprising that violence alone would not precipitate an Israeli withdrawal, and that they would have to exploit the gains of the *intifada* by combining it with a political process. This required a certain flexibility in policy, and the PLO, with the explicit backing of the local leadership in the Territories, embarked on this course in November 1988 by adopting the principle of a Palestinian state existing alongside Israel instead of in place of it.

Throughout 1989 the Palestinians and the PLO continued their efforts to further the political process and the dialogue with the US, even on the basis of the Israeli initiative of May 1989. The Palestinians were undoubtedly aware of the difficulties involved in the political process, and particularly the difficulties in beginning negotiations with Israel and pressuring Jerusalem to make policy concessions. They concluded that they must continue the *intifada*, particularly its violent aspect, yet at the same time operate to manipulate Israeli public opinion to their advantage. In this sense they viewed the March 1990 collapse of the Israeli unity government — due to the inability of the government to answer the Baker proposal regarding a meeting in Cairo that would initiate the process — as a victory for their cause.

Impact on Israel

As long as the intensity of *intifada* violence seemed to be decreasing during the second year, there was a tendency in Israel to 'tough it out.' This held true for the IDF forces serving in the Territories and the Israeli population that lived and traveled there. Yet the *intifada* continued to exact a heavy toll on Israel in a number of ways. A large segment of the army remained tied up with policing duties, a sharp rift prevailed within the population regarding the Palestinian question, new economic problems were created, and foreign relations were strained. By and large, it was only as a result of Israel's inability both to extricate itself from the *intifada* and to deal with American pressures, that it launched its own political initiative in May 1989. And it was Israel's inability to deliver on a peace process satisfactory to the United States, that eventually brought down the Israeli government in March 1990.

Conclusions

The progress of the *intifada* in its second year and the first months of its third year was extremely complicated from the Palestinians' point of view. They made progress in some ways and remained static in others. In addition to proving their ability to sustain such an uprising for over two years, they also succeeded in establishing institutions in the Territories that may surely be seen as 'self-rule in the making.' In contrast, the Israeli administration lost ground, and local bodies subservient to the civil administration increasingly developed an affinity with the populace and the PLO.

In contrast, incidents became less violent, even though they increased in number, as the IDF took effective counter-steps that reduced pressure on both soldiers and the civilian population living and traveling in the Territories. Civil disobedience continued, but was constrained by the fact that 100,000 Palestinian Arabs still had to make their living in Israel. The Palestinians themselves, fully aware of the problematic state of the *intifada*, analyzed it in their newspapers and consistently looked for new ways to give it impetus.

In many ways, the Israeli and Palestinian sides both reached a crossroads by early 1990. For the Palestinians, this came about because of their inability to sustain a high level of violence against Israel; for Israel, because of political difficulties stemming from its inability to provide a positive response to Secretary of State Baker's proposal for a Cairo meeting. The immediate danger for Israel was first of all political. But in the long range it involved the intensification of Palestinian enmity and increasing difficulty in being able to make territorial compromises.

Both sides now faced a variety of options, involving political moves as well as the continuing use of force. In view of the difficulty in launching violent acts that severely damage Israel, the Palestinians could show political flexibility that might either bring Israel to the bargaining table or render more difficult its relations with the US. But it was unlikely they would do so, as in their estimation they had already made sufficient concessions. They could also intensify violence within the framework of the *intifada*, for example through the widespread use of firearms against civilians. The Palestinians were also reluctant to take this step, which would defy PLO directives, because they perceived that a popular uprising without firearms had already advanced their cause far more effectively, and an escalation in violence of this nature could redound to their disadvantage. As long as they were not desperate, they were not likely to choose this option.

An intermediate option was a more controlled intensification of 'armed struggle' in parallel with the uprising, rather than through exploitation of demonstrations: more firing at soldiers and Israeli settlers, including ambushes on Israeli buses, and attacks on Jewish settlements. The Palestinians were liable to see this as a way to bolster the *intifada* indirectly and increase pressure on Israel. Indeed, this was already the principal means used by terrorist cells in the Territories. Were this tactic to escalate, it could precipitate a broad change in the struggle, perhaps even acts of revenge on the part of Jewish settlers against the Palestinians, and could hardly be beneficial for the Palestinians.

Finally, the *intifada* leadership might initiate additional actions to undermine Israeli rule in the Territories by means of mass resistance. Notably, none of the examples that follow seemed feasible by mid-1990; yet, were conditions to deteriorate, they might come to be viewed as acceptable risks by the Palestinians. Thus, they might send groups of thousands of women to "overcome" an IDF base in a refugee camp, or a command post, forcing the army either to leave and grant them a dramatic victory, or to open fire, with obvious consequences in Israeli and world public opinion. Because of the difficulty in finding thousands of women willing to endanger their lives, it is far more likely that an extremist organization like Hamas would do this than the PLO. Another such step might be non-compliance with curfews on towns and villages by masses of people (mostly women and children). If the IDF found no way to force the residents into observing the curfew, its deterrent force and its hold on the Territories would be substantially weakened. If it opened fire and killed many residents, women and children in particular, it would seriously harm Israel's international standing and particularly its relations with the US, and increase dissent inside Israel. Similarly, passive resistance to arrests by the security forces could be invoked by entire families against army units seeking to arrest a suspect. Or, large numbers of Palestinians could cease working in Israel, thereby foregoing the means to support their families — an unlikely possibility. Finally, a Beit Sahur-style tax revolt could also spread to many communities.

Again, it bears emphasis that such extreme options for action, with the risks they bear, did not seem likely by mid-1990. Yet options involving displays of mass opposition could become plausible and operational under certain circumstances: a) if and when the struggle, as we have known it thus far, greatly intensified; b) if the populace felt that it had little to lose and was willing to sacrifice more; and c) were the Palestinian leadership to be stronger, more unified and daring.

As for Israel's political options vis-a-vis the *intifada*, by the autumn of 1990 the Gulf Crisis — or, more precisely, the Palestinian attitude toward it — appeared to reduce the urgency of taking new decisions. That attitude was characterized by broad popular support for Saddam Hussein, and political efforts by the PLO to buttress the Iraqi position. The anger toward the PLO leadership that this generated in Washington and Cairo, along with the entire world's overall preoccupation with the Gulf, were likely to affect any new political initiative that might obligate Israel.

While this development clearly reduced the saliency of the Palestinian problem on the world agenda, it was equally clear that the problem would not go away. Even at the height of the early months of the Gulf Crisis the Soviet Union in particular, but also France and to some extent the United States, addressed the necessity of solving the Palestinian problem once the crisis was over. The international reaction to the deaths of 21 Palestinians in a clash with Israeli police on the Temple Mount in early October sharply strengthened international pressure. Hence it was highly likely that by some time in 1991 the issue would recapture its high international priority, possibly along with additional broader aspects of the Arab-Israel conflict. Conceivably, however, the PLO's stand in the Gulf Crisis, and particularly its support for Iraq in the face of a worldwide coalition, would reduce that organization's prospects for representing the Palestinians in renewed negotiations.

Accordingly, after two and a half months of the Gulf Crisis Israel confronted two political options for dealing with the Palestinian issue in the near term. First, it could maintain its initial waiting stance without taking any initiative until the crisis ended, on the assumption that impending developments might have far-reaching ramifications for the way in which Israel could deal with the problem. This entailed the risk that the United States, and possibly additional countries, might in the interim take initiatives not welcomed by Israel on the Palestinian issue, including an attempt to convene an international conference.

Alternatively, Israel could seek to exploit the relative weakness of the Palestinians and the PLO, and to avoid the prospect that an international conference would be convened (even after the termination of the Gulf Crisis), by taking a stronger initiative to implement its May 1989 proposal, with the agreement or cooperation of Palestinians from Judea, Samaria and Gaza.

9. Palestinian Armed Struggle

by Anat Kurz

The Issue of Palestinian Terrorism

The outbreak of the popular uprising in the West Bank and Gaza Strip shifted the focus of attention away from terrorist warfare as the salient feature of the Palestinian struggle against Israel. The Palestinian change of strategy toward an unarmed struggle, or one based on low-level violence carried out by the masses in the Territories, initiated a new phase in the protracted conflict. Moreover, the official PLO commitment of December 1988 to avoid terrorism added a new aspect to the strategic dilemma facing the PLO mainstream during the second year of the *intifada*. Preserving the image of unarmed struggle in the Territories, and of abstention from terrorism in general, became a key issue in the PLO's drive to advance its political prospects and preserve already achieved gains, such as the dialogue with the US. Further, the commitment publicly made by Arafat to "renounce terrorism" created an additional criterion for judging the PLO's ongoing international credibility and future ability to assume control over Palestinian affairs.

Perhaps most significantly, there were sharp differences among the principal actors involved in the political process — the US, the PLO and Israel — as to what constitutes a terrorist act in terms of tactics, targets and location. The three key actors also differed with regard to the degree of responsibility that could be attributed to the Arafat-led PLO mainstream, concerning the activities of diverse Palestinian groups whose subordination to the PLO was not always clear.

The Israeli position toward terrorism is the most comprehensive of the three. According to the Israeli Terrorism Prevention Act (1948), terrorism means violent acts that may result in death or injury, or threats to carry out such acts. This highly generalized categorization does not explicitly state that terrorism is politically motivated. Nor does it confine terrorist acts to assaults perpetrated in certain geographical areas or against certain targets.

In contrast, the nature of the objective that is attacked forms a major aspect of the American definition of terrorism. According to the Department of State's definition, terrorism is "premeditated, politically motivated violence perpetrated against noncombatant targets by subnational groups of clandestine state agents, usually intended to influence an audience."

As for the PLO approach, Arafat renounced terrorism, yet did not specify what acts were implied by the term. Addressing the UN General Assembly in Geneva on December 13, 1988 he condemned "terrorism in all forms" but also reiterated the Palestinian National Council's adherence to UN resolutions endorsing "the right of nations to resist foreign occupation."

In the event, during 1989 civil manifestations of the popular uprising in the Territories were accompanied by violent acts that fell within the definitions of terrorism set by both Israel and the US. Attacks carried out in the Territories and within pre-1967 Israel targeted both civilian and military targets. A considerable share of the acts perpetrated in Israel and across its borders during the period following Arafat's commitment, were carried out by elements associated with Arafat's own Fatah movement and with other PLO affiliates. Yet all these were declared legitimate by the PLO, which stated, "We reject the claim that the Palestinian *intifada* is terrorism....We also reject the claim that military actions against Israel are terrorist acts." Any ambiguity as to the legitimate venue of operations was clarified when Khalil al-Wazir (Abu Jihad) stated on December 20, 1988 that "within original Israel and the occupied territories, the Palestinians have the right to attack military targets."

Here the PLO mainstream attitude toward the *intifada* and the issue of armed struggle in the Territories is of interest. The official stand of the PLO and the PLO-backed Unified Leadership of the Uprising advocated confining the insurrection within the limits of popular, unarmed struggle. The major rationale behind this policy did not change since the early days of the *intifada*. It was to exploit all the political advantages of the popular struggle, while not providing Israeli authorities with the justification to quell it by massive force.

Differences concerning the issue of armed struggle have existed among diverse factions within the PLO, as well as among leaders of its main group, Fatah. The significance of armed struggle in gaining political and propaganda achievements for the *intifada* was not denied. Salah Khalaf, in a press conference held in January 1989, emphasized the importance of armed struggle in advancing a political resolution: "world public opinion is not only won by political and diplomatic action...(but) the continuation of the armed struggle (is)...decisive in bringing about changes in stands and also in finding a solution." Whereas announcements made by members of Fatah sometimes reflected a readiness to suspend armed struggle in anticipation of favorable political developments, declarations made by spokesmen of PLO radical groups persistently called for intensification of armed struggle, and emphasized its key role within the framework of the insurrection. Thus an announcement made by the PFLP following its conference in February 1989 in Damascus called "to continue the struggle in all forms, especially the armed struggle, until the legitimate rights of the Palestinian people are fulfilled."

Militant streams within Fatah itself appeared to gain dominance during the second year of the *intifada*. Concrete political developments — the Israeli-sponsored plan for elections in the Territories published in May, and subsequent contacts involving Egypt (and the PLO), the US and Israel concerning procedures for preliminary meetings that would prepare the elections — appeared at the time to some Palestinians likely to end up by excluding the PLO from the process. When the Fatah Revolutionary Council met in June in Tunis, some members expressed the fear that the *intifada* would fade away unless an escalation of the unrest were to stimulate the public debate in Israel and again direct world attention to the Territories. In early August a formal announcement was made at the Fifth Fatah Congress in Tunis, reaffirming dedication to the armed struggle and validating the military option, while nevertheless noting that "adherence to the armed struggle...does not conflict with political struggle and by no means cancels our political initiative."

Beyond Israel and the Territories, Fatah adopted a different approach, albeit with qualifications. It refrained from carrying out armed infiltration attempts into Israel from Lebanon. Indeed, PLO groups had by and large avoided participation in international terrorism since Arafat's pledge to abandon the international arena, given in November 1985 in Cairo.

Thus by renouncing terrorism at Geneva, Arafat essentially formalized previous commitments of one sort or another concerning a halt to terrorist activity in specific spheres: PLO-perpetrated terrorism in the international arena, cross-border activity by Fatah into Israel, and the resort to arms by elements associated with the PLO within the framework of the *intifada*.

Determining Arafat's responsibility for activities carried out by radical PLO groups turned out to be as complicated as interpreting the exact meaning of his renunciation of terrorism. The PLO mainstream sought to avoid the issue, with the risk it posed to PLO unity, by declaring cross-border infiltration attempts into Israel by organizations other than Fatah to be legitimate. Similarly, a total rejection of armed attacks carried out within Israel would have meant a drastic reversal of the traditional Palestinian perception of the legitimate course of struggle, and was therefore avoided.

In the initial stages of its contacts with the PLO, the US sought to persuade the organization to provide a broad, operative translation of Arafat's commitment and to assume responsibility for the relevant activities of its diverse member groups. The PLO was called upon to end the *intifada*, and Arafat was challenged by the administration regarding the activities of PLO-member groups in the Israeli border arena. The US also required the expulsion from the ranks of the organization of the Palestinian Liberation Front (PLF), held responsible for the hijacking of the Italian cruise ship Achille Lauro in 1985, and the dismantling of Fatah's Force 17.

None of these demands, however, were met. Even the pressure exercised by the US on Arafat in early 1989 to bring to a halt cross-border infiltration attempts carried out by PLO groups from Lebanon was eased throughout the year. In March 1989, Secretary of State James Baker maintained that attacks by the PLO against Israel in Southern Lebanon were not acts of terrorism requiring the cessation of US talks with the PLO. Moreover, the administration apparently accepted the PLO argument that attacks inside Israel and the Territories in some way constituted a legitimate expression of armed struggle against occupation, as did cross-border attacks against Israeli military targets. One assumption that presumably generated this development was that increased US pressure on Arafat on this aspect of the terrorism issue would shake his intra-PLO status, and might therefore leave the administration with no partner for negotiations.

By the end of the first year of Arafat's commitment, the linkage between PLO-perpetrated terrorism and the continuation of the dialogue between the organization and the US had been loosened. The issue of PLO groups' direct engagement in terrorism appeared to be less crucial, and formal definitions seemed to play a secondary role in influencing political moves. Thus in March

1990, a report issued by the US State Department stated that "the PLO has adhered to its commitment undertaken in 1988 to renounce terror," but called upon the organization to practice tighter control over the activities of its radical factions.

Israel regarded attacks perpetrated by PLO-affiliated elements as irrefutable indications of the lack of credibility of Arafat's undertaking. Intensive diplomatic efforts were conducted by Israeli government agencies throughout 1989 to prove the association between PLO groups in general, Fatah in particular, and terrorist acts. These were primarily aimed at convincing the administration to end its dialogue with the PLO and to exclude the organization from the political process. Israel, too, made specific distinctions. Thus, Israeli Defense Minister Yitzhak Rabin stated on February 19, 1990 that "any attempt to equate the *intifada* with terror is wrong and misleading." The uprising, he added could only be considered terrorism if the Palestinians were organized in armed terrorist squads, equipped with Kalashnikov rifles, hand grenades and explosives, and the use of those weapons had become "the most important element in the activity against us."

Israel did point, repeatedly, to instances of cross-border attacks from Lebanon by PLO-affiliated groups as clear violations of Arafat's commitment. Similarly, bombings and stabbings inside Israel and the Territories, as well as the numerous assassinations of Palestinians by Palestinians in the Territories, were cited.

The administration's dismissal of these allegations, as it pursued its dialogue with the PLO mainstream as a means of advancing the peace process, encountered growing congressional opposition throughout 1989 and early 1990. Hairsplitting attempts by administration spokesmen — e.g., the claim that DFLP cross-border attacks from Lebanon that targeted northern Israeli villages could not be considered terrorism against civilians because they had been thwarted by the IDF, hence the only Israeli 'target' involved was military — merely fueled the controversy.

Ultimately, it was precisely such an act — the attempted landing at central Israeli beaches on May 30, 1989 by Abul Abbas' PLF — that moved Washington to suspend its dialogue with the PLO.

The discussion that follows is intended to illustrate trends in the Palestinian armed struggle during the second year of the *intifada*. The volume of activity, as well as choices of tactics and target, reflect the atmosphere, mindsets and political considerations regarding the use of terrorism among Palestinian leaders and activists during the period under review. While the *intifada* formed the focus and core of related events and developments, Palestinian activity in different arenas led to distinct political ramifications regionally and internationally. Hence three major venues of activity — Israel and the administered territories, the border arena, and Southern Lebanon (where considerable Shi'ite and other non-Palestinian terrorist activity was also recorded) — are discussed separately. Because violent activity in the Territories is considered as part of an integrative analysis of the *intifada* in Chapter 8, our discussion of it here is limited to operational, organizational, and ideological aspects. Finally, Palestinian international terrorism in 1989 is discussed in a separate volume published by JCSS: *InTer: International Terrorism in 1989*.

Palestinian Terrorism in Israel and the Territories: The Armed Aspect of the Intifada

The figures indicate an increase in both unsophisticated as well as armed attacks, i.e., assaults with hatchets, knives and the like, as well as a growing reliance on firearms. Both developments strikingly corresponded with increased intra-Palestinian violence. Indeed, the employment of these weapons was much more frequent in attacks by Palestinians against fellow Arabs, than in confrontations with IDF troops in the Territories.

Activists involved in carrying out terrorist attacks against Israeli and Palestinian objectives were usually locally organized. Cells of this nature characterized the violence in the West Bank and Gaza Strip since the start of the uprising and even before. At the same time, most of the cells declared at least an ideological affiliation with Palestinian organizations, and in many instances coordinated their general course of activity and even specific operations with the organizations based outside of Israel. Many of the hundreds of cells whose organizational affiliation was identified during 1989 by the security forces were linked with Fatah, which enjoyed broader popular support in the Territories than the other Palestinian groups. Other active cells were affiliated with the Popular Front for the Liberation of Palestine (PFLP), the Democratic Front for the Liberation of Palestine (DFLP), and the fundamentalist Islamic Resistance Movement, *Hamas*.

Several dozen Fatah cells coordinated their activities with the organization abroad, primarily in Jordan. Most of the attacks perpetrated by the uncovered Fatah cells were carried out in the Territories, the great majority of them in the West Bank, while only a few took place within the pre-1967 borders of Israel, and most of these were minor or thwarted.

There were, however, indications that the organizations' leadership abroad as well as their local committees of activists did not always control the militant cells' participation in terrorist assaults. Spontaneous strike forces frequently carried out attacks in defiance of leadership directives with regard to targets and operational tactics. This radicalization probably was at least partially associated with the massive arrests conducted by security forces, insofar as they inflicted major blows on the more disciplined and restrained ranks of activists.

One attempt by the PLO to acquire influence over extremist elements was manifested in the formation of the Popular Army in the West Bank. By late 1988, paramilitary marches by masked youths wearing uniforms and carrying home-made arms were a common sight in the West Bank, mainly in the area of Nablus. This symbolic show of force by local elements was adopted by the leadership of the PLO and the *intifada* in January 1989. The PLO announced from Baghdad that it had initiated the creation of a popular army that was aimed at establishing "justice and law, and embodying the power of the people." Leaflet no. 32 of the Unified Leadership of the Uprising, issued on January 7 and broadcast by the Voice of Palestine from Algiers, praised the establishment of the "army." This time, however, earlier declarations that linked it exclusively with Fatah's Force 17 were not repeated, apparently as a result of pressure applied by other organizations, and especially the PFLP. Thus the Popular Army was declared "the army of the PLO, which is basically composed of the strike forces, comprises all parties, and obeys the orders of the Unified Leadership." The activities of the Popular Army, however, were essentially internally-oriented, and focused on enforcing the leadership's policy over the Palestinian population of the Territories, including calls for strikes and popular protests. Its violent aspect was mainly directed against Palestinians — and in many instances contradicted the leadership's explicit orders.

Similarly, activists bearing firearms were usually not involved in armed assaults against Israeli targets. Direct confrontations between troops and groups of masked youths, armed persons or fugitives were in most cases initiated by the soldiers and not planned as Palestinian attacks. On May 19, 1989, shots were fired at an IDF patrol pursuing a group of wanted activists in the area of Hebron. Responsibility for the incident was claimed by Abu Musa's faction of Fatah, which had repeatedly announced its intention to escalate the armed struggle in the Territories. The clash, which was the first of its kind since the start of the uprising, generated a pledge by Arafat to maintain the non-recourse to arms.

Dramatic incidents that took place in 1989 were relatively rare, the perpetrators did not belong to PLO groups, and the venue for the majority of them was pre-1967 Israel. They reflected a growing inclination toward self-initiated, risky acts of revenge, and attested to a limited capacity to perpetrate spectacular attacks within the Territories. Among the latter were a well-planned ambush on an IDF patrol near Gaza by a team of the Islamic Jihad in November 1989; the August kidnapping of an Israeli citizen in Tulkarem (an attempt to negotiate his release was thwarted when the captive was rescued); and the February and March kidnappings and subsequent murders of two soldiers near Ashkelon, north of the Gaza Strip by Hamas members who soon fled to Egypt. It bears emphasis that such attacks were exceptional, and did not reflect a shift in the overall direction of the struggle by radical *intifada* activists.

Additional spectacular assaults were also perpetrated by residents of the Territories who acted alone, without affiliation to any group. These included the May 1989 knife assault against Israelis in a Jerusalem bus station by a Hamas member, and the June suicide attack by a Gazan who seized the wheel of a Jerusalem-bound bus from Tel Aviv, and sent it crashing into an abyss. That incident, in which 15 persons were killed, accounted for a considerable share of the increase recorded in 1989 in the number of Jewish victims of Palestinian terrorist activity.

As in previous years, Palestinians from the Territories contributed considerably to the scope of incidents recorded within the Green Line. Thus some of the terrorist activity recorded in Jerusalem during 1989 was attributed to non-residents, usually Palestinians living in adjacent neighborhoods and villages. Jerusalem, in fact, was the only area of Israel in which a significant increase in violent attacks was evident during 1989. These were primarily arson attacks that targeted Israeli vehicles. Torching of fields and forests was one of the major sources of concern in the first year of the uprising, yet according to Israel Police statistics, a decrease of about 20 percent in such incidents was recorded the following year, accompanied by a 40 percent decrease in damage. Otherwise, there was no change in the scope of activity within Israel as compared with the previous year, 1988 (although notably 1988, the first year of the *intifada*, produced a significant increase compared with the years preceding the uprising).

At the same time, increased terrorist activity by Israeli Arabs continued, as the *intifada* spilled over from the Territories into pre-1967 Israel. The uprising, coupled with mounting religious zealotry, were major sources of inspiration and imitation by Israeli Arabs. The formation and activation of underground cells — sometimes in association with Palestinian organizations in the Territories and abroad — reflected this development, though there was no indication of a readiness by the Israeli Arab mainstream to adopt the methods of the uprising for advancing their civil and nationalist goals.

Extremist elements in the Territories were far from exhausting their potential for further escalation of terrorist activity by early 1990. Arm caches were maintained, and hardliner motivation remained high even when low-level violence and non-violent expressions of the *intifada* declined. The Islamic Jihad and Hamas, neither of them directed by considerations of political prestige, also saw an escalation of violence as a means of frustrating progress toward a negotiated settlement. Yet massive arrests conducted during the first two years of the *intifada* among leaders and activists of those organizations probably preempted any escalation of attacks. In any event, by the third year of the *intifada*, the link between violence and the image of the insurrection had become a genuine source of concern for the Palestinian leadership, as it focused increasingly on intra-Palestinian brutality.

Intra-Palestinian Terrorism

The second year of the *intifada* witnessed a significant change in the nature of the objectives of Palestinian violence in the Territories. Assaults against fellow Arabs gained dominance, and came to form a major feature of violence in the areas. The violent aspect of the uprising had in effect turned inward.

Intra-Palestinian violence featured diverse foci and manifestations. Threats were made on political and personal grounds; attacks aimed at inflicting property damage targeted the possessions of political rivals or persons accused of association with the Israeli authorities, including employees of the Civil Administration and the municipalities; there were clashes, usually involving the use of home-made arms, between rival organizations and factions; and, at the extreme, attacks against those accused of cooperation with the security forces. Persons suspected of such collaboration were kidnapped, interrogated, beaten, and in many instances murdered. Yet among those slain on the pretext of collaboration were many who had in effect been accused of immoral behavior — punished by *intifada* activists who regarded themselves as keepers of 'law and order' in the Palestinian street.

Assaults against persons accused of collaboration had increased dramatically by mid-1989. In an article written in response to claims condemning the "silence of the international and Palestinian human rights communities with respect to actions taken by Palestinians during the *intifada*" against "traitors and collaborators," Jonathan Kuttab, a West Bank lawyer, asked in September 1989 what action could be taken by "a national movement against such traitors, when the movement is largely underground?" His principal argument in defending the militant atmosphere among Palestinians was that "the population involved in the *intifada* is physically endangered by many collaborators....They provide the authorities with information that jeopardizes the general population. Hence, in addition to the need to provide sanctions that would punish or deter such individuals, there is also the need to protect the community."

Indeed, assaults against people accused of collaboration with the authorities were encouraged by the Palestinian leadership from the early stages of the *intifada*. Yet by the second year, as this activity became a daily reality and generated friction among Palestinians and loss of prestige for the struggle, it turned into a source of concern. Yet the declared policy of the PLO and the PLO-backed Unified Leadership of the uprising toward the phenomenon remained ambivalent. Prominent figures from the Territories, with few exceptions, avoided denouncing it; and leaders at the higher ranks, including Arafat, even claimed responsibility for ordering executions on behalf of the PLO. Documents discovered in October 1989 in the Gaza Strip included directives to local operatives by a Fatah activist based in Tunis and Amman to carry out attacks against those who cooperated with the authorities, but to conceal the organization's involvement. Khaled al-Hassan acknowledged in 1989 that attacks against collaborators followed the PLO line, though some attacks admittedly were carried out by people seeking personal revenge or were the result of overzealous decisions. In order to avoid repeating mistakes made during the Palestinian rebellion in 1936-9 against British rule, the current leadership, he noted, devoted great care to monitoring the phenomenon. His words, in effect, reflected a feeling among Palestinian leaders that the intracommunal violence in the Territories was getting out of control.

Accordingly, references to the killings issued by the *intifada* leadership focused on appeals to exercise restraint. Leaflet no. 44 of the Unified Leadership of the Intifada, broadcast by the Voice of the PLO from Baghdad on August 16, 1989, called upon activists in the Territories to refrain from killing collaborators unless accusations were soundly based, prior warnings had been given and the suspected person had been granted an opportunity to repent. Leaflet no. 46, distributed on September 26, called on Palestinians to continue harassment of "collaborators," yet appealed to avoid executions except for cases of "wide national consensus." In January 1990, masked youths declaring themselves "The General Security" and allegedly affiliated with Fatah, marched in the casbah of Nablus in protest against unbridled executions.

Yet these cells appeared to have little if any influence on activists dealing with accused collaborators. Indeed, those involved in executing accused traitors were usually members of strike forces affiliated with PLO organizations, such as the Fatah-affiliated "Black Panther," the PFLP-affiliated "Red Eagle," both of which operated in Nablus, and Fatah's "Eagles of the Revolution" in Gaza.

Future Developments

The possibility of the escalation of violence in the *intifada*, and the future role of the PLO's external leadership are likely to be closely intertwined. The frustration of the Palestinians' political aspirations, along with their growing difficulty in generating an immediate international response to occurrences in the Territories, were mentioned during the course of 1989-90 by PLO leaders as probable causes for a resort to armed struggle. Indeed, threats of this nature were repeatedly made from the start of the *intifada*, and were seen as attempts to prepare an alternative in the event of failure of the political process, or as retaliation for an Israeli crackdown in the Territories.

In fact specific and direct causes for any future escalation in the Territories are difficult to predict. Violence could erupt to discourage concrete political moves involving demands for further concessions by the Palestinians, or in reaction to continuing political stagnation. A regression in international awareness, or expressions of acute fatigue by Palestinians in the Territories could provoke radical elements to take extreme measures to revive the issue. Finally, Israeli political moves, and the reaction of security forces to growing militancy in the Territories, could interact with Palestinian activity and attitudes to produce escalation.

In 1989 the *intifada* leadership tread a fine line between the goal of maintaining the uprising's broad popular manifestations, and the need to control militant activists. Another critical dynamic was that between the leadership of the *intifada* in the Territories, and the PLO. One expression of these dynamics was the formation of the Popular Army by local elements and its subsequent adoption by the PLO. The most telling manifestation was the very outbreak of the *intifada*.

Cross-Border Palestinian Terrorism Against Israel

The limited feasibility of carrying out concerted terrorist campaigns within Israel has traditionally prompted the Palestinian organizations to resort to the border arena. This need became even more urgent after the outbreak of the uprising as diverse Palestinian exile groups strove to manifest their solidarity with the population of the Territories and at the same time compete for the leadership of the revitalized struggle.

Increased infiltration attempts were already evident during the early stages of the *intifada*, and this trend continued in waves throughout 1988 and 1989. In 1989 the total rate of infiltration attempts decreased, while remaining high compared to the years preceding the *intifada*. In all, 22 infiltration attempts into Israel and cross-border attacks were recorded during 1989: two from Egypt, six from Jordan and 14 from Lebanon.

A significant increase in infiltration attempts was noted along the Israel-Jordan border. Yet, as in the years preceding the *intifada*, the majority of attempts were launched from Southern Lebanon, where Palestinian organizations enjoyed relative freedom of action compared with other border arenas. Fatah was significantly active in the Lebanese border arena during the first months of the *intifada*, mainly against the backdrop of the PLO's self-imposed restrictions regarding the course of the armed struggle within Israel. During the following stages, radical factions of the PLO and pro-Syrian groups gained dominance in this sphere as it was transformed, in effect, into a testing ground for the credibility of Arafat's December 1988 pledge to halt terrorism.

Cross-Border Activity from Lebanon. The intensity of the cross-border campaign perpetrated from *Southern Lebanon* significantly declined throughout 1989. While ten infiltration attempts were perpetrated there from January to June 1989, only four were recorded during the following months. The campaign was carried out by PLO radical factions and by non-PLO groups that opposed both Arafat's public renunciation of terrorism in Geneva in December 1988, and a commitment to halt cross-border infiltrations specifically from South Lebanon into Israel, that he allegedly gave in late November. Thus infiltration attempts by the PFLP and DFLP were intended to bring about a halt to the US-PLO dialogue for which a renunciation of terrorism had formed a precondition.

The PLO mainstream was reluctant to denounce the cross-border campaign conducted by its opposition groups. In fact, the attacks were defended and officially described as military missions in order to qualify as a dimension of the armed struggle. In the event, a corresponding willingness to stretch its formal definitions of terrorism enabled the administration to ease pressure on Arafat concerning the continuation of incidents in the arena.

Other elements involved in the Lebanon border incidents were pro-Syrian groups that, unlike PLO organizations, have traditionally been motivated solely by armed struggle as their course of action. These were Tala'at Ya'akub's Palestine Liberation Front (PLF) which was responsible for five attempts (one carried out in cooperation with the PFLP, another with the PFLP and Hizballah), Ahmed Jibril's PFLP-GC responsible for one attempt, and the Palestinian Popular Struggle Front (PPSF) which carried out the

Table 15

Distribution of Infiltration Attempts from January-December 1989 by Perpetrating Organizations**

	Jan	Feb	Mar	Apr	May	Jun	Jul	Aug	Sep	Oct	Nov	Dec
<u>From Lebanon</u>												
PFLP		1	1		1		1					
PLF		1	1		1			1				
PFLP-GC			1									
DFLP		1	1			1		1				
PPSF				1								
Unknown				1					1			
		2*	4	2	1*	1	1	2	1			
<u>From Jordan</u>												
Fatah Rebels			1									
JI									1			
Jordanian soldier								1	2			
PLF									1			
			1					1	4			
<u>From Egypt</u>												
Fatah												1
JI			1									
			1									1
TOTAL		2	6	2	1	1	1	3	5			1

* Two infiltration attempts were joint operations by more than one organization: an infiltration attempt by the PFLP and PLF was carried out in South Lebanon in February; an attempt by the PFLP and PLF in cooperation with Hizballah was carried out in May in that arena. In addition, Fatah's involvement was alleged in a March infiltration by the Islamic Jihad from Egypt.

** Organizations surveyed:
DFLP — Democratic Front for the Liberation of Palestine
Fatah
Fatah rebels — Abu Musa's faction
JI — (Gaza-based) Islamic Jihad
PFLP — Popular Front for the Liberation of Palestine
PFLP-GC — PFLP-General Command
PLF — Palestine Liberation Front
PPSF — Palestinian Popular Struggle Front

only seaborne infiltration attempt into Israel perpetrated from Lebanon during 1989.

The decline in cross-border attempts from Southern Lebanon evident throughout 1989, however, may also be attributed to effective countermeasures invoked by the SLA and IDF in the region. Israeli troops in the security zone and routine activity by the SLA not only foiled all attempted attacks (only one terrorist cell, belonging to the DFLP, managed to get to the border fence), but presumably were instrumental in preempting additional attacks.

During 1989, 13 air raids were carried out by the IAF against Palestinian logistics and departure bases in Lebanon. Targeted in those raids were the PPSF, Jibril's PFLP-GC, Abu Nidal's Fatah Revolutionary Council (FRC), and the PLO factions DFLP, PFLP and PLF. The most frequented target in those raids was the PFLP-GC, whose strongholds were hit in six IAF operations inside Lebanon, including locations well behind Syrian lines in the Biq'a. Additional raids targeted positions in the area of Beirut, but the majority were conducted in the southern coastal region.

The association between Shi'ite and Palestinian organizations in Southern Lebanon was a dominant factor in facilitating the Palestinian infrastructure. During 1989 there were indications of greater freedom of movement provided to Palestinian organizations in the area by both Amal and Hizballah. The Shi'ites, for their part, were motivated to intensify ties with Palestinian elements by considerations related to their intracommunal rivalry for dominance in the region.

Hizballah's links with Palestinians, especially after late 1988, focused on radical, pro-Syrian elements. In contrast, Amal established links with radical and mainstream Palestinian groups alike. The Amal-Fatah accord, signed in December 1988 in the wake of the termination of the "camps war" in Lebanon, was mediated in part by the PFLP and DFLP. Their involvement in generating the agreement, which provided for a full ceasefire between Amal and Fatah as well as coordination of their activities in the western and central sections of South Lebanon, was allegedly directed by Syria, which sought to reinforce radical streams within Fatah itself. Amal granted Fatah approach routes to the Security Zone, provided guides and permitted teams actively involved in anti-Israel attacks in the region to use its positions as observation posts toward Israel. In early 1990 Amal's assistance to DFLP and PLF teams on their way to the Israeli border prompted an IAF raid against a village controlled by the militia south of Sidon.

Cooperation between Shi'ite and Palestinian organizations in Southern Lebanon was, for the Palestinians, primarily of pragmatic importance in facilitating their cross-border campaigns. The Palestinian motivation for this course of activity remained unchanged. The infiltration drive, therefore, was likely to continue and escalate in anticipation of any new developments in the Middle East political process. Continued stalemate in the political sphere, on the other hand, would generate greater pressure on the PLO mainstream to participate in a renewed border campaign in the region, even if this implied a reversal of Arafat's commitment from November 1988. This prospect, however, seemed less critical in 1990 than in early 1989, in view of the tolerance shown by the international community toward Palestinian activity in the Lebanese arena.

Two terrorist teams managed to cross the *Israel-Egypt border* in 1989. In March, a two-man Islamic Jihad cell initiated a shootout with IDF soldiers in Rafah. The terrorists said they had been recruited and directed by the Fatah office in Cairo. Four days before the second anniversary of the *intifada* in December, a five-man team was intercepted and killed at Har Harif in the Negev. The incursion was attributed to Fatah by official Israeli sources, and neither officially confirmed nor denied by the organization.

In any case, there remained doubts as to Fatah's association with the incidents. The Islamic Jihad and Fatah had indeed cooperated operationally for several years. Yet differences between the organizations had evolved by late 1988, and involvement in both incidents by Fatah personnel may well have been unauthorized, as indicated by the fact that in both cases no organization took credit for the infiltrations. In general, Fatah appeared to be exercising tight control over extremists among its ranks so as not to jeopardize its political collaboration with Cairo.

The Israel-Jordan border, which had been relatively calm for years, witnessed an increased volume of activity during 1989. Cross-border attacks and infiltrations were carried out by individuals seeking revenge for occurrences in the Territories, as well as by Palestinian organizations. Syria also sought to activate the arena against the backdrop of its cooling relationships with Amman, and reportedly encouraged the activity of radical Palestinian groups there. The latter, for their part, sought alternatives to the Israel-Lebanon border, where all their attacks had been foiled.

Palestinian organizations that took part in activity along the Israel-Jordan border during 1989, and were each responsible for one assault, were: Abu Musa's Fatah Rebels; Islamic Jihad; the Palestinian Liberation Front (which claimed responsibility for an attack that, according to Israeli sources, was perpetrated by the Islamic Jihad); and the PFLP. The remaining four incidents were carried out by individual disgruntled Jordanian soldiers.

In all, six infiltrations and two attacks from across the border were recorded during 1989. This trend of intensified activity continued throughout early 1990, with several additional shooting incidents in January, and an infiltration in April. The incidents took place the length of the border, from Lake Kinneret in the north to Eilat in the south.

The escalating attacks from Jordan generated concern on both sides of the border. Jordan stepped up its patrol activity, and reinforced its armed presence along the Jordan and Yarmoukh rivers and at the sensitive Jordan-Israel-Syria border junction. In October, security forces in Amman arrested members of the Syrian-backed PFLP accused of involvement in a September Katyusha attack on Israel from the area of the border triangle, and in March a Jordanian official pledged that Jordan would maintain its truce obligations with Israel.

Nevertheless, the long border between Israel and Jordan was likely to remain an attractive venue for Jordanians and Palestinians inspired by the *intifada*, as well as for Palestinian parties seeking to generate a deterioration in Jordanian-Israeli relations.

The Southern Lebanese Arena

Southern Lebanon, a portion of which is designated by Israel as a security zone, was the arena for militant activity by diverse groups in 1989-90. Shi'ite organizations, namely the Amal militia and Hizballah, were responsible for the majority of attacks. These were directed against the IDF presence in the area as well as against the Israeli-sponsored local militia, the Southern Lebanon Army (SLA). A few attacks targeted UNIFIL positions and troops.

For Palestinian groups and Lebanese leftist organizations the area served as a departure base for cross-border infiltration attempts and attacks against Israel. In fact, Southern Lebanon was the only territorial region in which the PLO enjoyed a relative measure of freedom of movement and direct access to the Israeli border. Southern Lebanon was also a major venue for intra-Shi'ite fighting between Amal and Hizballah for control over the Shi'ite populace, a factor that influenced the nature and scope of the struggle against Israel.

Shi'ite organizations were responsible for at least 133 attacks against the IDF, SLA and Israeli border settlements during 1989. This figure demonstrates a decrease in the volume of activity of Shi'ite organizations in comparison to updated data from 1988, when Shi'ites were responsible for 173 attacks. A decrease in the volume of Shi'ite activity was also evident during the first six months of 1990: 46 attacks were recorded during this period, while 66 were recorded during the same period in 1989.

The activity of Shi'ite organizations against the IDF and SLA was confined mainly to the security zone; they continued to refrain from infiltration attempts into Israel. Their involvement in activity along the Israeli border was limited to Katyusha rocket attacks, as well as occasional logistical support for infiltration attempts conducted by Palestinian groups. During 1989 Katyusha attacks against Northern Israel continued a long-term decline: 10 attacks in 1989 and 11 in 1988, compared to 24 in 1987. An additional four were recorded by June 1990. Most of these resulted in no injuries or damage inside Israel.

Among the Shi'ite elements, Amal continued to play the major role. It was responsible for 78 attacks during 1989, and for 13 additional ones by June 1990. The Shi'ites' preferred tactics were laying mines and roadside charges, and armed assaults. Direct confrontations between SLA or IDF troops and Shi'ite aggressors, however, were relatively rare during the period under review, and usually were not initiated by the latter.

The scope of armed assaults perpetrated by Hizballah was minor in 1989, and included mainly ambushes and artillery shelling. This relatively subdued level of activity stood in marked contrast to the large-scale frontal assaults carried out during 1987 and early 1988, apparently because this tactic had proven to be unsuccessful for Hizballah. The aggressive drive conducted at that time by the organization was aimed at gaining control over the Christian-controlled area linking Jezin and Southern Lebanon. It was curbed in mid-1988 by a major IDF operation at Maidoun, and was not resumed.

In 1989 Hizballah's concerted effort to strengthen its position in Southern Lebanon was concentrated in the western sector of the region, where it challenged Amal's dominance. The intensity of fighting between the two Shi'ite organizations apparently had direct implications for the volume of Hizballah's other activities, including attacks against the SLA, the IDF and the UNIFIL presence in the area. To these one must add a marked improvement in the SLA's operational capability to contain Hizballah military pressure — the result of a concentrated training effort.

Hizballah positions in the central and eastern sectors of Southern Lebanon, albeit north of the security zone, were targeted in five raids by the IAF and four by IDF ground forces, and at times by IDF artillery as well, during 1989 and early 1990. IDF pressure on Hizballah reflected Israel's constant drive against terrorist infrastructures in the region. The activity of Amal was by-and-large confined within the borders of the Security Zone, in part due to Amal's wish to avoid a major confrontation with the IDF. Nonetheless, enhanced cooperation between Amal and Palestinians — pro-Syrian radical groups as well as Fatah — reflected a growing inclination to risk such a confrontation, perhaps as a result of increased competition between Amal and Hizballah. It may also reflect growing militancy among local Amal leaders in the south, as well as Syrian encouragement.

Cooperation between Amal and radical Palestinian groups carrying out infiltration attempts into Northern Israel formed the backdrop for IAF raids against Amal positions on two occasions, in December 1988 and in February 1990. Amal retaliated with Katyusha attacks and threatened to attack objectives within Israel, a threshold it had not crossed by June 1990. Interestingly, the threat itself was apparently perceived as a 'green light' by Hizballah to conduct a Katyusha attack on the Galilee.

Lebanese leftist organizations were involved in 41 incidents in the south during 1989, and in 14 additional ones by June 1990. Several of these also involved pro-Syrian Palestinian elements. The Lebanese National Resistance Front (FNRL) — comprising the Lebanese Communist Party (LCP), the Lebanese Ba'ath Party, the Syrian Social Nationalist Party (SSNP) and radical Palestinians — increased its activity within the Security Zone in September 1989 to mark the seventh anniversary of its formation.

Southern Lebanon continued to serve as an arena for intra-Shi'ite fighting during 1989-1990. In January 1989 Amal and

Hizballah agreed to a ceasefire marking the end of fighting that had erupted between them in November the previous year. Yet the accord, and isolated instances of cooperation between Amal and Hizballah that it produced, primarily reflected the short-term tactical interests of Syria and Iran, as well as the two Shi'ite organizations. Like every other ceasefire in Lebanon, it soon broke down. Amal-Hizballah clashes for control over key sectors of the South continued well into 1990, with the PLO eventually exploiting the confrontation to improve its own positions.

To sum up, attacks against SLA and IDF forces in Southern Lebanon were motivated by-and-large by the opposition of local elements, primarily Shi'ite, to the Israeli presence in the region. Lebanese leftist groups and Palestinian elements were also active in the arena. The scope and volume of incidents was influenced by IDF retaliatory and preemptive measures, as well as by the operational capabilities of the Israeli-backed SLA. Yet periodical spurts of armed activity also reflected differences among the diverse organizations concerning strategic and tactical choices, and the Shi'ite groups' respective positions within the context of the intra-Lebanese balance of power. In particular, mounting tensions between Hizballah and Amal and varieties of Syrian and Iranian involvement, explained at least in part the decreased rate of attacks recorded in the area during the period under review.

10. Shi'ite International Terrorism and the Iranian Connection

by Anat Kurz

In recent years Shi'ite militancy — in its various arenas, choice of objectives and preferred modes of operation — has become one of the most salient trends in international terrorism. The phenomenon encompasses terrorist operations led by Iranian agents, as well as the activity of organizations motivated by Islamic fundamentalist zealotry, inspired and, in many instances, directed by Iran. The latter include mainly the Lebanese-based Hizballah, although Shi'ite groups from the Persian Gulf have also been involved.

If Shi'ite terrorist aims and methods are essentially a Middle East phenomenon with occasional strategic ramifications, they also at times play a key role in the shaky vicissitudes of relations between Iran and the West. Several distinct factors have been considered principal in producing periodical trends of Shi'ite involvement in international terrorism. Iranian political considerations — including those involving the power struggle within the regime in Tehran — and interests have played a major role in directing the course and scope of terrorist activity of actors inspired by Tehran. Terrorist activity of Shi'ite militant elements has also been influenced by developments taking place within the countries of origin of the terrorist groups, particularly Lebanon. In addition, the attitudes of victim states toward the challenges put forward by Iranian state-sponsored terrorism have also influenced the magnitude of terrorist attacks.

Overall, the incidents and related demands made by the perpetrators have been concentrated around two foci. One has been linked directly with interests of Shi'ite groups; the other mainly aimed at advancing Iranian interests. In many instances, such as the foreign hostages affair in Lebanon or in negotiations conducted during plane-hijacking episodes, the different — albeit not unrelated — foci of the demands clearly attested to the existence of two beneficiaries. Iran, however, has been the principal of them.

In terms of volume, Shi'ite international terrorism was marked during 1989 by a continuation of the trend of decline already evident the previous year. Though still considered major within the framework of international terrorism, Iranian state-agents and elements sponsored by Iran were held responsible for 36 international terrorist attacks in 1989, compared with 40 attacks in 1988 and 66 in 1987. Nevertheless, several attacks and terrorism-related developments that took place during this period focused world public awareness on the phenomenon of Iranian-inspired terrorism and its dramatic, sometimes disastrous, effects.

Attacks Against Persian Gulf States

In 1989, a series of anti-Saudi attacks, mainly targeting diplomatic objectives and personnel, was carried out over a broad geographical expanse: incidents were recorded in Asia (Thailand and Pakistan), the Middle East (Turkey, Saudi Arabia itself and Lebanon), and Western Europe (Belgium).

The campaign was attributed to Shi'ite groups persistently seeking revenge for the death of Iranian pilgrims during riots at the annual *hajj* in Mecca in July 1987, and for subsequent executions in Saudi Arabia of pro-Iranian Shi'ites convicted of terrorism — in September 1988 the Saudi authorities executed Shi'ites convicted of involvement in an attack on a petrochemical plant. At the time, the executions were prompted by a series of threats issued by Hizballah and other pro-Iranian groups, Hizballah Hijaz and Islamic Revolution in the Arab Peninsula. A statement made by Iranian Chairman of Parliament Mehdi Kharrubi, warned Saudi Arabia to expect acts of vengeance. The campaign was also thought to reflect the ongoing rift within the Iranian regime concerning the process of normalization of relations with Saudi Arabia, and was allegedly directed by hardliners seeking to bring that rapprochement to a halt.

The threats apparently materialized in a series of attacks against Saudi interests, including bombings in Mecca during the July 1989 pilgrimage. In September 1989, 16 Shi'ite extremists convicted of involvement in the July series of bombing attacks were executed, prompting a new wave of attacks against Saudi objectives in late 1989 and early 1990. A major disaster was prevented when a bomb was discovered, on November 23, 1989, aboard a Saudi airliner flying from Pakistan to Riyadh. This attempt too was attributed to Shi'ite extremists.

Iranian-sponsored terrorism in the arena of the Persian Gulf was aimed almost exclusively against Saudi Arabia. Kuwait, the objective for attacks in previous years, was not the target of any attack during 1989-1990. Whether or not this reflected a shift in Iranian regional policy, it apparently did not stem from any change in Kuwait's stance. Kuwait adhered to its refusal to free 15 pro-Iranian Shi'ite terrorists imprisoned in their country since 1983. In previous years the demand for their release was a major motive for Hizballah's terrorist operations worldwide against Kuwait as well as against the USA and France, and a prime condition for the release of hostages from Lebanon.

Mid-Air Explosions and the Palestinian Connection

As in the anti-Saudi campaign, revenge — accompanied by a wish to intimidate governments and institutions from acting against Iranian interests — was a principal motive for Iranian-directed attacks against western objectives. This presumably was the backdrop to the two most spectacular attacks of the period — the mid-air explosions of a PanAm airliner over Scotland in late December 1988 and of a French UTA plane over Niger in September 1989. In both cases direct Iranian involvement, as well as that of the Popular Front for the Liberation of Palestine-General Command (PFLP-GC), was strongly supported in disclosures made by western security agencies.

The downing of the IranAir airbus over the Gulf in July 1988 by the US Navy's *Vincennes* is thought to have formed a motive for the PanAm attack. That incident generated another terrorist attack when, on March 10, 1989, an improvised, unsophisticated charge went off in the car of the commander of the *Vincennes*. Responsibility for the attack, which did not result in casualties, was claimed by the Guardians of the Islamic Revolution, which also claimed responsibility for the downing of PanAm 103.

The attack against the UTA airliner was reportedly prompted by France's reluctance to fulfill obligations made to Iran in return for the release of hostages from captivity in Lebanon. Suspects in carrying out the attack included Shi'ite activists in West Africa, as well as Palestinian radical elements associated with Iran. The secretive nature of France's deals with Iran, and their implications for Paris' conciliatory stance toward terrorism as a whole, apparently explain the French government's noticeably low-key attitude toward the entire affair; the attack against the UTA airliner resulted in a remarkably lower public response than the international furor generated by the downing of the PanAm plane.

The Hostages Affair

The ongoing captivity in Lebanon of foreigners by Hizballah was for several years a major international issue. After 1987, however, a significant decline in world attention was evident concerning the affair. This derived at least in part from deliberate efforts by states involved to deny the captors propaganda gains associated with kidnappings — while nevertheless trying persistently to reach agreements with the captors and their sponsors. This state of affairs was primarily related to the attitudes toward the issue of the US and France, the two states whose citizens throughout the years were the most frequented targets for kidnappings.

After mid-1988, following negotiations between France and Iran as well as Hizballah, and subsequent concessions made by France, no French hostages remained captive in Lebanon. The French concessions included the repayment of a loan made by the late Shah in 1975; the improvement of diplomatic relations with Iran; the expulsion of members of the Iranian opposition-in-exile in Paris; and, in mid-1990 (long after the UTA downing), the release of Iranian sponsored Shi'ite terrorists from French jails.

The US administration, for its part, endorsed a low profile concerning the issue in May 1987. This policy was aimed at reestablishing America's leading role in the international struggle against state-sponsored terrorism, following the damage caused by the disclosure of the arms-for-hostages deals conducted with Iran during 1985-1986. It was also, to a great extent, a result of the evident failure of diverse measures — including the arms deals — to cause Hizballah and its sponsors to conclude the prolonged affair. Toward the end of the decade the issue, in fact, appeared to have reached a stalemate. Attempts were allegedly made by actors within the regime in Tehran to eliminate this source of friction with the West — at times generating new frictions between Iran and extremist Hizballah factions. Syria also made efforts, including direct military pressures upon Hizballah, to mediate the release of hostages, in the hope of scoring diplomatic points. All these efforts proved unsuccessful, although they did result in a reduction in the intensity of the kidnapping campaign.

In late July 1989 the issue was back in the headlines and on the agenda of governments — this time, however, as a result of an initiative taken by a victim state. In an effort to secure the release of three IDF soldiers held by Shi'ites in Lebanon since 1986, Israel captured Sheikh Abdel Karim Obeid, a prominent Hizballah leader in Southern Lebanon. Shortly thereafter a proposal was made to exchange him and 300 Shi'ite detainees held in Southern Lebanon by the SLA, in return for the release of the Israeli soldiers captured in Lebanon while on military missions there, along with all the other hostages held by Hizballah factions.

Hizballah threats to retaliate materialized in August, when it conducted a suicide carbomb attack against an IDF convoy in Southern Lebanon. The Obeid affair may have also been the catalyst for two incidents in the international arena, although other motives were not ruled out. On October 3, a prominent leader of the Jewish community was assassinated in Brussels. The incident was attributed to Abu Nidal's Fatah Revolutionary Council (FRC). And the premature explosion of a charge in London was linked by investigators to both the Rushdie affair (see below) and the abduction of Obeid; the Israel Embassy was mentioned as a probable target.

As a whole, however, Israeli and Jewish objectives abroad did not constitute a frequent target for Shi'ite terrorism during the period under review. Indeed, reluctance of Shi'ite terrorists to attack Israel in the international arena was in fact evident in previous years as well.

The abduction of Sheikh Obeid was harshly criticized by western and Arab states, as well as by the UN Secretary General. Tension between Israel and the US mounted dramatically following the announcement made by Hizballah on July 31 that it had executed an American hostage. The victim, whose hanged body was shown in a videotape publicized by the organization, was Lt. Col. William Higgins, who had been abducted on February 17, 1988 in Southern Lebanon. The Oppressed on Earth, considered a cover name for a faction of Hizballah, claimed responsibility for Higgins' abduction and alleged execution. It also threatened to execute another American hostage — Joseph Cicippio, held since September 12, 1986 — unless Israel freed Obeid. American combat ships embarked for the Eastern Mediterranean and the Gulf in a show of force aimed at deterring further executions.

Despite initial US condemnation of Israel generated by Hizballah's announcement of the assassination of Higgins, this development actually formed a turning point in the affair. Evidence produced by American security agencies that Higgins had in fact been dead since 1988, generated a lively controversy in the administration, Congress and the American public over the attitude adopted toward Israel and the issue in general. This contributed to an easing of tensions between Israel and the US, and also reduced fears that Higgins was the first in a series of hostages to be executed.

Attention then focused on Damascus and Tehran as possible partners for negotiating the release of hostages. Higgins' alleged execution was termed by Damascus "a crime that violated all humanitarian principles and norms." In contrast, threats to avenge the abduction of Obeid were made by Iranian Interior Minister Mohtashemi, who called on August 7 for attacks against American targets, noting that "The Hizballah people are spread today in clandestine cells over the western world and Israel in order to carry out Khomeini's will...." But there were also expressions in Tehran of a pragmatic readiness to work toward accommodation. The entire episode, which took place at a time when Soviet Foreign Minister Shevardnadze was visiting Tehran, seemed to hamper Iran's drive to break its international isolation. Thus Iranian President-elect Rafsanjani expressed "deep regret" over the reported death of the hostage, and actively intervened to achieve an extension of the deadline set by Hizballah for the execution of another hostage. On August 11 he stated that negotiations between the US and Iran over the release of hostages could begin "within days."

Yet contrary to Israeli official readiness to exchange Lebanese Shi'ite detainees for Israeli POWs, the US administration clung to its persistent refusal to negotiate deals with terrorists. It also refused to thaw frozen Iranian assets held in American banks, prior to the hostages' release. Still, statements made by the administration hinted at the probability that the release of hostages might permit the improvement of relations with Iran.

As the months passed, contradictory hints and statements regarding the possibility of coming releases were made by diverse factions in Tehran and within Hizballah. In general, the organization continued to insist on the freeing of Shi'ite prisoners held in Israel or jailed in other countries, while Iran's requests focused on its political and especially financial interests. Following discussions at an international tribunal in The Hague, US readiness to unfreeze $567 million of Iranian assets was reported in November 1989. Rumors about direct talks in Geneva between Iranian and American representatives reached the press several months later, in February 1990.

These negotiations culminated in April 1990 in the release of two American hostages: Robert Polhill, who was held by the Islamic Jihad for the Liberation of Palestine (considered a joint Shi'ite-Palestinian apparatus) since January 1987, and Frank Reed, held by Hizballah since September 1986. As in previous releases of hostages, Syria reaped diplomatic gains by highlighting its mediatory role and repatriating the captives via Damascus. Scarcely a month later, the US and Iran reached two agreements at The Hague which would eventually produce additional settlements of Iranian financial claims.

By May 1990, 15 westerners remained captive in Lebanon, of whom 11 were held by elements associated with Hizballah. They comprised six Americans, four Britons, two West Germans, one Italian, and two Swiss Red Cross employees. The latter two were the most recently abducted hostages — kidnapped on October 6, 1989 by Hizballah in cooperation with Abu Nidal's FRC, and held against the release from Swiss jail of a Shi'ite terrorist who had hijacked an Air Afrique airliner to Geneva in 1987. Also in 1989, Hizballah was involved in two incidents in which West German citizens were abducted; two of the victims remained in captivity. The kidnappings were perpetrated in order to influence the verdict delivered on May 17 in West Germany regarding a Hizballah member charged with involvement in the June 1985 hijacking of a TWA airliner to Beirut. (The terrorist, Mohammed Ali Hamadi, was nevertheless sentenced to life.)

The releases in April 1990 of the two American hostages raised hopes for further progress. No reciprocal steps by Israel or the US in return for their release became public, though one may speculate that some concessions had been agreed upon, and their materialization delayed until further moves were made by Hizballah. A prime benefactor of such deals, if they were made, was likely to be the organization itself. While demands it has repeatedly made concerning the fate of Shi'ites standing trial or imprisoned in diverse countries were by and large not met, indications have cumulated throughout the years about considerable sums of money received by Hizballah in return for conceding to Iranian pressures to release hostages.

To the extent these developments may be deemed positive, they could culminate in a gradual conclusion of the hostage affair, even though in its early stages Hizballah sought to exploit it for propaganda purposes. They were presumably made possible by the emergence of a pragmatic political atmosphere in Tehran, accompanied by a readiness to admit responsibility for the fate of hostages held by its proxy. This shift in the Iranian line also facilitated the Bush administration facing its first international crisis, and created a relatively convenient atmosphere for negotiations between the administration and Iran. Tehran's wish to rehabilitate its links with the western world — even a renewal of diplomatic relations with the US was mentioned as a condition for the release of hostages — may have persuaded American decision-makers that this time they would avoid the pitfalls associated with previous deals made with Tehran concerning the hostages affair.

The Rushdie Affair

While pragmatic considerations seemed to play a major role in directing the attitude of some key actors in Tehran's ruling elite toward the hostage crisis, the Rushdie affair was a reminder that religious zealotry and anti-western sentiments continued to exercise a primary influence over Iranian policy. True, the death sentence issued on February 14, 1989 against Salman Rushdie for allegedly blaspheming Islam in his book *The Satanic Verses* was delivered by Khomeini, and one may argue that the successors of the late leader would not have been so harsh in responding to the book. Yet the consent expressed by Muslim zealots throughout the world to the call by Khomeini to attack objectives associated with the publication of the book, offered a new manifestation of Tehran's influence over Muslim religious sentiments.

Mass demonstrations against the publication were held by enraged Muslims in Pakistan, India, Iran and Britain. Evidence accumulated during 1989 concerning plots by terrorists associated with Iran to carry it out. The threat against the life of the novelist generated a diplomatic crisis between Iran and the UK, and links between the two states were severed in March. In reaction to an EEC decision to withdraw heads of missions from Tehran, Iran recalled its envoys from all 12 EEC countries. Attacks against diplomatic objectives linked with the UK and against bookstores selling the book were perpetrated in countries around the globe. Most of these were minor and resulted in property damage only. They were attributed by and large to local Muslims inspired by Iran, but not acting at its behest. The more spectacular incidents were considered the work of terrorist elements directly associated with Iran. These included the assassination by Iranian agents of a Muslim leader accused of condemning the book too meekly, in March in Brussels; a carbomb attack near the British Embassy in Beirut that same month, attributed to Hizballah; and a Hizballah bomb plot, possibly targeting the Israel Embassy, that was foiled in London in August when the bomb detonated prematurely.

The Iranian drive to avenge publication of the book and execute its author was not confined to inciting Shi'ite elements. Two radical Palestinian organizations associated with Iran, the FRC and PFLP-GC, were also allegedly involved in schemes to carry out Khomeini's verdict.

Conclusion

The reduction in volume of Shi'ite international terrorism in 1989 was linked to several factors. These were the conclusion of the war in the Gulf, which resulted in decreased rates of activity by Iranian-directed elements against Gulf states that had sided with Iraq; considerations related to Iran's perceived wish to rehabilitate its relations with the West; and steps taken in recent years by western states to curb Iranian-sponsored terrorism by striking at the international Shi'ite terrorist infrastructure.

Yet the developments and incidents surveyed have also attested to the difficulty associated with predicting trends in Shi'ite international terrorism, due to unforeseen variables. Thus a major source of flux has been the ongoing power struggle within the regime in Tehran. It was reflected in different and at times contradictory policy lines concerning the West and regional conflicts in the Gulf. Another element was terrorist attacks perpetrated in cooperation with Palestinian radical elements. An additional source of concern has been the various degrees of independence practised by Shi'ite groups around the globe, and especially in Lebanon. This aspect of Shi'ite involvement in international terrorism was reflected in recent years, for example, in occasional Iranian difficulties in fulfillment of international obligations undertaken in return for concessions made by western states seeking the release of hostages.

In addition, there exists an international Shi'ite terrorist infrastructure that may be activated either independently or in coordination with Iran. It consists of Hizballah cells in diverse locations: Asia, the Middle East, Western Europe and West Africa; and local pro-Iranian activists, especially in Muslim states. It also encompasses an international Palestinian extremist infrastructure associated with Iran. This broad network of cells, which was mentioned by Mohtashemi when he announced the intention to avenge the capture of Sheikh Obeid by Israel, was also occasional ly activated against Iranian opposition figures living in exile abroad.

In 1987 the Hizballah infrastructure in Western Europe suffered major setbacks. Subsequently, moves were made by the organization to consolidate operational and logistical capabilities in the Ivory Coast and other countries in West Africa where Lebanese Shi'ites have settled, as substitute rear bases for activity in the West. Yet the European arena was not abandoned. In November 1989 a Hizballah network was uncovered in Spain. Police in Valencia seized large quantities of explosives and weapons (including surface-to-air missiles) sent from Sidon, and arrested persons directly linked with Hizballah. Additional arms shipments that originated in Lebanon reached Marseilles, France, and Larnaca, Cyprus.

Initial assessments concerning the discoveries in Spain linked them with alleged Hizballah plans to operate against the 1992 Barcelona Olympics. While this possibility cannot be ruled out, plots to operate much earlier, not necessarily in Spain and against diverse targets, seemed more likely. In this regard, the arms shipment to Spain may actually have been destined to reach French territory, in which case the interceptions foiled schemes to hit French objectives. Probable grounds for such attacks could be the refusal by France, prior to mid-1990, to free jailed pro-Iranian terrorists. A more immediate provocation may have been the perception of French support for the Lebanese Christian faction of General Michel Aoun against a pro-Syrian coalition.

PART II

REGIONAL MILITARY FORCES

Introductory Note

In Parts II and III the definition of high quality tanks includes the following tanks (mentioned in the text): T-72/improved T-72; Chieftain in Jordan and Oman (but not Chieftain Mk.5 in Iran and Kuwait); M-60 A3; Merkava. Similarly, the high quality interceptors include F-14, F-15 and MiG-25. High quality strike and multi-role aircraft include F-16, F-18, Mirage 2000, Tornado, MiG-29 and Su-24. Short range SAMs include all models which normally fulfill the task of providing air defense to ground forces, though the same weapons system may also be part of the Air Force or Air Defense Force. Defense expenditure figures include foreign military grants; arms transfers to and from Middle Eastern countries cover transfers during the most recent three years; numbers of weapons systems mentioned include systems in service and in storage; and bombers are included in numbers of total combat aircraft.

Acknowledgements

In addition to my colleagues at JCSS, I wish to thank a number of persons for their comments and assistance during the process of collecting and collating the data for Part II: Ofra Bengio, Uzi Rabbi and Yehudit Ronen of the Dayan Center for Middle Eastern and African Studies, Tel Aviv University; Haggai Erlich, Tel Aviv University; and JCSS researchers and research assistants whose aid was particularly valuable--Anat Kurz, David Tal, Sofia Kotzer, Yael Traiber, Orit Zilka, Maskit Burgin, Heda Rechnitz-Kijner, and especially Michal Harel and Anat Henefeld. Daniel Leshem, who served as principal research assistant to the JCSS Military Balance Project, deserves a very special word of praise and thanks.

Withal, I alone bear responsibility for any inaccuracies.

Z.E.

1. ALGERIA

BASIC DATA

Official Name of State: Democratic and Popular Republic of Algeria
Head of State: President Chadli Benjedid (also Supreme Commander of the Armed Forces and Defense Minister)
Prime Minister: Mouloud Hamrouche
Chief of General Staff: Brigadier General Khalid Nezzar
Commander of the Ground Forces: Brigadier General Ali Bouhadja (also Deputy Chief of the General Staff)
Commander of the Air Force and Air Defense Forces: Colonel Muhammad al-Mukhtar Bouteimine
Commander of the Navy: Rear Admiral Kamel Abd al-Rakhim
Area: 2,460,500 sq. km.

Population:		23,100,000
ethnic subdivision:		
Arabs	18,134,000	78.5%
Berbers	4,481,000	19.4%
Europeans	231,000	1.0%
Unknown	254,000	1.1%
religious subdivision:		
Sunni Muslims	22,869,000	99.0%
Christians and Jews	231,000	1.0%

GDP:
1987--$63.5 billion
1988--$54.1 billion

Balance of Payments (goods, services & unilateral transfer payments):

year	income	expenditure	balance
1986	$ 9.55 bil.	$11.78 bil.	-$2.23 bil.
1987	$10.23 bil.	$10.08 bil.	+$150 mil.

Defense Expenditure:
1986--$1.1 billion
1987--$1.2 billion

Foreign Military Aid and Security Assistance Received:
financial aid from:
USA--$150,000 grant (financing of military training)
military training:
foreign advisors/instructors from--Bulgaria; Cuba (unconfirmed); GDR, Pakistan, USSR (1000)
trainees abroad in--Britain (pilots for civilian aircraft), Egypt, France, Jordan, Tunisia (exchange of trainees), USSR
arms transfers from:
Brazil (ARVs); Britain (radars, target drones, patrol boats); Canada (aircraft training simulators); France (helicopters, ARVs, ATGMs); Italy (engines for Soviet

helicopters); Netherlands (transport aircraft); PRC (combat aircraft); USA (air traffic control equipment, radars); USSR (tanks, combat aircraft, SAMs)

Foreign Military Aid and Security Assistance Extended:
- financial aid to:
  - PLO--grant
- military training:
  - advisors/instructors in--Kuwait; POLISARIO
  - foreign trainees from--ETA (Spanish Basque separatists); Kuwait; Morocco; PLO-affiliated organizations; POLISARIO; Tunisia (part of an exchange program); Amal Lebanese militia
- arms transfers to:
  - Burkina Faso (Soviet-made fighter aircraft); POLISARIO
- facilities provided to:
  - Palestinian organizations (training camps); Chad anti-government groups (camps); POLISARIO (training, camps and operational facilities)

Cooperation in Arms Production/Assembly with:
Britain (naval vessels); Italy and Tunisia (diesel engines); France (trucks); Czechoslovakia (light transport aircraft)

INFRASTRUCTURE

Road Network:

length:	80,000 km
paved roads	60,000 km
gravel, crushed stone and earth tracks	20,000 km

main routes:
- Algiers--Oran
- Algiers--Sidi-bel-Abbes
- Oran--Oujda (Morocco)
- Sidi-bel-Abbes--Bechar--Tindouf--Atar (Mauritania)
- Bechar--Adrar--Gao (Mali)
- Algiers--Laghouat--Tamenghest (Tamanrasset)--Agadez (Niger)
- Algiers--Setif--Constantine
- Constantine--Biskra--Touggourt
- Constantine--Tebessa--Sousse (Tunisia)
- Algiers--Annaba--Tunis (Tunisia)
- Annaba--Tlemcen

Railway Network:

length:	3,890 km
standard gauge	2,632 km
narrow gauge	1,258 km

main routes:
- Algiers--Mostaganem--Oran
- Mostaganem--Sidi-bel-Abbes--Bechar--Kenadsa

Sidi-bel-Abbes--Oujda (Morocco)
Algiers--Constantine--Annaba--Tunis
Algiers--Laghouat
Constantine--Biskra--Touggourt
Annaba--Tebessa--Tunis

Airfields:

airfields by runway type:

permanent surface airfields	54
unpaved fields and usable airstrips	91
airfields by runway length:	
2440--3659 meters	29
1220--2439	73
under 1220	43
TOTAL	145

international airports: Algiers, Annaba, Constantine, Oran

major domestic airfields:
operational--Adrar, In Amenas, Bechar, Biskra, Borj Omar Driss, Ghardaia, El Golea, Laghouat, Ouargla, El Oued, Illizi, In Salah, Tamenghest, Timimoun, Tindouf, Touggourt
under construction--Ayn Guezzem, Batna, Bordj Bajdi Mokhtar, Setif

Airlines:

companies: Air Algerie (international and domestic);
aircraft:

Airbus A-310-200 (possibly on loan from Libya)	2
Boeing 737-200/737-200C	16
Boeing 727-200	10
Fokker F-27/F-27-400M/F-27-600	8
Lockheed L-100-30	3

Maritime Facilities:

harbors--Algiers, Annaba, Arziw, Bejaia, Beni Saf, Ghazaouet, Mostaganem, Oran (Wahran), Skikda (Philippeville)
anchorages--Cherchell, Collo, Dellys, Jijel, Nemours, Tenes (Port Breira)
oil terminals--Algiers, Annaba, Arzew, Bejaia, Oran, Skikda

Merchant Marine:

vessel type	number	DWT
LPG carrier	2	11,361
products tanker	6	155,199
LNG carrier	6	353,506
general cargo	13	155,954
tanker	6	24,831
bulk carrier	4	93,500
ro/ro	12	37,244
bunkering tanker	5	11,241
ferry	5	11,487

general cargo/container	14	104,344
chemical tanker	2	9,150
TOTAL	75	967,817

Defense Production:

army equipment:

production under license--diesel engines (with Italy and Tunisia); trucks (in collaboration with France)

air force equipment:

production under license--Czech ten passenger transport aircraft and four passenger light aircraft

naval craft:

tugs constructed; landing craft, gunboats and patrol boats under construction (under license from Britain) at Mers al-Kebir

ARMED FORCES

Personnel:

military forces--

	regular	reserves	total
army	170,000	150,000	320,000
air force	10,000	-	10,000
air defense	4,000 (unconf.)	-	4,000
navy	8,000	-	8,000
TOTAL	192,000	150,000	342,000

para-military forces--

gendarmerie	30,000

Army:

major units:

unit type	brigades	independent battalions
armored/tank	4	3
infantry, mechanized & motorized infantry	16	28
airborne/special forces	1	4
TOTAL	21	35

small arms:

personal weapons--

9mm MAT 49 SMG
9mm Vigneron SMG
9mm Uzi SMG
7.62mm AK-47 (Kalashnikov) AR
7.62mm AKM AR
7.62mm SKS (Simonov) SAR

machine guns--

14.5mm ZPU 14.5x4 HMG (employed in anti-aircraft role)
12.7mm D.Sh.K. 38/46 (Degtyarev) HMG
7.62mm SG-43/SGM (Goryunov) MMG
7.62mm RPD (Degtyarev) LMG

7.62mm PK/PKS (Kalashnikov) LMG
7.62mm (0.3") BAR LMG
light and medium mortars--
82mm M-43
light ATRLS--
RPG-7

tanks:		
model		number
high quality		
T-72		150
medium quality		
T-62		200
T-55		350
	(sub-total	550)
low quality		
AMX-13		50
T-54		150
	(sub-total	200)
TOTAL		900

APCs/ARVs:		
model		number
high quality		
BMP-2 (number unconfirmed)		450
BMP-1		650
Engesa E9	(unconfirmed)	50
	(sub-total	1150)
others		
AML-60		50
BRDM-2		150
BTR-40/50/60		600
BTR-152		100
M-3 (Panhard)		50
	(sub-total	950)
TOTAL		2100

artillery:	
self propelled guns and howitzers--	number
122mm M-1974 SP howitzer	70
towed guns and howitzers--	
152mm howitzer	50
130mm howitzer	
122mm D-30 howitzer	100
122mm M-1938 howitzer	40
85 mm M-1945/D-44 field/ AT gun	
mortars, heavy, over 160mm--	
160mm M-43 mortar	+
mortars, heavy, under 160mm--	
120mm M-43 mortar	
TOTAL	500
MRLs--	
240mm BM-24	20

140mm BM-14-16		20
122mm BM-21		60
TOTAL	(unconfirmed)	100
anti-tank weapons:		
missiles--		
AT-1 (Snapper)		
AT-3 (Sagger)		
AT-4 (Spigot)		
AT-5 (Spandrel; mounted on BMP-2 APC)		
BRDM-2 carrying AT-3 (Sagger) SP		
MILAN		
guns--		
85mm M-1945/D-44 field/AT gun		
76mm AT gun		
107mm B-11 recoilless rifle (unconfirmed)		
surface-to-surface missiles and rockets:		
model		launchers
FROG-7		
FROG-4		
TOTAL		25
army anti-aircraft defenses:		
missiles--		launchers
self propelled/mobile		
SA-6 (Gainful)		60
SA-8 (Gecko)		
SA-9 (Gaskin)		10
SA-13 (Gopher, unconfirmed)		
man-portable		
SA-7 (Grail)		
SA-14 (Gremlin, unconfirmed)		
short-range guns--		
57mm ZSU 57x2 SP		
23mm ZSU 23x4 SP (Gun Dish)		130
23mm ZU 23x2		
57mm M-1950 (S-60)		
37mm M-1939		

Air Force:

aircraft--general:	number
combat aircraft	341
transport aircraft	55
helicopters	128
combat aircraft:	
interceptors--	
high quality	
MiG-25 A/B/U (Foxbat)	26
others	
MiG-21 MF/bis/U (Fishbed)	115
Total	141

strike and multi-role aircraft--	
medium quality	
MiG-23/27 (Flogger B/D);	
MiG-23MF (Flogger G, unconfirmed)	70
Su-17/20 (Fitter C)	30
(sub-total	100)
others	
MiG-17 (Fresco), MiG-15	
and F-4 Shenyang	80
Su-7 BM/U (Fitter A)	20
(sub-total	100)
Total	200
transport aircraft:	
An-12 (Cub)	6
An-24 (Coke)/An-26(Curl)(possibly civilian a/c)	a few
Beechcraft Queen Air	5
Beechcraft King Air	2
Beechcraft Sierra 200	a few
Beechcraft Super King Air T-200T	
(employed in maritime patrol role)	6
C-130H & C-130H-30 Hercules	17
Fokker F-27 Mk 400/Mk 600	
(employed in maritime patrol role)	3
Gulfstream III	3
IL-76 (Candid)	4
IL-18 (Coot)	4
IL-14 (Crate)	4
Mystere Falcon 20	1
TOTAL	55
training and liaison aircraft:	
with ground attack/close air support capability--	
CM-170 Fouga Magister	20
L-39 Albatross	16
(sub-total	36)
others--	
Beechcraft T-34C (Turbo Mentor)	6
Yak-11 (Moose)	16
(sub-total	22)
TOTAL	58
on order: 16 L-39 Albatross	
helicopters:	
attack--	
Mi-24/Mi-25 (Hind)	37
heavy transport--	
Mi-6 (Hook)	10
medium transport--	
Mi-4 (Hound)	30
Mi-8/Mi-17 (Hip)	40
SA-330 Puma	5

(sub-total	75)
light transport--	
Alouette II/III	6
TOTAL	128
on order: French helicopters	
advanced armament:	
air-to-air missiles--	
AA-2 (Atoll)	
AA-6 (Acrid)	
AA-7 (Apex, unconfirmed)	
air-to-ground missiles--	
AT-2 (Swatter)	
AT-6 (Spiral)	
anti-aircraft defenses:	
long-range missiles--	
model	batteries
SA-2 (Guideline)/SA-3 (Goa)	41
long-range guns--	
100mm	
85mm	
military airfields:	15
Ain Ousira, Algiers, Bechar, Biskra, Boufarik, Oran, Ouargla, Tindouf, 7 additional	
aircraft maintenance and repair capability:	
for all models	

Navy:

combat vessels:	number
submarines--	
K class (Kilo)	2
R class (Romeo)	2
TOTAL	4
MFPBs--	
Ossa I	2
Ossa II	10
Total	12
missile corvettes--	
Nanuchka II	3
gun corvettes--	
C-58	1
ASW vessels--	
Koni class frigate	3
SO-1 large patrol craft	6
Total	9
mine warfare vessels--	
T-43 class minesweeper	1-2
gunboats/MTBs--	
Kebir class (Brooke Marine)	6
patrol craft--	
Baglietto Mangusta	6

Baglietto 20 GC (possibly with Coast Guard)	10
P-801 (possibly with customs service)	2
P-1200 (possibly with customs service)	3
Zhuk class	1
Chinese 25 meter patrol boat	3
Total .	25
on order: 3 Kebir class; 6 additional P-801, 1-2 additional C-58 gun corvettes	
landing craft:	
Polnochny class LCT	1
Brooke Marine 2,200 ton LSL	2
Total	3
auxiliary vessels:	
armed fishing	6
Niryat diving tender	1
Poluchat I class torpedo collecting	4
tankers	4
on order: one 180 ton research vessel from the Netherlands	

advanced armament:
  surface-to-surface missiles--
    SS-N-2 Styx
  surface-to-air missiles--
    SA-N-4

special naval forces:
  naval commando

naval bases: 3
  Algiers, Annaba, Mers al-Kebir

ship maintenance and repair capability:
  3 slipways belonging to Chantier Naval de Mers al-Kebir at Oran; 4 x 4,000-ton dry docks at Algiers; small graving dock at Annaba; small dry dock at Beni Saf.

2. BAHRAIN

BASIC DATA

Official Name of State: State of Bahrain
Head of State: Shaykh Isa ibn Salman al-Khalifa
Prime Minister: Khalifa ibn Salman al-Khalifa
Minister of Defense: Major General Khalifa ibn Ahmad al-Khalifa (also Deputy Commander in Chief of the Armed Forces)
Commander-in-chief of the Armed Forces: Shaykh Hamed ibn Isa al-Khalifa (also heir apparent)
Chief of the Bahraini Defense Forces: Brigadier General Abdullah ibn Salman al-Khalifa
Commander of the Air Force: Major Mohanna Fadel al-Naime
Commander of the Navy: Lieutenant Commander Youssuf Mulalah
Area: 676 sq.km. (estimate, including 32 small islands)

Population:		430,000
ethnic subdivision:		
Arabs	314,000	73.0%
Persians	39,000	9.0%
Southeast Asians, Europeans	77,000	18.0%
religious subdivision:		
Shi'ite Muslims	301,000	70.0%
Sunni Muslims	129,000	30.0%
nationality subdivision:		
Bahrainis	271,000	63.0%
Alien Arabs	43,000	10.0%
Alien non-Arabs		
Southeast Asians	56,000	13.0%
Iranians	34,000	8.0%
Others	27,000	6.0%

GDP:
1986--$3.0 billion
1987--$3.2 billion

Balance of Payments (goods, services & unilateral transfer payments):

year	income	expenditure	balance
1986	$3.37 bil.	$3.43 bil.	-$ 60 mil.
1987	$3.63 bil.	$3.78 bil.	-$150 mil.

Defense Expenditure:
1989--$184.6 million (unconfirmed)
1990--$193.9 million (unconfirmed)

Foreign Military Aid and Security Assistance Received:
military training:
foreign advisors/instructors/serving personnel from--Britain, Egypt, France, Jordan, Pakistan, USA
trainees abroad in--Britain, France, Egypt, Jordan, Kuwait, Saudi Arabia, USA
arms transfers from:
Britain (patrol craft, electronics); France (ARVs,

helicopters, AGMs); FRG (missile corvettes, helicopters); Italy (helicopters); Sweden (SAMs, via Singapore); USA (ATGMs, APCs, combat aircraft, SAMs, helicopters, tanks)

Foreign Military Aid and Security Assistance Extended:
- financial aid to:
  - Syria, Palestinian military organizations
- facilities provided to:
  - USA (naval facilities, storage facilities & intelligence installations)

forces deployed abroad in:
- Saudi Arabia (part of GCC rapid deployment force)

Joint Maneuvers with:
- GCC (members: Bahrain, Kuwait, Oman, Qatar, Saudi Arabia, UAE)

INFRASTRUCTURE

Road Network:

length:	475 km
paved roads	250 km
earth tracks	225 km

main routes:
- al-Manamah--Muharraq (airport)
- al-Manamah--Sitrah (oil terminal)
- al-Manamah--Budaiyah
- al-Manamah--Isa Town--Awali
- al-Manamah--Dhahran (Saudi Arabia); 25 km bridge causeway
- Awali--al-Zallaq
- Awali--Ras al-Yaman

Airfields:

airfields by runway type:	
permanent surface field	1
unpaved field	1
airfields by runway length:	
over 3660 meters	1
1220--2439	1
TOTAL	2

international airport: Bahrain (Muharraq)

Airlines:

companies:
- Gulf Air (international)--jointly owned by Bahrain, Oman, UAE and Qatar, with headquarters in Bahrain

aircraft:	
Boeing 767-300ER	6
Boeing 737-200	8
Lockheed L-1011-200 Tristar	3
Lockheed L-1011-100 Tristar	5
Lockheed L-1011-1 Tristar	3

on order: 12 Airbus A-321, 6 additional Boeing 767

BAHRAIN

Maritime Facilities:
harbors--Mina Sulman; Sitrah (ALBA aluminum terminal); Mina Manamah
oil terminal--Sitrah

Merchant Marine:

vessel type	number	DWT
bulk carrier	1	20,003

ARMED FORCES

Personnel:

military forces--	
army	8100
air force	700
navy	700
TOTAL	9,500

Army:

major units:

unit type	brigade	battalion	independent company
mechanized	1	1	
armored			1
TOTAL	1	1	1

small arms:
personal weapons--
9mm Model 12 Beretta SMG
machine guns--
light and medium mortars--
81mm L-16 A1

Tanks:

model	number
high quality	
M-60 A3	54

APCs/ARVs:

model	number
others	
M-3 (Panhard)	90
AML-90	
AT-105 Saxon	
Ferret	
Saladin	
on order: 80 M-113	
TOTAL	200

artillery:
towed guns and howitzers--

105mm howitzer	8

on order: 155mm M-198 A1 howitzer

anti-tank weapons:	
missiles--	launchers
BGM-71C Improved TOW	60
guns--	
120mm BAT L-4 recoilless rifle	
army anti-aircraft defenses:	
missiles--	launchers
man portable	
FIM-92A Stinger (number unconfirmed)	70
RBS-70	40-50

Air Force:

aircraft--general:	
combat aircraft	16
transport aircraft	1
helicopters	24-25
combat aircraft:	
strike and multi-role aircraft--	
high quality	
F-16C/D	4
medium and low quality	
F-5E/F	12
Total	16
on order: 12 F-16C/D, delivery in progress	
transport aircraft:	
Gulfstream II	1
helicopters:	number
maritime attack--	
SA-365 Dauphin	1-2
medium transport--	
AB-212	10
Bell 412	2
(sub-total	12)
light transport--	
500 MG	2
MBB BO-105	9
(sub-total	11)
TOTAL	24-25
advanced armament:	
air-to-air missiles--	
AIM-9P Sidewinder	
air-to-ground missiles--	
AS-15TT anti-ship missile	
military airfields:	1
Muharraq; a second AFB is under construction at Suman	
anti-aircraft defenses:	
on order: MIM-23B Improved HAWK SAMs; Cossor SSR and Plessey Watchman air traffic control radars for civilian and military use	

BAHRAIN

Navy:

combat vessels:	number
MFPBs--	
Lurssen TNC-45	4
missile corvettes--	
Lurssen 62 meter	2
gunboats/MTBs--	
Lurssen FPB-38 gunboat	2
patrol craft--	
Cheverton 50 ft. (15.3 meter)	1
Cheverton 27 ft. (8.2 meter)	3
Tracker	3
Fairey Marine Sword	4
Swift FPB-20	2
Wasp 30 meter	1
Wasp 20 meter	2
Wasp 11 meter	3
Total	19
on order: 2 additional TNC-45 MFPBs	
landing craft:	
150 ton Fairey Marine LCM	1
Tropmire Ltd. hovercraft	1
Loadmaster 60 ft. (18 meter) LCU	1
Swiftships 390 ton LCU	1
Total	4
on order: 14 British landing craft	

advanced armament:
- surface-to-surface missiles--
  - MM-40 Exocet
  - RGM-84A Harpoon

naval bases:
- Jufair

ship maintenance and repair capability:
- Arab Shipbuilding & Repair Yard (ASRY), a 500,000 DWT drydock engaged in repairs and construction (mainly supertankers; jointly owned by Bahrain, Kuwait, Qatar, Saudi Arabia, UA-each 18.84%, Iraq--4.7% and Libya--1.1%)

3. EGYPT

BASIC DATA

Official Name of State: The Arab Republic of Egypt

Head of State: President Muhammad Husni Mubarak

Prime Minister: Dr. Atif Sidqi

Minister of Defense and War Production: Major General Youssuf Sabri Abu Talib

Chief of the General Staff: General Saffi al-Din Abu Shenaf

Commander of the Air Force: Lieutenant General Ahmad Abd al-Rahman Nasser

Commander of the Air Defense Forces: Lieutenant General Mustafa Ahmad al-Shazli

Commander of the Navy: Vice Admiral Muhammad Sharif al-Sadiq

Area: 1,000,258 sq. km.

Population:		51,900,000
ethnic subdivision:		
Arabs	51,070,000	98.4%
Nubians	52,000	0.1%
Greeks, Italians, Armenians	519,000	1.0%
Others	259,000	0.5%
religious subdivision:		
Sunni Muslims	48,786,000	94.0%
Copts, other Christians	3,114,000	6.0%

GDP (figures unreliable, calculated according to the official exchange rate of 1.4286 per US dollar. In reality there are four exchange rates, giving a much lower value to the Egyptian pound than the official rate)

1986--$54.60 billion

1987--$62.93 billion

Balance of Payments (goods, services & unilateral transfer payments):

year	income	expenditure	balance
1986	$ 8.91 bil.	$10.78 bil.	-$1.87 bil.
1987	$10.85 bil.	$11.17 bil.	-$320 mil.

Defense Expenditure:

1988--$5.6 billion (unconfirmed)

1989--$6.8 billion (unconfirmed)

Foreign Military Aid and Security Assistance Received

financial aid from:

USA--$1.3 billion grant; Italy--$50 million grant or loan (unconfirmed); Arab aid (unconfirmed)

military training:

foreign advisors/instructors from-- France, USA

trainees abroad in--Britain, France, FRG, USA (over 500 men)

arms transfers from:

Belgium (LMGs); Brazil (trainer aircraft); Britain (ATGMs, helicopter parts, radio transceivers, tank guns, torpedoes, submarines on order); France (combat aircraft, ATGMs, helicopters, AAMs, SAMs, radar for AAGs); FRG (parts for Fahd APCs) ; Italy (helicopters, ECM, shipborne SAMs, Skyguard air defense systems); Libya (ten Czech-made trainer aircraft, a gift); North Korea (spare parts for Soviet arms; assistance to Egyptian production of SSMs, unconfirmed); PRC (artillery, a recent protocol to supply spare parts for all Soviet-made systems); Romania (artillery); Spain (APCs); Switzerland (AAGs); ; USA (APCs, ATGMs, combat aircraft, helicopters, early warning aircraft, radars, SAMs, tanks, RPVs and mini RPVs, fire control systems for submarines); USSR (spare parts for Soviet made weapons)

construction aid by:
USA (upgrading of airfields and dry docks)

maintenance of equipment in:
FRG (transport aircraft)

maintenance aid by:
USA (aircraft)

- Foreign Military Aid and Security Assistance Extended:

financial aid to:
Sudan ($42 million grant, given in arms, figure unconfirmed)

military training:
advisors/instructors in--Bahrain (retired personnel), Jordan (unconfirmed), Kuwait, Morocco (unconfirmed), Oman, Qatar, UAE, YAR, Zaire
foreign trainees from--Algeria, Bahrain, Chad, Djibouti, Iraq (400), Jordan, Kuwait (400), Morocco (unconfirmed), Oman, Pakistan, Qatar, Saudi Arabia, Senegal Tanzania, Tunisia, UAE, Zaire, Zimbabwe; Libya (unconfirmed)

arms transfers to:
Chad (small arms); Djibouti; Iraq (ammunition, trainer aircraft, spare parts, MRLs); Kenya (type unknown); Kuwait (Fahd APCs, Skyguard AA Systems); Morocco (mortars, APCs); Oman (APCs); Qatar (Fahd APCs, MRLs); Sudan (APCs); UAE (Fahd APCs, air defense systems); Uganda (type unknown, unconfirmed); YAR (unconfirmed); Zaire (Fahd APCs)

maintenance of equipment for:
Iraq (aircraft)

facilities provided to:
USA (airfields at Cairo West, Qena, Inshas); Iraq (naval vessels)

EGYPT

Cooperation in Arms Production/Assembly with:
Argentina and Iraq (development and production of SSM; cooperation possibly frozen in late 1989); Brazil (trainer aircraft); Britain (ATGMs, electronics); France (aircraft, electronics, helicopters, SP AAGs); FRG (Fahd APCs; companies involved in SSM production); Italy (Skyguard AAGs); North Korea (SSMs); USA (upgrading M-113 APCs, ammunition, electronics incl. radars, plans for M-1 tank assembly)

Joint Maneuvers with:
France, Italy, Jordan, Britain, UAE, USA

INFRASTRUCTURE

Road Network:

length:	29,000 km
paved roads	12,300 km
gravel and stone roads	2,500 km
improved earth roads	14,200 km

main routes:
- Cairo--Alexandria
- Cairo--Tanta--Alexandria
- Cairo--Isma'iliya
- Cairo--Suez
- Alexandria--Marsa Matruh--Tobruk (Libya)
- Alexandria--al-Alamein--Siwa (oasis)
- Marsah Matruh--Siwa (oasis)
- Isma'iliya--Bir Gafgafah--Beer Sheva (Israel)
- Kantara--al-Arish--Ashkelon (Israel)
- Sharm al-Shaykh--Eilat (Israel)
- Suez--Isma'iliya--Port Sa'id
- Cairo--al-Mansura--Damietta
- Cairo--al-Fayum
- Cairo--Asyut--Qena--Aswan
- Asyut--al-Kharga
- Suez--Hurghada--Ras Banas--Port Sudan (Sudan)
- Qena--Safaga

Railway Network:

length:	4,857 km
standard gauge	4,510 km
narrow gauge (0.75m.)	347 km

main routes:
- Cairo--Tanta--Alexandria
- Tanta--Damietta
- Cairo--Zagazig--Isma'iliya
- Cairo--Suez
- Suez--Isma'iliya--Port Sa'id
- Alexandria--Marsa Matruh--Salum
- Cairo--Asyut--Aswan
- Zagazig--al-Salahiya

Airfields:

airfields by runway type:

permanent surface fields	63
unpaved fields and usable air strips	22

airfields by runway length:

over 3660 meters	2
2440--3659	45
1220--2439	22
under 1220	16
TOTAL	85

international airports: Cairo, Aswan, Alexandria, Luxor

major domestic airfields: Abu Simbel, Asyut, Hurghada, Port Sa'id, Sharm al-Shaykh

Airlines:

companies: Egyptair (international); Misr Overseas Airways (international, charter and cargo); ZAS (Zarakani Aviation Services, cargo); Air Sinai (domestic, and to Israel); Petroleum Air Service (domestic, to oil fields); Transmed (charter)

aircraft:

Airbus A-300 B4/A-300-600	4
Boeing 767-200ER/300ER	5
Boeing 747-300 combi	2
Boeing 737-200	10
Boeing 707-320C	3
DHC-7 (Dash-7)	5
Fokker F-27/F-27-500	4
Lockheed Jetstar	2
MD-83	1

helicopters:

Bell 212 (including on lease)	11

on order: 2 Boeing 767-200ER, 2 MD-83, 5 Airbus A-300, 7 Airbus A-320, 6 Airbus A-321(unconfirmed); 5 Boeing 737-500

Maritime Facilities:

harbors--Adabiya, Alexandria, Damietta, al-Dikheila (under construction, partly operative), Port Sa'id, Safaga, Suez

anchorages--Abu Zneima, Kosseir, Marsa al-Hamra (al-Alamein), Marsa Matruh, Nuweiba, Ras Banas, Sharm al-Shaikh, al-Tur

oil terminals--Ras Gharib, Ras Shukeir , Wadi Fieran, Abu Qir

Merchant Marine:

vessel type	number	DWT
general cargo	89	503,066
crude carrier	1	38,177
oil tanker	6	150,298
bulk carrier	14	565,067
passenger/cargo	2	2,654

ro/ro	8	37,951
general cargo/container	7	49,859
multipurpose	2	25,200
ferry	4	3,581
reefer	3	16,591
bunkering tanker	6	14,731
TOTAL	142	1,407,103

Defense Production:

army equipment:

manufacture--120mm mortars (planned); 122mm Saqr 10/18/30 MRLs; Saqr 80 surface-to-surface rockets, still experimental; ammunition for artillery, tanks and small arms; mines; rifles; short-range SAMs; conversion of 122mm D-30 howitzers to SP howitzers, still experimental; conversion of 23mm AAGs to Sinai 23 SP AAGs; add-on armor to M-113 APCs; toxic gas (partly with assistance from a Swiss company)

production under license-- Dragon ATGMs, (under development); 130mm artillery pieces; British tank guns; tank tracks; upgrading of Soviet tanks (with British, USA and Austrian assistance); trucks and jeeps(with USA); Fahd APCs (with FRG components and assistance); Soviet design AAGs, MGs and small arms; tank (with USA, under development); minefield crossing systems (similar to Viper)

assembly--short-range SAMs, AAGs

air force equipment:

production under license--CBUs (US design); anti-runway bombs; parts for F-16; parts for Mirage 2000; aircraft fuel pods; aerial bombs

assembly--Alpha Jet trainers; SA-342 Gazelle helicopters; Embraer EMB-312 Tucano

naval craft:

assembly--US Swiftships patrol boats

electronics:

manufacture--Bassal artillery fire control system

production under license--AN/TPS-63 radars (assembly, with 30% of components locally produced); radio transceivers (in collaboration with France and Britain); SAM electronics (in collaboration with Britain); fire control system

ARMED FORCES

Personnel:

military forces--(not all reserves fully trained)

	regular	reserves	total
army	320,000	600,000	920,000
air force	25,000	20,000	45,000
air defense	70,000	60,000	130,000
navy	20,000	11,000	31,000

TOTAL	435,000	691,000	1,126,000

para-military forces--
coast guard--7,000
frontier corps--6,000

Army:

major units:

unit type	army corps HQ	divisions	independent brigades/ groups
all arms	2		
armored		4	3
mechanized		7	
infantry		1	11
airborne			2
special forces			3
TOTAL	2	12	19

small arms:

personal weapons--
- 9mm Aqaba SMG
- 7.62mm AK-47 (Kalashnikov) AR
- 7.62mm AKM AR
- 7.62mm Rashid SAR
- 7.62mm SKS (Simonov) SAR

machine guns--
- 14.5mm KPV HMG
- 14.5mm ZPU 14.5x4 HMG (in anti-aircraft role)
- 12.7mm D.Sh.K. 38/46 (Degtyarev)
- 12.7mm (0.5") Browning M2 HMG
- 7.62mm MAG (FN) LMG
- 7.62mm RPD (Degtyarev) LMG/Suez LMG
- 7.62mm SG-43/SGM (Goryunov) MMG/Aswan MMG

light and medium mortars--
- 82mm M-43
- 60mm (Hotchkiss-Brandt)

light ATRLs--
- RPG-2
- RPG-7

tanks (some in storage; Egypt has undertaken a commitment to the USA to keep no more than 2400-2500 tanks in units; the balance are stored):

model	number
high quality	
M-60 A3	850
medium quality	
M-60 A1	700
T-62	600
T-55 & T-54 (possibly some upgraded)	950
(sub-total	1650)
TOTAL	3100

on order: 555 M-1 A1 tanks, A1 tanks

APCs/ARVs:

model		number
high quality		
BMP-1		200
M-113 A2		1700
	(sub-total	1900)
others		
BMR-600		250
BRDM-2		
BTR-40/50/60/152		
Fahd		
OT-62		
	(sub-total	2200)
TOTAL		4100

on order: Fahd; Cadillac Gage Commando Scout ARV

artillery:

self propelled guns and howitzers--	number
155mm M-109 A2 SP howitzer	144
towed guns and howitzers--	
180mm S-23 gun (possibly phased out)	
152mm M-1943 (D-1) howitzer (possibly phased out)	
130mm M-46 gun/Type-59 gun	440
122mm D-30 howitzer	
122mm M-1938 howitzer (possibly phased out)	
100mm M-1955 field/AT gun	
mortars, heavy, over 160mm--	
240mm mortar	
160mm mortar	
mortars, heavy, under 160mm--	
120mm M-43 mortar	
107mm (4.2") M-30 SP mortar (on M-106 A2 carrier)	
TOTAL	2200

on order: 122mm D-30 SP (still under trial, designation AR122)

artillery/mortar-locating radars--
AN/TPQ-37

MRLs--
122mm BM-21
122mm BM-11
122mm Saqr 10/18/30

PGM--
155mm Copperhead projectiles (CLGP, unconfirmed)

on order: additional AN/TPQ-37 artillery and mortar-locating radar; 155mm Copperhead projectiles (CLPG, unconfirmed)

engineering equipment:
Bar mine-laying system
EWK pontoon bridges
GSP self-propelled ferries

M-123 Viper minefield crossing system
MT-55 bridging tanks
MTU-55 bridging tanks
Egyptian bridging tanks (on T-34 chassis, unconfirmed)
mine-clearing rollers
PMP folding pontoon bridges
PRP motorized bridges

armored recovery vehicles:
M-88 A1

AFV transporters:	1000
anti-tank weapons:	
missiles--	launchers
AT-3 (Sagger)	
BGM-71C Improved TOW	
BRDM-2 carrying AT-3 (Sagger)	
M-901 ITV SP (TOW under Armor)	
MILAN	
Swingfire	
TOTAL	1600-1800

on order: 180 BGM-71D TOW II launchers

guns--
107mm B-11 recoilless rifle (possibly phased out)

surface-to-surface missiles and rockets:

model	launchers
FROG-7	
SS-1 (Scud B)	
TOTAL	24

on order: Saqr 80, Badr 2000 (still under development, possibly discontinued)

army anti-aircraft defenses:

missiles--	launchers
self propelled/mobile	
Crotale	48
MIM-72A Chaparral	26
SA-6 (Gainful)	48
Skyguard AA system (missiles, radars and guns; Egyptian designation Amoun)	18
man-portable	
Ain al-Saqr	
SA-7 (Grail)	

short-range guns--	number
57mm ZSU 57x2 SP	
35mm Oerlikon-Buhrle 35x2 GDF-002	
23mm ZSU 23x4 SP (Gun Dish)	
23mm ZU 23x2	
Skyguard AA system (missiles, radars and guns; Egyptian designation: Amoun)	18
TOTAL	2500

on order: 8 additional Skyguard AA systems; Sinai 23 AA systems; 25 additional MIM-72A Chaparral

launchers
CW capabilities:
personal protective equipment, Soviet type
decontamination units
stockpile of gases

Air Force:

	number
aircraft--general:	
combat aircraft	541
transport aircraft	37
helicopters	198
combat aircraft:	
interceptors--	
high quality	
F-16A/B/C/D (multi-role, employed as interceptor)	79
Mirage 2000 (multi-role, employed as interceptor)	18
(sub-total	97)
medium and low quality	
F-7 Shenyang	60
F-6 Shenyang/FT-6	80
MiG-21 MF/U (Fishbed)	150
(sub-total	290)
Total	387
strike and multi-role aircraft--	
medium quality	
F-4E Phantom	33
Mirage 5	71
(sub-total	104)
others	
MiG-17 (Fresco, limited serviceability)	50
Total	154
on order: 40 F-16C/D; additional 40-50 F-16C/D; 20 Mirage 2000	
transport aircraft (older models partly grounded):	
Boeing 707 (3 to be converted to aerial tankers)	5
C-130H Hercules (including ELINT)	20
DHC-5D Buffalo	9
Mystere Falcon 20	3
TOTAL	37
training and liaison aircraft:	
with ground attack/close air support capability--	
Alpha Jet and Alpha Jet MS-2	43
L-29 (Delfin)	100
L-39 (Albatross)	10
(sub-total	153)
others--	
al-Gumhuriya	100

Embraer EMB-312 (Tucano)	40
PZL-104 Wilga 35/80	10
Yak-18 (Max)	35
(sub-total	185)
TOTAL	338
on order: 14 EMB-312	
helicopters:	
attack--	
SA-342 L/M Gazelle	80
heavy transport--	
CH-47C Chinook	15
Westland Commando Mk.2	25
(sub-total	40)
medium transport--	
Mi-8 (Hip)	
Mi-4 (Hound)	
(sub-total	55)
light transport--	
Hiller UH-12E	18
ASW--	
Westland Sea King Mk.47	5
TOTAL	198
on order: 2-4 UH-60A Black Hawk; 24 AH-64 Apache	
maritime surveillance aircraft:	
Beechcraft 1900C	6
miscellaneous aircraft:	
AEW/AWACS aircraft--	
E-2C Hawkeye AEW	5
target drones--	
Aerospatiale CT-20 target drone	
Beech AQM-37A target drone	
Beech MQM-107B target drone	
RPVs and mini-RPVs--	
Skyeye R450 mini-RPVs	48
Teledyne Ryan model 324 Scarab	29
on order: 70 TTL BTT-3 Banshee target drones; 27 additional Teledyne Ryan model 324 RPVs; an additional E-2C AEW	
advanced armament:	
air-to-air missiles--	
AIM-7F/7M Sparrow	
AIM-9 Sidewinder; AIM-9L; AIM-9P	
R-550 Magique	
R-530D Super	
air-to-ground missiles--	number
AGM-65 Maverick	1100
AM-39 Exocet (unconfirmed)	
AS-1 (Kennel)	
AS-5 (Kelt)	
AS-30L	

HOT
bombs--
CBU-7A
on order: 282 AIM-7M AAMs
aircraft shelters: in all operational airfields, for combat aircraft
military airfields: 21
Abu Suweir, Alexandria, Aswan, Beni Suef, Bilbeis, Cairo West, Fayid, Hurghada, Inshas, Janaklis, Kabrit, Luxor, al-Maza, al-Minya, Mansura, Marsah Matruh, Qena, Ras Banas, Tanta, 2 additional
aircraft maintenance and repair capability:
for all models

Air Defense Force:

radars:

AN/TPS-59	4
AN/TPS-63	9
P-15	+
Spoon Rest (P-12)	+
Tiger S (TRS-2100)	12

on order: AN/TPS-63 (to complete total to 42); an additional AN/TPS-59

long-range missiles:

model	batteries
MIM-23B Improved HAWK	12
SA-2 (Guideline) & SA-3 (Goa)	120
TOTAL	132

Navy:

combat vessels: (some older Soviet vessels may no longer be operational)	number
submarines--	
R class (Romeo)/Chinese R class (4 to be upgraded)	8
MFPBs--	
Hegu (Komar, made in PRC)	6
October	6
Ossa I	6
Ramadan	6
Total	24
gun destroyers--	
Z class	1
missile frigates--	
Descubierta class	2
Jianghu class	2
Total	4
mine warfare vessels--	
CMH-50	2-6
T-43 class minesweeper	3
T-301 class minesweeper	2

Yurka class minesweeper	4
Total	11-15
gunboats/MTBs (older vessels of limited serviceability)--	
Hainan class	8
Shanghai II	4
Shershen class MTB	6
Total	18
patrol craft--	
Bertram class 28 ft. (8.5 meter)	6
Crestitalia 110 ton (Nisr class)	6
de Castro 110 ton (Nisr class)	3
Swiftships 28.4 meter	9
Timsah class	12
Total	36
on order: 2 upgraded Oberon submarines	
landing craft:	
LCM	5
Polnochny class LCT	3
SMB-1 class LCU	2
SRN-6 hovercraft	3
Vydra class LCU	9
TOTAL	22
auxiliary vessels:	
Niryat diving support	2
Okhtensky (tug)	2
Poluchat II torpedo recovery	2
training (1 Sekstan, 1 4650-ton and 1 other)	3
Survey vessels	4
advanced armament:	
surface-to-surface missiles--	
Hai Ying-2 (HY-2)	
OTOMAT Mk.2 (also used for coastal defense)	
RGM-84A Harpoon	
SS-N-2 Styx	
surface-to-air missiles--	
Aspide	
advanced torpedoes--	
Stingray anti-submarine	
coastal defense:	launchers
SSC-2B Samlet coastal defense missile (probably no longer in service)	
OTOMAT coastal defense missile	
SSN-2 Styx converted to coastal defense role	
Total (unconfirmed)	30
on order: sub-Harpoon SSMs (for Romeo submarines)	
special maritime forces:	
divers and frogmen	
naval bases:	8

EGYPT

Abu Qir (naval academy), Alexandria, Hurghada, Marsa Matruh, Port Sa'id, Safaga, Suez; Berenice (Ras Banas)

ship maintenance and repair capability:

Alexandria (including construction up to 20,000 DWT), Port Sa'id

4. IRAN

BASIC DATA

Official Name of State: Islamic Republic of Iran

Supreme Religious and Political National Leader: Hojatolislam Ali Khamenei

Head of State (subordinate to national leader): President Hojatolislam Ali Akbar Hashemi Rafsanjani

Minister of Defense and Logistics of the Armed Forces: Akbar Turkan

Chief of Staff of the Armed Forces: Brigadier General Ali Shabazi

Commander-in-Chief of the Islamic Revolution Guards Corps (IRGC): Mohsen Rezai

Commander of the IRGC Ground Forces: Mustafa Izadi

Commander of the Air Force: Brigadier General Hussein Dehqan

Commander of the Navy: Rear Admiral Ali Shamkhani

Commander of the IRGC Naval Forces: Hussein Alai

Area: 1,647,240 sq. km.

Population:		51,250,000
ethnic subdivision:		
Persians	36,285,000	70.8%
Azeris	8,712,000	17.0%
Arabs	2,921,000	5.7%
Kurds	1,589,000	3.1%
Bakhtiaris	718,000	1.4%
Lurs and others	1,025,000	2.0%
religious subdivision:		
Shi'ite Muslims	47,662,000	93.0%
Sunni Muslims (incl. Kurds)	2,563,000	5.0%
Christians, Zoroastrians, Jews, Bahais and others	1,025,000	2.0%

GDP:

1984--$166.9 billion

1985--$168.1 billion

Balance of Payments (goods, services & unilateral transfer payments):

year	income	expenditure	balance
1983	$22.84 bil.	$18.47 bil.	+$4.37 bil.
1984	$18.16 bil.	$18.57 bil.	-$410 mil.

Defense Expenditure:

1989--$8.5 billion (unconfirmed)

1990--$8.6 billion

Foreign Military Aid and Security Assistance Received:

military training:

foreign advisors/instructors/serving personnel from--USSR, GDR, Bulgaria (unconfirmed), Cuba, Libya (unconfirmed), North Korea (several hundreds), PRC,

Syria, Afghanistan (dissidents, serving personnel)
trainees abroad in--France, GDR, North Korea (several hundreds), Pakistan (nuclear scientists, naval trainees), PRC, USSR; Cuba (unconfirmed)

arms transfers from:

Austria (AAGs, unconfirmed); Argentina (small arms, ammunition, high explosives, land mines); Belgium (small arms); Brazil (APCs, MRLs, unconfirmed); Britain (workshops, spare parts for tanks and ARVs, landrovers, radars); Czechoslovakia (tanks); Ethiopia (US-made combat aircraft); France (spare parts for MFPBs, artillery ammunition, rubber boats, trucks); FRG (trucks); GDR (combat aircraft, tanks); Greece (details unknown); Hong Kong (American aircraft spares and miscellaneous items); Italy (AAGs, optronics, ammunition, land mines, artillery pieces, spare parts for aircraft, naval guns, construction of harbor, naval mines via intermediaries); Libya (Soviet-made naval mines, Soviet-made SSMs); North Korea (artillery pieces, AAGs, small arms, naval mines, midget submarine, SAMs, AAMs, SSMs); Portugal (ammunition); PRC (artillery pieces, coastal defense SSMs, combat aircraft, SAMs, tanks; SSMs, unconfirmed); Romania (tanks, APCs); South Korea (aircraft spare parts, SAMs, unconfirmed); Sweden (explosives, patrol boats, trucks; SAMs via Singapore); Switzerland (trainer aircraft; AAGs and fire control, unconfirmed); Syria (Soviet-made small arms and ATGMs, AAGs, ammunition); Taiwan (artillery ammunition, mortars, small arms); USA (spare parts via Japan, unconfirmed); USSR & East European countries (AAGs, APCs, artillery pieces, small arms); Vietnam (US-made aircraft, helicopters, tanks, APCs, artillery pieces--war booty)

construction aid by:

Romania (naval base)

Foreign Military Aid and Security Assistance Extended:

financial aid to:

opposition groups in Bahrain, Iraq, Saudi Arabia--grants; Hizb Allah militia in Lebanon--grant; al-Amal movement in Lebanon--grant (unconfirmed); Syria--grant (free oil); Palestinian organizations (Fatah rebels--Abu Musa faction and since late 1989 also PFLP-GC)--grant; Afghan anti-government rebels; POLISARIO (unconfirmed); Tunisian anti-government fundamentalists--grant (unconfirmed); Egyptian anti-government fundamentalist groups--grant

military training:

foreign trainees from--Lebanon (Hizb Allah militia); Iraq, Bahrain, Saudi Arabia (opposition groups); Sudan; ASALA (Armenian Secret Army for the

Liberation of Armenia); Afghanistan (rebels); Egyptian anti-government fundamentalist groups; POLISARIO (unconfirmed)

advisors/instructors in--Algeria (POLISARIO units); Lebanon (IRGC personnel with Hizb Allah militia)

arms transfers to:

Afghan rebels; POLISARIO (via Algeria, type unknown)

facilities provided to:

Afghan rebels (training camps near Mashhad); radar facilities to USSR (unconfirmed); PFLP-GC (Palestinian organization, unconfirmed)

forces deployed abroad in:

Lebanon--1000-2000 revolutionary guards with Hizb Allah; 2 units in North Lebanon

Cooperation in Arms Production/Assembly with:

Czechoslovakia (artillery, ammunition, ATGMs); FRG companies (cooperation in production of toxic gas, unconfirmed)

INFRASTRUCTURE

Road Network:

length:	136,400 km
paved roads	40,066 km
gravel and crushed stone roads	46,866 km
improved earth tracks	49,468 km

main routes:

Teheran--Qom--Yazd--Kerman--Zahedan
Kerman--Shiraz--Bushehr
Shiraz--Ahwaz--Abadan
Bandar Khomeini--Ahwaz
Qom--Isfahan--Shiraz
Qom--Arak--Dezful--Ahwaz--Abadan
Qom--Hamadan
Teheran--Hamadan--Kermanshah--Ilam--al-Kut (Iraq)
Abadan--Basra (Iraq)
Kermanshah--Qasr-i Shirin--Baghdad (Iraq)
Dezful--Shahabad--Qasr-i Shirin
Shahabad--Kermanshah--Zanjan
Teheran--Zanjan--Tabriz--Jolfa--Nakhichevan (USSR)
Tabriz--Ardabil--Astara--Lenkoran (USSR)
Teheran--Mashhad
Mashhad--Ashkhabad (USSR)
Mashhad--Zahedan--Chah Bahar
Zahedan--Quetta (Pakistan)
Mashhad--Herat (Afghanistan)
Kerman--Bandar Abbas

Railway Network:

length:	4,601 km
standard gauge	4,509 km
1.676m gauge	92 km

main routes:
- Teheran--Qom--Isfahan--Yazd--Kerman
- Qom--Arak--Dezful--Ahwaz--Abadan
- Ahwaz--Basra (Iraq)
- Teheran--Zanjan--Tabriz--Jolfa--Nakhichevan (USSR)
- Teheran--Semnan--Mashhad
- Mashhad--Ashkhabad (USSR)
- Zahedan--Quetta (Pakistan)
- Tabriz--Malatya (Turkey)

Airfields:

airfields by runway type:

permanent surface fields	80
unpaved fields and usable airstrips	66

airfields by runway length:

over 3660 meters	16
2440--3659	17
1220--2439	68
under 1220	45
TOTAL	146

international airports: Teheran, Abadan

major domestic airfields: Abu Musa, Ardabil, Bandar Abbas, Bushehr, Chah Bahar, Gorgan, Isfahan, Kerman, Kharg Island, Mashhad, Rasht, Sanandaj, Shiraz, Tabriz, Yazd, Zahedan

Airlines:

companies: Iran Air (international, domestic and cargo), Iranian Assaman Airlines (domestic)

aircraft:

Aerocommander/Turbocommander/Shrike Commander	15
Airbus A-300 B2	4
Boeing 747-200F/SP/100B/200B	8
Boeing 737-200	4
Boeing 727-200	4
Boeing 727-100	2
Boeing 707-320C/707F	4
Britten Norman BN-2 Islander	2
Fairchild FH-227B	3
Fokker F-28-4000	2
Mystere-Falcon 20F	4
Piper Chieftain	2

Maritime Facilities:

harbors--Bandar Abbas, Bandar Anzelli, Bandar Lengeh (Lingeh), Chah Bahar, Khorramshahr (not in use due to war), Bandar Khomeini (formerly Bandar Shahpur; also referred to as Bandar Imam)

oil terminals--Bandar Abbas, Bushehr, Bandar Khomeini, Bandar Lengeh, Ganaveh, Kharg Island, Larak Island, Sirri Island

Merchant Marine:

vessel type	number	GRT
general cargo	40	381,000
tanker	15	651,000
TOTAL	55	1,032,000

(note: tanker figures do not include leased storage tankers)

Defense Production:

army equipment:
rifles (Heckler & Koch G-3 AR, under license); machine guns (MG-1A1, under license); artillery; MRLs; SSMs; small arms, mortars, and artillery ammunition; spare parts; trucks (assembly); toxic gas; gas masks; ATRLs (uncomfirmed); ATGMs (with assistance from Czechoslovakia)

air force equipment:
light aircraft (probably still under development); spare parts for aircraft

electronics:
radio transceivers (copy of USA model)

naval craft:
250 ton LCU (Foque 101), PBs, mines, 8.4 meter hovercraft

ARMED FORCES

Personnel:

military forces--

	regular	reserves	total
army	300,000	350,000	650,000
IRGC	300,000	895,000	1,195,000
Baseej	50,000	-	50,000
air force	35,000	-	35,000
navy	20,000	-	20,000
TOTAL	705,000	1,245,000	1,950,000

para-military forces--

Baseej (militiamen/boys)	+
gendarmerie	75,000

Army:

major units (including IRGC now integrated into Army; some units not fully organized):

unit type	army corps	divisions	independent brigades
all arms	3		
mechanized		1	
armored		6	
infantry		35	
paratroop/ special forces		1	3

airborne 2
TOTAL 3 43 5
(some divisions undermanned; about 13 army divisions, 30 IRGC divisions; IRGC divisions are smaller in size than army divisions, sometimes equivalent to the strength of one brigade)

small arms:
personal weapons--
11mm (0.45") M-3 A1 SMG
9mm Uzi SMG
7.62mm G-3 (Heckler & Koch) AR
7.62mm M-1 Garand SAR
7.62mm AK-47 (Kalashnikov) AR
machine guns--
12.7mm D.Sh.K. 38/46 (Degtyarev) HMG
12.7mm (0.5") Browning M2 HMG
7.62mm MG 1A1 LMG
7.62mm (0.3") Browning M-1919 MMG
7.62mm MAG (FN) (unconfirmed)
7.62mm PK/PKS (Kalashnikov) LMG
light and medium mortars--
81mm M-29
60mm M-19
light ATRLs--
3.5" M-20
RPG-7

tanks:

model	number
high quality	
T-72 (unconfirmed, captured)	a few
medium quality	
Chieftain Mk.3/Mk.5	
T-62	150
M-60 A1	
T-55/Type 69/Type 59	
low quality	
M-48/M-47	
Scorpion	
TOTAL (limited serviceability due to lack of spare parts)	600-700

on order: Type 69 (unconfirmed); T-72, T-55 (both unconfirmed)

APCs/ARVs:

model	number
high quality	
M-113	
BMP-1	
Engesa E9	
others	
BTR-40/50/60	

BTR-152	
Fox	
Ferret	
TOTAL	800
artillery:	
self propelled guns and howitzers--	
203mm M-110 SP howitzer	
175mm M-107 SP gun	
155mm M-109 SP howitzer	
towed guns and howitzers--	
203mm (8") M-115 howitzer	
155mm G-5 gun/howitzer	
155mm GHN-45 howitzer	140
155mm M-114 howitzer	
130mm M-46 gun/Type 59 gun	
105mm M-101 howitzer	
mortars, heavy, under 160mm--	
120mm M-65 mortar	
107mm (4.2") M-30 mortar	
TOTAL	1000
(approximately 2/3 high quality including SP guns & howitzers)	about 200
MRLs--	
355mm Nazeat	
333mm Shahin 2	
230mm Oghab	
180mm SS-40 Astros II (unconfirmed)	
130mm Type 63	
122mm BM-21	
107mm	
on order: 152mm and 122mm guns	
engineering equipment:	
pontoon bridges	
light infantry assault boats	
self-propelled pontoons	
anti-tank weapons:	
missiles--	launchers
AT-3 (Sagger)	
BGM-71A TOW	
M-47 Dragon	
SS-11/SS-12	
guns--	
106mm M-40 A1C recoilless rifle	
surface-to-surface missiles and rockets:	
SS-1 (Scud B)	3+
Iran-130 (unconfirmed)	
on order: Fajr 3 and possibly other SSMs	

army anti-aircraft defenses:	
missiles--	launchers
self propelled/mobile	
Rapier	45
Crotale (unconfirmed)	
man-portable	
FIM-92A Stinger (with IRGC)	a few
RBS-70	50
SA-7 (Grail)	
Tigercat	15
short-range guns--	
57mm ZSU 57x2 SP	
57mm	
40mm Bofors L-70 (unconfirmed)	
37mm	
35mm Contraves Skyguard ADS (unconfirmed)	
35mm Oerlikon-Bhurle 35x2 GDF-002	
23mm ZSU 23x4 SP (Gun Dish)	
23mm ZU 23x2	

on order: RBS-70 SAMs (unconfirmed); ZSU 23x4 AAGs (unconfirmed)

CW capabilities:

personal protective equipment for part of the armed forces

stockpile of gases

decontamination units

Air Force:

aircraft--general:(about 30% serviceable)	number
combat aircraft	214
transport aircraft	116
helicopters	400
combat aircraft:	
interceptors--	
high quality	
F-14A Tomcat (limited serviceability)	15
others	
F-7 (unconfirmed)	30
MiG-21 (Fishbed)	24
(sub-total	54)
Total	69
strike and multi-role aircraft--	
medium quality	
F-4 D/E/RF Phantom (limited serviceability)	50
others	
F-5 A/B/E	40
F-6	40
(sub-total	80)
Total	130

on order: 32 F-7; MiG-29, Su-24, MiG-23 (all

unconfirmed)	
transport aircraft:	
Aero Commander 690	2
Boeing 747	12
Boeing 737-200	3
Boeing 707 & KC-135 tanker (refuelling; including Boeing 707s in electronic surveillance/EW/CEW role)	14
C-130 E/H Hercules (including 2-3 in electronic surveillance role)	50
Cessna 310	5
Fokker F-27-400 M/F-27-600	16
Mystere Falcon 20	14
TOTAL	116
training and liaison aircraft:	
others--	
Beechcraft Bonanza F-33	50
Cessna 185	45
Pilatus PC-7 Turbo-Trainer	35
T-33	9
TOTAL	139
on order: 15 EMB-312, possibly delivered	
helicopters:	
attack--	
AH-1J Cobra	150
heavy transport	
CH-47C Chinook	60
CH-53D	
SA-321 Super Frelon	
medium transport--	
AB-214A	60
AB-205	75
AB-212	11
HH-34F (S-58, unconfirmed)	8
(sub-total	154)
light transport--	
AB-206 JetRanger	
ASW--	
SH-3D	32
TOTAL (limited serviceability)	400
maritime surveillance aircraft:	
P-3 Orion (unconfirmed)	2
advanced armament:	
air-to-air missiles--	
AIM-54A Phoenix (a limited number serviceable)	
AIM-9 Sidewinder	
AIM-7 Sparrow	
air-to-ground missiles--	
AGM-65 Maverick	

AS-12	
anti-aircraft defenses:	
radars--	
AR-3D	
long-range missiles--	batteries
HAWK / MIM-23B Improved HAWK	17
SA-2 (Guideline)	1
HQ-2J	4
TOTAL	22
on order: SA-2 or HQ-2J	
aircraft shelters--	
in some of the operational airfields	
military airfields:	20
Bandar Abbas, Birjand, Bushehr, Ghaleh-Marghi, Isfahan, Jegi, Kerman, Kharg Island, Khatami, Mehrabad, Murgeh, Qeshm, Shiraz, Tabriz, Teheran, 5 additional	

Navy:

combat vessels:	number
MFPBs--	
Combattante II (Kaman) class	10
missile destroyers--(possibly not all are in service)	
Battle class	1
Sumner class	2
Total	3
missile frigates--	
Vosper Mk.5	3
gun corvettes--	
PF-103 class	2
mine warfare vessels--	
MSC 292 & MSC 268 class minesweepers	3
Cape class minesweeper	2
Total	5
patrol craft--	
PGM-71 (improved) class	3
Cape (US coastguard)	3
Peterson Mk.II 50 ft. (15 meter)	56
Sewart 40 ft. (12 meter)	6
Boghammar (13 meter; IRGC)	51
Bertram 30.4 ft. and 20 ft.	12
Fateh boat	1
Total	132
landing craft:	
BH-7 (Wellington) class hovercraft	6
SRN-6 (Winchester) class hovercraft	8
Hengam class landing ship	4
750 ton LCT	3
LST (South Korean)	3
US LCU 1431	1
250 ton LCU	1

IRAN

TOTAL	26
auxiliary ships:	
Amphion class repair ship	1
Cargo Vessel (765 DWT)	5
harbor tanker (1700 ton full load)	1
Luhring Yard 3,250 DWT supply ship	2
Mazagon Docks 9430 ton water tanker	2
Swan Hunter replenishment ship	1
YW-83 class 1250 ton water tanker	1
Jansen research vessel	1

on order: 2 1350 ton maintenance ships from Japan

advanced armament:
- surface-to-surface missiles--
  - RGM-84 Harpoon
  - Seakiller
  - C-801
- surface-to-air missiles--
  - Standard
  - Seacat

coastal defense:	launchers
HY-2 (Silkworm) SSMs	100
C-801 SSM	100

special maritime forces:
- frogmen and divers
- A 30 ton Sea Horse midget submarine (made in North Korea); 2 Iranian midget submarines (unconfirmed)

naval bases: 8

Bandar Abbas, Bandar Anzelli, Bandar Khomeini, Bandar Lengeh, Bushehr, Chah Bahar, Farsi Island, Kharg Island

IRGC naval bases: 10

Abadan oil terminal, Abu Musa Island, al-Fayisiyah Island, Cyrus oilfield, Halul Island platform (unconfirmed), Larak Island, Qeshm Island (under construction), Rostam Island oilfield, Sir Abu Nu'air, Sirri Island

ship maintenance and repair capability:
- 1 MAN Nordhaman 28,000 ton floating dock

5. IRAQ

BASIC DATA

Official Name of State: The Republic of Iraq

Head of State: President Saddam Hussein (also Prime Minister and Supreme Commander of the Armed Forces)

Defense Minister: General Abd al-Jabbar Shanshal (also Deputy Supreme Commander of the Armed Forces)

Chief of the General Staff: Lieutenant General Nizar Abd al-Karim al-Khazraji

Commander of the Air Force: Lieutenant General Sab Hassan

Commander of the Navy: Rear Admiral Rahib Hassoun Rahib

Area: 438,446 sq. km.

Population: (not including 1.5-2 million Arab nationals, mostly Egyptians working in Iraq) 17,050,000

ethnic subdivision:		
Arabs	12,532,000	73.5%
Kurds	3,683,000	21.6%
Turkmens	409,000	2.4%
Others	426,000	2.5%
religious subdivision:		
Shi'ite Muslims	9,378,000	55.0%
Sunni Muslims (incl. Kurds)	7,161,000	42.0%
Christians, Yazidis and others	511,000	3.0%

GDP:
no GDP available since 1981

Balance of Payments (goods, services & unilateral transfer payments): not available

Defense Expenditure (figures unreliable)
1986--$10 billion (unconfirmed)
1987--$6-8 billion (unconfirmed)

Foreign Military Aid and Security Assistance Received:

financial aid from:
Kuwait, Qatar and UAE--grants and loans; Saudi Arabia--grants and loans, sums unknown; old debt extended by Saudis, Kuwaitis and Jordanians

military training:
foreign advisors/instructors/serving personnel from--Britain (30-40), Brazil, Egypt, France, India (unconfirmed), Jordan, Morocco, USSR and East European countries (1000, unconfirmed)
trainees abroad in--Britain, Egypt (400), France, Italy, Jordan, Turkey (unconfirmed), USSR

arms transfers from:
Austria (artillery pieces, via Jordan); Belgium (ammunition); Brazil (APCs, ARVs, trucks, MRLs, trainer aircraft via Egypt); Britain (electronic equipment, land rovers); Chile (aerial bombs); Denmark (landing craft); Egypt (ammunition, Soviet-made combat aircraft, ATGMs, small arms, tanks, APCs, SAMs, MRLs, mortars,

trainer aircraft, helicopters); Ethiopia (second-hand arms); France (combat aircraft, artillery pieces, ATGMs, SAMs, AGMs, AAMs); FRG (tank transporters); Greece (artillery ammunition); Italy (missile frigates and corvettes, aircraft electronics, artillery pieces, radars, helicopters, small arms, land mines, spare parts; chemicals for production of gas by private firms, unconfirmed); PRC (tanks, artillery pieces, APCs, combat aircraft; anti-ship AGMs, unconfirmed); Morocco (second-hand arms); North Korea (various items); Philippines (second-hand arms); Portugal (ammunition); South Africa (artillery pieces and ammunition, unconfirmed); Spain (mortar ammunition); Spain/FRG (helicopters); USA (civilian helicopters used for military purpose) ; USSR (combat aircraft, tanks, SSMs, helicopters, artillery pieces, ammunition, SAMs); Yugoslavia (small arms, MRLs, APCs)

support forces from:

volunteers serving with the Popular Army and Army--Arab nationals working in Iraq; volunteers from YAR, until December 1988, serving with the Army

use of facilities abroad:

Jordan (use of supply routes and harbor); Kuwait (use of harbors, overflight rights for combat aircraft); Saudi Arabia (use of harbors); Turkey (use of supply routes); Egypt (facilities for use by naval vessels); Mauritania (use of territory for test-firing SSMs)

construction aid by:

Belgium, India (railway construction), Yugoslavia (highways, power plant), Poland (highway construction)

maintenance of equipment in:

Egypt (aircraft)

Foreign Military Aid and Security Assistance Extended:

financial aid to:

PLO (al-Fatah, Abu al-Abbas faction of PLF, ALF); Iranian anti-government groups, including Mujahedeen Khalq

military training:

advisors/instructors in--Lebanon (with army loyal to Aoun's government); Sudan (technicians)

foreign trainees from--Lebanon (loyal to Aoun's government)

arms transfers to

PLO (ALF--small arms); Lebanon (tanks, artillery and MRLs to army loyal to Aoun's government, small patrol boats and other equipment to Lebanese Forces militia); Sudan (artillery pieces, ammunition, small arms) Jordan (tanks captured from Iran)

facilities provided to:

Palestinians (a camp for ALF, unconfirmed;

PLO--headquarter facilities; PLA forces); Jordan (facility for joint fighter aircraft squadron)

Cooperation in Arms Production/Assembly with:

Egypt (production of spares for Soviet arms); Egypt and Argentina (development of SSM, possibly discontinued now); Brazil (MRLs); companies from FRG, Italy and France (involved in SSM production); France (electronics); USSR (small arms, ammunition, assembly of T-72 tank, upgrading other tanks); Yugoslavia (small arms, ammunition); companies from Italy, FRG and other countries (assistance in toxic gas production); companies and experts from FRG, Brazil and France (assistance in producing an observation satellite); companies from Belgium and Britain (production of a "super-gun" to be capable of firing long range projectiles and rockets)

Joint maneuvers with:

Jordan

INFRASTRUCTURE

Road Network:

length:	13,720 km
paved roads	8,190 km
improved earth roads	5,530 km

main routes:

Baghdad--Kirkuk--Mosul
Baghdad--Mosul--al-Qamishli (Syria)--Diyarbakir(Turkey) /Mosul al Hasakah (Syria)
Baghdad--al-Hadithah--Qusaybah--Dir e-Zor (Syria) /Qusaybah--Palmyra (Syria)
Baghdàd--al-Rutbah--Damascus (Syria)
Baghdad--H-3--Mafraq (Jordan)
Baghdad--al-Hillah--al-Najaf--al-Samawah--Basra
Baghdad--al-Kut--al-Nasiriyah--Basra/al-Kut--al-Amarah --Basra
Basra--Abadan (Iran)
Basra--Kuwait
al-Najaf--Rafha (Saudi Arabia, on TAPline road leading also to Jordan)

Railway Network:

(some temporarily inoperative due to Iran-Iraq War)

length:	2,710 km
standard gauge	2,205 km
narrow gauge	505 km

main routes:

Baghdad--Mosul--al-Qamishli--Aleppo (Syria)/Mosul--al-Qamishli--Ankara (Turkey)
Baghdad--Kirkuk--Arbil (Irbil)
Baghdad--al-Nassiriya--Basra
Baghdad--al-Ramadi--al-Haditha--al-Qa'im (Syrian border

near Abu Kemal)
Kirkuk--al Hadithah
Baghdad--Mussayib--Karbala--Najaf--Kufa--Samawah--Basra--Umm Qasr

Airfields:

airfields by runway type:

permanent surface fields	65
unpaved fields and usable airstrips	31

airfields by runway length:

over 3660 meters	7
2440--3659	48
1220--2439	12
under 1220	29
TOTAL	96

international airports: Baghdad, Basra
major domestic airfields: Arbil (Irbil), H-3, al-Haditha, Kirkuk, Mosul

Airlines:

companies: Iraqi Airways (international and domestic)
aircraft:

Antonov An-12	5
Antonov An-24	3
Boeing 747-200C	3
Boeing 747-SP	1
Boeing 737-200C	2
Boeing 727-200	6
Boeing 707-320C	2
Ilyushin IL-76	30
Lockheed Jetstar II	6
Mystere Falcon 50	4
Mystere Falcon 20F	2
Piaggio P-166	4

on order: 10 Airbus (unconfirmed)

Maritime Facilities

(temporarily inoperative due to lack of peace settlement with Iran):
harbors--Basra, Umm Qasr
oil terminals--Khor al-Amaya, Faw, Mina al-Bakr

Merchant Marine

(flag carrying, operating from non-Iraqi ports due to lack of peace settlement with Iran):

vessel type	number	DWT
crude carrier	14	1,377,700
small tanker	2	17,083
general cargo/container	4	14,222
general cargo	9	96,062
training/cargo	1	12,650
ro/ro	3	11,955
reefer	1	9,247
ferry	1	1,223

barge	4	6,648
product tanker	2	16,388
TOTAL	41	1,563,178

Defense Production:

army equipment:

manufacture--small arms and artillery ammunition (with Soviet, Yugoslav and Italian assistance); electronics (with French assistance); toxic gas: mustard, tabun, sarin; biological weapons (unconfirmed); SSMs under development (some in cooperation with Argentina and Egypt and other foreign companies; possibly cooperation with Argentina discontinued); upgrading of Soviet-designed Scud B SSMs (with assistance from Egypt, companies and experts from FRG); "super-gun" capable of firing projectiles (with assistance from companies in Belgium and Britain)

production under license--ATRLs, rifles, artillery, MRLs (Brazilian and Yugoslav license); tank (Soviet model)

optronics:

development of a spy satellite (with assistance from Brazilian, French and other foreign companies)

aircraft armament:

production under license--Chile-designed Cardoen aerial CBU (unconfirmed); aerial bombs; mini RPVs (unconfirmed) ; AEW aircraft (Soviet, with French electronics)

naval craft:

small patrol boats; rubber boats

ARMED FORCES

Personnel:

military forces--

	regular	reserves (some on active duty)	total
army	355,000	680,000	1,035,000
air force	40,000		40,000
navy	5,000		5,000
TOTAL	400,000	680,000	1,080,000

a slow demobilization of reserves is in process since December 1988

para-military forces--

Popular Army--650,000-800,000

security troops

15,000 pro-Iraqi Iranians of the Iranian National Liberation Army, organized and based in Iraq

IRAQ

Army:

major units: (Some units not fully organized; all armored, mechanized and special forces--fully active and fully manned; infantry divisions--several not fully manned; reserve units have regular cadres).

unit type	army corps HQ	divisions	independent brigades
all arms	8		
armored		7	1
mechanized		3	
infantry/ special forces		40	14
TOTAL	8	50	15

small arms:

personal weapons--
- 7.62mm P.P.Sh. SMG
- 7.62mm AK-47 (Kalashnikov) AR
- 7.62mm SKS (Simonov) SAR
- 5.45mm AK-74 (Kalashnikov, unconfirmed) AR

machine guns--
- 14.5mm KPV HMG
- 14.5mm ZPU 14.5x4 HMG (in anti-aircraft role)
- 12.7mm D.Sh.K. 38/46 (Degtyarev) HMG
- 7.62mm SGM (Goryunov) MMG
- 7.62mm RPD (Degtyarev) LMG
- 7.62mm PK/PKS (Kalashnikov) LMG

light & medium mortars--
- 82mm M-43

light ATRLs--
- RPG-7

tanks:

model		number
high quality		
T-72/T-72M		1200
Assad Babil (improved T-55)		a few
medium quality		
T-62		1200
T-55/Type 59/Type 69/M-77		3400
	(sub-total	4600)
low quality		
PT-76		200
TOTAL		6000

APCs/ARVs:

model	number
high quality	
BMP-1	600
BMP-2	100
YW-531	+
Engesa EE-9/11	300

(sub-total 1800)

others
AML-90/60
BRDM-2
BTR-40/50/60
FUG-70
K-63
M-60P
M-3 (Panhard)
OT-62/OT-64
MT-LB (an artillery prime-mover, employed also as APC)

(sub-total 3200)

TOTAL 5000

on order: E3/9/11/17

artillery:
self propelled guns and howitzers--
210mm al-Faw howitzer (unconfirmed)
155mm M-109 SP howitzer (captured)
155mm GCT SP howitzer 85
155mm Majnoon howitzer/gun (unconfirmed)
152mm M-1973 SP howitzer
122mm M-1974 SP howitzer
towed guns and howitzers--
180mm S-23
155mm G-5 howitzer/gun 100
155mm GHN-45 howitzer/gun
155mm M-41
155mm M-114 A1 howitzer
152mm D-20
152mm M-1943 howitzer
130mm M-46 gun/ 130mm Type 59 gun
122mm D-30 howitzer/Saddam
122mm M-1938 howitzer
105mm M-56 Pack howitzer
105mm M-102
85mm field/AT gun
mortars, heavy, over 160mm--
160mm mortar
mortars, heavy, under 160mm--
120mm x 4 SP
120mm M-43 mortar
TOTAL 4500-5000
artillery ammunition carriers--
MT-LB (some MT-LB used as artillery prime-movers, command post vehicles, mortar carriers, MRL carriers and other tasks)
MRLs--
400mm Ababil-100
300mm SS-60 (also designated Sajeel-60)

262mm Ababil-50	
180mm SS-40 Astros (also designated Sajeel-40)	
132mm BM-13	
130mm	
128mm M-63	
127mm SS-30 Astros	
122mm BM-21/BM-11	
122mm Firos-25	
107mm	
on order: 155mm GCT SP howitzers; 300mm SS-60	
engineering equipment:	
MTU-55 bridging tanks	
GSP self propelled ferries	
mine-clearing rollers	
minefield crossing system (similar to Viper)	
PMP pontoon bridges	
TPP pontoon bridges	
Soviet-model tank-towed bridges	
AFV transporters:	2800
anti-tank weapons:	
missiles--	launchers
AT-3 (Sagger)	
AT-4 (Spigot)	
AT-5 (Spandrel, carried on BMP-2 APCs)	
BGM-71A TOW	
BRDM-2 (carrying AT-3 Sagger) SP	
M-3 (carrying HOT) SP	
VCR/ TH (carrying HOT) SP	100
MILAN	
Swingfire	
TOTAL	1500
guns--	
107mm B-11 recoilless rifle	
73mm SPG-9 recoilless gun	
surface-to-surface missiles and rockets:	
model	launchers
FROG-7	24
SS-1 (Scud B)	24
al-Hussein	+
al-Hussein stationary sites, at H-2	6
TOTAL	54+
on order: al-Abbas (under development), Badr 2000 (Iraqi version of Argentina's Condor II, possibly discontinued), Tamuz-1/al-Abid 2000 km. IRBM (still experimental)	
army anti-aircraft defenses:	
missiles--	launchers
self propelled/mobile	
SA-6 (Gainful)	
SA-8 (Gecko)	20

SA-9 (Gaskin) SP
SA-13 (Gopher)
Roland 90-100
man-portable
SA-7 (Grail)
SA-14 (Gremlin)
short-range guns-- number
57mm ZSU 57x2 SP
57mm
37mm
23mm ZSU 23x4 SP (Gun Dish)
23mm ZU 23x2
TOTAL (estimate) 1000
CW capabilities:
personal protective equipment
Soviet type unit decontamination equipment
stockpile of gasses: mustard, sarin, tabun
biological warfare capabilities:
toxins and other biological weapons

Air Force:

aircraft--general:	number
combat aircraft	705
transport aircraft	73
helicopters	576
combat aircraft:	number
interceptors--	
high quality	
MiG-25 (Foxbat)	30
MiG-29 (Fulcrum; multi-role aircraft employed in interceptor role; quantity unconfirmed)	40
(sub-total	70)
others	
MiG-21 MF/bis/U (Fishbed)/F-7	170
MiG-19/F-6	30
(sub-total	200)
Total	270
strike and multi-role aircraft--	
high quality	
Su-24 (Fencer C)	25
medium quality	
MiG-23 B (Flogger)/MiG-27	90
Mirage F-1B/EQ5/EQ2/EQ4	84
Su-20/22 (Fitter C/H)	110
Su-25 (Frogfoot)	50
(sub-total	334)
others	
F-6	30

Su-7B (Fitter A)		30
	(sub-total	60)
Total		419
bombers--		
Tu-22 (Blinder)		8
Tu-16 (Badger)/H-6 (B-6D)		8
Total		16
transport aircraft:		
An-2 (Colt)		10
An-12 (Cub, some converted to refuelling a/c)		10
An-24 (Coke)		6
An-26 (Curl)		9
IL-76 (Candid, some tankers)		24
Mystere Falcon 20		12
Tu-124A/Tu-134 (Crusty)		2
TOTAL		73
training and liaison aircraft:		
with ground attack/close air support capability--		
L-29 (Delfin)		42
L-39 (Albatross)		75
	(sub-total	117)
others--		
Embraer EMB-312 (Tucano)		80
MBB-223 Flamingo		16
Pilatus PC-7		52
Pilatus PC-9 (unconfirmed)		19
	(sub-total	167)
TOTAL		284
on order: Alpha Jet (unconfirmed)		
helicopters:		number
attack-- (part of Army Aviation)		
Alouette III (armed)		25
Mi-24/Mi-25 (Hind)		45
SA-342 Gazelle		60
MBB BO-105		30
	(sub-total	160)
maritime attack--		
SA-365 Dauphine 2		6
heavy transport--(mostly part of Army Aviation)		
AS-61		6
SA-321 Super Frelon (also employed in maritime attack role)		10
Mi-6 (Hook)		12
	(sub-total	28)
medium transport--(mostly part of Army Aviation)		
Mi-8/Mi-17 (Hip)		220
SA-330 Puma		10
Bell 214		40

Mi-2 (Hoplite) 10
(sub-total 280)
light transport--(part of Army Aviation)
Alouette III 22
Hughes 500D 28
Hughes 300C 28
Hughes 530F 24
(sub-total 102)
ASW--
AB-212 (unconfirmed)
TOTAL 576
on order: 6 AS-332 Super Puma; 6 BK-117; 6 SA-365 Dauphin 2
miscellaneous aircraft:
AEW/AWACS aircraft--
Adnan 1 AEW
advanced armament:
air-to-air missiles--
AA-2 (Atoll)
AA-6 (Acrid)
AA-7 (Apex)
AA-8 (Aphid)
R-530
R-550 Magique
Super 530D/F
air-to-ground missiles--
AM-39 Exocet
Armat (anti-radar)
AS-2 (Kipper, unconfirmed)
AS-4 (Kitchen)
AS-5 (Kelt)
AS-6 (Kingfish)
AS-7 (Kerry)
AS-9
AS-10 (laser-guided)
AS-12
AS-14 (Kedge)
AS-15TT anti-ship missile
AS-30L (laser-guided)
AT-2 (Swatter)
Hai Ying-2 (HY-2, Silkworm, air launched anti-ship version)
LX anti-ship missile (unconfirmed)
X-23 anti-radiation missile (unconfirmed)
bombs--
Belouga CBU
Cardoen CBU

anti-aircraft defenses:

long-range missiles--

model	batteries
SA-2 (Guideline)/ SA-3 (Goa)	60

aircraft shelters--

for all combat aircraft

military airfields: 20

Arbil, Balad, Basra, H-2, H-3, Habbaniyah, Kirkuk, Kut al-Amarah, Mosul, al Nasiriyah, al-Rashid (Baghdad), Shu'aiba, 8 additional

aircraft maintenance and repair capability:

repair of main models, with assistance from Soviet, Egyptian, and French technicians

Navy:

combat vessels:	number
MFPBs--	
Ossa I	
Ossa II	
Total	8
ASW vessels--	
SO-1 large patrol craft	3
mine warfare vessels--	
Nestin class minesweeper	3
T-43 class minesweeper	2
Yevgenia class coastal minesweeper	3
Total	8
gunboats/MTBs--	
P-6 MTB	6
patrol craft--	
Niryat II	4
PO-2 class	3
Poluchat I	2
SO-1	3
Thornycroft 100 ft. (PB-90, 30.5 meter)	3
Thornycroft 36 ft. (10.9 meter)	8
Thornycroft 21 ft. (6.4 meter)	4
Zhuk class	5
Total	32

on order: 4 Lupo class missile frigates and 6 Assad class missile corvettes (formerly Wadi class)--ready for delivery, but held in Italy

landing craft:	
Polnochny class LCT	2-3
SRN-6 (Winchester) hovercraft	6
Total	8-9

on order: 3 3500 ton LSTs (ready for delivery, but held in Denmark)

auxiliary vessels:

training frigate, 1850 ton (can carry SSMs)	1

IRAQ

746 ton harbor craft (former royal yacht) 1
Stromboli class support ship (held in Egypt)
advanced armament:
surface-to-surface missiles--
SS-N-2 Styx
on order: OTOMAT Mk.2
coastal defense:
Hai Ying-2 (HY-2, Silkworm)
naval bases: 3
Basra, Um Qasr , Faw (all damaged during the war)
ship maintenance and repair capability:
one 6,000 ton capacity floating dock (held in Egypt)

6. ISRAEL

BASIC DATA

Official Name of State: State of Israel
Head of State: President Haim Herzog
Prime Minister: Itzhak Shamir
Minister of Defense: Moshe Arens
Chief of the General Staff: Lieutenant General Dan Shomron
Commander of the Air Force: Major General Avihu Ben-Nun
Commander of Field Forces HQ: Major General Uri Sagui
Commander of the Navy: Rear Admiral Micha Ram
Area: 20,325 sq. km. including East Jerusalem and vicinity annexed in 1967 (not including Golan Heights, 1,100 sq. km., to which Israeli law was applied in 1981)

Population:		4,477,000
ethnic subdivision:		
Jews	3,658,000	81.7%
Arabs, Druze, and others (Armenian, Circassian, European)	819,000	18.3%
religious subdivision:		
Jews	3,658,000	81.7%
Muslims	636,000	14.2%
Christians	107,000	2.4%
Druze and others	76,000	1.7%

GDP:
1987--$34.9 billion
1988--$41.9 billion

Balance of Payments (goods, services & unilateral transfer payments):

year	income	expenditure	balance
1987	$18.67 bil.	$19.65 bil.	-$980 mil.
1988	$19.82 bil.	$20.50 bil.	-$700 bil.

Defense Expenditure:
1988--$5.1 billion
1989--$5.1 billion

Foreign Military Aid and Security Assistance Received:
financial aid from:
USA--$1.8 billion grant (1989)
military training:
trainees abroad in--USA, Britain, France, FRG
arms transfers from:
USA (tanks, SP artillery, naval SSMs, combat aircraft, attack helicopters, tank transporters); Belgium (LMGs); Britain (spare parts); France (spare parts, aircraft engines); FRG (tank transporters, trucks)

ISRAEL

Foreign Military Aid and Security Assistance Extended:
financial aid to:
South Lebanon militia--$20 million
military training:
advisors/instructors/technicians in--Colombia* (unconfirmed), Ecuador*, Ethiopia*, Liberia, Peru*, Singapore*, South Lebanon (SLA militia), Sri Lanka* (unconfirmed, until early 1990), Zaire
foreign trainees from--Colombia*, Lebanon (SLA militia), Liberia, Papua New Guinea, Sri Lanka* (until early 1990), Zaire
arms transfers to:
militias in Lebanon (small arms, tanks, artillery pieces); Argentina (aircraft sub-components, AAMs, aircraft radars, MRLs); Australia (conversion of Boeing 707 aircraft into aerial tankers, electronics); Brazil* (naval SSMs); Belgium* (naval tactical training center, ground forces radar); Cameroon* (transport aircraft); Canada (ammunition, mine clearing rollers); Chile* (AAMs, AAGs, tanks, artillery, mortars, night vision devices, MFPBs, radio transceivers, mini-RPVs); Colombia* (combat aircraft, small arms, radio transceivers); Ecuador* (AAMs); El Salvador* (transport aircraft); Ethiopia*; FRG (ammunition, electronic equipment, ECMs, mini-RPVs jointly produced); Guatemala (rifles); Haiti (Uzi SMGs, Galil rifles); Honduras* (transport aircraft); Ireland* (ballistic helmets; communications equipment); Italy (tank ammunition); Kenya (naval SSMs); Liberia (transport aircraft); Mexico (transport aircraft); Panama* (rifles, night vision equipment, radio transceivers until December 1989); Papua New Guinea (patrol craft, transport aircraft); Paraguay (transport aircraft); PRC*; Singapore* (SSMs, AAMs, naval tactical training center); Peru* (ARVs, helicopters, patrol boats); South Africa* (MFPBs, SSMs, rifles, refuelling aircraft, mini-RPVs); Spain* (tank guns, tank fire control systems, optronics and range finders); Sri Lanka* (patrol boats, small arms); Swaziland* (transport

*According to foreign and Israeli publications

aircraft); Switzerland (mini-RPVs jointly produced, tank ammunition); Taiwan* (AAMs, SSMs); Thailand (transport aircraft, mini-RPVs); UNITA* (Angolan anti-government rebels; captured Soviet arms); USA (parts, mini-RPVs, light AT rockets, tactical air-launched decoys, combat aircraft on lease, mine ploughs for tanks); Venezuela (MRLs); Zaire (small arms)

forces deployed abroad in:
Lebanon--units on a small scale in the security zone in South Lebanon (about 600 men)

Cooperation in Arms Production/Assembly with:
Argentina* (tank components, unconfirmed); Belgium (ground forces radar); Chile* (assistance in upgrading combat aircraft in Chile; provision of AAGs and turrets for Chilean-made SP AAG vehicle); Colombia* (assistance in upgrading combat aircraft in Colombia); FRG (joint production in FRG of mini-RPVs, joint development of an anti-radiation attack drone); South Africa* (joint production of a South African fighter aircraft); Switzerland* (cooperation in upgrading fighter aircraft; cooperation in production of mini RPVs in Switzerland); USA (aircraft, electronics, naval vessels, tank guns, terminal guidance bombs, ATBM, anti-radiation attack drone)

Joint Maneuvers with:
USA

INFRASTRUCTURE

Road Network:

length (paved): 4,760 km

main routes:
Tel Aviv--Jerusalem
Tel Aviv--Hadera--Haifa
Tel Aviv--Ashdod--Beer Sheva
Hadera--Afula--Tiberias/ Afula--Amiad--Rosh-Pina
Haifa--Tiberias
Haifa--Nahariya--Naqura (Lebanon)
Acre--Safed--Rosh Pina/Acre--Amiad
Rosh Pina--Kuneitra (Syria)
Tiberias--Metula--Marj Ayoun (Lebanon)
Beer Sheva--Eilat

*According to foreign and Israeli publications

Rafah (Rafiah)--Nitsana--Eilat
Eilat--Sharm al-Shaykh (Egypt)
Beer Sheva--Nitzana--Isma'iliya (Egypt)
Tel Aviv--Gaza--Kantara (Egypt)
Jerusalem--Hebron--Arad/Beer Sheva
Jerusalem--Nablus--Afula
Jerusalem--Allenby Bridge--Amman (Jordan)
Jerusalem--Jericho--Beit Shean/Jericho--Eilat

Railway Network:

length (standard gauge):	767 km

main routes:
Tel Aviv--Haifa
Haifa--Nahariya
Tel Aviv--Jerusalem
Tel Aviv--Beer Sheva--Oron
Kiryat-Gat--Ashkelon--Ashdod
Tel Aviv--Lod--Ashdod
Tel Aviv--Lod--Gaza (serviceable as far as Rafah)
Lod--Haifa

Airfields:

airfields by runway type:	
permanent surface fields	26
unpaved fields and usable airstrips	30
airfields by runway length:	
2440--3659 meters	6
1220--2439	11
under 1220	39
TOTAL	56

international airports: Ben Gurion (Tel Aviv), Eilat
major domestic airfields: Beer Sheva, Haifa, Jerusalem, Rosh Pina, Tel Aviv, Massada

Airlines:

companies: El Al (international); CAL (cargo); Arkia/Kanaf-Arkia (domestic and charter); Nesher (taxi and charter); Sun d'Or (charter); Shahaf (domestic and charter)

aircraft:	
Boeing 767/767ER	4
Boeing 757	4
Boeing 747-200B/200F/200B Combi/100F	9
Boeing 737-200	2
Boeing 707-320B/320C	3
Britten-Norman BN-2 Islander	1
DHC-6 Twin Otter	1
DHC-7 (Dash 7)	4
Piper Navajo/Chieftain	5

on order: 2 Boeing 757; 1 DHC-6 Twin Otter

Maritime Facilities:

harbors--Ashdod, Eilat, Haifa

anchorages--Tel Aviv-Yaffo
oil terminals--Ashkelon, Eilat, Haifa
coal terminal--Hadera

Merchant Marine:

vessel type	number	GRT
general cargo, including container	63	654,000
bulk carrier	22	580,000
other	17	885,000
TOTAL	102	2,119,000

Defense Production:

army equipment:
manufacture--
artillery pieces; small arms; ATGMs; ATRLs; electronic equipment; heavy, medium and light mortars; MRLs; artillery, mortar and small arms ammunition; mines; mine-clearing rollers; tanks; tank guns; tread width mine ploughs for tanks (TWMP); SP AAGs (Soviet gun, USA carrier)

aircraft and air ammunition:
manufacture--
AAMs; CBUs; TV and laser terminal guidance bombs; combat aircraft; light transport aircraft; naval patrol aircraft; mini RPVs; ultra-light aircraft; operational flight trainer systems; radars; upgrading of combat aircraft
production under license--
helicopter parts

naval craft and naval ammunition:
manufacture--
LCTs; MFPBs; patrol boats; SSMs
production under license--
patrol boats; torpedo components

electronics:
manufacture--
radars; direction finders; ELINT equipment; EW jammers; radio transceivers; audio/video microwave transceivers; radio voice scramblers and encryption units

optronics:
manufacture--
night vision devices, laser rangefinders and target designators

ISRAEL

ARMED FORCES

Personnel:

military forces--

	regular	reserves	total
army	133,000	365,000	498,000
air force	31,000	55,000	86,000
navy	10,000	10,000	20,000
TOTAL	174,000	430,000	604,000

para-military forces--
- Nahal--7,500
- border police--6,000

Army:

major units (including reserves):

unit type	divisions	independent brigades
armored	12	
mechanized/infantry/ territorial	4	8
airborne		5
TOTAL	16	13

anti-Intifada HQ: 2 divisional HQ for control of units engaged in anti-Intifada activities in Judea, Samaria and Gaza. These should not be counted as normal division HQs.

small arms:

personal weapons--
- 9mm Uzi SMG
- 7.62mm AK-47 (Kalashnikov)
- 7.62mm FAL/FN SAR
- 7.62mm Galil sniper rifle
- 7.62mm M-14 SAR
- 5.56mm Galil AR
- 5.56mm M-16 A1 & A2 AR

machine guns--
- 12.7mm (0.5") Browning M2 HMG
- 7.62mm (0.3") Browning M-1919 A1 MMG
- 7.62mm MAG (FN) LMG
- 5.56mm Minimi (FN) LMG
- 5.56mm Negev LMG

automatic grenade launchers--
- 40mm Mk.19

light and medium mortars--
- 81mm Soltam
- 60mm
- 52mm IMI

light ATRLs--
- M-72 LAW
- RPG-7

B-300

tanks:

model	number
high quality	
Merkava Mk.I/Mk.II/Mk.III	730
M-60 A3/upgraded M-60/Magach 7	600
(sub-total	1330)
medium quality	
Centurion/upgraded Centurion	1100
M-60/M-60 A1	800
M-48 A5	400
T-62	150
T-55 (upgraded)	80
(sub-total	2530)
TOTAL	3860

on order: additional Merkava Mk.III

APCs/ARVs:

model	number
high quality	
M-113 (various marks)	
Nagmashot*	100
RBY	
(sub-total	5100)
others	
M-2 & M-3 halftrack	
BTR-50	
OT-62	
BRDM-2	
(sub-total	3000)
TOTAL	8100

artillery:

self propelled guns and howitzers--	
203mm M-110 SP howitzer	
175mm M-107 SP gun	
155mm M-109 A1 & A2 SP howitzer	
155mm L-33 SP howitzer	
155mm M-50 SP howitzer	
towed guns and howitzers--	
155mm M-71 howitzer	
130mm M-46 gun	
122mm D-30 howitzer	
mortars, heavy, over 160mm--	
160mm SP mortar	
mortars, heavy, under 160mm--	
120mm mortar	250
TOTAL	1300

*According to foreign and Israeli publications

artillery/mortar-locating radars--
AN/TPQ-37
AN/PPS-15
MRLs--
290mm MAR 290
240mm
140mm
122mm BM-21
engineering equipment:
Gilois motorized bridges
M-123 Viper minefield crossing system
M-60 AVLB
mine-clearing rollers
mine layers
Pomins II portable mine neutralization system*
tank-towed bridges
TLB (trailer launched bridge)
Tread width mine ploughs (TWMP)
AFV transporters: +
anti-tank weapons:
missiles--
AT-3 (Sagger)
BGM-71A TOW and BGM-71C Improved TOW
M-47 Dragon
Mapats SP
Israeli BGM-71C Improved TOW SP
surface-to-surface missiles and rockets:

model	launchers
MGM-52C (Lance)	12
Jericho Mk. I/II SSM*	

army anti-aircraft defenses:

missiles--	launchers
self propelled/mobile	
MIM-72A Chaparral	ca. 50
man-portable	
MIM-43A Redeye	
SA-7 (Grail)	
short-range guns--	**number**
40mm Bofors L-70	
37mm	
ZU 23x2	
20mm M-163 A1 Vulcan SP	
20mm TCM-20 Hispano Suiza SP	
20mm Hispano Suiza	
TOTAL	900

on order: FIM-92A Stinger man portable SAMs

*According to foreign and Israeli publications

CW capabilities:
  personal protective equipment
  unit decontamination equipment
ground forces radars:
  AN/PPS-15

Air Force:

aircraft--general:	number
combat aircraft (including 80 in storage)	638
transport aircraft	91
helicopters	218
combat aircraft:	
interceptors--	
high quality	
F-15 Eagle	48
F-16A/B/C (multi-role, employed as interceptor)	123
Total	171
strike and multi-role aircraft--	
high quality	
F-16D	24
others	
F-4E/RF-4E Phantom	142
A-4 Skyhawk	120
Kfir C-2/TC-2/C-7/TC-7	101
(sub-total	363)
Kfir and A-4 Skyhawk (in storage)	ca. 80
Total (including aircraft in storage)	467
on order: 5 F-15D, 60 F-16C/D, upgraded F-4 designated Phantom 2000	
transport aircraft:	
Arava	10
Beechcraft Queen Air	12
Boeing 707	8
Boeing 707 tanker (refuelling)	2
C-130H Hercules	24
DC-3 Dakota (C-47)	20
Dornier Do-28	10
KC-130 tanker (refuelling)	2
Westwind 1124	3
TOTAL	91
on order: Beechcraft Bonanza A-36 (light executive aircraft)	
training and liaison aircraft:	
with ground attack/close air support capability--	
CM-170 Fouga Magister/Tzukit	90

others--		
Cessna U-206 (Stationair-6)		41
Piper Cub		35
	(sub-total	76)
TOTAL		166
helicopters:		
attack--		
AH-1G/1S Cobra		42
500MG Defender		35
	(sub-total	77)
naval attack/search & rescue--		
HH-65A Dolphin		2
heavy transport--		
CH-53		33
SA-321 Super Frelon		8
	(sub-total	41)
medium transport--		
Bell-212		58
light transport--		
AB-206 JetRanger/Bell-206L		40
TOTAL		218
on order: 19 AH-64 Apache		
maritime surveillance aircraft:		
Seascan (Westwind 1124N)		5
miscellaneous aircraft:		
AEW/AWACS aircraft--		
E-2C Hawkeye AEW		4
Boeing 707 AEW*		
ELINT and EW--		
Boeing 707 ELINT*		
Boeing 707 EW*		
target drones--		
Beech AQM-37A		
Beech BQM-107B		
RPVs and mini-RPVs--		
Mastiff (Tadiran) mini-RPV		
Pioneer mini-RPV		
Scout (IAI) mini-RPV		
MQM-74C Chuckar II RPV		
Teledyne Ryan 1241 RPV		
tactical air-launched decoys--		
Samson		
advanced armament:		
air-to-air missiles--		
AIM-9 Sidewinder; AIM-9L		

*According to foreign and Israeli sources

AIM-7 Sparrow
Python 3
R-530 Matra
Shafrir
air-to-ground missiles--
AGM-78D Standard ARM
AGM-65 Maverick
AGM-62A Walleye
AGM-45 A/B Shrike
Popeye (equivalent to AGM-142)
bombs--
CBU (including Tal-1)
runway-penetration bombs
Pyramid TV terminal-guidance bombs
Guillotine laser terminal-guidance bombs
on order: AIM-9M AAM
EW and CEW equipment:
chaff and flare dispensers for combat aircraft
on order: 20 AN/ALQ 131 electronic countermeasures systems
anti-aircraft defenses:
radars--
Elta
FPS-100
AN/TPS-43
long-range missiles--
model
HAWK
MIM-23B Improved HAWK
aircraft shelters--
in all operational airfields, for combat aircraft
military airfields: 11
Haifa, Hatzerim, Hatzor, Lod, Nevatim, Palmachim, Ramat David, Ramon, Tel Aviv, Tel Nof, Uvda
aircraft maintenance and repair capability:
maintenance on all models in service, partly in airfields, partly at Israel Aircraft Industries facilities

Navy:

combat vessels:	number
submarines--	
IKL/Vickers Type 206	3
MFPBs--	
Dvora	2
Sa'ar 2 and 3 class	9
Sa'ar 4 class (Reshef)	8
Sa'ar 4.5 class (Aliyah)	4
Total	23
missile-armed hydrofoils--	

Flagstaff 2
patrol craft--
Dabur class and a few Dvora (without missiles) 37
Kedma class (with Police Force) 4
PBR--Yatush 6
Total 47
on order: 3 Sa'ar 5 missile corvettes (delivery in 1993-95); additional Dvora patrol craft without missiles; 2 Type 209 submarines (delivery 1995)
landing craft:
Ash class LCT 6
Bat-Sheva class LST 1
LSM 1 class 3
Sealand Mk III hovercraft 2
US type LCM 3
TOTAL 15
auxiliary vessels:
support ship 1
swimmer delivery vehicles
advanced armament:
surface-to-surface missiles--
Gabriel 2 & 3
RGM-84A Harpoon
sub-Harpoon (unconfirmed)
anti-missile guns--
20mm Vulcan-Phalanx radar-controlled anti-missile gun
advanced torpedoes--
Mk.37 anti-submarine torpedoe
on order: NT-37E anti-submarine torpedo, Barak anti-missile missile
special maritime forces:
frogmen and divers
naval bases: 3
Ashdod, Eilat, Haifa
ship maintenance and repair capability:
repair and maintenance of all naval vessels in Haifa, partly in conjunction with Israel Wharves
Note: maritime surveillance aircraft and naval attack helicopters listed under Air Force

7. JORDAN

BASIC DATA

Official Name of State: The Hashemite Kingdom of Jordan
Head of State: King Hussein Ibn Talal al-Hashimi
Prime Minister: Mudar Badran (also Defense Minister)
Chief of the General Staff: General Fathi Abu Talib
Commander of the People's Army: Major General Hani al-Majaly
Commander of the Air Force: Major General Ihsan Shurdum
Area: 90,700 sq. (excluding West Bank; Jordan renounced all claims to this territory in July 1989)

Population:		2,850,000
ethnic subdivision:		
Arabs	2,793,500	98.0%
Circassians & Armenians	57,000	2.0%
religious subdivision:		
Sunni Muslims	2,668,000	93.6%
Greek Orthodox & other Christians	157,000	5.5%
Others	25,000	0.9%

GDP:
1986--$4.69 billion
1987--$4.98 billion

Balance of Payments (goods, services & unilateral transfer payments):

year	income	expenditure	balance
1986	$3.51 bil.	$3.55 bil.	-$ 40 mil.
1987	$3.62 bil.	$3.98 bil.	-$360 mil.

Defense Expenditure:
1987--$745 million (unconfirmed; including Arab aid)
1989--$850 million (unconfirmed)

Foreign Military Aid and Security Assistance Received:
financial aid from:
USA--$48 million grant (1990); $454 million Inter-Arab aid--grant (of which $360 million from Saudi Arabia); Japan--$100 million loan, for road construction
military training:
foreign advisors/instructors from--USA , USSR (a few); Egypt
trainees abroad in--Britain, Egypt, France, FRG, Pakistan, Saudi Arabia, USA, USSR
arms transfers from:
Australia (tank targets); Belgium (tank fire control systems); Brazil (APCs); Britain (bridging equipment, radars, ATRLs); France (combat aircraft, helicopters, AAMs, AGMs, artillery fire control systems, ATRLs); Spain (transport aircraft, trainer aircraft); USA (tanks, SP artillery, terminally guided artillery shells, ATGMs, AAGs, SAMs, helicopters); USSR (SAMs,

AAGs, APCs)
maintenance of equipment in:
FRG (transport aircraft)

Foreign Military Aid and Security Assistance Extended:
military training:
advisors/instructors in--Bahrain, Iraq, Kuwait, Oman, Qatar, UAE
foreign trainees from--Algeria, Bahrain, Iraq, Kuwait, Lebanon, Oman, PLO, Qatar, Saudi Arabia, Sudan, UAE, YAR
arms transfers to:
Iraq (ammunition); Badr unit of the PLA (small arms); Sudan (surplus obsolete arms)
facilities provided to:
Iraq (use of harbor, airfields and supply route, facility for joint fighter a/c squadron regularly stationed in Iraq); PLA (camp for Badr unit)

Cooperation in Arms Production/Assembly with:
Britain and USA (tank upgrading); USA (helicopter assembly)

Joint Maneuvers with:
USA (Special Forces, Air Force); Egypt; Britain; Iraq (training of a joint fighter aircraft squadron)

INFRASTRUCTURE

Road Network:

length:	7,500 km
paved roads	5,500 km
gravel and stone roads	2,000 km

main routes:
Amman--Ramtha--Dar'a (Syria)
Amman--Mafraq--Baghdad (Iraq)
Amman--Ma'an--Tabuk (Saudi Arabia)/Ma'an-- Aqaba
Amman--Allenby Bridge--Jerusalem (Israel)
Amman--al-Salt--Damiah Bridge--Nablus (West Bank)

Railway Network:

length (narrow gauge): 619 km

main routes:
Amman--Ramtha--Dar'a (Syria)
Amman--Ma'an--Aqaba/Ma'an--Haret Ammar (Saudi Arabian border)

Airfields:

airfields by runway type:	
permanent surface fields	14
unpaved fields and usable airstrips	5
airfields by runway length:	
over 3660 meters	2
2440--3659	14
1220--2439	1
under 1220	2

TOTAL	19

international airports: Amman (Queen Alia), Aqaba
major domestic airfields: Amman (Marka), Mafraq, Zarqa, Ma'an, H-5

Airlines:
companies: Royal Jordanian Airline (international and domestic)
aircraft:

Airbus A-310-300	4
Boeing 727-200	3
Boeing 707-320C	3
L-1011-500 Tristar	7

on order: 6 A-320 Airbus (delivery 1990); 3 additional A-310 (delivery 1989-90); 5 A-340 Airbus

Maritime Facilities:
harbors--Aqaba
oil terminals--Aqaba

Merchant Marine:

vessel type	number	DWT
Ro-ro	1	3,878
bulk carrier	2	43,832
TOTAL	3	47,710

Defense Production:
air force equipment:
assembly--Schweizer Model 330 helicopters, to begin 1990
optronics:
night vision devices (licenced production)

ARMED FORCES

Personnel:
military forces--(not all reserves are organized/ operational)

	regular	reserves	total
army	80,000	90,000	170,000
air force	9,700	--	9,700
navy	300	--	300
TOTAL	90,000	90,000	180,000

Army:
major units:

unit type	divisions	independent brigades
armored	2	
mechanized	2	
infantry		2
airborne/ special forces		1
TOTAL	4	3

para-military forces--
  one brigade of General Security Forces (gendarmerie)
  People's Army--40,000
small arms:
  personal weapons--
    7.62mm AK-47 (Kalashnikov) AR
    7.62mm G-3 (Heckler & Koch) AR
    5.56mm M-16 A1/A2 AR
  machine guns--
    12.7mm (0.5") Browning M2 HMG
    7.62mm (0.3") Browning M-1919 MMG
    7.62mm MAG (FN) LMG
    7.62mm M-60D GPMG/LMG
  light and medium mortars--
    81mm M-29
  light ATRLs--
    APILAS
    3.5" M-20 (being phased out)
    LAW-80

tanks: (including some in storage)

model	number
high quality	
Chieftain (Jordanian designation Khalid)	275
M-60 A3	100
(sub-total	375)
medium quality	
Centurion (improved, Jordanian designation Tariq)	290
M-60 A1	100
Chieftain (from Iran, captured by Iraq, in storage, not yet serviceable)	90
(sub-total	480)
low quality	
M-48 A1 (in storage, not operational)	260
TOTAL	1115

APCs/ARVs:

model	number
high quality	
BMP-2	25
M-113 A1/A2	1240
Engesa EE-11 (with Security Forces)	100
(sub-total	1365)
others	
Ferret	140
Saracen/Saladin (obsolete, in storage)	60
(sub-total	200)
TOTAL	1565

artillery:
  self propelled guns and howitzers--
    203mm M-110 A2 SP howitzer

155mm M-109 A2 SP howitzer	
155mm M-44 SP howitzer	
105mm M-52 howitzer	
towed guns and howitzers--	
203mm (8") M-115 gun	
155mm M-59 (Long Tom) gun	
155mm M-114 howitzer	
105mm M-102 A1 howitzer	
mortars, heavy, under 160mm--	
120mm mortar	
TOTAL	600
PGM--	
100 155mm Copperhead projectiles (CLGP)	
engineering equipment:	
bridges (British model)	
British mine-clearing ploughs and dozers attached to Chieftain and Centurion tanks	
AFV transporters: (unconfirmed)	200
anti-tank weapons:	
missiles--	launchers
BGM-71A TOW/BGM-71C Improved TOW	
M-47 Dragon	
M-901 ITV SP (TOW under armor)	
TOTAL	550
army anti-aircraft defenses:	
missiles--	launchers
self propelled/mobile	
MIM-43A Redeye	300
SA-8 (Gecko)	20
SA-13 (Gopher) SP	
man-portable	
SA-14 (Gremlin)	
short-range guns--	number
40mm M-42 SP (to be phased out)	+
23mm ZSU 23x4 SP (Gun Dish)	16
20mm M-163 A1 Vulcan SP	100
on order: Mistral SAMs (unconfirmed), 35mm 35x2 AAG (unconfirmed)	
CW capabilities:	
personal protective and decontamination equipment	

Air Force:

aircraft--general:	number
combat aircraft	107
transport aircraft	14
helicopters	68
combat aircraft:	
strike and multi-role aircraft--	
medium quality	
Mirage F-1 C/E	34

others
F-5 E/F 73
TOTAL 107
on order: 12 Mirage 2000 (delivery - end of 1990)

transport aircraft:
- Boeing 727 1
- C-130 Hercules 6
- CASA C-212 2
- Mystere Falcon 50 3
- Sabreliner 75A 2
- TOTAL 14
- on order: C-130; 1 CASA C-212; 2 CASA/Nurtanio CN-235

training and liaison aircraft:
- with ground attack/close air support capability--
  - CASA C-101 15
- others--
  - AS-202 Bravo 20
  - Cessna 318 (T-37) 10
  - BAe-SA-3-125 Bulldog 19
  - (sub-total 49)
- TOTAL 64

helicopters:
- attack--
  - AH-1G/1S Cobra 24
- medium transport--
  - S-76 18
  - UH-60A Black Hawk 3
  - AS-332 Super Puma 11
  - (sub-total 32)
- light transport--
  - Alouette III 1
  - 500 MG 8
  - MBB BO-105 (with Police) 3
  - BK-117 +
  - (sub-total 12)
- TOTAL 68
- on order: AS-332 Super Puma (unconfirmed)
- miscellaneous aircraft:
  - target drones--
  - on order: 82 TTL BTT-3 Banshee target drone, 2 launchers

advanced armament:
- air-to-air missiles--
  - AIM-9B/E/J/N/P Sidewinder
  - R-550 Magique
- air-to-ground missiles--
  - AS-30L
- bombs--
  - Belouga CBU
  - Durandal anti-runway bombs

anti-aircraft defenses:

radars--

model	units
AN/TPS-43	
AN/TPS-63	
Marconi S711	5

on order: Marconi radars (Britain)

long-range missiles--

model	batteries
MIM-23B Improved HAWK	14

aircraft shelters--
for all combat aircraft

military airfields: 6
Amman (Marka), Azrak, H-4, H-5, Ja'afar, Mafraq

aircraft maintenance and repair capability:
repair and maintenance of all models, possibly with French/American technical help

Navy:

combat vessels:	number
patrol craft--	
Bertram class (Enforcer)	
38 ft. (11.6 meter)	4

on order: 3 VT Hawk patrol boats, 3 12 meter patrol boats; all deliveries 1990

special maritime forces:
a few divers

naval base:
Aqaba

8. KUWAIT

BASIC DATA

Official Name of State: State of Kuwait
Head of State: Emir Jabir al-Ahmad al-Sabah
Prime Minister: Sa'ad Abdullah al-Sabah (also Crown Prince)
Minister of Defense: Nawaf al-Ahmad al-Jabir al-Sabah
Chief of the General Staff: Major General Mazyad Abd al-Rahman al-Sani
Commander of the Ground Forces: Colonel Abd al-Aziz al Barghash
Commander of the Air Force and Air Defense Forces: Brigadier General Daud al-Ghanim
Acting Commander of the Navy: Commander Kawas al-Salih
Area: 24,280 sq. km.

Population:		1,870,000
ethnic subdivision (number of aliens not reliable):		
Arabs	1,500,000	80.2%
Persians	94,000	5.0%
Southeast Asians	39,000	2.1%
Europeans	168,000	9.0%
Others	69,000	3.7%
religious subdivision:		
Sunni Muslims	1,029,000	55.0%
Shi'ite Muslims	561,000	30.0%
Christians, Parsis, Hindus and others	200,000	15.0%
nationality subdivision:		
Kuwaitis	729,000	39.0%
Aliens		
other Arabs	729,000	39.0%
Southeast Asians	168,000	9.0%
Iranians	76,000	4.0%
Others	168,000	9.0%

GDP:
1986--$17.12 billion
1987--$19.54 billion

Balance of Payments (goods, services & unilateral transfer payments):

year	income	expenditure	balance
1987	$15.22 bil.	$10.54 bil.	+$4.68 bil.
1988	$15.80 bil.	$11.09 bil.	+$4.71 bil.

Defense Expenditure:
1987--$1.40 billion (unconfirmed)
1989--$1.56 billion (unconfirmed)

Foreign Military Aid and Security Assistance Received:
military training received:
foreign advisors/instructors from--Algeria, Britain, Egypt, France, FRG, India, Jordan, Pakistan, USA,

USSR
trainees abroad in--Algeria, Britain, Egypt (400), France, FRG, Jordan, Pakistan, Saudi Arabia, UAE, USA, USSR
arms transfers from:
Austria (small arms); Britain (APCs, tanks, trainer aircraft, naval patrol craft, landing craft); Egypt (APCs, AA systems on order); France (radars, combat aircraft, helicopters, SP artillery, ATGMs); FRG (AFV transporters, MFPBs); Hungary (electronics, probably in collaboration with USSR, unconfirmed); Japan (tugs); USA (APCs, patrol boats, SAMs, combat aircraft on order); USSR (surface-to-surface rockets, SAMs, AAGs, APCs)

Foreign Military Aid and Security Assistance Extended:
financial aid to:
Iraq--grants and loans, old debt extended; Jordan--grant; Palestinian organizations--grants; Syria; Tunisia
military training:
foreign trainees from--Bahrain, Qatar (including student pilots), UAE
facilities provided to:
Iraq--use of harbors, wartime overflight rights for Iraqi aircraft, possibly continued

Joint Maneuvers with:
GCC (members: Bahrain, Kuwait, Oman, Qatar, Saudi Arabia, UAE)

INFRASTRUCTURE

Road Network:

length:	2,600 km
paved roads	2,300 km
gravel and improved earth roads	300 km

main routes:
Kuwait--al-Jahrah--Raudhatain--Basra (Iraq)
Kuwait--al-Jahrah--Hafar al-Batin (Saudi Arabia)
Kuwait--al-Ahmadi
Kuwait--Fahaheel--Mina al-Ahmadi--Mina Saud--Ras Tanura (Saudi Arabia)

Airfields:

airfields by runway type:	
permanent surface fields	4
airfields by runway length:	
2440--3659 meters	4
TOTAL	4

international airport: Kuwait
major domestic airfields: al-Ahmadi

Airlines:

companies: Kuwait Airways (international)

aircraft:

Airbus A-300 C4-600	1
Airbus A-310-200	5
Boeing 767-200ER	3
Boeing 747-200 combi	4
Boeing 727-200	3
Gulfstream III	2

on order: 4 Boeing 767-200ER

Maritime Facilities:

harbors--Shuwaikh (Kuwait City); Shuaiba, Mina al-Ahmadi
anchorage--Khor al-Mufatta
oil terminals--Mina al-Ahmadi/Sea Island; Mina Abdullah; Mina Saud (Zour)

Merchant Marine:

vessel type	number	DWT
crude carrier	2	176,101
gas tanker (LPG)	1	61,401
product tanker	7	306,270
asphalt tanker	1	4,225
bunkering tanker	1	18,949
chemical tanker	1	4,925
general cargo/container	16	379,091
container	5	155,471
livestock carrier	6	148,195
TOTAL	40	1,254,028

ARMED FORCES

Personnel:

military forces--

army	16,000-18,000
air force	2,200
navy	2,100
TOTAL	20,300-22,300

Army:

major units:

unit type	brigades
armored	1
mechanized	2
tactical reserve brigade	1
TOTAL	4

small arms:

personal weapons--
9mm Sterling Mk.4 SMG
7.62mm CAL/FAL (FN) SAR
7.62mm SSG-69 sniping rifle

machine guns--
7.62mm Browning M-1919 MMG
7.62mm MAG (FN) LMG

light and medium mortars--

81mm
tanks:
model | number
medium quality
Chieftain 165
Centurion 40
Vickers Mk.1 70
TOTAL 275
on order: 200-230 M-84
APCs/ARVs:
model | number
high quality
BMP-2 245
M-113
V-150 Commando
others
AT-105 Saxon
Saladin/Saracen/Ferret
Fahd 40
TOTAL 725
on order: 60 additional Fahd (delivery in progress)
artillery:
self propelled guns and howitzers--
155mm M-109 A2 SP howitzer 18
155mm Mk. F-3 (AMX) SP howitzer 40
TOTAL 58
MRLs--
on order: Soviet MRLs (unconfirmed); 7 US made MLRS
AFV transporters: 30
anti-tank weapons:
missiles--
AT-4 Spigot (unconfirmed)
BGM-71A Improved TOW
HOT
M-901 ITV (TOW under Armor) 56
M-47 Dragon
Vigilant
surface-to-surface missiles and rockets:
model | launchers
FROG-7 4
army anti-aircraft defenses:
missiles-- | launchers
self propelled/mobile
SA-8 (Gecko) 4
SA-9 (Gaskin)
man portable
SA-7 (Grail)

short-range guns--
40mm Bofors L-70/L-60
35mm Oerlikon-Buhrle 35x2 GDF-002
23mm ZSU 23x4 SP (Gun Dish)
20mm Oerlikon GAI
on order: Crotale SAMs (unconfirmed); 10 Skyguard (Amoun) air defense systems (3 batteries); additional 23x4, SA-14
CW capabilities:
personal protective equipment
decontamination units

Air Force:

	number
aircraft--general:	
combat aircraft	60
transport aircraft	7
helicopters	44
combat aircraft:	
strike and multi-role--	
medium quality	
Mirage F-1B/C	30
others	
A-4 KU/TA-4 KU Skyhawk II	30
TOTAL	60
on order: 40 F-18	
transport aircraft:	
Boeing 737-200	1
C-130-30 Hercules/L-100-30	4
DC-9	2
TOTAL	7
training and liaison aircraft:	
with ground attack/close air support capability--	
BAC-167 Strikemaster Mk.83	8
Hawk	12
TOTAL	20
on order: 16 S-312 Tucano (British made EMB-312)	
helicopters:	
attack--	
SA-342K Gazelle	28
medium transport--	
AS-332 Super Puma	6
SA-330 Puma	10
(sub-total	16)
TOTAL	44
on order: SA-365N maritime attack	
miscellaneous aircraft:	
target drones--	
TTL BTT-3 Banshee (unconfirmed)	

advanced armament:
  air-to-air missiles--
    AIM-9M Sidewinder
    R-550 Magique
    Super R-530D/F
  air-to-ground missiles--
    AS-11
    AS-12
    HOT (unconfirmed)
  on order: AM-39 Exocet air-to-ship missiles, 300 AGM-65G Maverick AGMs, 200 AIM-7 Sparrow AAMs, 120 AIM-9 Sidewinder AAMs
anti-aircraft defenses:
  radars--
    French-made radar
    AN/TPS-32
    AR-15
  on order: AN/TPS-63
  long-range missiles--

model	batteries
MIM-23B Improved HAWK	4

aircraft shelters:
  in both airfields, for combat aircraft
  on order: Shahine 2 (unconfirmed); SA-8
military airfields: 2
  al-Ahmadi (Ahmad al-Jaber AFB), al-Jahra (Ali al-Salem AFB)

Navy:

combat vessels:	number
MFPBs--	
Lurssen FPB-57	2
Lurssen TNC-45	6
Total	8
patrol craft--	
Halter Marine	1
Vosper Thornycroft 78 ft. (24 meter)	10
Vosper Thornycroft 56 ft. (17 meter)	5
Thornycroft 50 ft. (15 meter)	8
Vosper Thornycroft 36 ft. (11 meter)	8
Magnum Sedan 27.3 ft. (8.3 meter)	7
Seagull class	5
Total	44

  on order: 20 Magnum Sedan patrol boats; 5 additional Seagull PBs

landing craft:	
Loadmaster 350 ton LCT	4
Vosper 320 ton logistic support	3
Vosper Thornycroft 170 ton LCU	3

KUWAIT

TOTAL	10
on order: 6 SRN-6 hovercraft	
auxiliary vessels:	
tugs (Hayashikane)	2
tugs (Cheverton)	2
launch (Cheverton)	6
advanced armament:	
surface-to-surface missiles--	
MM-40 Exocet	
on order: additional MM-40 Exocet	
special maritime forces:	
Frogmen and divers	
naval bases:	
Kuwait City, Ras al-Qulayah	2
ship maintenance and repair capability:	
Kuwait City (Shuwaikh harbor)--190 meter floating dock; repair capacity 35,000 DWT	

9. LEBANON

BASIC DATA

Official Name of State: Republic of Lebanon

Head of State: President Elias al-Herawi (recognized by a part of the population)

Prime Ministers: Dr. Salim al-Houss (recognized by Muslims and Herawy supporters)

Defense Minister: Albert Mansour (loyal to Herawi)

Commander-in-Chief of the Armed Forces: Lieutenant General Michel Aoun (recognized by Christians); Admiral Emile Lahoud (loyal to al-Herawi)

Commander of the Air Force: Brigadier General Mahmoud Mater (loyal to Herawi)

Commander of the Navy: Rear Admiral Alberto al-Rharib (loyal to Christian PM Aoun)

Area: 10,452 sq.km.

Population: (estimate; all data uncertain)		3,100,000
ethnic subdivision:		
Arabs	2,805,500	90.5%
Armenians	139,500	4.5%
Kurds	46,500	1.5%
Others	108,500	3.5%
religious subdivision:		
Shi'ite Muslims	992,000	32.0%
Sunni Muslims	651,000	21.0%
Druze	186,000	6.0%
Alawis	31,000	1.0%
Christians		
Maronites	651,000	21.0%
Greek Orthodox	248,000	8.0%
Greek Catholic	155,000	5.0%
Armenians (Orthodox and Catholics)	124,000	4.0%
Others	62,000	2.0%
nationality subdivision:		
Lebanese	2,703,200	87.2%
Palestinians	350,300	11.3%
Others	46,500	1.5%

GDP:
- 1976--$3.29 billion
- 1977--$3.34 billion (latest year available)

Defense Expenditure:
- 1982--$272 million
- 1985--$229 million

Foreign Military Aid and Security Assistance Received:

financial aid from:

France--$1.16 million grant for trainees in France; FRG--grant (unconfirmed); Italy--loan; Saudi Arabia--

(at least $7 million); other Arab states--grant; Syria (to Herawi--grant); USA--$300,000 grant (1989)

military training:

foreign instructors/advisors from-- France (with army loyal to Christian government of Aoun); Iraq (with army loayl to Christian government of Aoun, unconfirmed, for a short period in 1989)

trainees abroad in-- France, Italy; Syria (Muslim officers from army units loyal to Muslim government of Herawi)

arms transfers from:

France (helicopters); Switzerland (AAGs, small arms); UAE (vehicles, small arms); Iraq (tanks, artillery to part of army loyal to Aoun and Lebanese Forces militia); Syria (tanks, artillery, MRLs to al-Amal and other militias)

Foreign Forces from:

Syria (30,000-40,000 in Biq'a, Tripoli area and Beirut); UNIFIL (5,800 in South Lebanon); Palestinian organizations (see Part II Chapter 13); limited (600) Israeli observation units in the security zone in South Lebanon; 1000 Islamic Revolution Guards Corps (IRGC) troops in the Syrian-held Biq'a

INFRASTRUCTURE

Road Network:

length:	7,370 km
paved roads	6,270 km
gravel and stone roads	450 km
improved earth tracks	650 km

main routes:

Beirut--Sidon--Tyre--Naqurah--Haifa (Israel)
Beirut--Tripoli--Tartus (Syria)/Homs (Syria)
Beirut--Zahlah--Ba'albek--Homs
Beirut--Shtaurah--Damascus (Syria)
Tyre--Bint J'bail
Zahlah--Shtaurah--Marj Ayoun--Metulla (Israel)
Marj Ayoun--Jezzin--Sidon
Ba'albek--Tripoli

Railway Network:

length: (partly not in use)	378 km
standard gauge	296 km
narrow gauge	82 km

main routes:

Beirut--Sidon
Beirut--Tripoli--Homs
Beirut--Zahlah--Rayaq--Homs/Rayaq--Damascus (narrow gauge)

Airfields:

airfields by runway type:

permanent surface fields	5
unpaved fields and usable airstrips	3

airfields by runway length:

2440--3659 meters	3
1220--2439	2
under 1220	3
TOTAL	8

international airports: Beirut

major domestic airfields: Rayaq, Kleiat, Khalat (landing strip)

Airlines:

companies: Middle East Airlines (international); Trans-Mediterranean Airways (cargo)

aircraft:

Boeing 747/747-200B Combi	3
Boeing 720B	4
Boeing 707-320C	15

Maritime Facilities:

harbors--Beirut, Juniah, Sidon, Tripoli, Tyre

anchorages--al-Abde, Chekka, Salata, al-Minya, al-Jiya, Naqura, Khalde, Sill al-Ouzai, 5 others

oil terminals--Sidon, Tripoli

Merchant Marine:

vessel type	number	DWT
general cargo	48	251,989
bulk carrier	6	146,273
livestock carrier	8	62,835
ro/ro	2	3,922
container	2	4,573
tanker	2	21,960
reefer	3	3,952
bitumen tanker	1	2,049
TOTAL	72	497,553

ARMED FORCES

Personnel:

military forces (estimate)--

army	34,000
air force	800
navy	500
TOTAL	35,300

(about 15,000 loyal to General Aoun, the balance to the Herawi government)

para-military forces--

gendarmerie	7,000

LEBANON

Army:

major units:

infantry & special forces (partly skeleton, undermanned or disorganized): 10 brigades

(1, 2, 6, 11 and 12 brigades loyal to Herawi. 5, 8, 9 and 10 brigades loyal to Aoun. 7 brigade commanded by Colonel Paul Faris is "neutral" in the Aoun-Herawi conflict)

small arms:

personal weapons--
- 9mm MAT 49 SMG
- 9mm Sterling SMG
- 7.62mm FAL (FN) SAR
- 7.5mm M-49/56 SAR
- 5.56mm CAL (FN) AR (unconfirmed)
- 5.56mm HK-33 (Heckler & Koch) AR
- 5.56mm M-16 A1 AR
- 5.56mm SG-540 AR

machine guns--
- 12.7mm (0.5") Browning M2 HMG
- 7.62mm (0.3") Browning M-1919 MMG
- 7.62mm MAG (FN) LMG
- 7.62mm M-60D GPMG
- 7.5mm AA-52 MMG
- 7.5mm Chatellerault M-24/29 LMG

light and medium mortars--
- 81mm Hotchkiss-Brandt
- 81mm M-29
- 60mm Hotchkiss-Brandt

light ATRLs--
- RPG-7
- 89mm M-65

tanks:

model	number
medium quality	
AMX-13/105mm gun	20
M-48 A1/M-48 A5	100
T-55 (unconfirmed)	40
(sub-total	160)
low quality	
AMX-13/75mm gun	30
M-3 (Panhard VTT)	
TOTAL	190

APCs/ARVs:

model	number
high quality	
AML 90	
AMX-VCI	
M-113 A1/A2	

VAB	95
V-150 Commando	
(sub-total	300)
others	
Saracén/Saladin	100
TOTAL	400
on order: 85 M-113/M-577 A1; VAB	
artillery:	
towed guns and howitzers--	
155mm M-198 howitzer	
155mm M-114 howitzer	
155mm M-50 howitzer	
122mm D-30	
105mm M-102 howitzer	
mortars, heavy, under 160mm--	
120mm Brandt M-50 & M-60 mortars	
TOTAL	180
anti-tank weapons:	
missiles--	launchers
BGM-71A TOW	
MILAN	
SS-11	
TOTAL	150-200
guns--	
106mm M-40 A2 recoilless rifle	
army anti-aircraft defenses:	
missiles--	
man-portable	
FIM-92A Stinger (unconfirmed, with Aoun's government)	
short-range guns--	
40mm M-42 SP	
20mm	

Air Force:

aircraft--general:	number
combat aircraft	14
transport aircraft	3
helicopters	31
combat aircraft:	
interceptors--	
medium quality	
Mirage III BL/EL (grounded)	10
strike and multi-role aircraft--	
low quality	
Hawker Hunter F-70/T-66 (controlled by Herawi)	4
transport aircraft:	
Hawker Siddeley Dove	1
Turbo-Commander 690B	2
TOTAL	3

training and liaison aircraft:
  with ground attack/close air support capability--
    CM-170 Fouga Magister 5
  others--
    BAe SA-3-120 Bulldog 5
  TOTAL 10
helicopters (some grounded):
  attack--
    SA-342 Gazelle 4
  medium transport--
    AB-212 0
    SA-330 Puma 9
(sub-total 17)
  light transport--
    Alouette II
    Alouette III
(sub-total 10)

TOTAL
31
advanced armament:
  air-to-air missiles--
    Matra R-530
military airfields: 5
  Rayaq, Kleiat, Khalat (landing strip), Beirut, Idma (helicopter port occupied by Lebanese Forces militia)
aircraft maintenance and repair capability:
  routine repairs for existing models

Navy:

combat vessels:	number
patrol craft--	
Ch. Navals de l'Esterel 124.7 ft. (38 meter)	1
Byblos class 66 ft. (20.1 meter)	3
Tracker II class	1
Aztec class (9 meter)	5
12 meter PB	4
TOTAL	14

note: additional patrol craft--see below, Lebanese Forces Militia

landing craft:
  EDIC class LCT 2
naval bases: 2
  Beirut, Juniah
ship maintenance and repair capability:
  a 55-meter slipway for light craft repairs

LEBANON

Non-Government Military Forces

military force/organization	armed personnel*
Lebanese Forces: Combination of various Christian militias (led by Samir Geagea)	10,000 (8,000 regulars +2,000 reserves)
Lebanese Forces splinter group (led by Eli Hobeiqa, under Syrian patronage)	a few hundred
Druze Community Forces, under Walid Jumblatt, and non-Druze followers	14,000 (4000 regulars + 10,000 reserves)
Al-Amal (Shi'ites)	7,000-8,000
Hizb Allah (pro-Iran Shi'ites)	5,000
Tripoli-based pro-Syrian militias (Arab Democratic Party Militia, also known as Farsan al-Arab, or Arab Cavalry)	a few hundred
Army of South Lebanon (pro-Israel, commanded by Major General Antoine Lahd)	2,500
Communist Labor Organization	a few hundred
"Giants" (Franjieh)	1,000
Islamic Unification Movement and Islamic Resistance (Tripoli)	a few hundred
Lebanese Communist Party	500
Socialist Arab Ba'ath Party (pro-Iraqi)	a few hundred
Socialist Arab Ba'ath Party (pro-Syrian)	a few hundred
Syrian Social Nationalist Party (SSNP; pro-Syrian terror and suicide squads)	1,000
Independent Nasserites (Murabitun)	a few hundred
Popular Nasserite Organization (in Sidon, led by Mustapha Saad)	

*All figures are estimated, with wide margins of error

LEBANON

Palestinian Organizations (see Part II/Ch.13, "Palestinian Military and Para-Military Forces")

Note: 1000 Iranian IRGC personnel in Lebanon--listed above under Foreign Forces

Tanks, APCs and Artillery in Non-Government Militias

militia	tanks	APCs	artillery pieces
Lebanese Forces	100 T-54, a few M-48 AMX-13 & Sherman	80 including M-113	100 including 155m and 130mm
Al-Amal	50 T-54/T-55, some AMX-13	a few M-113	a few 122mm; a few 130mm
Druze Community Forces	50 T-54, a few M-48	several score including M-113	several score including 122mm and 130mm guns, 122mm BM-21 MRLs and 107mm MRLs
Army of South Lebanon	45 Sherman & T-54	a few M-113	30 including 155mm
Hizb Allah		several M-113	several including 130mm

Aircraft:
Lebanese Forces--3 SA-342 Gazelle helicopters

Militias deploying naval vessels (patrol boats):
Lebanese Forces-about 25 vessels, including 2 Dvorah patrol boats, 1 18 meter patrol craft, 1 tracker II, and about 20 small boats of up to 10 meter

10. LIBYA

BASIC DATA

Official Name of State: The Great Socialist People's Libyan Arab Jamahiriya (Jamahiriya is an Arabic term, meaning "public" or "polity of the masses")

Head of State (leader; does not hold any other title) Colonel Muammar al-Qaddafi (in practice also in charge of the Defense Ministry and Commander-in-Chief of the Armed Forces)

Deputy Head of State (second in the hierarchy; equivalent to Prime Minister): Major Abd al-Sallam Jallud

Secretary-General of the General People's Committee (equivalent to the Cabinet): Zaydallah Aziz al-Salihi

Commander-in-Chief of the Armed Forces: Colonel Abu-Bakr Yunis Jaber

Chief of Staff of the Army: Colonel Faraj al-Hidayri

Inspector General of the Armed Forces: Colonel Mustapha al-Kharrubi

Commander of the Air Force: Colonel Salih Abdullah Salih

Commander of the Navy: Captain Abdullah al-Latif al-Shakshuki

Area: 1,759,540 sq. km.

Population:		4,230,000
ethnic subdivision:		
Arabs	3,904,000	92.3%
Berbers	169,000	4.0%
Black Africans	106,000	2.5%
Europeans and others	51,000	1.2%
religious subdivision:		
Sunni Muslims	4,103,000	97.0%
Christians	127,000	3.0%
nationality subdivision:		
Libyans	3,693,000	87.3%
Egyptians	351,000	8.3%
Tunisians	102,000	2.4%
Others	84,000	2.0%

GDP:

1985--$24.33 billion
1986--$20.62 billion

Balance of Payments (goods, services & unilateral transfer payments):

year	income	expenditure	balance
1985	$10.88 bil.	$ 8.80 bil.	+$2.08 bil.
1986	$ 6.44 bil.	$ 6.60 bil.	-$160 mil.

Defense Expenditure:

1988--$1.20 billion (unconfirmed)
1989--$1.20 billion (unconfirmed)

LIBYA

Foreign Military Aid and Security Assistance Received:

military training:

foreign advisors/instructors/serving personnel from--Britain (non-governmental technicians); Cuba; France; Italy; North Korea; Pakistan; Palestinian personnel from PFLP-GC; Syria (pilots); USSR and East European countries; GDR (200 until January 1990, 50 since then); Yugoslavia; Indians and other foreigners residing in Libya drafted into armed forces

trainees abroad in--USSR, other East European countries; France (unconfirmed); Italy; Netherlands (civil aircraft pilots); Portugal (unconfirmed); Sweden; Syria; Turkey (unconfirmed); Yugoslavia (unconfirmed); Egypt (unconfirmed)

arms transfers from:

Austria (artillery pieces, possibly for Iran, unconfirmed; small arms); Brazil (APCs, ARVs; light transport aircraft, maritime surveillance aircraft, and MRLs, unconfirmed); Czechoslovakia (trainer and transport aircraft); France (spare parts for French-made systems, three combat aircraft); FRG (floating dock); company from FRG: aerial refuelling systems; Greece (spare parts for American and French-made aircraft, unconfirmed); Italy (electronics, spares for aircraft) ; Netherlands (transport aircraft); Spain (recoilless rifles, unconfirmed; ammunition); Sweden (explosives); Turkey (LST, patrol boats); USSR (combat aircraft, tanks, SAMs, SSMs, missile corvettes, naval mines); Yugoslavia (trainer aircraft)

maintenance performed abroad in:

Malta (for corvettes); France (SAMs); Poland (landing craft); Italy (aircraft, helicopter engines)

construction aid by:

India (airfields)

Foreign Military Aid and Security Assistance Extended:

financial aid to:

BR (Italy, unconfirmed); Chadian CDR group (opposed to government) until Dec. 1989; ETA (Basque separatists, Spain)--grant; IRA (Irish Republican Army); Iran; various Lebanese militias; M-19 (Colombian anti-government group); MORO Front (Philippine Muslims); "Nasserite Egyptian Revolution" (Egyptian anti-government group); Palestinian organizations (PFLP-GC and Abu Musa faction of Fatah); Sudan--grant (money and oil); Syria--grant

military training:

advisors/instructors/serving personnel in--Sudan; Surinam (100, number unconfirmed); Uganda; Nicaragua (unconfirmed)

foreign trainees from--Abu Musa faction of Fatah and

PFLP-GC groups; ANC and PAC (South African anti-government organizations); Burkina Faso; Chad anti-government rebels; Dominican Republic anti-government rebels; ETA; Kanak (anti-French Socialist National Liberation Front of New Caledonia, unconfirmed); Malta (unconfirmed); MORO Front; Reunion (MIR, Movement for Independence of Reunion, a French-governed island in the Indian Ocean, unconfirmed); SWAPO (Namibian anti-government guerrillas); Syria (pilots); "African Islamic Foreign Legion" (anti-government personnel from Gambia, Senegal, Mali & Niger); Yemeni, Egyptian, Sudanese, Tunisian, and Iraqi anti-government groups

arms transfers to:

Burkina Faso (Brazilian-made ARVs, Italian-made trainer aircraft); Chile anti-government groups (unconfirmed); Egypt (Czech-made trainer aircraft, a gift); Iran (APCs, ARVs, other Soviet weapons; Soviet-made SSMs; Austrian artillery, unconfirmed); IRA (small arms, HMGs; SA-7 missiles--unconfirmed); Kurdish rebels in Iraq (small arms); Nicaragua (small arms, unconfirmed); Palestinian military organizations (MRLs, SAMs, artillery pieces); Somali anti-government guerrillas (small arms); Sudan (small arms, aircraft spares, combat aircraft); SWAPO (small arms); Syria (Soviet AAMs); Togo (Brazilian ARVs)

facilities provided to:

Chad anti-government organizations (camps); Palestinian organizations (PFLP-GC, camps, until September 1989); USSR (use of naval bases at Bardiyah & Tobruk, unconfirmed; use of Ouqba ben Nafi AFB, unconfirmed)

forces deployed abroad in:

Chad--troops with the anti-Habre rebels in northern Chad; Sudan--a few aircraft supporting Sudanese forces in Southern Sudan, 3,000 soldiers in Western Sudan (Darfur province)

Joint Maneuvers with:

USSR (naval maneuvers)

Cooperation in Arms Production/Assembly with:

companies from FRG and Japan (toxic gas); Italy (assembly of light aircraft, unconfirmed); upgrading SSMs, possibly development of SSMs, with individual experts hired mainly from FRG

INFRASTRUCTURE

Road Network:

length:	19,300 km
paved roads	10,800 km
gravel, stone & improved earth roads	8,500 km

main routes:

Tripoli--Benghazi--Tobruk--Bardiyah
Tripoli--Misratah (Misurata)--Waddan--Sabha (Sebha)--Marzuq (Murzuq)
Tripoli--Tunis (Tunisia)
Tripoli--Ghadams (Ghadames)--Ghat
Tobruk--Alexandria (Egypt)
Benghazi--Zighan--Kufra
Tripoli--Nalut--Sabha
Sabha--Ghat
Tobruk--Jaghbud
Bardiyah--Jaghbud

Airfields:

airfields by runway type:

permanent surface fields	48
unpaved fields and usable airstrips	67

airfields by runway length:

over 3660 meters	6
2440--3659	28
1220--2439	39
under 1220	42
TOTAL	115

international airports: Tripoli, Benghazi (Baninah)
major domestic airfields: Ghadams (Ghadames), Ghat, Kufra, Marsa al-Brega, Misratah, Sabha, Surt (Sidra, Sirt), Tobruk

Airlines:

companies: Jamahiriya Libyan Arab Airlines (international, domestic, cargo and charter)

aircraft:

Airbus A-310	2
Boeing 727-200	10
Boeing 707-320C	5
DHC-6 Twin Otter	5
Fokker F-27-600/500/400	16
Fokker F-28-4000 (including a/c on lease)	3
Ilyushin IL-76T	21
L-100-20	4

on order: 3 Tu-154M (unconfirmed)

Maritime Facilities:

harbors--Benghazi, Derna, Misratah, Tobruk, Tripoli
anchorages--Kasr Ahmed
oil terminals--Surt (Sidra), Marsa al-Brega, Marsa al-Hairqa (Tobruk), Ras Lanuf, Zawiyah, Zueitinah

Merchant Marine:

vessel type	number	DWT
crude carrier	8	1,032,273
product tanker	2	61,315
general cargo	5	28,950
general cargo/container	6	58,635
ferry	3	10,807

ro/ro	4	12,059
chemical tanker	1	5,390
TOTAL	29	1,209,429

Defense Production:

army equipment:

toxic gas

aircraft and air ammunition:

assembly of a light aircraft (assisted by foreign experts hired individually)

ARMED FORCES

Personnel:

military forces--

	regular	reserves	total
army	85,000	30,000	115,000
air force	9,000		9,000
navy	8,000		6,500
TOTAL	102,000	30,000	132,000

para-military forces--

"People's Resistance"--one battalion

Army:

major units:

unit type	divisions	brigades	independent battalions
armored/tank	2-3	2	3
mechanized/ infantry	2-4	2	8
paratroop			13
Republican Guard		1	
TOTAL	5-7	5	24

small arms:

personal weapons--

9mm Model 12 Beretta SMG
9mm L-34 A1 SMG
7.62mm AK-47 (Kalashnikov) AR
7.62mm SKS (Simonov) SAR
7.62mm FAL (FN) SAR
5.45mm AK-74 (Kalashnikov) AR

machine guns--

12.7mm D.Sh.K. 38/46 (Degtyarev) HMG
7.62mm MAG (FN) LMG
7.62mm PK/PKS (Kalashnikov) LMG
7.62mm RPD (Degtyarev) LMG
7.62mm SGM (Goryunov) MMG

light and medium mortars--

82mm M-43

light ATRLs--

RPG-7

LIBYA

tanks:

model	number
high quality	
T-72	300
medium quality	
T-62	800
T-55	1500
(sub-total	2300)
TOTAL (including about 1500 in storage)	2600

APCs/ARVs:

model	number
high quality	
BMP-1/BMP-2	800
Engesa EE-9/11	300
Fiat Type 6614/6616	100-200
M-113 A1	100-200
others	
BTR-50/60	
BRDM-2	
OT-62	
OT-64	
Saladin	
TOTAL (approximately 2/3 high quality, about half in storage)	2000
on order: EE-9/11	

artillery:

self propelled guns and howitzers--	
155mm M-109 SP howitzer	18
155mm Palmaria SP howitzer	200
152mm M-1973 SP howitzer	
122mm M-1974 SP howitzer	
towed guns and howitzers--	
155mm GHN-45 howitzer (possibly transferred to Iran, unconfirmed)	
152mm M-1943 howitzer	
130mm M-46 gun	
122mm D-30 howitzer	
122mm M-1938 howitzer	
105mm M-101 howitzer	
mortars, heavy, over 160mm--	
240mm mortar	
160mm mortar	
mortars, heavy, under 160mm	
120mm mortar	
TOTAL	2000
MRLs--	
140mm	
130mm M-51	
122mm BM-21/RM-70	

107mm Type 63	
on order: 155mm Palmaria SP howitzer; 180mm SS-40 Astros II MRL	
AFV transporters:	1000
anti-tank weapons:	
missiles--	launchers
AT-3 (Sagger)	
AT-4 (Spigot)	
AT-5 (Spandrel)	
BRDM-2 carrying AT-3 (Sagger) SP	
MILAN	
SS-11	
Vigilant	
TOTAL	2000
guns--	
106mm recoilless rifle	
surface-to-surface missiles and rockets:	
model	launchers
FROG-7	28
SS-1 (Scud B)	72
TOTAL	100
army anti-aircraft defenses:	
missiles--	launchers
self propelled/mobile	
Crotale	30
SA-6 (Gainful)	100
SA-8 (Gecko)	20
SA-9 (Gaskin)	60
SA-13 (Gopher)	
man portable	
SA-7 (Grail)	
SA-14 (Gremlin)	
short-range guns--	number
57mm	
40mm Bofors L-70	
30mm 30x2 M-53/59 SP	
23mm ZSU 23x4 SP (Gun Dish)	
23mm ZU 23x2	
TOTAL	450
on order: 30mm Artemis (unconfirmed)	
CW capabilities:	
personal protective equipment, Soviet type	
decontamination units	
ABC protection of SSM sites	
stockpile of gases, including mustard; Sarin (unconfirmed)	

Air Force:

aircraft--general:	number
combat aircraft (some in storage)	543

transport aircraft	139+
helicopters	177
combat aircraft:	
interceptors--	
high quality	
MiG-25 and MiG-25R (Foxbat)	80
medium quality	
MiG-21 bis (Fishbed)	50
Total	130
strike and multi-role aircraft--	
high quality	
Su-24 (Fencer C)	6
medium quality	
MiG-23/27 (Flogger, incl. MiG-23G)	190
Su-20/22 (Fitter C)	100
Mirage F-1	30
Mirage 5	80
(sub-total	400)
Total	406
on order: MiG-29; 9 Su-24	
bombers--	
Tu-22 (Blinder)	7
transport aircraft:	
An-26 (Curl)	36
Boeing 707	1
C-130H Hercules/L-100-20/L-100-30	10
C-140 Jetstar	1
DHC-6 Twin Otter	10
Fokker F-27-600	8
Fokker F-28 (unconfirmed)	a few
G-222L	20
IL-76 (Candid)	28
L-410 UVP	19
Mystere Falcon 20	6
TOTAL	139+
on order: 25 EMB-121	
training and liaison aircraft (some in storage):	
with ground attack/close air support capability--	
G-2AE Galeb/J-1 Jastreb	150
L-39 Albatross	170
(sub-total	320)
others--	
SIAI--Marchetti SF-260 M/L	150
TOTAL	470
helicopters:	number
attack--	
Mi-24/Mi-25 (Hind, number unconfirmed)	40
heavy transport--	
CH-47C Chinook	18
SA-321 Super Frelon (also	

employed in ASW role) 8
(sub-total 26)
medium transport--
AB-212 5
Mi-2 (Hoplite) 35
Mi-8/Mi-17 (Hip) 25
(sub-total 65)
light transport--
Alouette III 12
AB-206 JetRanger 5
(sub-total 17)
ASW--
Mi-14 (Haze) 29
TOTAL 177
advanced armament:
air-to-air missiles--
AA-2 (Atoll)
AA-6 (Acrid)
AA-7 (Apex)
AA-8 (Aphid)
R-550 Magique
Super 530D/F
air-to-ground missiles--
AS-14 (Kedge)
AT-2 (Swatter)
AT-6 (Spiral)
anti-aircraft defenses:
radars--
Square Pair
long-range missiles-- (some in storage)

model		batteries
SA-2 (Guideline) & SA-3 (Goa)		93
SA-5 (Gammon)		6
TOTAL	(unconfirmed)	99

on order: additional SA-5 (possibly delivered)
aircraft shelters--
for combat aircraft
military airfields: 18
al-Adem , al-Bayda, Benghazi (Baninah), Beni Walid, al-Bumbah, Ghurdabiyah (Sirte), Jufra, Kufra, Ma'atan al-Sarra, Misratha, Mu'atiga, Ouqba ben Nafi (al-Watiyah), Ouzu, Sabhah, Tripoli International, al-Watiyah, Zawiyah, 2 additional
aircraft maintenance and repair capability:
foreign technicians employed for all models

Navy:

combat vessels: number
submarines--
F class (Foxtrot) 6

LIBYA

MFPBs--	
Combattante II	9
Ossa II	12
Susa (Vosper 100 ft.)	3
Total	24
missile frigates--	
Vosper Thornycroft Mk.7	1
Koni (with SS-N-2C SSMs; usually in ASW role)	2
(sub-total	3)
missile corvettes--	
Assad class (formerly Wadi class)	4
Nanuchka class	3
Total	7
gun corvettes--	
Vosper Thornycroft Mk.1B (Tobruk)	1
mine warfare vessels--	
Natya class minesweepers	8
patrol craft--	
Garian class	4
Poluchat	1
Thornycroft 100 ft. (30.5 meter)	3
Thornycroft 78 ft. (23.5 meter)	1
SAR-33	14
Total	23
on order: 4 Rade Koncar MFPBs	
landing craft:	
C-107 LCT	2
PS-700 class LST	2
Polnochny class LCT	3
TOTAL	7
auxiliary vessels:	
LSD-1 class logistic support ship	1
maintenance & repair craft, ex-British LCT	1
Mala midget submarine	6
remotely controlled explosive motor craft	50-125
ro/ro transport ship, 3100 ton	1
Yelva diving-support ship	1
advanced armament:	
surface-to-surface missiles--	
OTOMAT Mk.2	
SS-N-2 Styx/SS-N-2C	
SS-12	
surface-to-air missiles--	
Seacat	
Aspide	
SA-N-4	
mines--	
Soviet-made acoustic mines; magnetic mines	

(unconfirmed)

naval bases: 6

al-Khums, Benghazi, Misratah, Ras Hillal, Tobruk, Tripoli

ship maintenance and repair capability:

facilities at Tripoli with foreign technicians for repair of vessels up to 6000 DWT; a 3200 ton lift floating dock; and floating docks at Benghazi and Tobruk

11. MOROCCO

BASIC DATA

Official Name of State: Kingdom of Morocco

Head of State: King Hassan II (also Minister of Defense, Commander-in-Chief of the Armed Forces and Chief of the General Staff)

Prime Minister: Azzedine Laraki

Inspector General of the Armed Forces: General Idriss Bin-Issa

Commander of the Air Force: Major General Muhammad Kabaj

Inspector of the Navy: Captain Lahcen Ouhirra

Area: 622,012 sq. km., including the former Spanish Sahara (409,200 sq. km. excluding this territory)

Population:		23,910,000
ethnic subdivision:		
Arabs	14,250,000	59.6%
Berbers	9,444,000	39.5%
Europeans and others	216,000	0.9%
religious subdivision:		
Sunni Muslims	23,599,000	98.7%
Christians	263,000	1.1%
Jews	48,000	0.2%

GDP:
- 1985--$11.85 billion
- 1986--$14.76 billion

Balance of Payments (goods, services & unilateral transfer payments):

year	income	expenditure	balance
1987	$5.96 bil.	$5.79 bil.	+$170 mil.
1988	$7.01 bil.	$6.55 bil.	+$460 mil.

Defense Expenditure:
- 1986--$750 million
- 1987--$850 million

Foreign Military Aid and Security Assistance Received:

financial aid from:

Saudi Arabia--grant; Kuwait, Qatar, UAE--grants, finance of purchase of 24 Mirage 2000s from France and various arms from Spain; USA--$42.8 million grant (1990)

military training:

foreign advisors/instructors from--USA, Belgium, France; Egypt (unconfirmed)

trainees abroad in--USA, Belgium, France, Spain; Egypt (unconfirmed)

arms transfers from:

Austria (recovery vehicles, tanks); Brazil (APCs); Britain (artillery pieces); Canada (jeeps); Egypt (mortars; APCs on order, unconfirmed); France (ATGMs, combat aircraft, naval SSMs, naval vessels, tank transporters); FRG (light transport aircraft); Italy (helicopters, vehicles and mines, shipborne SAMs); South Africa (APCs); Spain (AFVs, mortars, MRLs, naval vessels, electronic equipment, night vision devices, communications equipment); Switzerland (trainer aircraft); USA (ATGMs, SAMs, tanks, tank transporters)

maintenance of equipment in:
France (aircraft)

construction aid by:
USA (improving airfields)

Foreign Military Aid and Security Assistance Extended:

military training:
advisors/instructors/serving personnel in--Iraq (unconfirmed), UAE
foreign trainees from--Angola (UNITA, anti-government group in Angola, unconfirmed)

facilities provided to:
USA (use of Sidi Slimane, Ben Guerir [Marrakech] and Casablanca airfields in emergencies; permission for space shuttle to land at Benguerir AFB; use of communications center at Kenitra; storage and use of naval facilities at Mohammedia)

Joint Maneuvers with:
Belgium (joint training of pilots in both countries), France, Spain, USA

Cooperation in Arms Production/Assembly with:
Portugal (aircraft industry, overhauls and production of a light trainer aircraft, unconfirmed)

INFRASTRUCTURE

Road Network:

length:	58,000 km
paved roads	25,750 km
gravel, crushed stone roads and earth tracks	32,250 km

main routes:
Rabat--Tangier
Tangier--Tetouan--Nador--Oran (Algeria)
Ceuta--Tetouan--Kenitra--Rabat
Rabat--Meknes--Fez--Oujda--Oran
Oujda--Bouarfa--Bechar (Algeria)
Rabat--Casablanca--Marrakech
Casablanca--Safi--Agadir--Tarfaya--L'Ayoun--Bir Moghreim (Mauritania)

Railway Network:

length (standard gauge):	1,891 km

main routes:
Rabat--Casablanca--Marrakech

Rabat--Sidi Kacem--Tangier
Rabat--Sidi Kacem--Meknes--Fez--Oujda--Sidi-bel-Abbes (Algeria)

Airfields:

airfields by runway type:

permanent surface fields	26
unpaved fields and usable airstrips	45

airfields by runway length:

over 3660 meters	2
2440--3659	14
1220--2439	28
under 1220	27
TOTAL	71

international airports: Agadir, Casablanca (Nouasseur), Fez, Marrakech, Oujda, Rabat (Sale), Tangier
major domestic airfields: L'Ayoun, Casablanca (Arfa), Ouarzazate, Sidi Ifni, Smara-Ferduja, Tantan, Tarfaya

Airlines:

companies: Royal Air Maroc (international & domestic)
aircraft:

Boeing 757-200	2
Boeing 747-200 Combi/747SP	2
Boeing 737-200/737-200C	7
Boeing 727-200	8
Boeing 707-320C	2

on order: 10 Boeing 737-400/500, delivery 1990-94; 3 ATR-42

Maritime Facilities:

harbors--Agadir, L'Ayoun (Fousbucra Port), Casablanca, El Jedida/Jorf al-Asfar, Kenitra, Mohammedia, Nador, Safi, Tangier
anchorages--Essaouira (Mogador), Larache, Martil (Tetouan)
oil terminals--Agadir, Kenitra, Mohammedia, Safi

Merchant Marine:

vessel type	number	DWT
crude carrier	1	6,211
small tanker	2	12,254
chemical tanker	14	216,742
general cargo	3	7,421
bulk carrier	4	163,291
reefer	13	75,999
passenger/cargo	1	1,398
ferry	1	3,180
ro/ro	3	11,082
general cargo/container	6	20,627
TOTAL	48	518,205

MOROCCO

Defense Production:

army equipment:

small arms ammunition; assembly of trucks

aircraft and air ammunition:

trainer aircraft

ARMED FORCES

Personnel:

military forces--

army	170,000
air force	15,000
navy and marines	6,000
Total	191,000

para-military forces-

gendarmerie--8,000; internal security forces--3,000

Army:

major units:

unit type	brigades/ regiments	indep. battalions	indep. companies
armored		5	
mechanized	4	1	
infantry	4		
camel corps		10	
desert cavalry	(unconfirmed)	1	
paratroops	1		
commando		3	
armored car			4
TOTAL	9	20	4

small arms:

personal weapons--

9mm MAT 49/56 SMG
9mm Model 38/49 Beretta SMG
7.62mm AK-47 (Kalashnikov) AR
7.62mm G-3 AR
7.5mm MAS 49/56 SAR

machine guns--

14.5mm ZPU 14.5x4 HMG (in anti-aircraft role)
14.5mm ZPU 14.5x2 HMG (in anti-aircraft role)
12.7mm (0.5") Browning M2 HMG
7.62mm M-60 D GPMG
7.62mm MAG (FN) LMG
7.62mm RPD (Degtyarev) LMG
7.5mm AA-52 MMG
7.5mm Chatellerault M-24/29 LMG

light and medium mortars--

82mm M-43
81mm ECIA

81mm M-29
60mm M-2
light ATRLs--
RPG-7
89mm Strim-89
3.5" M-20 (Bazooka)

tanks:

model		number
medium quality		
M-48 A5		110
SK-105 (Kurassier)		80
	(sub-total	190)
low quality		
AMX-13		50
T-54		10
	(sub-total	60)
TOTAL		250

on order: 108 M-60 A3; M-48 A5; SK-105 (Kurassier)

APCs/ARVs:

model		number
high quality		
AMX-10RCM		37
Engesa EE-9/EE-11 (unconfirmed)		60
M-113 A1/A2		460
M-3 (Panhard, unconfirmed)		
Ratel 20/90		60
Steyr 4K 7FA (unconfirmed)		
VAB		394
	(sub-total	+1011)
others		
AML-90/AML-60		200
EBR-75		25
Eland		+
M-3 half-track		100
M-8 ARV		55
OT-62		50
UR-416		15
	(sub-total	445)
TOTAL		1456+

on order: 140 M-113, additional AMX-10RCM; Fahd (unconfirmed)

artillery:

	number
self propelled guns and howitzers--	
155mm M-109 A1 SP howitzer	56
155mm Mk. F-3 (AMX) SP howitzer	48
105mm Mk. 61 SP howitzer	24
100mm SU-100 SP gun	
towed guns and howitzers--	
155mm M-114 howitzer	70
152mm howitzer	12

Item	Number
130mm M-46 gun	12
105mm Light Gun	36
105mm M-101 howitzer	
85mm M-1945/D-44 field/AT gun	
mortars, heavy, under 160mm	
120mm mortar	
TOTAL	410
MRLs--	
140mm Teruel	
122mm BM-21	36
anti-tank weapons:	
missiles--	
AT-3 (Sagger)	
BGM-71A TOW	
HOT/HOT Commando	
M-47 Dragon	480
MILAN	82
TOTAL	1000
guns--	
106mm M-40 A2 recoilless rifle	
90mm recoilless rifle	
army anti-aircraft defenses:	
missiles--	launchers
self propelled/mobile	
MIM-72A Chaparral	36
man-portable	
SA-7 (Grail)	
short-range guns--	number
57mm M-1950 (S-60)	
37mm M-1939	35
23mm ZU 23x2	200
20mm M-163 Vulcan SP	55
20mm	
TOTAL	290+

Air Force:

Item	Number
aircraft--general:	number
combat aircraft	67
transport aircraft	48
helicopters	151
combat aircraft:	
strike and multi-role aircraft--	
medium quality	
Mirage F-1/F-2B	34
others	
F-5E/F-5F	20
F-5A/B	10
RF-5E	3
(sub-total	33)
TOTAL	67

MOROCCO

on order: 10 Mirage F-1; F-16 (unconfirmed)	
transport aircraft:	
Beechcraft King Air	9
C-119 (not serviceable)	5
C-130H Hercules (including C-130H with SLAR, employed for electronic surveillance)	17
DC-3 Dakota (C-47)	8
Dornier DO-28 D-2	3
Gulfstream	1
KC-130 refuelling	3
Mystere Falcon 20	2
TOTAL	48
on order: 7 CN-235	
training and liaison aircraft:	
with ground attack/close air support capability--	
Alpha Jet	22
CM-170 Fouga Magister	22
(sub-total	44)
others--	
AS-202/18A Bravo	12
Beechcraft T-34C	12
Broussard	9
(sub-total	33
TOTAL	77
on order: 20 Gepal IV; Bragg ultra-light aircraft (unconfirmed)	
helicopters:	
attack--	
SA-342 Gazelle	25
heavy transport--	
CH-47C Chinook	12
medium transport--	
AB-212	11
AB-205	30
Kaman HH-43B Huskie	4
SA-330 Puma	36
(sub-total	81)
light transport--	
Alouette III	8
AB-206 JetRanger	23
SA-315B Lama	2
(sub-total	33)
TOTAL	151
on order: SA-342; AB-206; 24 500MG or 530MG	
miscellaneous aircraft:	
counter insurgency--	
OV-10 Bronco	4
RPVs and mini-RPVs--	
Skyeye R4E-50 mini-RPV	

advanced armament:
  air-to-air missiles--
    AIM-9J Sidewinder 320
    R-530
    R-550 Magique
    Super 530D
  air-to-ground missiles--
    AGM-65 Maverick 380
    HOT
anti-aircraft defenses:
  radars--
    AN/TPS-43 16
    AN/TPS-63
  long-range guns--
    100mm M-49 (possibly no longer in service)
military airfields: 12
  Agadir, Ben Guerir, Casablanca (Nouasseur), Fez, Kenitra, Larache, L'Ayoun, Marrakech, Meknes, Oujda, Rabat, Sidi Slimane
aircraft maintenance and repair capability:
  for all existing models

Navy:

combat vessels:	number
MFPBs--	
Lazaga	4
missile frigates--	
Descubierta	1
mine warfare vessels--	
Sirius class	1
gunboats/MTBs--	
PR-72 class	2
P-200D Vigilance (Cormoran)	6
Total	8
patrol craft--	
P-32	6
VC large patrol craft	1
Le Fougeux (modified), 53 meter	1
CMN 40.6 meter	1
Acror 46 (with customs)	18
Osprey-55	2
Total	32

on order: 2 additional Osprey-55 (Fredrickshavn Vaerft) gunboats, delivery 1990; 4 P-32 patrol boats; an additional Descubierta missile frigate (unconfirmed, possibly two frigates)

landing craft:	
Batral LSL	3
EDIC LCT	1

MOROCCO

TOTAL	4
auxiliary vessels:	
Cargo ship, 1500 GRT	2
advanced armament:	
surface-to-surface missiles--	
MM-40 Exocet	
MM-38 Exocet	
naval bases:	6
Agadir, Casablanca, Kenitra, Dakhla, Safi, Tangier	
ship maintenance and repair capability:	
at Casablanca--156 meter dry-dock, repairs up to 10,000 DWT; at Agadir--minor repairs	

12. OMAN

BASIC DATA

Official Name of State: Sultanate of Oman

Head of State: Sultan Qabus bin Said (also Prime Minister and Minister of Defense)

Deputy Prime Minister for Security and Defense: Fahr ibn Taymur al-Bu-Said

Minister of State for Defense: Brigadier General Mutasim Ibd Hamud al-Bu-Saidi

Chief of the General Staff: Lieutenant General Hamad Ibn Said al-Aufi

Commander of the Ground Forces: Major General Khamis Ibn Hamid al-Kalabani

Commander of the Air Force: Major General Erik P. Bennett (unconfirmed); Acting Commander of the Air Force: Brigadier General Talib Bin Marin

Commander of the Navy: Rear Admiral H.M. Balfour

Area: 212,200 sq.km.

Population:		1,380,000
ethnic subdivision:		
Arabs	1,205,000	90.6%
Others (Africans, Persians, Southeast Asians)	125,000	9.4%
religious subdivision:		
Ibadi Muslims (Kharadjites)	1,035,000	75.0%
Sunni Muslims	259,000	18.8%
Shi'ite Muslims, Hindus	86,000	6.2%

GDP:

1985--$10.01 billion

1986--$7.28 billion

Balance of Payments (goods, services, & unilateral transfer payments):

year	income	expenditure	balance
1986	$3.47 bil.	$4.49 bil.	-$1.02 bil.
1987	$4.35 bil.	$3.49 bil.	+$860 mil.

Defense Expenditure:

1989--$1.3 billion

1990--$1.4 billion

Foreign Military Aid and Security Assistance Received:

financial aid from:

Saudi Arabia--grant

military training:

foreign advisors/instructors/serving personnel from--Britain (several hundred officers and NCOs, 200 of whom are seconded from the British forces, the balance hired on a personal basis); Egypt; Jordan; Pakistan; USA

trainees abroad in--Britain, France, FRG, Jordan, Saudi Arabia
arms transfers from:
Austria (small arms); Britain (tanks, artillery pieces, combat aircraft, training aircraft, aircraft radars and navigation systems, MFPBs, landing ship, radars, target drones); Egypt (jeeps, APCs); France (ATGMs, AAMs, naval SSMs); USA (AAMs, SP artillery)
Foreign Military Aid and Security Assistance Extended:
financial aid to:
PLO (unconfirmed)
facilities provided to:
USA (airfields at Masirah, Seeb, Khasab, Thamarit; storage facilities; naval facilities at Masirah and Jazirat Ghanam; communications center); Britain (use of airfields)
Joint Maneuvers with:
Britain, Egypt, GCC (members: Bahrain, Kuwait, Oman, Qatar, Saudi Arabia, UAE)

INFRASTRUCTURE

Road Network:

length:	16,900 km
paved roads	2,200 km
gravel, improved earth roads and tracks	14,700 km

main routes:
Muscat--Ras al-Khaimah/Dubai--Abu Dhabi (UAE)
Muscat--Izki--Fuhud/Izki--Salalah
Muscat--Sur
Muscat--Fujairah (UAE)
Hajma--Ras al-Daqm
Muscat--Khasab (Mussandam Peninsula)

Airfields:

airfields by runway type:	
permanent surface fields	6
unpaved fields and usable airstrips	108
airfields by runway length:	
over 3660 meters	1
2440--3659	4
1220--2439	55
under 1220	54
TOTAL	114

international airport: Muscat (Seeb)
major domestic airfield: Salalah

Airlines:

companies: Gulf Air (international)--jointly owned by Bahrain, Qatar, UAE and Oman (aircraft listed under Bahrain); Oman Aviation Service (domestic)
aircraft (excluding Gulf Air):

Beechcraft Super King Air 200	1
Boeing 727 (Sultan's personal aircraft)	1
Cessna Citation II	1
DHC-6 Twin Otter	2
Fokker F-27-500	4

Maritime Facilities:

harbors--Mina Oabus, Mina Raysut (Salalah)

oil terminals--Mina Fahal, Riyam

ARMED FORCES

Personnel:

military forces--

army	18,700
air force	5,000
navy	3,500
TOTAL	27,200

para-military forces--

tribal force--5,000

Police/Border police--7,000 (operating aircraft, helicopters and patrol boats)

Army:

major units:

unit type	brigades	independent battalions
royal guard		1
armored		1
armored reconnaissance		1
infantry (partly mechanized)	2	2
paratroop/ special forces		1
TOTAL	2	6

small arms:

personal weapons--

9mm Sterling Mk.4 SMG

7.62mm FAL (FN) SAR

5.56mm M-16 A1 AR

5.56mm AUG Steyr AR

machine guns--

7.62mm (0.3") Browning M-1919 MMG

7.62mm MAG (FN) LMG

light and medium mortars--

81mm L-16 A1

60mm Hotchkiss-Brandt

light ATRLs--

on order: LAW-80

OMAN

tanks:	
model	number
high quality	
Chieftain	34
medium quality	
M-60 A1	6
low quality	
Scorpion	30
TOTAL	70
on order: 20 Chieftain (unconfirmed)	
APCs/ARVs:	
model	number
high quality	
V-150 Commando	20
VAB	14
VBC-90	6
(sub-total	40)
others	
AT-105 Saxon	15
Fahd	7
(sub-total	22)
TOTAL	62
artillery:	
self propelled guns and howitzers--	
155mm M-109 A2 SP howitzer	12
towed guns and howitzers--	
155mm FH-70	12
130mm Type 59 gun	12
105mm Light Gun	36
105mm M-102 howitzer	36
25 lb. (87mm) howitzer (possibly phased out)	18
mortars, heavy, under 160mm	
120mm mortar	12
107mm (4.2") M-30 SP mortar	12
TOTAL	150
on order: 155mm Palmaria SP howitzer	
anti-tank weapons:	
missiles--	
BGM-71A Improved TOW	
MILAN	
army anti-aircraft defenses:	
missiles--	launchers
self propelled/mobile	
Rapier	24
Tigercat (unconfirmed)	
man-portable	
Blowpipe	
Javelin	28

short-range guns--	
40mm Bofors L-60 (unconfirmed)	12
23mm ZU 23x2	
20mm VDAA SP	9
on order: Rapier; Javelin (unconfirmed)	

Air Force:

aircraft--general:	number
combat aircraft	39
transport aircraft	41
helicopters	32
combat aircraft:	
strike and multi-role aircraft--	
medium quality	
SEPECAT Jaguar S(O) Mk.1/Mk.2/T2	22
others	
Hawker Hunter FGA-6/FR-10/T-67	17
TOTAL	39
transport aircraft:	
BAe-111	3
Britten-Norman BN-2 Defender/Islander	6
C-130H Hercules	3
DC-8	1
DC-10	1
DHC-5D Buffalo	4
Dornier Do-228-100 (used by police air wing for maritime surveillance & border patrol)	2
Gulfstream	1
Learjet (in police service)	1
Merlin IV	2
Mystere Falcon 20	1
Mystere Falcon 10	1
Short Skyvan Srs 3M (some employed in maritime patrol role)	15
TOTAL	41
on order: 1 C-130H; additional DHC-5D	
training and liaison aircraft:	
with ground attack/close air support capability--	
BAC-167 Strikemaster Mk.82	12
Hawk	8
(sub-total	20)
others--	
AS-202 Bravo	4
PC-6 Turbo-Porter	
(sub-total	4+)
TOTAL	24+
on order: 24-30 Hawk (number unconfirmed)	

OMAN

helicopters:	number
medium transport--	
AB-205	19
AB-212B/Bell 212	3
AB-214	5
AS-332 Super Puma	2
(sub-total	29)
light transport--	
AB-206 JetRanger	3
TOTAL	32
on order: Westland HAS Mk.1 Sea King ASW helicopters (unconfirmed)	
miscellaneous aircraft:	
target drones--	
TTL BTT-3 Banshee (original number supplied)	53
advanced armament:	
air-to-air missiles--	
R-550 Magique	
AIM-9P/AIM-9J Sidewinder	
bombs--	
BL-755 CBU	
anti-aircraft defenses:	
radars--	
AR-15	
S-713 Martello 3D	2
S-600	
Watchman	
aircraft shelters--	
for all combat aircraft, at Masirah and Thamarit	
military airfields:	6
Khasab (Musandam Peninsula), Masirah, Muscat (Seeb), Nizwa, Salalah, Thamarit	

Navy:

combat vessels:	number
MFPBs--	
Province class	4
gunboats/MTBs--	
Brooke Marine 123 ft. (37.5 meter)	4
patrol craft (police service):	
CG 27 87.6 ft. (26.7 meter)	2
Vosper Thornycroft 75 ft. (22.9 meter)	5
Watercraft & Shoreham 45.6 ft. (13.9 meter)	3
P-2000	1
P-1903	1
Vosper 25 meter (with Navy)	4
Cheverton 27 ft. (8.2 meter)	8
Total	24
on order: P-2000 patrol boats (unconfirmed)	

OMAN

landing craft:	
Brooke Marine 2000 ton landing ship-logistics/tank	1
Brooke Marine 2200 ton landing ship-logistics/tank	1
Lewis Offshore 85 DWT LCU	1
Impala Marine 75 DWT LCU	1
Cheverton 45 DWT LCU	2
Cheverton 30 DWT LCU	1
TOTAL	6
on order: Skima 12 hovercraft (unconfirmed)	
auxiliary vessels	number
Brooke Marine 900 ton royal yacht	1
Conoship Groningen 1380 DWT coastal freighter	1
survey craft, 23.6 ton	1
advanced armament:	
MM-38 Exocet SSM	
MM-40 Exocet SSM	
naval bases:	4
Mina Raysut (Salalah), Khasab (Musandam Peninsula), Muscat, Wudam	
ship maintenance and repair capability:	
Muscat	

13. PALESTINIAN MILITARY AND PARA-MILITARY FORCES

On November 15, 1988, in Algeria the PNC proclaimed an independent Palestinian state, which has in reality no control over territory. For all intents and purposes this has not altered the status of Palestinian forces, which remain as diverse and devoid of central authority as ever. The chairman of the PLO Executive Committee and designated president of the state is Yasir Arafat, who also heads Fatah, the largest constituent organization. Seven major organisations are members of the PLO institutions: Fatah, PLF, ALF, PFLP, DFLP, PPSF and PCP. Palestinian military and para-military forces not belonging to the PLO are FRC (Abu Nidal), Fatah rebels, PFLP-GC and al Sa'iqa. They are not controlled by the PLO executive organizations mentioned under Armed Forces.

The PFLP and DFLP both returned to the PLO in April 1987, and obtained seats on its Executive Committee, which grew accordingly from 10 to 15 members. The small Palestinian Communist Party also became a formal member of the PLO, with a representative on the Executive Committee. The anti-Arafat Palestine National Salvation Front was left with only four members: al-Sa'iqa, Fatah Rebels, PFLP-GC and PPSF. PPSF is the only organization that belongs to the PLO and to the Palestine National Salvation Front.

The PLF is part of the mainstream PLO. The PLF faction led by Tal'at Ya'qub (now deceased) formally agreed to merge with the Abu al-Abbas PLF in 1987. It is not clear to what extent the unification materialized.

In early 1990 several of Abu Nidal's close associates seceded from the FRC, and named themselves "Fatah Revolutionary Command--Emergency Command." Their posture is closer to that of Fatah (Arafat).

Although the PLO attempts to coordinate the activities of its member organizations, it lacks operational control. In practice, the military forces of all organizations are responsible only to their own leadership.

Palestinian forces may be divided into four categories: a) quasi-regular units of the various organizations; b) terror squads; c) the regular Palestinian Liberation Army (PLA); and d) militias which occasionally supplement the quasi-regular units.

PALESTINIAN FORCES

The quasi-regular forces of Fatah have been scattered among a number of Arab countries. Movement back to Lebanon from Tunisia, Algeria, Iraq, Yemen, and PDRY proceeded apace in 1989-90; we count the members of the various organizations as single entities regardless of their presumed location. All organizations (except for Fatah, the Abu Abbas faction of the PLF and the ALF) were deployed in Syria and Lebanon. Militiamen remained concentrated mainly in Lebanon. Terror squads continued their operations mainly from Lebanon, directed against Israel, and occasionally against targets elsewhere in the world. They also operated from Algeria, Iraq, Libya, and Syria.

ARMED FORCES

Personnel:

quasi-regular forces--

organization	commander	armed personnel (estimate)
PLO		
Arafat Loyalist:		
Al-Fatah	Yasir Arafat	8,000
Palestine Liberation Front (PLF)	Mahmud al-Zaidan, alias Abu al-Abbas	less than 300
Arab Liberation Front (ALF)	Abd al-Rahim Ahmad	300
Democratic Front for the Liberation of Palestine (DFLP)	Naif Hawatmeh	800-1,200
Popular Front for the Liberation of Palestine (PFLP)	Dr. George Habash	800-1,200
Palestine Popular Struggle Front (PPSF)	Dr. Samir Ghusha	600
Palestine National Salvation Front (pro-Syrian, anti-Arafat):		
Al-Fatah rebels	Muhammad Said Musa, alias Abu Musa	2,500
Popular Front for the Liberation of Palestine--General Command (PFLP--GC)	Ahmad Jibril	600-800

Al-Sa'iqa	Dr. Issam al-Qadi	1,000
Secessionist organizations belonging neither to the Arafat Loyalists nor to the Palestine National Salvation Front:		
Abu Nidal Faction (al-Fatah Revolutionary Council-FRC)	Sabri al-Bana, alias Abu Nidal	1,000
FRC-Emergency Command (Secessionists from Abu Nidal)		ca. 200
Popular Front for the Liberation of Palestine--Special Command (PFLP-SC)	Salim Abu Salem, alias Abu Muhammad	100
TOTAL, all organizations		16,500

Approximate Deployment, mid-1990 (all organizations):

country		number
Lebanon:		
Biq'a		1,500
Mount Lebanon Area		1,400
Tripoli & Northern Lebanon		800
Beirut & vicinity		4,000
South Lebanon (Tyre, Sidon & vicinity)		4,000
	(sub-total	11,700)
Syria (excluding PLA)		2,500
Other:		
Algeria		500
Iraq		2,000
PDRY		500
Sudan		500
Tunisia (administrative personnel)		100
YAR		1,500
	(sub-total	5,100)
TOTAL		19,300
terror squads		about 200
PLA Force in Jordan		2,000
militias		10,000+

Ground Forces:

major units--	brigades
PLA	
in Syria & Syrian-occupied Lebanon	2
in Jordan	1

in Iraq 1
TOTAL 4

quasi-regular forces of the major organizations

	brigades	battalions	companies
Al-Fatah	3		
PFLP		6	
PFLP-GC			5-6
Al-Sa'iqa		5	
DFLP		8	
PLF			(estimate) 2
TOTAL, all organizations	3	19	7-8

small arms:
personal weapons--
9mm P.P.Sh.41 SMG
7.62mm AK-47 (Kalashnikov) AR
7.62mm AKM AR
7.62mm Type 56 AR
7.62mm SSG-69 sniping rifle
5.56mm HK-33 Heckler & Koch AR
5.56mm M-16 A1 AR
machine guns--
14.5mm ZPU 14.5x4 HMG (in anti-aircraft role)
14.5mm ZPU 14.5x2 HMG (in anti-aircraft role)
12.7mm D.Sh.K. 38/46 (Degtyarev) HMG
7.62mm SGM (Goryunov)
7.62mm RPD (Degtyarev) LMG
7.62mm RPK LMG
7.62mm PK/PKS (Kalashnikov) LMG
light and medium mortars--
82mm M-43
light ATRLs--
M-72 LAW
RPG-7

tanks:
model
medium quality
T-55/improved T-54

APCs/ARVs:
model
high quality
M-113 a few
medium and low quality number
BTR-152
BRDM-2 (also an SP ATGM carrying AT-3 Sagger)
UR-416
TOTAL a few

artillery:
towed guns and howitzers--

155mm M-1950 howitzer
130mm M-46 gun
122mm D-30 howitzer
122mm M-1938 howitzer
105mm M-102 howitzer
100mm M-1955 field/AT gun
85mm M-1945/D-44 field/AT gun
mortars, heavy, over 160mm--
160mm mortar
mortars, heavy, under 160mm--
120mm mortar
TOTAL (unconfirmed) 80
MRLs--
122mm BM-21
122mm BM-11
107mm
improvised MRLs on light vehicles
TOTAL 50
anti-tank weapons:
missiles-- launchers
AT-3 (Sagger)
MILAN
TOTAL 200
guns--
107mm B-11 recoilless rifle
106mm M-40 A2 recoilless rifle
82mm B-10 recoilless rifle
57mm gun
army anti-aircraft defenses:
missiles-- launchers
self propelled/mobile
SA-9 (Gaskin) SP a few
man-portable
SA-7 (Grail)
short-range guns--
23mm ZSU 23x4 SP (Gun Dish)
23mm ZU 23x2
20mm 20x3 M-55 A4

Air Units:
The PLO-affiliated organizations have no air force. The so-called "Fatah Air Force" is designated Force 14. About 200 Palestinians have reportedly undergone training as fighter and helicopter pilots in Libya, YAR, Romania, Pakistan, Cuba, North Korea and the USSR. Other PLO members have learned to fly commercial aircraft in civilian flight schools in Romania, Yugoslavia and several western countries. Some are now flying diverse aircraft, including MiG-23 and MiG-21 fighters, in Libya. Two Palestinian pilots were killed flying a MiG-21 and a

MiG-23 for the Libyan Air Force in Northern Chad (1987); one of them was identified as belonging to Jibril's PFLP-GC. Helicopters flown include the Mi-24, Mi-8, CH-4 and AS-321. Transport aircraft flown include the Fokker F-27. Some PLO airmen have reportedly flown aircraft and helicopters in Nicaragua for the Nicaraguan government.

PLO terrorists have trained with hot air balloons and hang-gliders equipped with auxiliary motors. Hang-gliders have been used twice in action, in 1981 and in 1987. It is estimated that the PFLP-GC and Abu al-Abbas fraction of the PLF have purchased around 80 ultra-light aircraft.

In recent years a concentration of Palestinian pilots and affiliated personnel was reportedly located in YAR and at Kamran Island (an island legally part of PDRY, but practically controlled by YAR, off the shore of Saleef). The PLO has de facto control of an airline company registered in Guinea Bissau, where Palestinians fly commercial aircraft.

Naval Forces:

swimmer-delivery vehicles
underwater demolition squads 50 men
small boat units 200 men
(concentrated in YAR, at Kamran Island in PDRY, in Libya and in Annaba, Algeria)

Foreign Military Aid and Security Assistance Received:

financial aid from:
Algeria; Bahrain; Iran (to Fatah rebels--Abu Musa, and since late 1989 also to PELP-GC), Iraq (to al-Fatah, Abu al-Abbas faction of PLF, ALF, 15th May organization); Kuwait; Libya (to PFLP, PFLP-GC, PLF, al-Fatah rebels); Saudi Arabia ($86 million annually to al-Fatah); Syria (to al-Sa'iqa, PFLP-GC, al-Fatah rebels, Abu Nidal, PLF [Abd al-Fateh al-Ghanem and Tal'at Ya'qub factions only], PPSS); UAE

military training:
trainees abroad in--Algeria, Bulgaria, Cuba, Czechoslovakia, GDR, Hungary, Iraq, Libya, North Korea, Pakistan, PDRY, Syria, USSR, Yugoslavia

arms transfers from:
Algeria (small arms); Iraq (small arms); Libya (MRLs, SAMs, artillery pieces); North Korea (artillery pieces); PDRY (Soviet arms); PRC (small arms); Saudi

Arabia (small arms and ammunition, trucks); Syria (tanks); USSR and other East European countries (tanks, SAMs, MRLs); Yugoslavia (AAGs; small arms--unconfirmed)

support forces from:

Japan and various European countries (individual volunteers)

Foreign Military Aid and Security Assistance Extended:

military training, sabotage instruction, and cooperation extended by the PLO and affiliated organizations to the following non-Palestinian organizations:

ANC and PAC (South Africa, unconfirmed)

The Nicaraguan government (formerly FSLN--Front Sandinista de Liberacion Nacional)

Hizb Allah in Lebanon

SWAPO anti-South African guerrillas in Namibia

Tamil guerrillas in Sri Lanka

14. QATAR

BASIC DATA

Official Name of State: State of Qatar

Head of State: Shaykh Khalifa ibn Hamad al-Thani (also Prime Minister)

Minister of Defense: Major General Shaykh Hamad ibn Khalifa al-Thani (also Heir Apparent and Commander in Chief of the Armed Forces)

Chief of the General Staff: Colonel Shaykh Hamad ibn Abdullah al-Thani

Commander of the Ground Forces: Colonel Muhammad Rashid Sharaan

Commander of the Air Force: Lieutenant Colonel Ahmad Abdullah al-Kawari

Commander of the Navy: Commander Said al-Swaydi

Area: 10,360 sq. km.

Population:		330,000
ethnic subdivision:		
Arabs	132,000	40.0%
Pakistanis	59,000	18.0%
Indians	59,000	18.0%
Persians	33,000	10.0%
Others (mostly Southeast Asians)	47,000	14.0%
religious subdivision:		
Sunni Muslims	232,000	70.3%
Shi'ite Muslims	80,000	24.3%
Others	18,000	5.4%
nationality subdivision:		
Qataris	83,000	25.0%
Alien Arabs	66,000	20.0%
Alien Non-Arabs		
Southeast Asians (Indians, Pakistanis, Chinese, Thais, Filipinos, others)	112,000	34.0%
Iranians	53,000	16.0%
Others	16,000	5.0%

GDP:
- 1985--$6.3 billion
- 1986--$4.95 billion

Defense Expenditure:
- 1990--$200 million (estimate)

Foreign Military Aid and Security Assistance Received:

military training:

foreign advisors/instructors/serving personnel from--Britain, Egypt, France, Jordan, Kuwait, Pakistan trainees abroad in--Britain, Egypt, France, Jordan, Kuwait, Pakistan, Saudi Arabia

arms transfers from:

Britain (helicopters, SAMs, target drones); Egypt (APCs, MRLs); France (tanks, APCs, MFPBs, naval SSMs, combat aircraft, artillery pieces, anti-ship AGMs)

Foreign Military Aid and Security Assistance Extended:

financial aid to:

Jordan, Syria, Lebanon, Palestinian organizations--grants; Iraq--loans

Joint Maneuvers with:

GCC members (Bahrain, Kuwait, Oman, Qatar, Saudi Arabia, UAE)

INFRASTRUCTURE

Road Network:

length:	840 km
paved roads	490 km
gravel roads	350 km

main routes:

Doha--Umm Sa'id

Doha--Salwa--al-Hufuf (Saudi Arabia)

Doha--Dukhan--Umm Bab (oil fields)

Doha--al-Ruwais--Zubara

Airfields:

airfields by runway type:	
permanent surface fields	1
unpaved fields and usable airstrips	3
airfields by runway length:	
over 3660 meters	1
1220--2439	2
under 1220	1
TOTAL	4

international airports: Doha

Airlines:

companies: Gulf Air--jointly owned by Oman, Qatar, Bahrain and UAE (listed under Bahrain)

Maritime Facilities:

harbors--Doha

oil terminals--Halul Island, Umm Sa'id

Merchant Marine:

vessel type	number	DWT
crude tanker	1	137,676
tanker	1	63,132
general cargo/container	8	147,677
bunkering tanker	1	5,390
container	3	95,542
TOTAL	14	449,417

QATAR

ARMED FORCES

Personnel:

military forces--

army	6,000
air force	300
navy	500
TOTAL	6,800

Army:

major units:

unit type	regiments	battalions
armored/tank		1
guard infantry	1	
infantry		5
TOTAL	1	6

small arms:
  personal weapons--
    7.62mm G-3 AR
    7.62mm L-1 A1 SAR
  machine guns--
    7.62mm MAG (FN) LMG
  light and medium mortars--
    81mm

tanks:

model		number
medium quality		
AMX-30		24

APCs/ARVs:

model		
high quality		
AMX-10P		30
VAB		158
VPM 81 mortar carrier		4
V-150 Commando		8
	(sub-total	200)
others		
Fahd		6-10
Ferret		10
Saracen		25
	(sub-total	41-45)
TOTAL		245

on order: Engesa APCs, ARVs (unconfirmed); 6 French armored vehicles (command post, medical evacuation vehicles)

artillery:

self propelled guns and howitzer--	
155mm Mk. F-3 (AMX) SP howitzer	6
towed guns and howitzers--	
25 lb. (87mm) howitzer	8

TOTAL	14
on order: 6 additional 155mm Mk. F-3 SP howitzers	
MRLs--	
122mm BM-21	
anti-tank weapons:	
missiles--	
MILAN	
guns--	
84mm Carl Gustaf light recoilless rifle	
army anti-aircraft defenses:	
missiles--	launchers
self propelled/mobile	
Rapier	18
Roland 2	9
Tigercat	5
man-portable	
Blowpipe	6
FIM-92A Stinger	12
on order: Crotale SAMs (possibly delivered)	

Air Force:

aircraft--general:	number
combat aircraft	17
transport aircraft	4
helicopters	37
combat aircraft:	
strike and multi-role aircraft--	
medium quality	
Mirage F-1E/B	14
others	
Hawker Hunter FGA-78/T-79	3
TOTAL	17
transport aircraft:	
Boeing 707	2
Boeing 727	1
Britten-Norman BN-2 Islander	1
TOTAL	4
training and liaison aircraft:	
with ground attack/close air support capability--	
Alpha Jet	6
helicopters:	
attack--	
SA-342 Gazelle (employed as light helicopter)	12
heavy transport--	
Westland Commando Mk.2/3	12
medium transport--	
Westland Lynx	3
Westland Whirlwind Series 3	2
(sub-total	5)

maritime attack--
Westland Sea King (in attack role) 8
TOTAL 37
on order: AS-332 Super Puma
miscellaneous aircraft:
target drones--
TTL BTT-3 Banshee RPV/target (unconfirmed)
advanced armament:
air to ground missiles--
AM-39 Exocet
anti-aircraft defenses:
long-range missiles--
on order: MIM-23B Improved HAWK (possibly delivered); 4 Thomson CSF (TRS-2100) radars
military airfields: 1
Doha

Navy:

combat vessels:	number
MFPBs--	
Combattante III	3
patrol craft--	
Vosper Thornycroft 110 ft. (33.5 meter)	6
Whittingham & Mitchell 75 ft. (22.5 meter)	2
Damen "Polycat 1450"	6
Keith Nelson type 44 ft. (13.5 meter)	2
Fairey Marine Spear class	25
Fairey Marine Interceptor class	
Fast assault and rescue craft	2
P-1200	7
Total	50
landing craft:	
48.8 meter LCT	1
advanced armament:	
MM-40 Exocet SSM	
coastal defense: launchers	
MM-40 Exocet coastal defense missiles	3x4
naval bases:	2
Doha, Halul Island (under construction)	

15. SAUDI ARABIA

BASIC DATA

Official Name of State: The Kingdom of Saudi Arabia

Head of State: King Fahd ibn Abd al-Aziz al-Saud (also Prime Minister)

First Deputy Prime Minister and Heir Apparent: Crown Prince Abdullah ibn Abd al-Aziz al-Saud (also Commander of the National Guard)

Defense and Aviation Minister: Prince Sultan ibn Abd al-Aziz al-Saud (also Second Deputy Prime Minister)

Chief of Staff of the Armed Forces: General Muhammad Salih al-Hammad

Commander of the Ground Forces: Lieutenant General Youssuf Abd al-Rahman al-Rashid (also Deputy Chief of Staff of the Armed Forces)

Commander of the Air Force: Lieutenant General Ahmad Ibrahim al-Buheiri

Commander of the Air Defense Forces: Major General Prince Khalid ibn Sultan

Commander of the Navy: Vice Admiral Talal Ibn Salem al-Mufadhi

Area: 2,331,000 sq.km. (approximation; some borders undefined or undemarcated)

Population (estimate):		8,500,000
ethnic subdivision:		
Arabs	7,769,000	91.4%
Afro-Arabs	425,000	5.0%
Others	306,000	3.6%
religious subdivision:		
Sunni Muslims	7,829,000	92.1%
Shi'ite Muslims	425,000	5.0%
Others (mainly Christians)	246,000	2.9%
nationality subdivision:		
Saudis	6,681,000	78.6%
Yemenis	969,000	11.4%
Palestinians	60,000	0.7%
Americans	42,000	0.5%
Others (Thais, Filipinos, Chinese, Indians, Pakistanis, other Arabs)	748,000	8.8%

GDP:

1986--$ 75.46 billion

1987--$ 71.47 billion

Balance of Payments (goods, services & unilateral transfer payments):

year	income	expenditure	balance
1986	$33.97 bil.	$45.86 bil.	-$11.89 bil.

SAUDI ARABIA

1987 $36.44 bil. $46.01 bil. -$ 9.57 bil.

Defense Expenditure:
- 1987--$16.2 billion
- 1990--$13.8 billion

Foreign Military Aid and Security Assistance Received:
- military training:
  - foreign advisors/instructors/serving personnel from--Britain, Egypt, France, FRG, India, Japan, Jordan, Morocco (1000, unconfirmed), Pakistan, PRC, Syria, Turkey, USA (partly civilian)
  - trainees abroad in--Britain, France, Jordan, Pakistan, PRC, Switzerland, Turkey, USA
- arms transfers from:
  - Austria (small arms); Britain (combat aircraft, trainer aircraft, hovercraft, SSB radio transceivers, helicopters and minesweepers); France (APCs, radars, SAMs, SP artillery, anti-ship AGMs, frigates on order); FRG (small arms, electronics, EW equipment); Italy (helicopters) ; PRC (SSMs); Spain (transport aircraft, trucks); Switzerland (trainer aircraft); USA (AAMs, AGMs, ATGMs, artillery pieces, AWACS aircraft, combat aircraft, aircraft engines, SAMs, tanks, transport aircraft, aircraft simulators, trucks)
- support forces from:
  - Bangladesh (unconfirmed), Pakistan (a few hundred); USA (AWACS and refuelling aircraft, until May 1989); GCC rapid deployment force (10,000 men, mostly from Saudi Arabia, but some from Bahrain, Kuwait, Oman, Qatar, and UAE)
- construction aid by:
  - South Korea, USA, Britain
- maintenance of equipment in:
  - France (naval vessels)

Foreign Military Aid and Security Assistance Extended:
- financial aid to:
  - Jordan, $360 million--grant; Lebanon, Morocco, PLO, Somalia--grants; Sudan, Syria-- grant; YAR, Iraq--grant and loan, old debt extended, Pakistan, Mauritania--grant, Turkey--loan
- military training:
  - advisors/instructors/technicians in--YAR
  - foreign trainees from--Bahrain, Djibouti, Jordan, Kuwait, Mauritania, Oman, Qatar, Somalia, Sudan, Tunisia, UAE, YAR
- arms transfers to:
  - PLO (ammunition, small arms)
- construction aid to:
  - Sudan (construction/upgrading of airfield)

Cooperation in Arms Production/Assembly with:
- Britain (electronics, AAMs); France (electronics); FRG

(small arms and ammunition, ATGMs; unconfirmed reports--development of SSMs or upgrading of SSMs)

Joint Maneuvers with:

GCC (members: Bahrain, Kuwait, Oman, Qatar, Saudi Arabia, UAE); France; Pakistan

INFRASTRUCTURE

Road Network:

length:	80,000 km
paved roads	35,000 km
gravel and improved earth and roads	50,000 km

main routes:

- Jiddah--al-Qunfudhah--Jizan--Hodeida (YAR)
- Jiddah--Medina--Tabuk--Ma'an (Jordan)/Yanbu--Wajh--Haql--Aqaba (Jordan)
- Tabuk--Sakhakh--Badanah (on TAPline road)
- Jiddah--Mecca
- Mecca--Ta'if--Qal'at Bishah--Khamis Mushayt/Qal'at Bishah--Najran
- Mecca--Ta'if--Abha--Khamis Mushayt
- Riyadh--Buraydah--Ha'il/Buraydah--Medina
- Riyadh--al-Hufuf--Dhahran/al-Hufuf--Doha (Qatar)
- Dhahran--al-Dammam--Qatif--Ras Tanura--Jubayl--al-Qaysumah--H-5 (Jordan) (TAPline)
- Dhahran--al-Manamah (Bahrain): 25 km bridge causeway
- Riyadh--al-Kharj--al-Sulayyil--Najran
- Najran--San'a (YAR)
- Rafha (on TAPline road)--al-Najaf (Iraq)

Railway Network:

length (standard gauge):	886 km

route:

Riyadh--al-Hufuf--Abqaiq--Dhahran--al-Dammam

Airfields:

airfields by runway type:	
permanent surface fields	62
unpaved fields and usable airstrips	114
airfields by runway length:	
over 3660 meters	12
2440--3659	29
1220--2439	98
under 1220	37
TOTAL	176

international airports: Dhahran, Jiddah, Medina, Riyadh

major domestic airfields: Abha/Khamis Mushayt, al-Dammam, Arrar, Bishah, Gassim, Qurayat, Ha'il, al-Hufuf, Jawf, Jizan, Mecca, Najran, al-Qaysumah, Rafha, Sharawra, Tabuk, Ta'if, Turayf, Wajh, Wadi al-Dawasir, Yanbu

Airlines:

companies: Saudia (international and domestic)

aircraft:

Airbus A-300-600	11
Boeing 747-100/747-300/747-SP/747-200F	21
Boeing 737-200/737-200C	19
Cessna Citation II	2
Gulfstream II	5
Gulfstream III	6
Gulfstream IV	2
Lockheed L-1011-200 Tristar	17
Mystere Falcon 900	1

Maritime Facilities:

harbors--al-Dammam (King Abdul Aziz Port), Jizan, Jiddah (Jiddah Islamic Port), Jubayl, Ras al-Mish'ab, Ras Tanura, Yanbu (King Fahd Port); al-Duba (under construction)

oil terminals--Halul Island, Ju'aymah (offshore oil terminal), Ras Tanura, Yanbu

Merchant Marine:

vessel type	number	DWT
crude carrier	12	2,279,954
general cargo	5	24,912
bulk carrier	2	83,287
ore/oil	1	264,591
general cargo/container	7	166,005
ro-ro	14	232,262
product tanker	4	138,460
livestock carrier	5	110,183
container	3	75,691
gas tanker (LPG)	1	61,803
cement carrier	2	53,838
reefer	4	24,748
depot tanker	4	158,372
cement storage	3	207,394
bunkering tanker	29	112,870
ferry	7	10,701
passenger/cargo	1	2,494
chemical tanker	2	47,762
small tanker	1	2,440
methanol tanker	1	42,825
storage tanker	1	36,964
TOTAL	109	4,137,556

Defense Production:

army equipment:

production under license--G-3 ARs

manufacture--small arms ammunition, electronic components

planned: tanks, under license; tank guns, under FRG license; electronic equipment, under British, French and US license and cooperation; APCs; Artillery and AAMs in cooperation with Britain; ATGMs, in cooperation with FRG

electronics:
assembly--radio transceivers

ARMED FORCES

Personnel:

military forces--

army	45,000
air force	15,000
navy (including a marine unit)	7,800
national guard (regular)	25,000
royal guards	2,000
TOTAL	94,800

para-military forces--

Mujahidun (affiliated with national guard)	29,000
coast guard	6,500

Army and National Guard:

major units:

unit type	brigades/ regiments	independent battalions
armored	2	
mechanized	6	
Royal Guard Infantry	1	
infantry		19
marines (unconfirmed)		1
airborne/special force	1	
TOTAL	10	20

small arms:
personal weapons--
9mm Model 12 Beretta SMG
7.62mm FAL (FN) SAR
7.62mm G-3 AR
7.62mm SSG-69 sniping rifle
5.56mm AUG Steyr AR
5.56mm HK-33 Heckler & Koch AR
5.56mm M-16 A1 AR
machine guns--
7.62mm (0.3") Browning M-1919 A1 MMG
automatic grenade launchers--
40mm Mk.19
light and medium mortars--
81mm
light ATRLs--
M-72 LAW

tanks:

model	number
high quality	
M-60 A3	100
medium quality	

M-60 A1	150
AMX-30	300
(sub-total	450)
TOTAL	550

on order: 150 kits to upgrade M-60 A1 to M-60 A3 standard, delivery in process; 315 M-1 A2

APCs/ARVs:

model	number
high quality	
AMX-10	450
M-113 A1/A2	1000
V-150 Commando	1000
(sub-total	2450)
others	
AML-60/90	200
BMR-600 (with marines)	140
Fox/Ferret	200
M-3 (Panhard)	150
UR-416	+
(sub-total	+690)
TOTAL	3140+

on order: V-150 & V-300; 200 M-2/M-3 Bradley with BGM-71C Improved TOW (delivery 1991); 300 Mowag Piranha 8x8 APCs

artillery:

self propelled guns and howitzers--	
155mm M-109 A2 SP howitzer	224
155mm GCT SP howitzer	51
towed guns and howitzers--	
155mm FH-70 howitzer	72
155mm M-198 howitzer	36
105mm M-56 Pack howitzer	
105mm M-101 howitzer	
mortars, heavy, under 160mm	
107mm (4.2") M-30 mortar	
TOTAL	700

on order: 93 M-992 ammunition carriers from the USA; 50 155mm GHN-45 from Austria; 27 additional 155mm M-198

MRLs:

180mm SS-40 Astros

127mm SS-30 Astros II

on order: 300mm SS-60 ASTROS II, 180mm SS-40 ASTROS II, and 127mm SS-30 Astros II; 40 MLRS

engineering equipment:

M-123 Viper minefield crossing system

M-69 A1 bridging tanks

bridging equipment

AFV transporters:	600

anti-tank weapons:	
missiles--	launchers
AMX-10P SP (carrying HOT)	
BGM-71C Improved TOW	
M-47 Dragon	
TOTAL	700
guns--	
90mm Mecar light gun (unconfirmed)	
on order: BGM-71D (TOW II)	
surface-to-surface missiles and rockets	launchers
CSS-2 SSM (East Wind, IRBM, number unconfirmed)	8-12
army anti-aircraft defenses:	
missiles--	launchers
self propelled/mobile	
Crotale	12+
Shahine	12
man-portable	
FIM-92A Stinger	400
MIM-43A Redeye	
short-range guns--	number
35mm Oerlikon-Buhrle 35x2 GDF-002	
30mm AMX DCA 30 (twin 30 mm) SP	
20mm M-163 Vulcan SP	72
on order: Stinger SAM; Gepard 35mm SP AAG; 60 30mm 30x2 Wildcat SP AAGs; Shahine II; 1500 Mistral SAMs	
CW capabilities:	
personal protective equipment	
decontamination units	

Air Force:

aircraft--general:	number
combat aircraft	226
transport aircraft	73
helicopters	141
combat aircraft:	
interceptors--	
high quality	
F-15 C/D Eagle	60
Tornado ADV	16
(sub-total	76)
strike and multi-role aircraft--	
high quality	
Tornado IDS	40
medium or low quality	
F-5E/F	85
F-5A/B	15
RF-5E	10
(sub-total	110)
Total	150

on order: 20 Tornado ADV, 8 Tornado IDS, part of the Yamama I agreement, delivery in process; 12-14 F-15; additional 48 Tornado IDS and Tornado ADV, part of the Yamama II agreement (unconfirmed; order possibly cancelled)

transport aircraft:	
Boeing 747	1
Boeing 737	1
Boeing 707	2
C-130E/H Hercules	34
CN-235	2
KC-130H tanker (refuelling)	8
KE-3/Boeing 707 tanker (refuelling)	8
L-100/L-100-30HS (unconfirmed)	9
Gates Learjet 35 (employed in target-towing role)	3
Gulfstream III	1
Mystere Falcon 20	2
VC-140 JetStar (equivalent to C-140 JetStar)	2
TOTAL	73
on order: 2 CN-235; Super King Air 200	
training and liaison aircraft:	
with ground attack/close air support capability--	
BAC-167 Strikemaster	27
Hawk	30
(sub-total	57)
others--	
BAe Jetstream 31 (employed as cockpit training a/c for Tornado pilots)	2
Cessna 172 G/H/L	12
Pilatus PC-9	30
(sub-total	44)
TOTAL	101
on order: additional 30 Hawk, including 20 Hawk-200, part of Yamama II	
helicopters:	
attack-- (part of Army Aviation)	
OH-58D (Combat Scout, AHIP)	15
maritime attack--	
SA-365 Dauphin 2	24
heavy transport--	
SH-3 (AS-61A)	3
KV-107/KV-107 IIA-17	16
(sub-total	19)
medium transport--	
AB-212 (unconfirmed)	35
SA-365N Dauphin 2 (employed in medical evacuation role)	6
UH-60A Black Hawk/Desert Hawk (part of Army	

Aviation)	12
(sub-total	53)
light transport--	
AB-206 JetRanger	30
TOTAL	141

on order: 12 AS-332 Super Puma, naval attack configuration; additional 80 British helicopters, reportedly UH-60A (WS-70) and other models

miscellaneous aircraft:

AEW/AWACS aircraft--	
E-3A AWACS	5
target drones--	
TTL BTT-3 Banshee	
RPVs and mini-RPVs--	
MQM-74C Chukar II RPV	

advanced armament:

air-to-air missiles--	number
AIM-7F Sparrow	850
AIM-9J/P Sidewinder	
AIM-9L Sidewinder	
Red Top	
Sky Flash	
Firestreak	
air-to-ground missiles--	
AGM-65A Maverick	2400
AS-15TT anti-ship missile	
Sea Eagle anti-ship missile	
bombs--	
laser-guided bombs	3000
CBU	1000
BL-755 CBU	
JP-233 anti-runway bombs	

on order: AS-15TT air-to-sea missile, 100 AGM-84 Harpoon air-to-sea missile, AIM-9M AAMs, 995 AIM-9L AAMs, 671 AIM-9P-4 AAMS, ALARM anti-radiation missiles, AM-39 Exocet air-to-sea missiles

anti-aircraft defenses:

radars--	
AN/FPS-117	17
AN/TPS-43	
AN/TPS-59 (unconfirmed)	
AN/TPS-63 (unconfirmed)	
long-range missiles--	
model	batteries
MIM-23B Improved HAWK	15
aircraft shelters--	
for combat aircraft	

military airfields: 20

Abqaiq, al-Sulayil, Dhahran (King Abd al-Aziz), Jiddah (Amir Abdullah), Khamis Mushayt, al-Kharj, Medina,

Riyadh, Sharawrah, Tabuk, Ta'if (King Fahd), 9 additional
aircraft maintenance and repair capability:
for all models, dependent on foreign technicians

Navy:

combat vessels:	number
MFPBs--	
PGG-1 class (Peterson Builders)	9
missile frigates--	
F-2000	4
missile corvettes--	
PCG-1 class (Tacoma Boatbuilding)	4
mine warfare vessels--	
MSC-322 class minesweeper	4
gunboats/MTBs--	
Jaguar class MTB	3
patrol craft-- (some serving with coast guard)	
Blohm & Voss 38.9 meter (with coast guard)	4
P-32	8
USCG-Type 95 ft. (29 meter)	1
Skorpion class (with coast guard)	15
Rapier class 50 ft. (with coast guard)	12
Naja 12	20
Total	60

note: coast guard has 110 additional small patrol craft

on order: 2 26-meter (80 ton) Abeking & Rasmussen patrol boats; 6 Sandown minehunters (1 launched August 1989, undergoing refit and trials in Britain); 3 Lafayette class frigates

landing craft:	
LCM-6 class	8
SRN-6 class hovercraft (with coast guards)	24
US LCU 1610 class LCU	4
26 ton LCM	4
TOTAL	40
auxiliary vessels:	
training ship, 350 ton	1
royal yacht, 1450 DWT	1
royal yacht, 650 ton	1
Durance class tanker, 10,500 ton	2
advanced armament:	
surface-to-surface missiles--	
OTOMAT Mk.2	
RGM-84A Harpoon	120
surface-to-air missile--	
Crotale Navale	
Mistral	
anti-missile guns--	

20mm Vulcan-Phalanx radar-controlled
advanced torpedoes--
F-17P
coastal defense:
OTOMAT coastal defense missile
special maritime forces:
frogmen and divers
naval bases (including Coast Guard): 12
al-Dammam, al-Haql (coast guard), Jiddah, Jizan, Jubayl, Makna (coast guard), al-Qatif, Ras al-Mish'ab, Ras Tanurah, al-Sharma, al-Wajh, Yanbu
ship maintenance and repair capability:
repair of vessels, dependent on foreign experts; 22,000 ton and 62,000 ton floating docks at Dammam; 45,000 ton and 16,000 ton floating docks at Jiddah; docks work mostly for commercial vessels
coast guard:
small patrol boats 120

16. SOUTH YEMEN (PDRY)

BASIC DATA

Official Name of State: The People's Democratic Republic of Yemen (PDRY). On May 22, 1990, YAR and PDRY proclaimed their formal unification as one state. The unification is to include a two-and-a-half year transition period. Merger of the armed forces has begun. Here PDRY and YAR are still treated as two separate entities.

Head of State: President Haydar Abu Bakr al-Attas (also Chairman of the Supreme People's Council)

Prime Minister: Yasin Said Numan

Defense Minister: Colonel Salih Ubayd Ahmad Ali

Chief of the General Staff: Colonel Haytham Qasim Tahir

Commander of the Air Force: Major Ali Muthanna Hadi

Commander of the Navy: Commander Ali Qasim Talib

Area: 287,500 sq. km. (borders with Saudi Arabia, Oman and YAR partly undemarcated and/or disputed)

Population		2,510,000
ethnic subdivision:		
Arabs	2,430,000	96.8%
Somalis	35,000	1.4%
Others	45,000	1.8%
religious subdivision:		
Sunni Muslims	2,502,000	99.7%
Hindus	6,000	0.2%
Others	2,000	0.1%

GDP:

No GDP available since 1980

Balance of Payments (goods, services & unilateral transfer payments):

year	income	expenditure	balance
1987	$544 mil.	$674 mil.	-$130 mil.
1988	$535 mil.	$918 mil.	-$383 mil.

Defense Expenditure:

1983--$171 million (estimate)

1984--$194 million (estimate)

Foreign Military Aid and Security Assistance Received:

financial aid from:

USSR (for repair of refineries damaged in January 1986 coup d'etat); Saudi Arabia--grant

military training:

foreign advisors/instructors from--Cuba (unconfirmed), GDR (left in May 1990), North Korea, Syria, USSR

trainees abroad in--USSR, Syria, East European countries

arms transfers from:
USSR and East European countries (combat aircraft, small arms, tanks)

Foreign Military Aid and Security Assistance Extended:

military training:
foreign trainees from--Palestinian organizations, (PFLP-GC, al-Fatah, PFLP); ASALA (Armenians); Japanese Red Army (JRA);

arms transfers to:
Palestinian organizations (artillery, tanks, small arms)

facilities provided to:
Palestinian organizations and other terrorist groups (training camps); USSR (airfields, naval base at Socotra)

INFRASTRUCTURE

Road Network:

length:	5,600 km
paved roads	1,700 km
gravel and stone roads	630 km
earth tracks	3,270 km

main routes:
Aden--Shuqra--Lawdar/Shuqra--al-Mukalla
Aden--Musaymir--Ta'iz (YAR)
al-Mukalla--al-Qatn--Tarim
al-Mukalla--al-Riyan--Salalah (Oman)

Airfields:

airfields by runway type:	
permanent surface fields	7
unpaved fields and usable airstrips	23
airfields by runway length:	
2440--3659 meters	11
1220--2439	11
under 1220	8
TOTAL	30

international airport: Aden (Khormaksar)

major domestic airfields: Ataq, Bayhan al-Qasab, al-Ghaydah, Lawdar, al Mukalla/al-Riyan, Mukayris, al Qatn, Qishin, Seiyun/Tarim

Airlines:

companies: Alyemda--Democratic Yemen Airlines (international and domestic)

aircraft:	
An-26	1
Boeing 737-200C	2
Boeing 707-320C	2
DHC Dash 7	2
Tupolev Tu-154	1

Maritime Facilities:

harbors--Aden, al-Mukalla

oil terminal--Aden

Merchant Marine:

vessel type	number	DWT
general cargo	1	1,723
tanker	1	3,184
TOTAL	2	4,907

ARMED FORCES

Personnel:

military forces--		
army		24,000
air force		2,500
navy		1,000
TOTAL		27,500
para-military forces--		
popular militia	(unconfirmed)	15,000

Army:

major units: (not all fully operational/fully organized)

unit type	brigades
armored	1
mechanized	3
infantry (mostly skeleton or undermanned)	8
TOTAL	12

small arms:

personal weapons--

7.62mm AK-47 (Kalashnikov) AR

7.62mm SKS (Simonov) SAR

machine guns--

12.7mm D.Sh.K. 38/46 (Degtyarev) HMG

7.62mm PK/PKS (Kalashnikov) LMG

7.62mm RPD (Degtyarev) LMG

7.62mm SG-43 (Goryunov) MMG

light and medium mortars--

82mm M-43

light ATRLs--

RPG-7

tanks:

model	number
medium quality	
T-62	
T-55	
low quality	
T-54	
TOTAL	480-500

SOUTH YEMEN

APCs/ARVs:	
model	number
high quality	
BMP-1	
others	
BTR-40/50/60	
BTR-152	
Ferret (possibly phased out)	
Saladin (possibly phased out)	
TOTAL	450
artillery:	
towed guns and howitzers--	
130mm M-46 gun	
122mm D-30 howitzer	
122mm M-1938 howitzer	
100mm M-1955 field/AT gun	
85mm M-1945/D-44 field/AT gun	
mortars, heavy, over 160mm--	
160mm mortar	
mortars, heavy, under 160mm--	
120mm mortar	
TOTAL	350
MRLs--	
122mm BM-21	
anti-tank weapons:	
missiles--	
AT-3 (Sagger)	
guns--	
85mm M-1945/D-44 field/AT gun (see artillery)	
107mm B-11 recoilless rifle (unconfirmed)	
TOTAL	220
surface-to-surface missiles and rockets:	
model	launchers
FROG-7	12
SS-1 (Scud B)	6
TOTAL	18
army anti-aircraft defenses:	
missiles--	
self propelled/mobile	
SA-6 (Gainful)	
SA-9 (Gaskin, unconfirmed)	
man-portable	
SA-7 (Grail)	
short-range guns--	
57mm ZSU 57x2 SP	
57mm	
37mm	
23mm ZSU 23x4 SP (Gun Dish)	
23mm ZU 23x2	

SOUTH YEMEN

Air Force:

aircraft--general:	number
combat aircraft	130
transport aircraft	18
helicopters	69
combat aircraft:	number
interceptors--	
medium quality	
MiG-21 (Fishbed)	45
strike and multi-role aircraft--	
medium quality	
MiG-23/27 (Flogger B/D)	25
Su-20/22 (Fitter C)	40
(sub-total	65)
others	
MiG-17 (Fresco)	10
MiG-15 UTI	5
(sub-total	15)
Total	80
bombers--	
IL-28 (Beagle)	5
transport aircraft:	
An-24/26 (Coke/Curl)	10
DC-3 Dakota (C-47)	4
IL-14 (Crate)	4
TOTAL	18
training and liaison aircraft:	
with ground attack/close air support capability--	
L-39 Albatross (unconfirmed)	a few
helicopters:	
attack--	
Mi-24/Mi-25 (Hind)	20
medium transport--	
Mi-4 (Hound)	4
Mi-8/Mi-17 (Hip)	45
(sub-total	49)
TOTAL	69
advanced armament:	
air-to-air missiles--	
AA-2 (Atoll)	
air-to-ground missiles--	
AT-2 (Swatter)	
anti-aircraft defenses:	
long-range missiles--	
model	batteries
SA-2 (Guideline)	6
SA-3 (Goa)	3
TOTAL	9

military airfields: 14+
Aden (Khormaksar), al-Anad, al-Ansab (Nisab), Ataq, Bayhan al-Qasab, al-Dali, Ghor Ubayd, Ir-Fadhl, Lawdar, al-Mukalla, Mukayris, Perim Island, Socotra, Zamakh

Navy:

combat vessels:	number
MFPBs--	
Ossa II	6
ASW vessels--	
SO-1 class 2	
gunboats/MTBs--	
P-6 MTB	2
patrol craft--	
Fairey Marine Spear	3
Fairey Marine Interceptor	1
Fairey Marine Tracker 2	1
Zhuk class	2
Total	7
landing craft:	
Ropucha class LST	1
Polnochny class LCT	2
T-4 LCM	3
TOTAL	6

advanced armament:
SS-N-2 Styx SSM

coastal defense:
land-based SS-N-2C Styx

naval bases: 4
Aden, al-Mukalla, Perim Island, Socotra

ship maintenance and repair capability:
National Dockyards, Aden (4,500-ton floating dock and 1,500-ton slipway)

17. SUDAN

BASIC DATA

Official Name of State: The Republic of Sudan

Prime Minister and Head of the National Salvation Revolutionary Command Council: Lieutenant General Omar Hassan al-Bashir (also Defense Minister)

State Minister at the Ministry of Defense: Major General Uthman Muhammad al-Hassan

Chief of the General Staff: Lieutenant General Ishaq Ibrahim Umar

Commander of the Air Force: Major General Ali Youssuf Ahmad al-Badri

Commander of the Air Defense: Major General Abd al-Haliq Ibrahim

Commander of the Navy: Rear Admiral Fathi Ahmad Ali

Area: 2,504,530 sq. km.

Population:		23,800,000
ethnic subdivision:		
Arabs	9,996,000	42.0%
Nilotics, Negroes and others	13,804,000	58.0%
religious subdivision:		
Sunni Muslims	16,660,000	70.0%
Animists	4,760,000	20.0%
Christians (Coptic, Greek Orthodox, Catholic, Protestant)	1,190,000	5.0%
Not known	1,190,000	5.0%
Refugees:(excluded from total)	1,200,000	
Ethiopians	800,000	
Chadians	150,000	
Ugandans	250,000	

GDP:
- 1986--$8.80 billion
- 1987--$11.08 billion

Balance of Payments (goods, services & unilateral transfer payments):

year	income	expenditure	balance
1987	$ 591 mil.	$1.02 bil.	-$429 mil.
1988	$ 815 mil.	$1.26 bil.	-$445 mil.

Defense Expenditure:
- 1987--$420 million (unconfirmed)
- 1989--$235 million

Foreign Military Aid and Security Assistance Received:

financial aid from:

Egypt--$42 million grant of arms; Kuwait; Libya--grant, oil shipments; PRC--$30 million loan (possibly civilian); Saudi Arabia--grant

military training:
foreign advisors/instructors from--Britain, Egypt, Iraq (technicians), USA (including aircraft maintenance personnel); Yugoslavia (unconfirmed)
trainees abroad in--Egypt, Jordan, Iran, Iraq, Saudi Arabia, Libya, USA, FRG, Turkey (unconfirmed) Yugoslavia
arms transfers from:
Brazil (transport aircraft); Canada (transport aircraft); Egypt (ATGMs, APCs); France (artillery pieces); Iraq (artillery pieces, MRLs, ammunition, small arms); Jordan (obsolete weapons); Libya (small arms, aircraft spares, trucks; combat aircraft, unconfirmed); PRC (tanks, artillery, APCs); Romania (helicopters); USA (tanks, SP AAGs); Spain/FRG (helicopters); Turkey (small arms, FRG-designed)
support forces from:
Egypt (engineering units); Libya (two or more aircraft flying close air support missions; troops in Western Sudan)
construction aid from:
USA, Saudi Arabia (airport)
maintenance of equipment in:
USA (aircraft); Jordan (civil aircraft)

Foreign Military Aid and Security Assistance Extended:
military training:
advisors/instructors in--
UAE
foreign trainees from--
Eritrean rebels; Kuwait, Jordan, Qatar, UAE; Egypt (unconfirmed, part of an exchange program)
arms transfers to:
Eritrean rebels
facilities provided to:
Eritrean rebels (camps, unconfirmed); Palestinian organizations (al-Fatah forces evacuated from Lebanon, camps)

Joint Maneuvers with:
Egypt

INFRASTRUCTURE

Road Network:

length:	47,000 km
paved roads	2,000 km
gravel and crushed stone roads	4,000 km
earth tracks	41,000 km

main routes:
Khartoum--Shendi--Atbara--Suakin--Port Sudan
Atbara--Wadi Halfa (Egyptian border)
Atbara--Merowe--Wadi Halfa

Khartoum--Kassala--Asmara (Ethiopia)
Khartoum--Wad Medani--Gedaref--Gondar (Ethiopia)
Kosti--Malakal--Juba--Kampala (Uganda)/Juba--Niangara (Zaire)
Khartoum--al-Dueim--Rabak/Kosti
Kosti--Gedaref--Kassala--Port Sudan
Kosti--al-Obeid--al-Fasher--al-Geneina--Abeche (Chad)
Port Sudan--Hurghada (Egypt)

Railway Network:

length:	5,516 km
narrow gauge (1.067 meter)	4,800 km
1.6096 meter gauge (plantation line)	716 km

main routes:
Khartoum--Wadi Halfa
Khartoum--Atbara--Port Sudan
Khartoum--Sennar--Kosti--El Obeid
Khartoum--Wad Medani--Sennar--Damazin/Sennar--Kosti--Babanusa
Babanusa--Nyala
Babanusa--Wau

Airfields:

airfields by runway type:	
permanent surface fields	8
unpaved fields and usable airstrips	70
airfields by runway length:	
2440--3659 meters	4
1220--2439	31
under 1220	43
TOTAL	78

international airport: Khartoum
major domestic airfields: Atbara, Dongola, El Fasher, El Geneina, Juba, Kassala, Malakal, Merowe, Myala, El Obeida, Port Sudan, Wadi Halfa, Wau

Airlines:

companies: Sudan Airways (international, charter, domestic), Trans Arabian Air Transport (cargo), Nile Safaris Cargo (cargo charter)

aircraft:	
Boeing 737-200C/737-200	2
Boeing 707-320C	8
DC-8-50F	1
Fokker F-27-200/600	3
Fokker F-50	2

on order: 2 additional Fokker F-50 (unconfirmed)

Maritime Facilities:

harbor--Port Sudan, Suakin

Merchant Marine:

vessel type	number	DWT
general cargo	4	38,694

multi-purpose	2	25,810
general cargo/container	5	60,555
TOTAL	11	125,059

ARMED FORCES

Personnel:

military forces--	
army	50,000
air force (including air defense)	5,500
navy	700
TOTAL	56,200
para-military forces--	
popular defense units	3,500
border guards	2,500
Sudan People's Liberation Army (SPLA), anti-government rebels in control of parts of Southern Sudan (estimate)	30,000

Army:

major units:

unit type	divisions	brigades
armored	1	2
infantry	4	10
airborne		1
republican guard		1
TOTAL (partly skeleton or undermanned)	5	14

small arms:

personal weapons--
- 9mm Sterling SMG
- 7.62mm AK-47 (Kalashnikov) AR
- 7.62mm G-3 (Heckler & Koch) AR
- 7.62mm SKS (Simonov) SAR

machine guns--
- 12.7mm D.Sh.K. 38/46 (Degtyarev) HMG
- 7.62mm MG-3
- 7.62mm RPD (Degtyarev) LMG
- 7.62mm SGM (Goryunov) MMG

light and medium mortars--
- 82mm M-43

light ATRLs--
- RPG-7

tanks:

model	number
high quality	
M-60 A3	20
medium quality	
T-55/Type 59 (number unconfirmed)	170

low quality		
T-54		70
M-47		15
M-41		55
Type 62		70
	(sub-total	210)
TOTAL		400
APCs/ARVs:		
model		number
high quality		
M-113		80
V-150 Commando		54
AMX-VCI		a few
	(sub-total	134+)
others		
al-Walid		20+
AML-90		6
BTR-50		
BTR-152		200
Ferret		60
M-3 (Panhard, unconfirmed)		
OT-64		
OT-62		
Saladin		50
	(sub-total	716)
TOTAL		850+
on order: 60 Fahd APCs (unconfirmed)		
artillery:		
self propelled guns and howitzers--		
155mm Mk. F-3 (AMX) SP howitzer		11
towed guns and howitzers--		
155mm M-114		12
130mm Type 59		10
122mm M-1938 howitzer		
105mm M-101 howitzer		
100mm M-1955 field/AT gun		
25 lb. (87mm) howitzer		
85mm M-1945/D-44 field/AT gun		
mortars, heavy, under 160mm--		
120mm mortar		
TOTAL		250
MRLs--		
122mm Saqr		
anti-tank weapons:		
missiles--		
BGM-71C Improved TOW (unconfirmed)		
Swingfire		
AT-3 (Sagger)		

army anti-aircraft defenses:
missiles--
man-portable
SA-7 (Grail)
MIM-43A Redeye

short-range guns--	number
40mm Bofors L-60	80
37mm M-1939	80
23mm ZU 23x2	+
20mm M-163 A-1 Vulcan SP	8
20mm M-167 Vulcan (number unconfirmed)	32
TOTAL	200+

Air Force:

aircraft--general: (low serviceability)	number
combat aircraft	59
transport aircraft	30
helicopters	67
combat aircraft:	
interceptors--	
medium and low quality	
F-6 Shenyang	23
MiG-21 (Fishbed)	8
Total	31
strike and multi-role aircraft--	
medium and low quality	
F-5E/F	5
MiG-23 (Flogger)	3
MiG-17 (Fresco)/Shenyang F-5	20
Total	28
transport aircraft:	
An-24 (Coke)	5
C-130H Hercules (some being overhauled in USA)	5
CASA C-212 (some employed in maritime surveillance role)	6
DHC-5D Buffalo	3
DHC-6 Twin Otter	1
EMB-110 P-2	6
Fokker F-27	4
TOTAL	30
on order: 2 C-212	
training and liaison aircraft:	
with ground attack/close air support capability--	
BAC-145 Jet Provost	5
BAC-167 Strikemaster	3
TOTAL	8

helicopters:	number
medium transport--	
Mi-4 (Hound)	3

Mi-8 (Hip)	14
SA-330 Puma/IAR-330 Puma	24
Bell 212/AB-212	4
(sub-total	45)
light transport--	
MBB BO-105 (possibly serving police)	22
TOTAL	67

advanced armament:
  air-to-air missiles--
    AIM-9M Sidewinder
    AA-2 (Atoll)
anti-aircraft defenses:
  long range missiles--

model	batteries
SA-2 (Guideline)	5

military airfields: 13
  Atbara, Dongola, al-Fasher, al-Geneina, Juba, Khartoum, Malakal, Merowe, al-Obeid, Port Sudan, Wad Medani, Wadi Sayidina, Wau

Navy:

combat vessels:	number
patrol craft--	
PBR (Yugoslav) 115 ft. (35 meter)	3
Abeking and Rasmussen 75.2 ft. (22.9 meter)	3
Sewart class	4
Total	10

on order: six 11 meter patrol boats from Spain (unconfirmed)

landing craft:
  DTM-221 LCT 2

naval base:
  Port Sudan

18. SYRIA

BASIC DATA

Official Name of State: The Arab Republic of Syria
Head of State: President Hafez al-Assad
Prime Minister: Mahmoud al-Zuebi
Defense Minister: Lieutenant General Mustafa al-Tlass
Chief of the General Staff: General Hikmat Shihabi
Commander of the Air Force: Major-General Ali Mulakhafji
Commander of the Navy: Rear Admiral Mustafa Tayara
Area: 185,680 sq. km.

Population:		11,340,000
ethnic subdivision:		
Arabs	9,972,000	88.0%
Kurds	907,000	8.0%
Armenians and others	461,000	4.0%
religious subdivision:		
Sunni Muslims	7,768,000	68.5%
Alawis	1,474,000	13.0%
Shi'ite Muslims	171,000	1.5%
Druze	340,000	3.0%
Christians (Greek Orthodox, Gregorian, Armenian Catholics, Syrian Orthodox, Greek Catholics)	1,474,000	13.0%
Others	113,000	1.0%

GDP (figures unreliable; calculated according to the official rate of exchange of 3.925 Syrian Pounds per US dollar in 1986, and 11.225 Syrian Pounds per US dollar in 1987)
1986--$25.55 billion
1987--$11.25 billion

Balance of Payments (goods, services & unilateral transfer payments):

year	income	expenditure	balance
1986	$2.62 bil.	$3.15 bil.	-$530 mil.
1987	$2.95 bil.	$3.14 bil.	-$190 mil.

Defense Expenditure:
1987--$3.35 billion
1989--$1.47 billion, unreliable figure due to unrealistic rates of exchange; could be as high as $ 3.3 billion

Foreign Military Aid and Security Assistance Received:
financial aid from:
joint Arab fund-- partly from Saudi Arabia; Libya--loan
military training:
foreign advisors/instructors from--USSR (2000), Bulgaria, Cuba, Hungary, GDR, North Korea

trainees abroad in--USSR, other East European countries, France, Libya
arms transfers from:
France (ATGMs, helicopters); USSR (SP artillery, combat aircraft, helicopters, coastal defense SSMs, naval vessels, SAMs, SSMs, tanks, submarines)
Foreign Military Aid and Security Assistance Extended:
financial aid to:
Palestinian organizations (al-Fatah rebels, al-Sa'iqa, PPSF, PLF and PFLP-GC)--grants; Lebanese army loyal to Herawi
military training:
advisors/instructors/serving personnel in--Libya (pilots), Palestinian units (al-Sa'iqa), PDRY, al-Amal militia in Lebanon
foreign trainees from--Palestinian organizations, PDRY, Libya, al-Amal Lebanese militia, Lebanon (Shi'ite Army officers)
arms transfers to:
Palestinian military forces (tanks, artillery pieces, small arms); al-Amal and other militias in Lebanon (tanks, artillery, MRLs); Lebanese army loyal to Herawi (artillery; tanks, unconfirmed)
facilities provided to:
USSR (use of Latakia and Tartus harbor, T-4 airfield); al-Fatah rebels, PPSF, PFLP-GC, PFLP, DFLP, al-Sa'iqa and PLF (camps); PKK (Kurdish anti-Turkish group; camps in Syrian held parts of Biq'a, Lebanon and in northern Syria)
forces deployed abroad in:
Lebanon--30,000-40,000 in Biq'a, northern Lebanon (Tripoli area), and Beirut
Cooperation in Arms Production/Assembly with:
North Korea (upgrading SSMs, unconfirmed)

INFRASTRUCTURE

Road Network:

length:	27,000 km
paved roads	21,000 km
gravel and crushed stone roads	3,000 km
improved earth tracks	3,000 km

main routes:
Damascus--Homs--Hama--Aleppo
Tartus--Banias--Latakia
Latakia--Aleppo--Dir e-Zor--Qusaybah (Iraq)
Tartus--Homs--Palmyra--Qusaybah
Banias--Hama
Damascus--Beirut (Lebanon)
Damascus--Palmyra--Dir e-Zor--al-Hasakah-- al-Qamishli
Damascus--al-Rutbah (Iraq)

Damascus--Dar'a--Ramtha (Jordan)
Damascus--Kuneitra--Rosh Pina (Israel)
Tartus--Tripoli (Lebanon)

Railway Network:

length:	1,997 km
standard gauge	1,686 km
narrow gauge	311 km

main routes:
Aleppo--Adana (Turkey)
Aleppo--Latakia
Aleppo--Hama--Homs--Tripoli (Lebanon)/Homs--Zahlah (Lebanon)/Homs--Damascus
Aleppo--al-Qamishli--Mosul (Iraq)
Aleppo--Dir e-Zor--al-Qamishli
Damascus--Dar'a--Ramtha (Jordan)
Damascus--Beirut (Lebanon)
Latakia--Tartus
Latakia--Aleppo
Tartus--Homs
Dir e-Zor--Abu Kemal

Airfields:

airfields by runway type:	
permanent surface fields	24
unpaved fields and usable airstrips	70
airfields by runway length:	
2440--3659 meters	21
1220--2439	4
under 1220	69
TOTAL	94

international airports: Aleppo, Damascus, Latakia
major domestic airfields: Dir e-Zor, Palmyra, al-Qamishli, al-Hasakah

Airlines:

companies: Syrian Arab Airlines (international and domestic)

aircraft:	
Boeing 747 SP	2
Boeing 727-200	3
Caravelle 10B (Super Caravelle)	2
Tupolev Tu-134	7
Tupolev Tu-154	3

Maritime Facilities:

harbors--Latakia, Tartus
anchorages--Arwad, Jablah, Banias
oil terminals--Banias, Latakia, Tartus

Merchant Marine:

vessel type	number	DWT
general cargo	11	51,290

SYRIA

Defense Production:

army equipment:

ammunition; toxic gases; chemical warheads for SSMs (unconfirmed); upgrading of tanks; upgrading of SSMs (with assistance from North Korea, unconfirmed)

ARMED FORCES

Personnel:

military forces--

	regular	reserves	total
army	306,000	100,000	406,000
air force & air defense	80,000	37,500	117,500
navy	4,000	2,500	6,500
TOTAL	390,000	140,000	530,000

Beyond 100,000 trained reserves, Syria can mobilize another 900,000 reserves, not currently organized

para-military forces--

Workers' Militia	400,000

Army:

major units:

unit type	army corps HQ	divisions	independent brigades/ groups
all arms	2		
armored		6	1
mechanized		3	1
infantry/ special forces		1	
airborne/ special forces			7
TOTAL	2	10	9

note: 2 new divisions being organized

small arms:

personal weapons--

9mm Model 23/25 SMG
7.62mm AK-47 (Kalashnikov) AR
7.62mm AKM AR
7.62mm SKS (Simonov) SAR
5.45mm AK-74 (Kalashnikov, unconfirmed) AR

machine guns--

12.7mm D.Sh.K. 38/46 (Degtyarev) HMG
7.62mm PK/PKS (Kalashnikov) LMG
7.62mm RPD (Degtyarev) LMG
7.62mm SG-43 (Goryunov) MMG
7.62mm SGM (Goryunov) MMG

light and medium mortars--

82mm M-43

SYRIA

- light ATRLs--
  - RPG-7
- tanks: (some in storage)
  - model — number
    - high quality
      - T-72/Improved T-72 — 1100
    - medium quality
      - T-62 — 1000
      - T-55 — 2100
      - (sub-total 3100)
    - TOTAL — 4200
    - on order: Improved T-72
- APCs/ARVs: (some in storage)
  - model
    - high quality
      - BMP-1
      - BMP-2 — several scores
      - (sub-total 2200)
    - others
      - BTR-152
      - BTR-40/50/60
      - BRDM-2
      - (sub-total 1600)
    - TOTAL — 3800
- artillery: (some in storage)
  - self propelled guns and howitzers--
    - 152mm M-1973 SP howitzer
    - 122mm M-1974 SP howitzer
    - 122mm (Syrian)
  - towed guns and howitzers--
    - 180mm S-23 gun
    - 152mm M-1943 howitzer
    - 152mm D-20
    - 130mm M-46 gun
    - 122mm D-30 howitzer
    - 122mm D-74 gun
    - 122mm M-1938 howitzer
  - mortars, heavy, over 160mm--
    - 240mm mortar
    - 160mm mortar
  - mortars, heavy, under 160mm--
    - 120mm mortar
  - TOTAL — 2300
  - MRLs--
    - 240mm BM-24
    - 140mm BM-14-16
    - 122mm BM-21
- engineering equipment:
  - MTU-55 bridging tanks
  - MTU-67 bridging tank

MT-55 bridging tanks	
tank-towed bridges	
mine-clearing rollers	
AFV transporters:	800
anti-tank weapons:	
missiles--	launchers
AT-3 (Sagger)	
AT-4 (Spigot)	
AT-5 (Spandrel) mounted on BMP-2	
BRDM-2 carrying AT-3 (Sagger) SP	
MILAN	
TOTAL	2000
guns--	
73mm SPG-9 recoilless gun	
surface-to-surface missiles and rockets:	
model	launchers
FROG-7	24
SS-1 (Scud B)	18
SS-21 (Scarab)	18
TOTAL	60
on order: additional SSMs	
army anti-aircraft defenses:	
missiles--	
self propelled/mobile	
SA-6 (Gainful)	
SA-8 (Gecko)	
SA-9 (Gaskin)	
SA-13 (Gopher)	
man-portable	
SA-7 (Grail)	
SA-14 (Gremlin)	
SA-16	
short range guns--	number
57mm ZSU 57x2 SP	
57mm M-1950 (S-60)	
23mm ZSU 23x4 SP (Gun Dish)	
23mm ZU 23x2	
TOTAL	1000
CW capabilities:	
personal protective equipment, Soviet type	
unit decontamination equipment	
stockpiles of nerve gas, including Sarin	
chemical warheads for SSMs	
biological warfare capabilities:	
biological weapons and toxins (unconfirmed)	

Air Force:

aircraft--general:	number
combat aircraft	620
transport aircraft	32

Item		Number
helicopters		290
combat aircraft:		
interceptors--		
high quality		
MiG-25 and MiG-25R (Foxbat)		45
MiG-29 (Fulcrum, multi-role, employed as interceptor)		20
	(sub-total	65)
others		
MiG-21 MF/S/bis/U (Fishbed)		
MiG-23 ML/MF/MS		
	(sub-total	275)
Total		340
strike and multi-role aircraft--		
high quality		
Su-24 (Fencer)		20
medium quality		
MiG-23 U/BN (Flogger)		
Su-20/22 (Fitter C)		
	(sub-total	215)
others (limited serviceability)		
MiG-17 (Fresco)		
Su-7B (Fitter A)		
	(sub-total	45)
Total		280
on order: additional MiG-29 (Fulcrum, total order 80); Su-24 (Fencer, total order 48), delivery in progress		
transport aircraft:		number
An-24/26 (Coke/Curl)		
IL-14 (Crate)		
IL-18 (Coot)		
IL-76 (Candid)		
Mystere Falcon 20		
Yak-40 (Codling)		
TOTAL		32
training and liaison aircraft:		
with ground attack/close air support capability--		
L-29 Delfin		60
L-39 Albatross		100
	(sub-total	160)
others--		
MBB 223 Flamingo		43
Piper Navajo		2
Yak-11 (Moose)		
Yak-18 (Max)		
	(sub-total	45+)
TOTAL		205+

helicopters:
  attack--
    Mi-24/Mi-25 (Hind) 60
    SA-342 Gazelle 55
    (sub-total 115)
  medium transport--
    Mi-8 (Hip)/Mi-17 (Hip H) 130
    Mi-4 (Hound, limited serviceability) 10
    Mi-2 (Hoplite, limited serviceability) 10
    (sub-total 150)
  ASW--
    Kamov Ka-25 (Hormone) 5
    Mi-14 (Haze) 20
    (sub-total 25)
  TOTAL 290
miscellaneous aircraft:
  AEW/AWACS aircraft--
    Tu-126 (Moss) AEW, operated with Soviet aid (unconfirmed)
  RPVs and mini-RPVs--
    Soviet-made RPVs
advanced armament:
  air-to-air missiles--
    AA-2 (Atoll)
    AA-6 (Acrid)
    AA-7 (Apex)
    AA-8 (Aphid)
    AA-10 (Alamo, unconfirmed)
    AA-11 (Archer, unconfirmed)
  air-to-ground missiles--
    AS-11
    AS-12
    AT-2 (Swatter)
    AT-6
    HOT
anti-aircraft defenses:
  radars--
    Long Track•
    P-15 Flat Face
    P-12 Spoon Rest
  long-range missiles--

model	batteries
SA-2 (Guideline) & SA-3 (Goa)	100
SA-5 (Gammon)	8
TOTAL	108

  aircraft shelters--
    in all airfields, for combat aircraft only
military airfields: 21
  Aleppo, al-Qusayr, Blay, Damascus (international), Damascus (Meze), Dir e-Zor, Dumayr, al-Suweida, Hama,

Khalkhala, Latakia, Nassiriyah, Palmyra, Sayqal, Shayarat, T-4, 5 additional

aircraft maintenance and repair capability:

for all models in service

Navy:

combat vessels:	number
submarines	
R class (Romeo)	3
MFPBs--	
Komar	5
Ossa I	6
Ossa II	10
Total	21
ASW vessels--	
Petya II submarine chaser frigate	2
mine warfare vessels--	
T-43 class minesweeper	1
Vanya class minesweeper	2
Yevgenia class minesweeper	4
Total	7
patrol craft--	
Zhuk class	6
Natya (formerly a minesweeper)	1
Total	7
landing craft:	
Polnochny B class LCT	3
auxiliary vessels:	
training ship (al-Assad)	1
Poluchat torpedo recovery vessel	1
advanced armament:	
SS-N-2 Styx/SS-N-2C SSM	
coastal defense:	
SSC-1B Sepal coastal defense missile	
SSC-3 coastal defense missile	
naval bases:	3
Latakia, Minat al-Baida, Tartus	
ship maintenance and repair capability:	
repairs at Latakia	

note: ASW helicopters listed under Air Force

19. TUNISIA

BASIC DATA

Official Name of State: The Republic of Tunisia

Head of State: President General Zine al-Abedine Ben Ali (also Defense Minister)

Prime Minister: Hamid al-Karoui

Minister of Defense: Abdullah al-Kallal

Chief of the General Staff: General Muhammad Said al-Katib

Commander of the Ground Forces : General Muhammad Hadi Bin Hassin

Commander of the Air Force: Major General Riva Atar

Commander of the Navy: Vice Admiral Habib Fadhila

Chief of Staff of the Navy: Captain al-Shazli al-Sharif

Area: 164,206 sq. km.

Population:		7,810,000
ethnic subdivision:		
Arabs/Berbers	7,654,000	98.0%
Europeans	62,000	0.8%
Others	94,000	1.2%
religious subdivision:		
Sunni Muslims	7,654,000	98.0%
Christians	78,000	1.0%
Others, including Jews	78,000	1.0%

GDP:
- 1987--$9.60 billion
- 1988--$10.03 billion

Balance of Payments (goods, services & unilateral transfer payments):

year	income	expenditure	balance
1987	$3.89 bil.	$3.95 bil.	- $60 mil.
1988	$4.97 bil.	$4.75 bil.	-$220 mil.

Defense Expenditure:
- 1986--$417 million
- 1987--$520 million (unconfirmed)

Foreign Military Aid and Security Assistance Received:

financial aid from:
Saudi Arabia--grant; USA--$30 million grant

military training:
foreign advisors/instructors from--USA; France (unconfirmed)
trainees abroad in--Algeria, Egypt, France, Saudi Arabia, USA

arms transfers from:
Austria (light tanks, small arms); Belgium (small arms); Brazil (APCs, ARVs); Britain (patrol craft, target drones); France (helicopters, naval SSMs); Italy

(trainer aircraft, APCs); USA (artillery pieces, SAMs, tanks, transport aircraft)

Foreign Military Aid and Security Assistance Extended:
- military training:
  - foreign trainees from--Algeria (part of an exchange program)
- arms transfers to:
  - Palestinian organizations (unconfirmed)
- facilities provided to:
  - France (radar station); PLO/Fatah (camps)

Cooperation in Arms Production/Assembly with:
- Algeria and Italy (diesel engines); South Korea (patrol craft)

Joint Maneuvers with:
- France, USA; Spain (unconfirmed)

INFRASTRUCTURE

Road Network:

length:	17,700 km
paved roads	9,100 km
gravel roads and improved earth tracks	8,600 km

main routes:
- Tunis--Bizerta
- Tunis--Annaba (Algeria)
- Tunis--Kairouan--Gafsa--Tozeur--Touggourt (Algeria)
- Tunis--Sousse--Sfax--Gabes--Tripoli (Libya)
- Sousse--Kasserine
- Gabes--Gafsa

Railway Network:

length:	2,051 km
standard gauge	465 km
narrow gauge (1.0 meter)	1,586 km

main routes:
- Tunis--Bizerta
- Tunis--Annaba (Algeria)
- Tunis--Kasserine--Gafsa--Tozeur
- Tunis--Sousse--Sfax--Gabes
- Sfax--Gafsa--Tozeur

Airfields:

airfields by runway type:	
permanent surface fields	13
unpaved fields and usable airstrips	16
airfields by runway length:	
2440--3659 meters	6
1220--2439	8
under 1220	15
TOTAL	29

international airports: Jerba, Monastir, Sfax, Tabarka, Tozeur, Tunis (Carthage)

domestic airfields: Gafsa; Gabes (under construction)

TUNISIA

Airlines:

companies: Tunis Air (international and domestic), Tunisavia (domestic), Air Liberte Tunisie

aircraft:

Airbus A-300 B4-200	1
Boeing 737-200C/737-200	4
Boeing 727-200	8
DHC-6 Twin Otter	2
Mystere-Falcon 20C	1
Piper Cheyenne II	1

on order: 1 Airbus A-300 B4-200, 3 A-320, 2 Boeing 737-500

helicopters:

SA-316B Alouette III	1
SA-330 Puma	1
SA-365N/365C Dauphin 2	2

Maritime Facilities:

harbors--Bizerta, Gabes, La Goulette (Tunis), Sousse, Sfax, Zarzis (under construction)

oil terminals--Ashtart, Bizerta (Menzel Bourguiba), Gabes, La Goulette (Tunis), Sekhira

Merchant Marine:

vessel type	number	DWT
general cargo	6	42,011
passenger ferry	1	3,372
chemical tanker	6	58,267
crude carrier	1	37,224
small tanker	1	9,976
bulk carrier	3	58,581
gas tanker (LPG)	1	9,996
ro/ro cargo	2	5,296
TOTAL	21	224,723

Defense Production:

army equipment:

production under license--

diesel engines (with Italy and Algeria)

naval craft:

production--

20 meter patrol craft, with assistance from South Korea

ARMED FORCES

Personnel:

military forces--

army	33,000
air force	2,500
navy	4,500
TOTAL	40,000

reserves: some (unconfirmed)

para-military forces--

gendarmerie	2,000
national guard	5,000

Army:

major units:

unit type	regiments/brigades
armored reconnaissance	1
infantry/mechanized	2
commando/paratroops	1
Sahara Drigade	1
TOTAL	5

small arms:

personal weapons--
- 9mm Model 38/49 Beretta SMG
- 9mm Sterling SMG
- 7.62mm FAC (FN) SAR
- 5.56mm AUG Steyr AR

machine guns--
- 7.62mm (0.3") Browning M-1919 MMG
- 7.62mm MAG(FN)LMG

light and medium mortars--
- 82mm
- 81mm
- 60mm

light ATRLs--
- 89mm Strim-89

tanks:

model		number
high quality		
M-60 A3		54
medium quality		
M-48 A3		15
SK-105 (Kurassier)		54
	(sub-total	69)
low quality		
AMX-13		50
M-41		15
	(sub-total	65)
TOTAL		188

APCs/ARVs:

model		number
high quality		
Engesa EE-11/EE-9		20
Fiat Type 6614		110
M-113 A1/A2/M-125/M-577		100
V-150 Commando		a few
Steyr 4K 7FA (unconfirmed)		a few
	(sub-total	230+)

others
AML-60/AML-90 25
EBR-75 15
Saladin 20
(sub-total 60)
TOTAL 290+
on order: Fahd

artillery:
self propelled guns and howitzers--
155mm M-109 howitzer 18
105mm M-108 howitzer 10
(sub-total 28)
towed guns and howitzers--
155mm M-114 howitzer (unconfirmed) 18
105mm M-101 howitzer 50
25 lb. (87mm) howitzer
(sub-total 68)
TOTAL 96+
on order: 57 155mm M-198 howitzers

AFV transporters:
on order: US-made transporters

anti-tank weapons:
missiles-- launchers
BGM-71A TOW 100
M-901 ITV SP (TOW under armor) 35
MILAN

army anti-aircraft defenses:
missiles--
self propelled/mobile
MIM-72A Chaparral
man-portable
RBS-70
SA-7 (Grail)
short-range guns-- number
40mm
37mm
on order: 26 20mm M-163 Vulcan SP AAG; Egyptian AD systems (unconfirmed)

Air Force:

aircraft--general: number
combat aircraft 11
transport aircraft 8
helicopters 31

combat aircraft:
strike and multi-role aircraft--
medium and low quality
F-5E/F-5F 11
on order: 4-12 additional F-5E/F-5F

transport aircraft:

C-130H Hercules	4
other	4
TOTAL	8
training and liaison aircraft:	
with ground attack/close air support capability--	
Aermacchi MB-326 B/KT/LT	10
others--	
Rockwell T-6	12
SIAI-Marchetti SF-260WT/C	17
SIAI-Marchetti S-208	2
(sub-total	31)
TOTAL	41
on order: EMB-312 (unconfirmed), Alpha Jet (unconfirmed)	
helicopters:	
medium transport--	
AB-205/Bell-205	18
SA-330 Puma	1
(sub-total	19)
light transport--	
Alouette III	6
AS-350 Ecureuil	6
(sub-total	12)
TOTAL	31
advanced armament:	
air-to-air missiles--	
AIM-9J Sidewinder	
military airfields:	7
Bizerta, Gabes, Gafsa, Jerba, Monastir, Sfax, Tunis	
aircraft maintenance and repair capability:	
routine maintenance and repairs	

Navy:

combat vessels:	number
MFPBs--	
Combattante III	3
P-48	3
Total	6
gun frigates--	
Savage class	1
ASW vessels--	
Le Fougeux class corvette	1
mine warfare vessels--	
Adjutant class minesweeper	2
gunboats/MTBs--	
Shanghai II gunboat	2
patrol craft--	
Vosper Thornycroft 103 ft. (31 meter)	2
Ch. Navals de l'Esterel 83 ft. (25 meter)	6

Lurssen 23 meter	4
Total	12
auxiliary vessels:	
tug	3
advanced armament:	
MM-40 Exocet	
SS-12	
naval bases:	5
Bizerta, Kelibia, Sfax, Sousse, Tunis	
ship maintenance and repair capability:	
4 drydocks and 1 slipway at Bizerta; 2 pontoons and 1 floating dock at Sfax. Capability to maintain and repair existing vessels.	

20. UNITED ARAB EMIRAES (UAE)

BASIC DATA

Official Name of State: United Arab Emirates*

Head of State: President Shaykh Zayid ibn Sultan al-Nuhayan, Emir of Abu Dhabi (also Supreme Commander of the Armed Forces)

Prime Minister: Shaykh Rashid ibn Said al-Maktum, Emir of Dubai (also Vice President)

Minister of Defense: Shaykh Muhammad ibn Rashid al-Maktum

Commander-in-Chief of the Armed Forces: Brigadier General Sultan ibn Zayid

Chief of the General Staff: Brigadier General Muhammad Said al-Badi

Commander of the Ground Forces: Major General Abid Ali al-Abed al-Khatabi

Commander of the Air Force and Air Defense Forces: Brigadier General Shaykh Muhammad ibn Zayd al-Nuhayan

Commander of the Navy: Commodore Hazza Sultan al-Darmaki

Area: approximately 82,900 sq. km. (borders with Oman, Saudi Arabia and Qatar partly undemarcated and/or disputed)

Population:		1,500,000
ethnic subdivision:		
Arabs	750,000	50.0%
Southeast Asians	657,000	43.8%
Others (Europeans, Persians)	93,000	6.2%
religious subdivision:		
Sunni Muslims	938,000	62.5%
Shi'ite Muslims	225,000	15.0%
Others	337,000	22.5%
nationality subdivision:		
UAE nationals	285,000	19.0%
Alien Arabs	345,000	23.0%
Southeast Asians (Indians, Pakistanis, Thais, Filipinos)	750,000	50.0%
Others (Europeans, Iranians)	120,000	8.0%

GDP:
1987--$23.70 billion
1988--$23.84 billion

Defense Expenditure:
1986--$1.58 billion
1989--$1.59 billion

*The UAE consists of seven principalities: Abu Dhabi, Dubai, Ras al-Khaimah, Sharjah, Umm al-Qaiwain, Fujairah and Ajman.

Foreign Military Aid and Security Assistance Received:
- military training:
  - foreign advisors/instructors/serving personnel from--Britain, Egypt, France, Jordan, Morocco, Pakistan, USA (some civilians)
  - trainees abroad in--Britain, Egypt, France, Jordan, Pakistan, Saudi Arabia, USA
- arms transfers from:
  - Brazil (APCs); Britain (APCs, artillery pieces, mobile workshops, SAMs, trainer aircraft, AFV transporters); Egypt (APCs, air defense systems on order); France (combat aircraft, tanks, AGMs, AAMs); FRG (tank transporters); Italy (trainer aircraft, transport aircraft); Spain (transport aircraft); Sweden (SAMs via Singapore); Switzerland (trainer aircraft); USA (aircraft training simulator, transport aircraft, SAMs, light reconnaissance vehicles, radio systems)
- support forces from:
  - Morocco (5000, unconfirmed)
- construction aid by:
  - Britain (naval base)

Foreign Military Aid and Security Assistance Extended:
- financial aid to:
  - Syria, Morocco, Palestinian organizations; Jordan--grant; Iraq--loan
- military training:
  - foreign trainees from--Bahrain, Kuwait, Qatar, YAR (unconfirmed)
- facilities provided to: USA (storage facilities)

Forces Deployed Abroad in:
- Saudi Arabia (part of GCC rapid deployment force)

Joint Maneuvers with:
- GCC (members: Bahrain, Kuwait, Oman, Qatar, Saudi Arabia, UAE)

INFRASTRUCTURE

Road Network:

length:	2,000 km
paved roads	1,800 km
gravel and improved earth tracks	200 km

main routes:
- Abu Dhabi--Jebel Dhanna
- Abu Dhabi--Bu Hasa
- Abu Dhabi--Muscat (Oman)
- Abu Dhabi--Dubai--Sharjah--Ajman--Ras al-Khaimah
- Dubai--Muscat
- Ajman--Fujairah--Muscat
- Ajman--Daba al-Bay'ah (Oman)

UAE

Airfields:

airfields by runway type:

permanent surface fields	19
unpaved fields and usable airstrips	14

airfields by runway length:

over 3660 meters	7
2440--3659	4
1220--2439	6
under 1220	16
TOTAL	33

international airports: Abu Dhabi, Dubai, Fujairah, Ras al-Khaimah, Sharjah

major domestic airfields: Jebel Dhanna, Mina Khor Fakkan

Airlines:

companies: Gulf Air (international)--jointly owned by UAE, Oman, Qatar and Bahrain, listed under Bahrain); Emirates Air Services (domestic and international)

aircraft (excluding Gulf Air):

Airbus A-300-600R	2
Airbus A-310-300	2
Boeing 727-200	3

on order: 2 Airbus A-300-600, 3 Airbus A-310-300

Maritime Facilities:

harbors--Mina Zayd (Abu Dhabi), Mina Jebel Ali (Dubai), Mina Rashid (Dubai), Mina Sakr (Ras al-Khaimah), Mina Khalid (Sharjah), Fujairah, Mina Khor Fakkan (Sharjah)

anchorages--Abu Bukhoosh (Abu Dhabi), Ras al-Khaimah

oil terminals--Dasa Island (Abu Dhabi), Halat al-Mubarras (Abu Dhabi), Jebel Dhanna (Abu Dhabi), Mina Rashid (Dubai), Fateh Oil Storage Terminal (Dubai), Mubarak Oil Terminal (Sharjah)

Merchant Marine:

vessel type	number	DWT
crude carrier	3	330,717
product tanker	6	218,215
general cargo	7	40,162
container	7	211,569
tanker	5	94,659
storage tanker	1	12,125
reefer	1	2,540
GC/container	5	118,536
bunkering tanker	5	108,609
cement carrier	2	26,486
TOTAL	42	1,163,618

Defense Production:

naval craft:

construction of patrol boats at Ajman (with British cooperation)

UAE

ARMED FORCES

Personnel:

military forces--	
army	42,000
air force	1,500
navy	1,500
TOTAL	45,000

Army:

major units:

unit type	brigades
armored	2
mechanized	1
infantry	3
TOTAL	6

small arms:
- personal weapons--
  - 9mm Sterling Mk.4 SMG
  - 7.62mm AK-47 (Kalashnikov) AR (unconfirmed)
  - 7.62mm FAL (FN) SAR
- machine guns--
  - 7.62mm (0.3") Browning M-1919 MMG
  - 7.62mm MAG (FN) LMG
- light and medium mortars--
  - 81mm L-16 A1

tanks:

model		number
medium quality		
AMX-30		100
OF-40 Lion MK.2		36
	(sub-total	136)
low quality		
Scorpion		80
TOTAL		216

APCs/ARVs:

model		number
high quality		
AMX-VCI		
AMX-10P		
Engesa EE-11 Urutu		30
M-3 (Panhard)		
VAB		20
VBC-90		
	(sub-total	430)
others		
AML-60/AML-90		
AT-105 Saxon		8
Fahd		50
Ferret		

Saladin	
Saracen	
Saxon (possibly with police)	
Shoreland Mk.2	
(sub-total	235)
TOTAL	665
on order: M-113 A2; EE-11; M-998 Hummer light reconnaissance vehicle	
artillery:	
self propelled guns and howitzers--	
155mm Mk. F3 (AMX) SP howitzer	20
towed guns and howitzers--	
105mm Light Gun	50
105mm M-102 howitzer	50
105mm M-56 Pack howitzer	12
(sub-total	112)
mortars, heavy, under 160mm--	
120mm mortar	12
TOTAL	144
MRLs--	
Firos	a few
anti-tank weapons:	
missiles--	launchers
BGM-71B Improved TOW	24
Vigilant	
guns--	
120mm BAT L-4 recoilless rifle	
84mm Carl Gustaf M-2 light recoilless rifle	
army anti-aircraft defenses:	
missiles--	launchers
self propelled/mobile	
Crotale	9
Rapier	
Skyguard AA system	
Tigercat	
man-portable	
Blowpipe	
Javelin (unconfirmed)	
RBS-70	
SA-7 (Grail)	
short-range guns--	
2x30mm M-3 VDA SP	
2x20mm GCF-BM2 SP	
on order: additional Crotale SAMs; Mistral SAMs	
CW capabilities:	
personal protective equipment	

Air Force:

aircraft--general:	number
combat aircraft	60

transport aircraft	32
helicopters	66
combat aircraft:	
strike and multi-role aircraft--	
high quality	
Mirage 2000	23
medium quality	
Mirage V--AD/RAD/DAD	16
Mirage III	10
(sub-total	26)
others	
Hawker Hunter	11
TOTAL	60
on order: 12 additional Mirage 2000	
transport aircraft:	
BAe-125	1
Boeing 707	3
Boeing 737	1
Britten-Norman BN-2 Islander	5
C-130H Hercules/L-100-30	6
CASA C-212 (employed in EW role)	4
DHC-4 Caribou	3
DHC-5D Buffalo	5
G-222	1
Gulfstream II	1
Mystere Falcon 20	1
VC-10	1
TOTAL	32
on order: G-222	
training and liaison aircraft:	
with ground attack/close air support capability--	
Aermacchi MB-326 KD/LD	8
Aermacchi MB-339	5
Hawk	16
(sub-total	29)
others--	
Cessna 182 Skylane	1
Pilatus PC-7	23
SIAI-Marchetti SF-260 WD	7
(sub-total	31)
TOTAL	60
on order: SF-260; 12 Aermacchi MB-339 (unconfirmed); 12 Hawk (unconfirmed)	
helicopters:	number
attack--	
SA-342K Gazelle	13
medium transport--	
AB-205/Bell 205	10
AB-212	3
AB-214	4

AB-412	
AS-332 Super Puma (2 in naval attack role)	8
SA-330 Puma	8
(sub-total	33)
light transport--	
AB-206 JetRanger/Bell 206L	6
Alouette III	7
AS-350 Ecureuil	1
BO-105 (employed in liaison role)	6
(sub-total	20)
TOTAL	66
on order: 30 A-109, A-129 (unconfirmed); 3 AB-412	
miscellaneous aircraft:	
AEW/AWACS aircraft--	
on order: E-2C Hawkeye AEW (unconfirmed), BN-Defender AEW	2
ELINT and EW--	
on order: C-130 EW	
target drones--	
TTL BTT-3 Banshee	
RPVs and mini-RPVs--	
Beech MQM-107A RPV	20
advanced armament:	
air-to-air missiles--	
AIM-9L Sidewinder	
R-550 Magique	
air-to-ground missiles--	
AS-11	
AS-12	
AM-39 Exocet	
anti-aircraft defenses:	
radars--	
AN/TPS-70	3
Watchman	
long-range missiles--	batteries
MIM-23B Improved HAWK	7
aircraft shelters--	
for combat aircraft at Abu Dhabi and Jebel Ali AF bases	
military airfields:	8
Abu Dhabi, al-Dhafra, Batin (Abu Dhabi), Dubai, Fujairah, Jebel Ali (Dubai), Ras al-Khaimah, Sharjah	

Navy:

combat vessels:	
MFPBs--	number
Lurssen TNC-45	6
patrol craft-- (some with coast guard)	
Vosper Thornycroft type 110 ft. (33.5 meter)	6

Camcraft 77 ft.	5
Camcraft 65 ft.	16
Watercraft 45 ft.	10
Cantieri Posillipo 68 ft.	1
Keith Nelson type 57 ft. (17.4 meter)	3
Cheverton 50 ft. (15.3 meter)	2
Keith Nelson (Dhafeer) class 40.3 ft. (12.3 meter)	6
Fairey Marine Spear	6
Boghammar (13 meter) police boat	3
P-1200	10
Baglietto GC-23 (serving coast guard)	4
Total	72

on order: 2 Lurssen 62 meter missile corvettes; 2 additional Lurssen TNC-45 MFPBs

landing craft:

Siong Huat 40 meter landing craft logistics 1

on order: 2 54 meter LCTs from Vosper QAF, Singapore

auxiliary vessels:

Cheverton Type tenders 2

on order: 2 Crestitalia 30-meter diver support vessels

advanced armament:

surface to surface missiles--

MM-40 Exocet SSMs

on order: 30 mm Vulcan-Goalkeeper anti-missile guns

special maritime forces:

a unit of frogmen, divers

naval bases: 13

Ajman, Dalma (Abu Dhabi), Fujairah, Mina Jebel Ali (Dubai), Mina Khalid (Sharjah), Mina Khor Fakkan (Sharjah), Mina Rashid (Dubai), Mina Sakr (Ras al-Khaimah), Mina Sultan (Sharja), Mina Zayd (Abu Dhabi), al-Qaffay Island (under construction), Taweelah Samha (under construction)

21. YEMEN (YAR)

BASIC DATA

Official Name of State: The Yemeni Arab Republic (YAR). On May 22, 1990, YAR and PDRY proclaimed their formal unification as one state. The unification is to include a two-and-a-half year transition period. Merger of the armed forces has begun. Here PDRY and YAR are still treated as two separate entities.

Head of State: President Colonel Ali Abdullah Salih

Prime Minister: Abd al-Aziz Abd al-Ghani

Chief of the General Staff: Major General Abdullah Hussayn al-Bashari until May 22, 1990

Commander of the People's Army: Lieutenant Colonel Abdullah Naji Daris

Commander of the Air Force: Ahmad al-Shaykh

Commander of the Navy: Commander Abd al-Karim Muharram

Area: 194,250 sq. km. (borders with Saudi Arabia and PDRY partly undemarcated and/or disputed)

Population:		7,530,000
ethnic subdivision:		
Arabs	6,777,000	90.0%
Afro-Arabs	602,000	8.0%
Others	151,000	2.0%
religious subdivision:		
Sunni Muslims	3,727,000	49.5%
Shi'ite Zaydi Muslims	3,614,000	48.0%
Shi'ite Isma'ili Muslims	53,000	0.7%
Others	136,000	1.8%

GDP:

1986--$3.98 billion (unreliable, due to several rates of exchange)

1987--$4.21 billion (unreliable, due to several rates of exchange)

Balance of Payments (goods, services & unilateral transfer payments):

year	income	expenditure	balance
1986	$893 mil.	$1.02 bil.	-$127 mil.
1987	$1.07 bil.	$1.52 bil.	-$450 mil.

Defense Expenditure:

1987--$414 million (unconfirmed)

1988--$620 million (unconfirmed)

Foreign Military Aid and Security Assistance Received:

financial aid from:

Libya--grant; Kuwait--grant; Saudi Arabia--grant; USA--$1 million grant

military training:

foreign advisors/instructors from--Cuba, Egypt, USA

(60, unconfirmed); USSR (500, unconfirmed); Saudi Arabia
trainees abroad in--Jordan, Saudi Arabia, USA, USSR
arms transfers from:
USSR (tanks, combat aircraft, SAMs, SSMs); Saudi Arabia (US-made arms, in coordination with the USA)
maintenance of equipment in:
USSR (aircraft)
Foreign Military Aid and Security Assistance Extended:
military training:
foreign trainees from--PLO organizations
facilities provided to:
al-Fatah (Palestinian): camps, use of airfield and naval facilities at Kamran Island; 15,000 anti-government troops from PDRY, loyal to former President Ali Nasser Muhammad, until the May 22, 1990 union

NFRASTRUCTURE

Road Network:

length:	22,275 km
paved roads	1,775 km
gravel and stone roads	500 km
earth and light gravel tracks	20,000 km

main routes:
San'a--Hodeida
San'a--Ta'iz--al-Mukha (Mocha)
Hodeida--Zabid--al-Mukha/Zabid--Ta'iz
Ta'iz--Aden (PDRY)
San'a--Sa'dah--Abha (Saudi Arabia)
Hodeida--al Saleef--Jizan (Saudi Arabia)

Airfields:

airfields by runway type:	
permanent surface fields	4
unpaved fields and usable airstrips	11
airfields by runway length:	
2440--3659 meters	9
1220--2439	3
under 1220	3
TOTAL	15

international airports: Hodeida, San'a
major domestic airfields: Kamran Island, Sa'dah, Ta'iz

Airlines:

companies: Yemenia--Yemen Airway Corporation (international and domestic)
aircraft:

Boeing 737-200	1
Boeing 727-200	4
DHC-7 Dash 7	2

YEMEN

Maritime Facilities:

harbors--Hodeida

anchorages--al-Mukha (harbor planned); al-Saleef (harbor under construction)

oil terminals--Hodeida

ARMED FORCES

Personnel:

military forces--

army	35,000+
air force	1,500
navy	800
TOTAL	37,300+

Army:

major units: (not all fully operational/fully organized)

unit type	brigades
armored	6
mechanized	3
infantry (mostly skeleton or undermanned)	9
commando/paratroops	1
special forces	1
central guards	1
TOTAL	21

small arms:

personal weapons--
- 7.62mm AK-47 (Kalashnikov) AR
- 7.62mm SKS (Simonov) SAR

machine guns--
- 12.7mm D.Sh.K. 38/46 (Degtyarev) HMG
- 7.62mm PK/PKS (Kalashnikov) LMG
- 7.62mm RPD (Degtyarev) LMG
- 7.62mm SG-43 (Goryunov) MMG

light and medium mortars--
- 82mm M-43

light ATRLs--
- RPG-7
- M-72 LAW

tanks:

model		number
medium quality		
T-62		50
M-60 A1		64
T-55		450
	(sub-total	564)
low quality		
T-54		136
T-34	(unconfirmed)	100
	(sub-total	236)
TOTAL		800

YEMEN

APCs/ARVs:	
model	number
high quality	
M-113 Al and its derivatives	100
others	
AML-90	
BTR-40/50/60	
BTR-152	
al-Walid	
Ferret	
Saladin	
(sub-total	400)
TOTAL	500
artillery:	number
self propelled guns and howitzers--	
100mm SU-100 gun	
towed guns and howitzers--	
155mm M-114 howitzer	
122mm D-30 howitzer	
122mm M-1938 howitzer	
105mm M-102 howitzer	
76mm M-1942 divisional gun	
mortars, heavy, under 160mm--	
120mm mortar	
TOTAL	320
MRLs--	
122mm BM-21	60
anti-tank weapons:	
missiles--	
BGM-71A Improved TOW	
M-47 Dragon	
Vigilant	
guns--	
85mm M-1945/D-44 field/AT gun	
82mm recoilless rifle	
75mm recoilless rifle	
57mm gun	
surface-to-surface missiles--	launchers
SS-21	4
army anti-aircraft defenses:	
missiles--	
self propelled/mobile	
SA-6 (Gainful)	30
SA-9 (Gaskin)	
man-portable	
SA-7 (Grail)	
short-range guns--	number
57mm S-60	
37mm M-1939	
23mm ZSU 23x4 SP (Gun Dish)	40

23mm ZU 23x2	
20mm M-163 Vulcan SP	20
20mm M-167 Vulcan	52
Air Force:	
aircraft--general:	
combat aircraft (some in storage)	118
transport aircraft	24
helicopters	43+
combat aircraft:	
interceptors--	
medium quality	
MiG-21 (Fishbed)	48
strike and multi-role aircraft--	
medium quality	
Su-20/22 (Fitter C)	20
others	
F-5E/B	15
MiG-17 (Fresco)	32
MiG-15 (Faggot/Midget, in training role)	3
(sub-total	50)
TOTAL	70
transport aircraft:	
An-12 (Cub)	1
An-24/An-26 (Coke/Curl)	5
C-130H Hercules	4
DC-3 Dakota (C-47)	3
Fokker F-27	5
IL-14 (Crate)	4
Short Skyvan Srs. 3	2
TOTAL	24
training and liaison aircraft:	
others--	
Yak-11 (Moose)	18
helicopters:	
attack--	
Mi-24 (Hind)	a few
medium transport--	
AB-212	5
AB-204	2
AB-205	2
Mi-8 (Hip)	25
Mi-4 (Hound)	1
(sub-total	35)
light transport--	
AB-206 JetRanger	6
Alouette III/SA-315 Lama (unconfirmed)	2
(sub-total	8)
TOTAL	43+

advanced armament:
  air-to-air missiles--
    AIM-9M Sidewinder
    AA-2 (Atoll)
  air-to-ground missiles--
    AT-2 (Swatter)
anti-aircraft defenses:
  long-range missiles--

model		batteries
SA-2 (Guideline)		4
SA-3		3
MIM-23B Improved HAWK	(unconfirmed)	5
TOTAL		12

military airfields: 3
  Hodeida, San'a (Martyr Dilmy AFB); Kamran Island (unconfirmed)

Navy:

combat vessels:	number
mine warfare vessels--	
Yevgenia class	3
patrol craft--	
Poluchat class (unconfirmed)	1
Zhuk class	5
Broadsword class (unconfirmed)	3
Total	9
landing craft:	
Ondatra LCU	2
T-4 LCM	2
Total	4
naval bases:	2

  Hodeida; anchorage at Kamran Island (unconfirmed)

PART III

COMPARATIVE TABLES
GLOSSARY OF WEAPONS SYSTEMS
LIST OF ABBREVIATIONS
CHRONOLOGY
MAPS

Table 1. Major Armies of the Middle East

Country	Year	Personnel (thousands)			Divisions			Indep.Brigades		
		Reg.	Res.	Total	Armor	Mech.	Inf.	Armor	Mech.	Inf./ Para./ Com./ Terr.
Egypt	1989-90	320	600	920	4	7	1	3	-	16
	1988-89	320	600	920	4	7	1	3	-	16
Iran*	1989-90	650	1245	1895	6	1	36	-	-	5
	1988-89	700	1245	1945	6	1	36	-	-	5
Iraq**	1989-90	355	680	1035	7	3	40	1	-	14
	1988-89	555	480	1035	7	3	45	-	-	14
Israel	1989-90	133	365	498	12	-	4	-	-	13
	1988-89	130	365	495	12	-	-	-	-	25
Jordan	1989-90	80	90	170	2	2	-	-	-	3
	1988-89	80	60	140	2	2	-	-	-	3
Libya	1989-90	85	30	115	3	4	-	2	2	1
	1988-89	85	30	115	3	4	-	2	2	1
Saudi	1989-90	70	-	70	-	-	-	2	6	2
Arabia#	1988-89	70	-	70	-	-	-	2	6	2
Syria	1989-90	306	100	406	6	3	1	1	1	7
	1988-89	306	300	606	6	3	1	1	-	7

Note: plus sign indicates precise number unknown;
minus sign indicates no entry.

* Army and IRGC, excluding Baseej reserves

** excluding Popular Army

Army and National Guard

For classification of tanks according to quality see introductory note Part II.

Indep.Battalions			Tanks						
Armor	Mech.	Inf./ Para. Com./ Terr.	High Quality	Others	Total	APCs & ARVs	Guns & Mortars	ATGM Launchers	SSM Launchers
-	-	-	850	2250	3100	4100	2200	1600-1800	24
-	-	-	850	1550	2400	4100	2200	1600-1800	24
-	-	-	+	+	700	800	1000	+	+
-	-	-	+	+	700	1000	1000	+	+
-	-	-	1200	4800	6000	5000	4700	1500	54+
-	-	-	1000	5000	6000	5000	4700	1500	48+
-	-	-	1330	2530	3860	8100	1300	+	12
-	-	-	1210	2600	3810	8100	1300	+	12
-	-	-	375	740	1115	1565	600	550	-
-	-	-	375	740	1115	1565	600	550	-
3	8	13	300	2300	2600	2000	2000	2000	100
3	8	13	300	2500	2800	2000	2000	2000	100
-	-	19	100	450	550	3140+	700	700	8-12
-	-	19	100	450	550	3140+	700	700	20
-	-	-	1100	3100	4200	3800	2300	2000	00
-	-	-	1000	3100	4100	3800	2300	2000	60

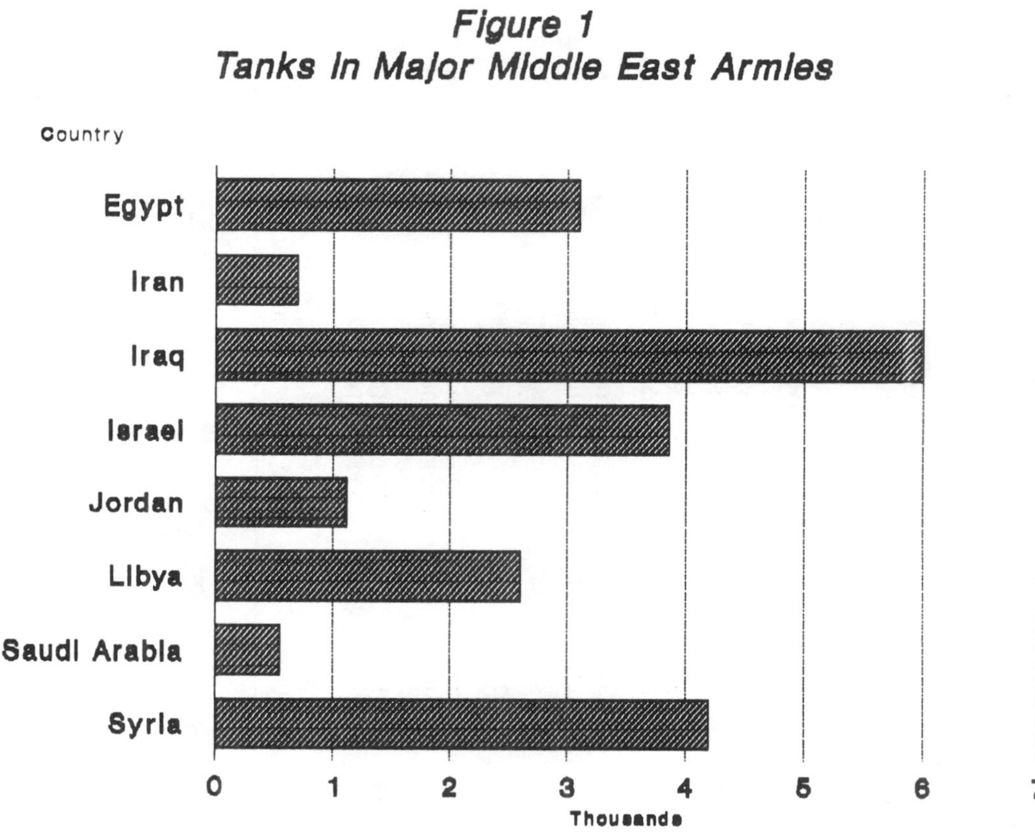

Figure 1
Tanks in Major Middle East Armies

Figure 2
*Surface-to-Surface Missiles & Rockets In Service In Middle East Armies**

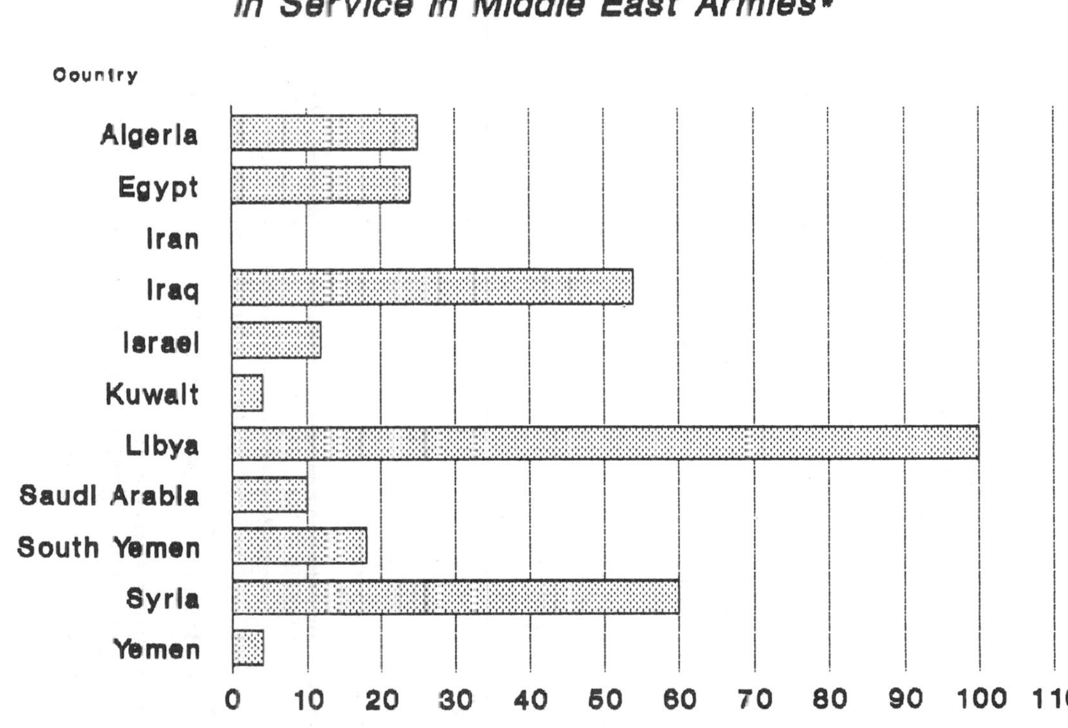

*by number of launchers

Table 2. Major Air Forces of the Middle East

Country	Year	Personnel (thousands)			Interceptors		Strike & Multi-Role Aircraft	
		Reg.	Res.	Total	High Quality	Others	High Quality	Others
Egypt	1989-90	95	80	175	97	290	-	154
	1988-89	107	85	192	98	290	-	154
Iran***	1989-90	35	-	35	15	69	-	130
	1988-89	35	-	35	15	18	-	130
Iraq	1989-90	40	-	40	70	200	25	394
	1988-89	40	-	40	56	200	15	412
Israel	1989-90	31	55	86	171	-	24	443
	1988-89	30	55	85	171	-	24	440
Jordan	1989-90	9.7	-	9.7	-	-	-	107
	1988-89	9.7	-	9.7	-	-	-	107
Libya	1989-90	9	-	9	80	50	6	400
	1988-89	9	-	9	80	50	6	400
Saudia Arabia	1989-90	15	-	15	76	-	40	110
	1988-89	15	-	15	64	-	20	110
Syria	1989-90	80	37.5	117.5	65	275	20	260
	1988-89	80	37.5	117.5	65	280	-	305

Note: plus sign indicates precise number unknown; minus sign indicates no entry.
For classification of combat aircraft according to quality see introductory note, part II.
* including 24 maritime attack
** classification of long range SAMs has been changed. See introductory note to part II.
*** 30% of aircraft serviceable

including Air Defense Forces)

Bombers	Total Combat A/C	Transport Aircraft	Helicopters: Attack	Helicopters: Transport +ASW	Helicopters: Total	Military Airfields	Long-Range SAM Batteries **
-	541	37	80	118	198	21	132
-	542	34	80	118	198	21	132
-	214	116	150	250	400	20	22
-	163	120	+	+	250	13	22
16	705	73	160	416	576	20	60
22	705	86	160	425	585	20	60
-	638	91	77	141	218	11	+
-	635	91	77	143	220	11	+
-	107	14	24	44	68	6	14
-	107	14	24	45	69	6	14
7	543	139+	40	137	177	18	99
7	543	139+	40	137	177	18	97
-	226	73	39*	102	141	20	15
-	194	73	24*	90	114	20	15
-	620	32	115	175	290	21	108
-	650	32	115	175	290	21	68

Figure 3
Major Air Weapons Systems in the Middle East

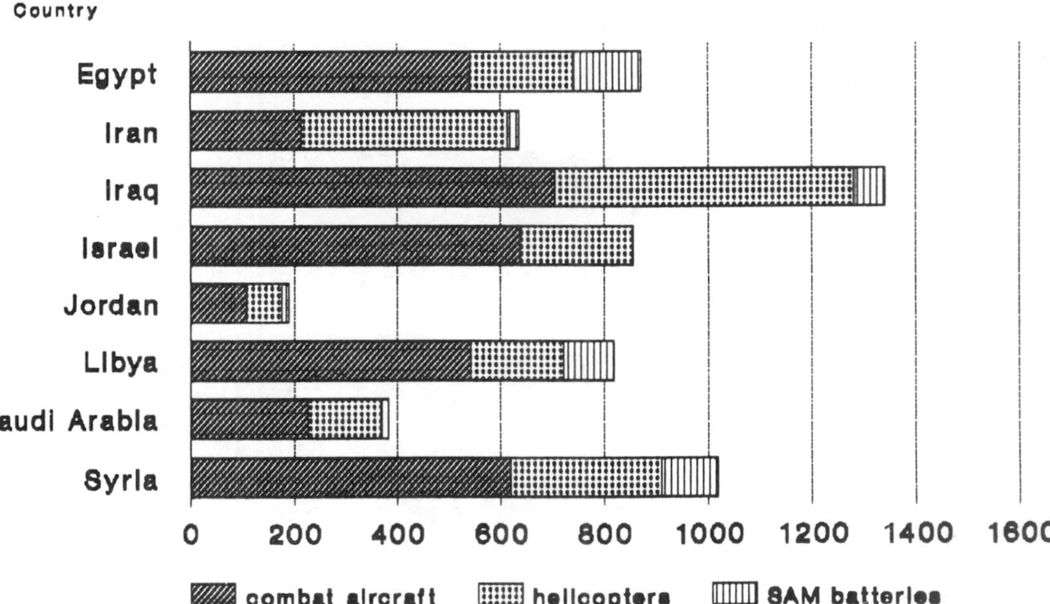

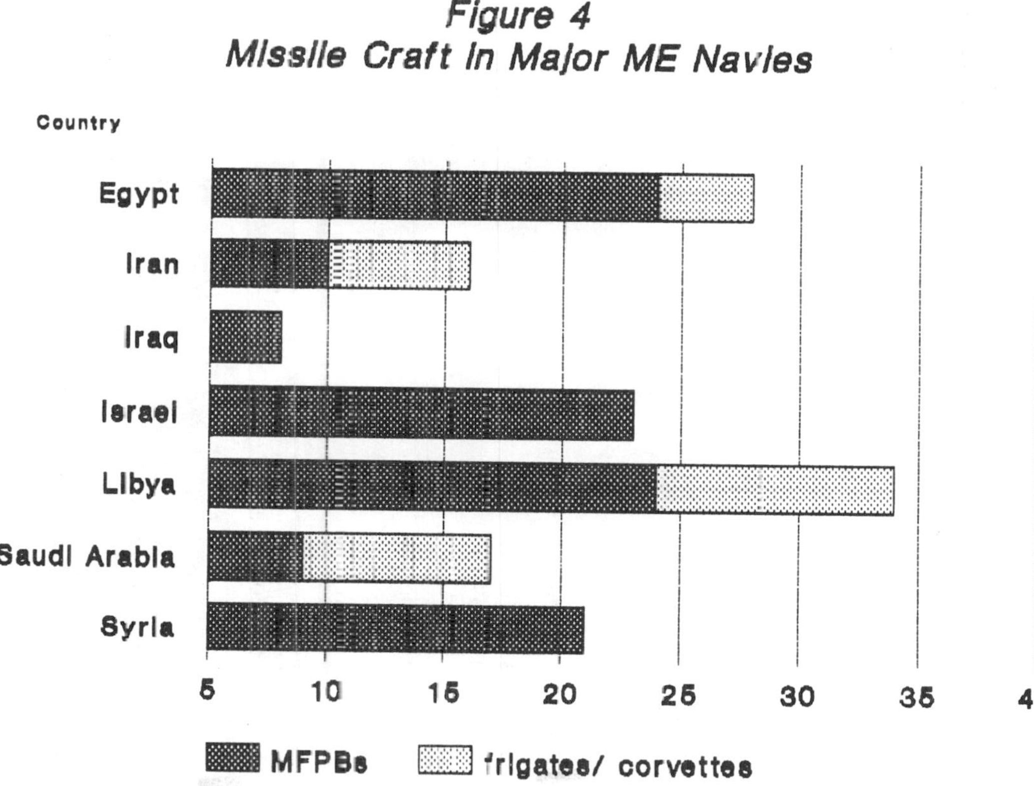

Figure 4
Missile Craft in Major ME Navies

Table 3. Major Navies of the Middle East

Country	Year	Personnel (thousands) Reg.	Res.	Total	Sub-Marines	MFPBs	Missile Destroyers, Frigates & Corvettes	SSMs
Egypt	1989-90	20	15	35	8	24	4	Harpoon, Otomat, Styx
	1988-89	20	15	35	10	25	4	Harpoon, Otomat, Styx,HY-
Iran	1989-90	20	-	20	-	10	6	Harpoon, Seakille C-801
	1988-89	20	-	20	-	10	6	Harpoon, Seakille C-801
Iraq	1989-90	5	-	5	-	8	-	Styx
	1988-89	5	-	5	-	8	-	Styx
Israel	1989-90	10	10	20	3	23+2 hydro-foils	-	Gabriel, Harpoon
	1988-89	10	10	20	3	24+2 hydro-foils	-	Gabriel, Harpoon
Libya	1989-90	8	-	8	6	24	10	Otomat, SS-12, Styx
	1988-89	6.5	-	6.5	6	24	10	Otomat, SS-12, Styx
Saudi Arabia	1989-90	7.8	-	7.5	-	9	8	Harpoon, Otomat 2
	1988-89	7.5	-	7.5	-	9	8	Harpoon, Otomat 2
Syria	1989-90	4	2.5	6.5	3	21	-	Styx
	1988-89	4	2.5	6.5	3	21	-	Styx

Note: minus sign indicates no entry.

Gun Destroyers, Frigates & Corvettes	ASW Vessels	Mine Warfare	MTBs & Gunboats	Patrol Craft	Landing Craft	Hover-Craft	Naval Bases
1	-	11-15	18	36	19	3	8
1	-	9	18	36	24	3	8
2	-	5	-	132	12	14	9
2	-	5	-	131	12	13	9
-	3	8	6	32	2-3	6	3
-	3	8	6	32	2-3	6	3
-	-	-	-	47	13	2	3
-	-	-	-	47	13	2	3
1	-	8	-	23	7	-	5
1	-	8	-	23	7		5
-	-	4	3	60	16	24	12
-	-	4	3	56	16	24	12
-	2	7	-	7	3	-	3
-	2	8	-	7	3	-	3

Table 4. The Israel-Syria Military Balance

Army

Country	Personnel (thousands)			Divisions			Indep. Brigades		
	Reg.	Res.	Total	Armor	Mech.	Inf.	Armor	Mech.	Inf./ Para./ Com./ Terr.
Israel	133	365	498	12	-	4	-	-	13
Syria	306		406	6	3	1	1	1	7

Air Force and Air Defense

Country	Personnel (thousands)			Interceptors		Strike & Multi-Role Aircraft	
	Reg.	Res.	Total	High Quality	Others	High Quality	Others
Israel	31	55	86	171	-	24	443
Syria	80	37.5	117.5	65	275	20	260

Navy

Country	Personnel (thousands)			Sub-marines	MFPBs	Missile Destroyers, Frigates & Corvettes	SSMs
	Reg.	Res.	Total				
Israel	10	10	20	3	23 +2 hydro-foil	-	Gabriel, Harpoon
Syria	4	2.5	6.5	3	21	-	Styx

Note: plus sign indicates precise number unknown; minus sign indicates no entry.
For classification of tanks, long-range SAMs and combat aircraft according to quality see introductory note, Part II.

Tanks	APCs & ARVs	Guns & Mortars	ATGM Launchers	SSM Launchers
3860	8100	1300	+	12
4200	3800	2300	2000	60

Total Combat	Transport Aircraft	Helicopters: Attack	Helicopters: Transport + ASW	Helicopters: Total	Military Airfields	Long-range SAM Batteries
[illegible]38	91	77	141	218	11	+
[illegible]20	32	115	175	290	21	108

ASW Vessels	Mine Warfare Vessels	Patrol Craft	Landing Craft	Hover-Craft	Naval Bases
-	-	46	13	2	3
2	7	7	3	-	3

Table 5. Eastern Front-Israel Military Balance

Full participants: Israel, Syria, Jordan, Palestinian forces.
Partial participants: Saudi Army (two brigades) and Air Force (two fighter squadrons and one transport squadron); Kuwaiti Air Force (one squadron);

Army

	Personnel (thousands)			Divisions			
	Reg.	Res.	Total	Armor	Mech.	Inf.	Total
Eastern Front	571	190	761	11	9	2	22
Israel	133	365	498	12	-	4	16
Ratio, 1989-90	4.3:1	0.5:1	1.5:1	0.9:1	*	0.5:1	1.4:1
Ratio, 1988-89	4.1:1	1:1	1.8:1	0.8:1	*	*	1.7:1

Air Force and Air Defense

	Personnel (thousands)			Interceptors		Strike & Multi-Role Aircraft	
	Reg.	Res.	Total	High Quality	Others	High Quality	Others
Eastern Front	107	37.5	144.5	130	345	80	477
Israel	31	55	86	171	-	24	443
Ratio, 1989-90	3.5:1	0.7:1	1.7:1	0.8:1	*	3.3:1	1.1:1
Ratio, 1988-89	3.3:1	0.7:1	1.6:1	0.8:1	*	0.7:1	1.2:1

Navy

	Personnel (thousands)			Sub-marines	MFPBs	Missile Destroyers, Frigates & Corvettes	SSMs
	Reg.	Res.	Total				
Eastern Front	12.5	2.5	15	9	45	10	Styx, Otomat
Israel	10	10	20	3	25**	-	Gabriel, Harpoon
Ratio, 1989-90	1.3:1	0.3:1	0.8:1	3:1	1.8:1	*	*
Ratio, 1988-89	1.1:1	0.3:1	0.7:1	3:1	1.7:1	*	*

Note: the constellation of full and partial participants presented here is only one of several reasonable possibilities; it reflects neither an absolute certainty nor the maximum force which all countries involved are thought to be capable of deploying.

Iraq (seven divisions, 30 SSM launchers, 200 combat aircraft, 100 helicopters); various militias in Lebanon; Libyan Army (one mechanized division, three mechanized brigades, 20 SSM launchers), Libyan Air Force (two squadron of combat aircraft, one of attack helicopters), and the entire Libyan Navy.

Indep.Brigades								
Armor	Mech.	Inf./ Para./ Com./ Terr.	Total	Tanks	APCs & ARVs	Guns & Mortars	ATGM Launchers	SSM Launchers
2	5	13	20	7500	7800	3800	4250	110
-	-	13	13	3860	8100	1300	+	12
*	*	1:1	1.5:1	1.9:1	1:1	2.9:1	*	9.2:1
*	*	0.7:1	0.7:1	1.8:1	0.9:1	2.9:1	*	9.2:1

Bombers	Total Combat A/C	Transport Aircraft	Helicopters			Military Airfields	Long-range SAM Batteries
			Attack	Transport +ASW	Total		
4	1036	77	179	292	471	35	132
-	638	91	77	141	218	11	+
*	1.6:1	0.8:1	2.3:1	2.1:1	2.2:1	3.2:1	*
*	1.5:1	1:1	2.3:1	1.8:1	2:1	2.7:1	*

Gun Destroyers, Frigates & Corvettes	ASW Vessels	Mine Warfare Vessels	MTBs & Gunboats	Patrol Craft	Landing Craft	Hover-Craft	Naval Bases
1	2	15	-	33	10	-	10
-	-	-	-	46	13	2	3
*	*	*	*	0.7:1	0.8:1	*	3.3:1
*	*	*	*	0.6:1	0.8:1	*	2.7:1

Note: plus sign indicates precise number unknown, minus sign indicates no entry.
indicates no basis for calculation
** including 2 hydrofoils
For classification of tanks, SAMs and combat aircraft according to quality see introductory note, Part II.

Table 6. Arab-Israel Military Balance (Israel vs.

Full participants: Israel, Syria, Jordan, Palestinian forces, Egypt, Libyan Navy. Partial participants: Saudi Army (two brigades) and Air Force (two squadrons); Iraq (seven divisions, 30 SSM launchers, 200 combat aircraft, 100 helicopters); Kuwaiti Air Force (one squadron); Algerian army (two brigades) and Air Force (2 squadrons of

Army

	Personnel (thousands)			Divisions			
	Reg.	Res.	Total	Armor	Mech.	Inf.	Total
Arab Coalition	901	790	1691	15	16	3	34
Israel	133	365	598	12	-	4	16
Ratio, 1989-90	6.7:1	2.2:1	2.8:1	1.3:1	*	0.8:1	2.1:1
Ratio, 1988-89	6.6:1	2.6:1	3.7:1	1.2:1	*	*	2.7:1

Air Force and Air Defense

	Personnel (thousands)			Interceptors		Strike & Multi-Role	
	Reg.	Res.	Total	High Quality	Others	High Quality	Others
Arab Coalition	205	117.5	322.5	227	635	80	661
Israel	31	55	86	171	-	24	443
Ratio, 1989-90	6.6:1	2.1:1	3.8:1	1.3:1	*	3.3:1	1.5:1
Ratio, 1988-89	7:1	2.2:1	3.9:1	1.5:1	*	1.7:1	1.6:1

Navy

	Personnel (thousands)			Sub-marines	MFPBs	Missile Destroyers, Frigates & Corvettes	SSMs
	Reg.	Res.	Total				
Arab Coalition	32.5	17.5	50	17	70	14	Styx, Otomat Harpoon
Israel	10	10	20	3	25**	-	Gabriel Harpoon
Ratio, 1989-90	3.3:1	1.8:1	2.5:1	5.7:1	2.8:1	*	*
Ratio, 1988-89	3.1:1	1.8:1	2.4:1	6.3:1	2.8:1	*	*

Note: the constellation of full and partial participants presented here is only one of several reasonable possibilities; it reflects neither an absolute certainty nor the maximum force which all countries involved are thought to be capable of deploying.

Arab Coalition, including Egypt and Iraq)

fighter a/c), Moroccan Army (one brigade) and Air Force (one squadron), Libyan Army (one mech. div., 3 mech. brig., 5 para. battalions) and Air Force (two squadrons of combat a/c and one helicopter squadron).

Indep .Brigades				Tanks	APCs & ARVs	Guns & Mortars	ATGM Launchers	SSM Launchers
Armor	Mech.	Inf./ Para./ Com./ Terr./	Total					
6	6	29	41	10800	12100	6100	5000	140
-	-	13	13	3860	8100	1300	+	12
*	*	2.2:1	3.2:1	2.8:1	1.5:1	4.7:1	*	11.6:1
*	*	1.4:1	2:1	2.4:1	1.4:1	4.6:1	*	11.2:1

Bombers	Total Combat A/C	Transport Aircraft	Helicopters			Military Airfields	Long-range SAM Batteries
			Attack	Transport +ASW	Total		
4	1607	118	259	414	637	56	286
-	638	91	77	141	218	11	+
*	2.5:1	1.3:1	3.4:1	3.0:1	3.1:1	5.1:1	*
*	2.5:1	1.5:1	3.4:1	2.7:1	3:1	4.6:1	*

Gun Destroyers, Frigates & Corvettes	ASW Vessels	Mine Warfare Vessels	MTBs & Gunboats	Patrol Craft	Landing Craft	Hover-Craft	Naval Bases
2	2	26-30	18	69	29	3	18
-	-	-	-	46	13	2	3
*	*	*	*	1.5:1	2.2:1	1.5:1	6:1
*	*	*	*	1.4:1	2.6:1	1.5:1	5.3:1

Note: plus sign indicates precise number unknown; minus sign indicates no entry. The classification of tanks, SAMs and combat aircraft according to quality was changed in 1987 and 1988--see introductory note, Part II.
* indicates no basis for calculation. ** including two hydrofoils.

Table 7. Arab-Israel Military Balance 1984-1990

Full participants: Egypt, Jordan, Syria, Lebanese militias, Palestinian forces.
Partial participants: Algeria, Kuwait, Libya, Morocco, Saudi Arabia; in 1990--also Iraq

Army

	Divisions							
	Armor		Mech.		Inf.		Total	
	84	90	84	90	84	90	84	90
Arab Coalition	10	15	10	16	3	3	23	34
Israel	11	12	-	-	-	4	11	16
Ratio	0.9:1	1.3:1	*	*	*	0.8:1	2.1:1	2.1:1

Air Force & Air Defense

	Interceptors				Strike & Multi-Role Aircraft			
	High Quality		Others		High Quality		Others	
	84	90	84	90	84	90	84	90
Arab Coalition	130	227	620	635	496	80	354	661
Israel	40	171	-	-	445	24	185	443
Ratio	3.25:1	1.3:1	*	*	1.1:1	3.3:1	1.9:1	1.5:1

Navy

	Submarines		MFPBs		Missile Destroyers, Frigates & Corvettes	
	84	90	84	90	84	90
Arab Coalition	18	17	67	70	8	14
Israel	3	3	24	25	-	-
Ratio	6:1	5.7	2.8:1	2.8:1	*	*

Note: plus sign indicates precise number unknown; minus sign indicates no entry.
* indicates no basis for calculation.

Independent Brigades 84	Independent Brigades 90	Tanks 84	Tanks 90	APCs & ARVs 84	APCs & ARVs 90	GUNs & Mortars 84	GUNs & Mortars 90	ATGM Launchers 84	ATGM Launchers 90	SSM Launchers 84	SSM Launchers 90
51	41	8065	10800	8470	12100	6050	6100	5150	5000	54	140
20	13	3650	3860	8000	8100	1000	1300	+	+	+	+
2.5:1	2.1:1	2.2:1	2.8:1	1.1:1	1.5:1	6:1	4.7:1	*	*	*	*

Total Combat A/C 84	Total Combat A/C 90	Helicopters: Attack 84	Helicopters: Attack 90	Helicopters: Transport +ASW 84	Helicopters: Transport +ASW 90	Helicopters: Total 84	Helicopters: Total 90	Military airfields 84	Military airfields 90	Long-range SAM Batteries 84	Long-range SAM Batteries 90
1635	1607	161	259	324	414	485	673	48	56	304	286
670	638	55	77	133	141	188	218	11	11	+	+
.4:1	2.5:1	2.9:1	3.4:1	2.4:1	2.9:1	2.6:1	3:1	4.4:1	5.1:1	*	*

Gun Destroyers, Frigates & Corvettes 84	Gun Destroyers, Frigates & Corvettes 90	Landing Craft 84	Landing Craft 90	Naval Bases 84	Naval Bases 90
8	2	36	29	17	18
-	-	13	13	3	3
*	*	2.8:1	2.2:1	5.7:1	6:1

Table 8. The Iran-Iraq Military Balance

Army

Country	Personnel (thousands)			Divisions			Indep.Brigades		
	Reg.	Res.	Total	Armor	Mech.	Inf.	Armor	Mech.	Inf./ Para./ Com./ Terr./
Iran*	650	1245	1895	6	1	36	-	-	5
Iraq**	355	680	1035	7	3	40	1	-	14

Air Force and Air Defense

Country	Personnel (thousands)			Interceptors		Strike & Multi-Role Aircraft	
	Reg.	Res.	Total	High Quality	Others	High Quality	Others
Iran*	35	-	35	15	18	-	130
Iraq	40	-	40	56	200	15	412

Navy

Country	Personnel (thousands)			Sub-marines	MFPBs	Missile Destroyers, Frigates & Corvettes	SSMs
	Reg.	Res.	Total				
Iran	20	-	20	-	10	6	Harpoon, Seakiller C-801
Iraq	5	-	5	-	8	-	Styx

Note: plus sign indicates precise number unknown; minus sign indicates no entry.
* Army and IRGC; serviceability of Iranian aircraft 30%
** excluding Popular Army.
***For classification of tanks, long range SAMs and combat aircraft according to quality see introductory note, part II.

Tanks	APCs & ARVs	Guns & Mortars	ATGM Launchers	SSM Launchers
700	800	1000	+	+
[illegible]000	5000	4700	1500	54+

[illegible]ombers	Total Combat a/c	Transport Aircraft	Helicopters: Attack	Helicopters: Transport	Helicopters: Total	Military Airfields	Long-range SAM Batteries***
-	163	120	150	250	400	20	22
22	705	86	160	425	585	20	60

Gun Destroyers, Frigates & Corvettes	ASW Vessels	Mine Warfare Vessels	MTBs & Gunboats	Patrol Craft	Landing Craft	Hover-Craft	Naval Bases
2	-	5	-	131	12	13	9
-	3	8	6	32	2-3	6	3

Table 9. The USA in the Middle East: Financial Aid

Country	US Financial Aid ($millions)			US Arms (major items) Granted or Sold
	Grants	Loans	Total	
Algeria	.15	-	-	air traffic control equipment, radars
Bahrain	-	-	-	ATGMs, combat aircraft, helicopters, tanks
Egypt	1,300	-	1,300	tanks, APCs, artillery, RPVs, helicopters, combat aircraft, SAMS, naval SSMs, early warning aircraft, radars
Iraq	-	-	-	helicopters (allegedly civilian)
Israel	1,800	-	1,800	tanks, APCs, artillery, combat aircraft, SAMs, naval SSMs, tank transporters, attack helicopters
Jordan	48	-	48	tanks, ATGMs, artillery, SAMs, AAGs, helicopters, terminally guided artillery shells
Kuwait	-	-	-	SAMs, APCs, patrol boats, combat a/c on order
Lebanon	.3	-	.3	-
Morocco	42.8	-	42.8	tanks, ATGMs, SAMs, tank transporters
Oman	-	-	-	SP artillery, AAMs
Saudi Arabia	-	-	-	tanks, APCs, artillery, ATGMs, combat aircraft, transport aircraft, SAMs, AAMs, AGMs, AWACS
Sudan	-	-	-	tanks, AAGs
Tunisia	30	-	30	tanks, SAMs, transport aircraft, artillery
UAE	-	-	-	transport aircraft, SAMs, aircraft training simulator, light reconnaissance vehicles, radio systems
Yemen (YAR)	1	-	1	

Military), Arms Sales, Advisors, Trainees and Facilities

US Advisors Present	Trainees in US	Facilities Provided to US	Joint maneuvers with USA
-	?	-	-
+	+	naval, intelligence & storage facilities	-
+	+	use of airfields	+
-	-	-	-
-	+	-	+
+	+	-	+
+	+	-	-
-	-	-	-
+	+	use of airfields, naval communications and storage facilities	+
+	-	use of airfields, naval, communications and storage facilities	-
+	+	-	-
+	+	-	-
+	+	-	+
+	+	-	-
+	+	-	-

Table 10. The USSR in the Middle East: Arms Sales, Advisors, Trainees and Facilities

Country	Soviet Arms (major items) Granted or Sold	Soviet Advisors Present	Trainees in USSR	Facilities Provided to
Algeria	tanks, combat aircraft, SAMs, missile corvette, submarine	+	+	-
Egypt	spare parts for Soviet weapons	-	-	-
Iran*	APCs, AAGs, small arms, artillery	+	+	?
Iraq	tanks, artillery, SAMs, SSMs, combat aircraft, artillery pieces, helicopters	+	+	-
Jordan	SAMs, AAGs, APCs	+	+	-
Kuwait	surface-to-surface rockets, SAMs, AAGs, APCs	+	+	-
Libya	tanks, APCs, artillery, SSMs, combat aircraft, SAMs, naval vessels, naval mines	+	+	use of airfield & naval facilities (unconfirmed)
Palestinian Org's.	small arms, tanks, artillery, MRLs, SAMs	-	+	-
South Yemen (PDRY)	small arms, tanks, combat aircraft	+	+	use of airfields & naval facilities
Syria	small arms, tanks, artillery, SSMs, combat aircraft, helicopters, SAMs, naval vessels, coastal defense missiles	+	+	use of airfields & naval facilities
Yemen (YAR)	SSMs, tanks, SAMs, combat aircraft	+	+	-

* via North Korea and East European countries

Table 11. France in the Middle East: Arms Sales, Advisors and Trainees

Country	French Arms (major items) Granted or Sold	French Advisors Present	Trainees in France
Algeria	ARVs, ATGMs, helicopters	-	+
Bahrain	ARVs, helicopters, AGMs	+	+
Egypt	ATGMs, combat aircraft, helicopters, SAMs, AAMs, radars for AAGs, night vision devices, AGMs	+	+
Iran	artillery ammunition, spare parts for MFPBs, rubber boats	-	+
Iraq	ATGMs, combat aircraft, helicopters, AGMs, SAMs, AAMs, artillery pieces	+	+
Israel	spares (via intermediaries), a/c engines	-	+
Jordan	combat aircraft, AAMs, AGMs, helicopters, radars, ATRL, artillery fire control sys.	-	+
Kuwait	SP artillery, ATGMs, combat aircraft, helicopters, radars	+	+
Lebanon	helicopters	+	+
Libya	3 combat aircraft, spare parts	?	?
Morocco	tank transporters, ATGMs, combat aircraft, helicopters, AAMs, naval vessels, naval SSMs	+	+
Oman	ATGMs, naval SSMs, AAMs	-	+
Qatar	tanks, APCs, artillery, combat aircraft, helicopters, MFPBs, naval SSMs, anti-ship AGMs	+	+
Saudi Arabia	APCs, SP artillery, ATGMs, radars, SAMs, anti-ship AGMs, frigates on order	+	+
Sudan	artillery pieces	-	-
Syria	ATGMs, helicopters, naval survey vessels	-	+
Tunisia	helicopters, naval SSMs	+	+
UAE	tanks, combat aircraft, AAMs, AGMs	+	+

Table 12. Britain in the Middle East: Arms Sales, Advisors, Trainees, and Cooperation in Arms Production.

Country	British Arms (major items) Granted or Sold	British Advisors Present	Trainees in Britain	Cooperation in arms production
Algeria	radars, target drones naval vessels	+	+	naval vessels
Bahrain	naval craft, electronics	+	+	
Egypt	ATGMs, helicopter spares, radio transceivers, torpedoes, tank guns	-	+	ATGMs, helicopter parts, tank guns, electronics
Iraq	-	-	+	-
Israel	spare parts	-	+	-
Jordan	bridging equipment, radars, ATRLs	-	+	upgrading of tanks
Kuwait	tanks, APCs, naval vessels, trainer aircraft	+	+	-
Libya	-	non gvt. personnel on individual basis	-	-
Morocco	artillery pieces	-	-	-
Oman	tanks, artillery pieces, combat and training aircraft, ground and a/c radars, MFPBs, landing craft, navigation systems, drones	1000, some seconded, others hired	+	-
Qatar	helicopters, SAMs, drones	+	+	+
Saudi Arabia	combat and trainer aircraft, hovercraft, radio transceivers, helicopters, minesweepers	+	+	-
Sudan	-	+	-	-
Tunisia	naval patrol craft, target drones	-	-	-
UAE	APCs, artillery pieces, SAMs, workshops, trainer aircraft, tank transporters	-	+	-

Table 13. Surface-to-Surface Missiles and Rockets in Service in Middle Eastern Armies (by Number of Launchers)

Country	Model				
	FROG 7/4	SS-1 Scud	SS-21 Scarab	other	total number
Algeria	24	-	-	-	25
Egypt	+	+	-		24
Iran	-	+	-	Iran-130	not known
Iraq	24	24	-	6+ al-Hussein	54+
Israel	-	-	-	MGM-52C Lance, Jericho I, II*	12 ?
Kuwait	4	-	-	-	4
Libya	+	+	-	-	100
Saudi Arabia	-	-	-	CSS-2	10
Syria	24	18	18	-	60
South Yemen (PDRY)	12	6	-	-	18
Yemen (YAR)	-	-	4	-	4

*according to foreign sources

GLOSSARY OF WEAPONS SYSTEMS

ARMY

AA Guns, Short Range

(caliber, designation, NATO codename if relevant, SP when relevant, tracked or wheeled when relevant, country of origin)

57mm ZSU 57x2 SP, tracked, USSR
57mm M-1950 (S-60), USSR
40mm M-42 (twin 40mm) SP, tracked, USA
40mm Bofors L-70, Sweden
40mm Bofors L-60, Sweden
37mm M-1939, USSR
35mm Contraves Skyguard, see below, Air Defense Systems
35mm Gepard SP, FRG
35mm Oerlikon-Buhrle 35x2 GDF-002, Switzerland; may be part of 35mm Skyguard system
30mm AMX DCA 30 (twin 30mm) SP, tracked, France
30mm Artemis (twin 30mm), Greece, based on 30mm Mauser AAG, FRG
30mm 30x2 M-53/59 SP, wheeled, Czechoslovakia
30mm Oerlikon, Switzerland
30mm 30x2 Wildcat SP, wheeled, FRG
23mm ZSU 23x4 (Gun Dish) SP, tracked, USSR (Soviet designation Shilka)
23mm ZU 23x2, USSR
20mm TCM-20x2 SP (on M-3 halftrack), France (gun)/Israeli mounting of gun on US-made halftrack
20mm Oerlikon GAI, Switzerland 20mm Hispano-Suiza, France
20mm M-163 A1 Vulcan SP, USA
20mm M-167 Vulcan, USA
20mm 20x2mm SP (mounted on Panhard VCR 6x6), France
20mm 20x3 M-55 A4, Yugoslavia
20mm VDAA SP (mounted on VAB 6x6), France

Air Def. Sys., short-range

(caliber of gun, designation, missiles, SP when relevant, country of origin)

35mm Skyguard (Contraves Skyguard) 2x35, Aspide or RIM-7M Sparrow SAM, SP, Italy (gun--Switzerland, SAM--Italy or USA, chassis and radar--Italy or Austria); Egyptian designation Amoun
23mm Nile 23, 2x23, 4xSA-7, SP, Egypt (gun + SAM--USSR or Egypt, chassis--USA, radar--France)
23mm Sinai 23, see 23mm Nile 23

Anti-Tank Guns

(caliber, designation, recoilless if relevant, country of origin)

120mm BAT L-4 recoilless rifle, Britain
107mm B-11 recoilless rifle, USSR
106mm M-40 A1C/A2 recoilless rifle, USA/Israel
100mm M-1955 gun (field/AT gun), USSR; see guns and howitzers
90mm light gun, low recoil gun, Belgium; used on AFVs
85mm M-1945/D-44 field/AT gun, USSR; see guns and howitzers
84mm Carl Gustaf light recoilless rifle, Sweden
82mm B-10 recoilless rifle, USSR
73mm SPG-9 recoilless gun, USSR
76mm M-1942 divisional gun (ZIS-3), USSR; (field/AT gun, see guns and howitzers)
75mm M-20 recoilless rifle, USA
57mm AT gun, Czechoslovakia

APCs/ARVs

(designation, tracked or wheeled, APC or ARV, amphibious if relevant, ATGM equipped if relevant, country of origin)
al-Walid, wheeled APC, Egypt
AML-60, wheeled ARV, France
AML-90, wheeled ARV, France
AMX-10 R/S/P, tracked, amphibious APC, France
AMX-VCI, tracked APC, France
AT-105 Saxon, wheeled APC, Britain
BMP-1, tracked, amphibious, ATGM-equipped APC (usually AT-3 Sagger), with 73mm gun, USSR
BMP-2, tracked, amphibious, ATGM equipped APC (usually AT-5 Spandrel), with 30mm cannon, USSR
BMR-600, wheeled, amphibious APC, Spain
BRDM 2, wheeled, amphibious, ATGM-equipped ARV, USSR
BTR-40, wheeled, amphibious ARV, USSR
BTR-50, tracked, amphibious APC, USSR
BTR-60, wheeled, amphibious APC, USSR
BTR-152, wheeled APC, USSR
Cadillac Gage Commando Scout, ARV (occasionally ATGM-equipped), USA
EBR-75, wheeled ARV, France
Eland, wheeled ARV, South Africa/licensed production of French AML-90/AML-60
Engesa EE-3 Jararaca, wheeled ARV, Brazil
Engesa EE-9 Cascavel, wheeled ARV, Brazil
Engesa EE-11 Urutu, wheeled, amphibious APC, Brazil
Engesa EE-17 Sucuri, wheeled, amphibious tank destroyer, Brazil
Fahd, wheeled APC, Egypt (FRG collaboration)
Ferret, wheeled ARV, Britain
Fiat Type 6614, wheeled, amphibious APC, Italy
Fiat Type 6616, wheeled, amphibious ATGM-equipped ARV, Italy
Fox, wheeled, amphibious ARV, Britain
FUG-70, see above, BRDM-2, usually without ATGM, Hungary

(licensed production of Soviet BRDM-2)
K-63, tracked, amphibious, APC, PRC
M-2, half-tracked APC, USA
M-3, half-tracked APC--see M-2
M-3 (Panhard, VTT), wheeled, amphibious APC (occasionally 4xHOT are added, see Anti-Tank Missiles), France
M-8 (WWII Greyhound), ARV USA
M-60P, APC, Yugoslavia
M-125, derivative of M-113, 81mm mortar carrier, USA
M-901 ITV (TOW under armor), tracked, amphibious ATGM-equipped ARV (tank destroyer) (based on M-113 APC), USA; see also under ATGM
M-113 A1/A2, tracked, amphibious APC, USA/Italy (licensed production)
M-125, derivative of M-113, 81mm mortar carrier, USA
M-577/M-577 A1, tracked artillery command post vehicle (based on M-113 APC), USA
Mowag Piranha 8x8, wheeled, amphibious, APC, Switzerland
MT-LB, USSR; see under Artillery Ammunition Carriers
OT-62, APC, Czechoslovakia, see BTR-50
OT-64, wheeled APC, Czechoslovakia
RAM, wheeled ARV, Israel; improvement of RBY-2
Ratel 20, wheeled APC, South Africa
Ratel 90, same as Ratel 20 with a 90mm gun and turret, South Africa
RBY/RBY-2, wheeled ARV, Israel
Saladin, wheeled ARV, Britain
Saracen, wheeled APC, Britain
Shoreland Mk.2/Mk.3, wheeled ARV, Britain
Steyr 4K 7FA tracked APC, Austria
Type 77, Chinese copy of Soviet BTR-50, PRC; see BTR-50
UR-416, wheeled APC, FRG
V-150 Commando, wheeled, amphibious ATGM-equipped ARV/APC, USA
V-300, wheeled APC, USA
VAB, wheeled amphibious APC, France
VBC-90, wheeled ARV, France; derivative of VAB, with a 90mm gun
VCR/TH, wheeled, amphibious, ATGM-equipped APC/tank destroyer (see anti-tank missiles), France
YW-531, tracked, amphibious APC, PRC

Army AA Defense--missiles

(designation, NATO codename if relevant, SP when relevant, man-portable if relevant, range, country of origin)
Ain al-Saqr (Egyptian-improved version of Soviet SA-7), man-portable, 4.4 km, Egypt
Blowpipe, man-portable, Britain
Crotale SP, 9 km, France; see also Shahine 2
FIM-92A Stinger, man-portable, 5.4 km, USA

MIM-43A Redeye, man-portable, 3 km, USA
MIM-72A Chaparral SP, 8 km, USA
Mistral (Matra Mistral), man-portable, 6 km, France
Rapier, 6 km, Britain
RBS-70, 5 km, Sweden
Roland, 6 km, France
SA-6 Gainful, SP, 3-21 km, USSR
SA-7 Grail , man-portable, 3.5 km (Soviet designation Strella), USSR
SA-8 Gecko, SP, 11 km, USSR
SA-9 Gaskin SP, 28 km, USSR
SA-11 Gadfly, SP, 28 km, USSR
SA-13 Gopher SP, 10 km, (Soviet designation Strella 10) USSR
SA-14 Gremlin, man-portable, 6-7 km (unconfirmed), USSR
Shahine 2/Crotale Shahine 2, SP, 13km, France; improvement of Crotale listed above
Shahine 2 ATTS (Air Transportable Towed System); a towed version of Shahine 2
Tigercat, Britain

Artillery Ammunition Carriers

(designation, tracked or wheeled, armored, country of origin)
M-992, tracked USA
MT-LB, tracked, armored, USSR; also serves as prime mover for towed artillery and APC

Artillery/mortar locating radars

(designation, country of origin)
AN/TPQ 37, USA
AN/PPS-15, USA

ATGMs

(anti-tank guided missiles, designation, NATO codename if relevant, SP if relevant, range, country of origin)
AT-1 Snapper, 500-2300m., USSR
AT-2 Swatter, 600-2500m., USSR
AT-3 Sagger, 500-3000m. (Soviet designation Malyutka), USSR
AT-4 Spigot, 2000m., USSR
AT-5 Spandrel, 3600m., USSR
AT-6 Spiral, USSR
BGM-71A TOW/BGM-71C Improved TOW, 65-3750m. (range of Improved TOW), USA
BGM-71D TOW II, USA; improvement of BGM-71C
BRDM-2 carrying AT-3 (Sagger) SP, 500-3000m., USSR
Dragon III, 1500m.,USA; improved M-47A
HOT, 75-4000m., France/FRG
HOT Commando, HOT mounted on a Peugeot P-4 4x4 jeep-like

vehicle, France

Israeli BGM-71C Improved TOW SP, 65-3750m; derivative of M-113 APC, USA; missile and APC, USA; mounting and hydraulics--Israel

M-3 (Panhard) carrying HOT SP, 75-4000m., France; see also APC

M-47A Dragon, 1000m., USA

M-901 ITV SP (TOW under armor), BGM-71A TOW, 65-3750m., derivative of M-113 APC, USA; see also APC/ARV

Mapats, 4500m., Israel; laser-beam riding Israeli improvement of US-made BGM-71A TOW

MILAN, 25-2000m., France/FRG

SS-11, 500-3000m., France

SS-12, 6000m., France (can be employed as ATGM or as anti-ship missile launched from ground, helicopter or ship)

Swingfire 300-4000m., Britain/Egypt

T-1/T-16 SP, ATGM system/tank destroyer (unconfirmed), USSR

Vigilant, 200-1375m., Britain

VCR/TH carrying HOT SP, 75-4000m., France; see also APC

Automatic grenade launchers

(caliber, designation, country of origin)

40mm Mk.19, USA

Engineering equipment

(designation, type, country of origin)

Bar mine-laying system, Britain

EWK pontoon bridge (Faltschwimmbrucke), FRG

Gilois motorized bridge, France

GSP self-propelled ferry, USSR

M-69 Al bridging tank, USA

M-123 Viper minefield-crossing system, USA

MT-55 bridging tank, USSR

MTU-55 bridging tank, USSR

PMP pontoon bridge, USSR

Pomins II, portable (infantry) mine neutralization system, Israel

PRP motorized bridge, USSR

TLB, trailer launched bridge, Israel

Guns & Howitzers, SP

(caliber, designation, gun or howitzer, range, country of origin)

210mm al-Faw, 57 km (with base bleed and RAP ammunition), Iraq (with assistance of companies from Belgium and Britain)

203mm/8" M-110 Al SP howitzer, 16.8 km, USA

175mm M-107 SP gun, 32.7 km, USA

155mm Mk. F-3 (AMX) SP howitzer, 18 km, France
155mm GCT SP howitzer, 23.5 km, France
155mm M-109 A1/A2 SP howitzer, 21 km, Israel
155mm L-33 (Sherman/Soltam) SP howitzer, 21 km, Israel
155mm M-50 (Sherman) SP howitzer, 17.5 km, Israel (gun-France; chassis-USA, improved in Israel)
155mm M-44 SP howitzer, 14.6 km, USA
155mm Palmaria SP howitzer, 24 km, Italy
152mm M-1973 SP howitzer, 18 km, USSR
122mm M-1974 SP howitzer, 15.3 km, USSR
122mm D-30 SP howitzer, 16 km, USSR (gun)/Egypt (conversion to SP with British/US aid)
122mm ISU SP gun, 16 km, USSR
105mm M-108 SP howitzer, 11.5 km, USA
105mm M-52 SP howitzer, 11.3 km, USA
105mm Mk.61 SP howitzer, 15 km, France
100mm SU-100 SP gun, USSR

Guns & Howitzers, Towed

(caliber, designation, gun or howitzer, range, country of origin)
203mm/8" M-115 howitzer, 16.8 km, USA
180mm S-23 gun, 32 km, USSR
155mm M-41 gun, 30 km, Iraq/Austria; a combination of the 130mm gun and Austrian 155mm tubes
155mm FH-70 howitzer, 24 km, FRG
155mm G-5 gun/howitzer, 30 km, South Africa
155mm GHN-45 howitzer/gun, 17.8 km, Austria
155mm M-198 A1 howitzer, 18.1 km, USA
155mm M-114 A2 howitzer, 14.6 km, USA
155mm M-1950 howitzer, 17.5 km, France
155mm M-71 gun/howitzer, 24 km, Israel
155mm M-59 (Long Tom) gun, 22 km, USA
152mm D-20 howitzer/gun, 18 km, USSR
152mm M-1943 (D-1) howitzer, USSR
130mm M-46 gun, 27.1 km, USSR
130mm Type 59 gun, 27.4 km, PRC; copy of Soviet 130mm M-46
122mm M-1938 howitzer, 11.8 km, USSR
122mm D-30 howitzer, 16 km, USSR
122mm Saddam, Iraq/USSR (Soviet 122mm D-30 produced in Iraq)
105mm Gun, 17.2 km, Britain
105mm M-102 A1 howitzer, 11.5 km, USA
105mm M-101 A1 howitzer, 11.3 km, USA
105mm M-56 Pack howitzer, 10.6 km, Italy
100mm M-1955 gun, 21 km (field/AT gun), USSR
25 lb. (87mm) howitzer, 12.2 km, Britain
85mm M-1945/D-44 gun, 15.8 km (field/AT gun), USSR
76mm M-1942 divisional gun (ZIS-3), 13.3 km, USSR

Light ATRLs

(designation, effective range, country of origin)
APILAS (APILAS Manurhin), 400m., France
LAW-80, 500m., Britain
M-72 A1/A2 LAW, 300m., USA
RPG-2, 150m., USSR
RPG-7, 500m., USSR
89mm M-65, Spain
89mm Strim-89, 360m., France
3.5" M-20 (Bazooka), 110m., USA

Machine Guns

(caliber, designation, type, country of origin)
14.5mm KPV HMG, USSR
14.5mm ZPU 14.5x4 HMG, USSR; employed in anti-aircraft role
14.5mm ZPU 14.5x2 HMG, USSR; employed in anti-aircraft role
12.7mm D.Sh.K. 38/46 (Degtyarev) HMG, USSR
12.7mm (0.5") Browning M2 HMG, USA
7.62mm Aswan MMG, Egypt; a copy of Soviet 7.62mm SG-43
7.62mm MAG (FN) LMG, Belgium
7.62mm PK/PKS (Kalashnikov) LMG, USSR
7.62mm PKT (Kalashnikov) LMG, USSR
7.62mm RPD (Degtyarev) LMG, USSR
7.62mm RPK LMG, USSR
7.62mm Suez, Egypt; copy of Soviet 7.62mm RPD
7.62mm (0.3") Browning M-1919 MMG, USA
7.62mm (0.3") BAR (Browning) LMG, USA
7.62mm MG 1A1/1A3 LMG, Iran (licensed production of FRG's MG-3)
7.62mm MG-3, LMG, FRG
7.62mm M-60 D GPMG/LMG, USA
7.62mm SG-43 (Goryunov) MMG, USSR
7.62mm SGM (Goryunov) MMG, USSR
7.5mm AA-52/M2 MMG, France
7.5mm Chatellerault M-24/29 LMG, France
5.56mm Minimi (FN) LMG, Belgium
5.56mm Negev LMG, Israel

Mortars, heavy, over 160mm

(caliber, designation, SP if relevant, range, country of origin)
240mm M-240, 9.7 km, USSR
160mm M-43/53, 5.1 km, USSR
160mm M-66 SP, 9.3 km, Israel

Mortars, heavy, under 160mm

(caliber, designation, SP if relevant, range, country of origin)

120mm M-43, 5.7 km, USSR

120mm Brandt M-50/M-60, 6.6 km (unconfirmed), France

120mm M-65, 6.3 km, Israel; also available as SP, mounted on US-made M-2 halftrack

120mm x 4 SP, 11.5 km, Iraq; mounted on Soviet made MT-LB carrier

107mm (4.2") M-30 SP/towed (SP on M-106 A2 carrier, a derivative of M-113 APC), 5.6 km, USA

Mortars, Light and Medium

(caliber, designation, range, country of origin)

82mm M-41/43, 2550 m., USSR

81mm Hotchkiss Brandt, 4550 m. (unconfirmed), France

81mm M-29, 4590 m., USA

81mm Soltam, 4100 m. (short barrel), 4900 m. (long barrel), Israel

81mm ECIA, Spain

81mm L-16 A1, 5660 m., Britain

60mm Hotchkiss-Brandt, 2050 m., France

60mm M-2, 2550 m., Israel

60mm M-19, 1810 m., USA

52mm IMI, 420 m., Israel

MRLs

(caliber, designation, number of launchers, range, country of origin)

400mm Ababil-100, 4, 100 km, Iraq/copy or improvement of Yugoslavia's 262mm LRSV M-87

355mm Nazeat, 90 km, Iran

333mm Shahin 2, 20 km, Iran

300mm SS-60, 4, 68 km, Brazil

290mm (MAR 290), 4, 25 km (unconfirmed), Israel

262mm Ababil-50, 12, 50 km, Iraq/copy of Yugoslavia's 262mm LRSV M-87

240mm BM-24, 12, 10.2 km, USSR

230mm Oghab, 3, 40 km (unconfirmed), Iran; copy of PRC's Type 83 273mm rocket

180mm SS-40 Astros II, 16, 35 km, Brazil

140mm BM-14-16, 16, 9.8 km, USSR

140mm RPU-14, 16, 9.8 km, USSR

140mm Teruel, 40, 18.2 km, Spain

132mm BM-13-16, 16, 9 km, USSR

130mm M-51 (=130mm RM-130), 32, 8.2 km, Romania/USSR

130mm M-51, 32, 8.2 km, Czechoslovakia

130mm Type 63, 19, 10.4 km, PRC

128mm M-63, 32, 8.5 km, Yugoslavia
127mm SS-30 Astros II, 32, 30 km, Brazil
122mm BM-11, 30, North Korea; a variant of Soviet BM-21
122mm BM-21, 40, 20.8 km, USSR
122mm Firos-25, 40, 25 km, Italy
122mm RM-70, 40, 20.4 km, Czechoslovakia; similar to Soviet BM-21
122mm Saqr 30, 22.5 km, Egypt
122mm Saqr 10 and Saqr 18, short range versions of Saqr 30, Egypt
107mm RM-11, 8.1 km, North Korea
107mm, Iraq; copy of 107mm from PRC or RM-11 from North Korea
MLRS, USA

Personal Weapons

(caliber, designation, type, country of origin)
11mm (0.45") M-3 A1 SMG, USA
9mm Aqaba SMG, Egypt (improved Port Sa'id)
9mm Carl Gustaf Model 45 SMG, Sweden
9mm L-34 A1 SMG, Britain
9mm MAT 49/56 SMG, France
9mm Mini Uzi SMG, Israel
9mm Model 12 Beretta SMG, Italy
9mm Model 23/25 SMG, Czechoslovakia
9mm Model 38/49 Beretta SMG, Italy
9mm Port Sa'id SMG, Egypt (copy of Swedish Carl Gustaf)
9mm P.P.Sh. 41/42/43 SMG, USSR (also available in 7.62mm caliber)
9mm Sterling Mk.4 SMG, Britain
9mm Uzi SMG, Israel; produced under licence in Belgium
9mm Vigneron M2 SMG, Belgium
7.62mm AK-47/AKM (Kalashnikov) AR, USSR
7.62mm FAL (FN) SAR, Belgium
7.62mm L-1 A1 SAR, Britain
7.62mm FAC (FN) SAR, Belgium; similar to 7.62mm CAL/FAL, above
7.62mm FAL (FN) SAR, Belgium; same as 7.62mm CAL/FAL, above
7.62mm Galil sniper rifle, Israel
7.62mm G-3 (Heckler & Koch) AR, FRG/Iran (licensed production)
7.62mm M-1 Garand SAR, USA
7.62mm M-14 SAR, USA
7.62mm Rashid SAR, Egypt
7.62mm SKS (Simonov) SAR, USSR
7.62mm SSG-69 sniper rifle (Steyr), Austria
7.62mm Type 56 AR, PRC; Chinese copy of Soviet AK-47
7.5mm MAS 49/56 SAR, France
5.56mm AR-180 SAR, USA
5.56mm AUG Steyr AR, Austria
5.56mm CAL (FN) AR, Belgium

5.56mm Galil AR, Israel
5.56mm HK-33 (Heckler & Koch) AR, FRG
5.56mm M-16 A1/A2 AR, USA
5.56mm SG-540 AR, Switzerland

Recovery Vehicles

(designation, APC/tank chassis, country of origin)
M-578 A1 APC, USA
M-88 A1 Recovery Tank, USA
T-55 Recovery Tank, USSR
T-62 Recovery Tank, USSR

SS Missiles & Rockets

(designation, NATO codename if relevant, range, circular error probability (CEP), payload, country of origin)
al-Hussein (Iraqi modified SS-1), 600-700 km, 180kg (unconfirmed), USSR/Iraq
CSS-2 (East Wind) IRBM, 1500 km, 2045 kg, (with conventional warhead), PRC
FROG-4, 45 km, USSR
FROG-7 (Soviet designation Luna), 60 km, 450 kg, 500m, USSR
Iran-130, 130 km, Iran
Jericho I, 450 km, 500 kg (according to foreign publications), Israel
Jericho II, 800 km, 500 kg (according to foreign publications), Israel
MGM-52C Lance, 75 km (with conventional warhead), 225 kg, USA
M-9, 600 km (unconfirmed), PRC
Saqr 80, 80 km, 200 kg, Egypt; launched from FROG-7 launcher
SS-1 Scud B, 280 km, 800-1000 kg, 1000m, USSR
SS-21 Scarab, 80 km, 100m, USSR
Tamuz 1, 2000 km, Iraq (with assistance from German, Italian and French experts)

Tanks

(designation, caliber of gun, weight, country of origin)
AMX-13 LT, 75mm/105mm, 14.5 ton, France
AMX-30 MBT, 105mm, 36 ton, France
Assad Babil, T-55 with Iraqi upgrading, including 125mm gun, USSR/Iraq
Centurion MBT, 105mm, 52 ton, Britain
Chieftain Mk.3/Mk.5 MBT, 120mm, 52.3 ton, Britain
Khalid--Jordanian designation for Chieftain; see above
M-41 LT, 76.2mm, 24 ton, USA
M-47 A1/2/5 MBT, 90mm, 44 ton, USA
M-48 A1/5 Patton MBT, 90mm/105mm, 46.6 ton, USA
M-60/M-60 A1/A2/A3 MBT, 105mm, 49 ton, USA
M-77 MBT (improved Soviet T-55), Romania
M-84 MBT, Yugoslavia; licensed production of Soviet T-72

Merkava Mk.1/Mk.2 MBT, 105mm, 56 ton, Israel
Merkava Mk.3 MBT, 120mm, 59 ton, Israel
OF-40 Lion MBT, 105mm, 43 ton, Italy; heavily reliant on FRG's Leopard 1 in design and components
Osorio (EE-T1) MBT, 105mm/120mm, Brazil
PT-76 amphibious LT, 76mm, 14 ton, USSR
Ramses II MBT, 105mm, 36 ton (unconfirmed), Egypt; Soviet T-54/T-55 upgraded with USA model gun and USA stabilizer, laser range finder, fire control and night vision
Scorpion LT, 76mm, 7.8 ton, Britain
SK-105 (Kurassier; also Jagdpanzer) LT/tank destroyer, 105mm, 18 ton, Austria
T-34 Medium Tank, 85mm, 32 ton, USSR
T-54 B/C MBT, 100mm, 36 ton, USSR
T-55 B/C/D MBT, 100mm, 36 ton, USSR
T-62 MBT, 115mm, 37.5 ton, USSR
T-72 MBT, 125mm, 41 ton, USSR
Type-59 (=T-55), PRC
Type-62 Medium Tank, 85mm, 21 ton, PRC
Type-69, improved Type-59, above, PRC
Vickers Mk.1 MBT, 105mm, 38.1 ton, Britain

AIR FORCE

AA Guns, Long Range (caliber, designation, country of origin)
100mm M-49, USSR
85mm M-44, USSR

AEW/AWACS Aircraft
(designation, NATO codename if relevant, derivation if relevant, function, speed, range, radar range, country of origin)
E-3A Sentry, AWACS, Boeing 707, 853 km/h., 6 hrs. endurance, radar range 370 km, USA
E-2C Hawkeye, AEW, 602 km/h., 6 hrs. 6 min. endurance, radar range 250 km, USA
TU-126 Moss, AWACS, TU-114, 850 km/h., 12,550 km, USSR

Air-to-Air Missiles (AAMs)
(designation, NATO codename if relevant, guidance systems, effective range, country of origin)
AA-1 Alkali, semi-active radar guidance, 6-8 km, USSR
AA-2 Atoll, infra-red homing, 5-6.5 km, USSR
AA-2 Advanced Atoll, active radar homing, 5-6.5 km, USSR
AA-6 Acrid, infra-red guidance, 37 km, USSR
AA-7 Apex, infra-red or semi-active guidance, 27 km, USSR
AA-8 Aphid, 5-7.4 km, USSR
AA-10 Alamo, radar homing, 20-34 km, USSR
AA-11 Archer, active terminal radar, 39-68 km, USSR
AIM-7/AIM-7E/F Sparrow III, semi-active radar guidance, 44 km, USA
AIM-9B Sidewinder, infra-red homing, now obsolete, USA
AIM-9E/F Sidewinder, infra-red guidance, USA; improved AIM-9B
AIM-9J Sidewinder, USA; advanced version of AIM-9E with enhanced dogfight capability
AIM-9L Sidewinder, infra-red guidance and active laser fuse, 18 km, USA
AIM-9M Sidewinder, similar to AIM-9L, with improved target acquisition and lock-on capabilities, USA
AIM-9P/P4 Sidewinder, improved AIM-9B, USA
AIM-54A Phoenix, semi-active radar guidance and fully active radar during terminal guidance, 44 km, USA
Firestreak, infra-red homing, 1.8 km, Britain
Python 3, infra-red guidance, 15 km, Israel
Red Top, infra-red homing, 12 km, Britain
R-530 (Matra R-530), infra-red guidance version/semi-active radar version, 18 km, France
R-550 Magique, infra-red guidance, 10 km, France

Shafrir, infra-red guidance, 5 km, Israel
Sky Flash, semi-active radar, 40 km, Britain
Super 530D/F (improved R-530), semi-active homing radar, 25 km, France

Air-to-Ground Missiles(AGMs)

(designation, NATO codename if relevant, function, guidance, range, country of origin)
AGM-45A/B Shrike, anti-radar/SAM sites, radar-guidance, 12-16 km, USA
AGM-62A Walleye, anti-ship/airbase/bridge, TV-guided, USA
AGM-65A/B Maverick, anti-tank/hard target, TV-guided, USA
AGM-65C Maverick (=65A/B guided by Laser designator), USA
AGM-78D Standard ARM anti-radar/SAM site, passive radar homing, USA
AGM-84, anti-ship missile, air-launched variant of RGM-84A Harpoon SSM, USA; see Navy
AGM-114 Hellfire, helicopter-borne, ATGM, guidance by Laser designator, USA
ALARM, air-launched anti-radar missile, Britain
AM-39, anti-ship, radio and radar guided, 50-70 km, France; air-launched derivative of the MM-38 & MM-40 Exocet SSMs
Armat, air launched anti-radar missile, homing on radar emission, France; enhanced successor version of French-British AS-37
AS-1 Kennel, anti-ship/hard target, radar guidance, 90 km, USSR
AS-2 Kipper, autopilot command override, active terminal homing, 160 km, USSR
AS-4 Kitchen, inertial guidance with radar terminal homing, 400 km, USSR
AS-5 Kelt, anti-ship and hard target, radar guidance, 160 km, USSR
AS-6 Kingfish, inertial guidance, 240 km, USSR
AS-11, anti-ship, wire-guided (optical/tracked navigation), 3 km, France, helicopter-launched anti-ship & anti-tank version of SS-11 ATGM
AS-12, anti-ship, wire-guided (optical/tracked navigation), 6 km, France; helicopter-launched anti-ship version of the SS-12 ATGM
AS-14 Kedge, anti tank/hard target, mid-course guidance and electro-optical homing, 30km, (unconfirmed), USSR
AS-15TT, anti-ship, radar and radio-guided, 14.4 km, France; helicopter-launched
AS-30, radio-guided, 11.2 km, France
AS-30L, laser-guided, France
LX, anti-ship missile (unconfirmed), USSR
Sea Eagle, anti-ship missile, inertial navigation and radar homing, 100 km, Britain

X-23, anti-radiation missile (unconfirmed), USSR

Aircraft, Bombers

(designation, NATO codename, maximum speed, range, armament, country of origin)

H-6 (B-6D), copy of Soviet Tu-16, PRC

IL-28 Beagle, 900 km/h., 2260 km, 2040 kg. bombs, 4x23mm gun, USSR

Tu-16 Badger, 945 km/h., 4800 km, Kelt AGM/9000 kg. bombs, 2x2x23mm gun, USSR

Tu-22 Blinder, Mach 1.4, 2250 km, Kitchen AGM and bombs, 1x23mm gun, USSR

Aircraft, Counter-insurgency

IA-58/IA-66 Pucara, counter-insurgency/trainer (turboprop), 2x20mm gun, 4x7.62mm MG, 1000 kg. bombs, Argentina

OV-10 Bronco (also Rockwell OV-10 Bronco), counter-insurgency/surveillance aircraft, FLIR sensor, laser designator, 272 kg. weapon pods/20mm guns/bombs, 463 km/h., 367 km (combat radius with weapon load), USA

Aircraft, Interceptors

(designation, NATO codename if relevant, maximum speed, combat radius, armament, country of origin)

F-6 Shenyang (=MiG-19), PRC; see also aircraft, strike & multi-role, & MiG-19, below

F-7 Shenyang (=MiG-21), PRC; see MiG-21, below

F-14A Tomcat, Mach 2.4, 4xAIM-7 or 4xAIM-54A Phoenix + 4xAIM-9, 1x20mm gun, USA

F-15A/B/C/D Eagle, Mach 2.5+, 1000 km, 4xAIM-7/4xAIM-9, 1x20mm gun, USA

FT-6, PRC; two-seater training version of F-6; also JJ-6, copy of Soviet MiG-19 UTI

MiG-19 PF/PFM Farmer C/D, 1452 km/h., 685 km, 2xAA-2 Atoll AAM, 2 or 3x30mm gun, USSR

MiG-21 MF/S/U Fishbed, Mach 2.1, 1100 km, 2xAA-2 Atoll AAM/Advanced Atoll, 1x23mm gun, USSR

MiG-23 ML/MF/MS Flogger B/E, Mach 2.3, 1200 km, 5xAA-7 Apex/AA-8 Aphid AAM, 1x23mm gun, USSR

MiG-25 Foxbat A/B/E/U, Mach 2.8, 1450 km, 4xAA-8 Aphid/AA-6 Acrid AAM, USSR

MiG-25R, reconnaissance version of MiG-25

Mirage III C/E/BL/EL, Mach 2.2, 1200 km, 1xR530/2xAIM-9, 2x30mm gun, France

Su-27 Flanker A, Mach 2.3, 1500 km, 6-8xAA-10 AAM, 23mm gun, USSR

Tornado (Panavia Tornado) ADV, Mach 2.2, radius 620 km, AIM-9L, Sky Flash AAM, 1x27mm Mauser cannon, Britain, FRG and Italy (joint production); see also Aircraft, Strike and

Multi-Role
Xian J-7, copy of MiG-21, PRC; export version designated F-7 Shenyang, see above

Aircraft, Maritime Surveillance

(designation, jet/turboprop, speed, endurance, range, sonar, radar, country of origin)

EMB-111N Bandeirante, based on EMB-110 transport aircraft, turboprop, 360 km/h., 2940 km, sea patrol radar, Brazil

P-3 Orion, turboprop, 608 km/h., 3 hours on station, 3835 km, sonar (ARR-72), APS-115 radar, USA; may carry depth bombs

Westwind I/Sea Scan/ 1124 Sea Scan, based on Westwind 1124, maritime reconnaissance aircraft, 872 km/h., 6 hrs. 30 min. endurance, equipped with search radar, Israel

Beechcraft 1900C, derivative of commuter/light transport aircraft employed in Egypt in ELINT and/or maritime surveillance role, USA; see Aircraft, Transport and Executive

Aircraft, Strike & Multi-Role

(designation, NATO codename if relevant, maximum speed, combat radius/range, armament, country of origin)

A-4 A/B/D/E/J/KU Skyhawk, 1085 km/h., 3200 km, 2x20mm gun, 4,500 kg. bombs, USA (A-4E data)

F-4 D/E Phantom, Mach 2+, 1145 km, 4xAIM-7 + 4xAIM-9, 1x20mm gun, 7250 kg. bombs, USA

F-4 Shenyang (=MiG-17), PRC, see MiG-17

F-5 A/B/E/F (Tiger II), Mach 1.64, 890 km, 2xAIM-9, 2x20mm gun, 3.17 ton bombs, USA (F-5E data)

F-6 Shenyang, PRC (copy of Soviet MiG-19 interceptor); see MiG-19, Aircraft, Interceptors

F-16 A/B/C/D Fighting Falcon, Mach 1.95, 925 km, 2xAIM-9, 1x20mm gun, 6.8 ton bombs, USA

Hawker Hunter FGA-6/F-70/FR-10/T-66/T-67, Mach 0.8, 4x30mm gun, 0.5 ton bombs, Britain

J-1 Jastreb, light attack version of SOKO G-2 Galeb; see Aircraft, Training

Kfir C-2/TC-2/C-7/TC-7, Mach 2.3, 768 km, 2xShafrir AAM, 2x30mm gun, 3150 kg. bombs, Israel

MiG-15 Faggot, 1070 km/h., 1400 km, 1x37mm gun, 2x23mm gun, USSR; also employed as advanced trainer

Mig-17 Fresco, 1145 km/h., 1400 km, 1x37mm gun, 2x23mm gun, 500 kg. bombs, USSR

MiG-23 S/BN/U Flogger A/F/C/S/G, Mach 2.3, 1200 km, AA-7 Apex & AA-8 Aphid AAMs, 1x23mm twin barrel gun, USSR; see also Aircraft, Interceptors

MiG-27 Flogger D, Mach 1.6, ca. 500 km, AA-7 Apex & AA-8 Aphid AAMs, 1x23mm twin barrel gun, USSR

MiG-29 Fulcrum, Mach 2.8 (unconfirmed), USSR
Mirage 5/50, Mach 2.2, 1300 km, 2xAIM-9 AAM/2xR-530, 2x30mm gun, up to 4000 kg. bombs, France
Mirage F-1 B/C/D/E, Mach 2.2, AIM-9/R-530 and R-550 Magique, AS-30 AGM, 2x30mm gun, 3600 kg. bombs, France
Mirage F-1 EQ5 = F-1 E equipped to fire AM-39 Exocet ASM, France
Mirage 2000, Mach 2.2+, 1480 km with external tanks and bombs, 2xSuper R-530 AAM and 2xR-550 Magique AAM, 2x30mm gun, up to 5000 kg. bombs, France
RF-4E Phantom, reconnaissance version of F-4E
RF-5E Northrop Tiger II, reconnaissance/photography version of F-5E (unarmed), USA
SEPECAT Jaguar S/E-01, Mach 1.6, 1408 km, 2xR-550 Magique or 2xAIM-9 AAM or AS 37 AGM, 1-2x30mm gun, 3600 kg. bombs, Britain and France
Su-7 BM/U Fitter A/B, Mach 1.6, 480 km, 2x30mm gun, 1 ton bombs, USSR
Su-20/22 Fitter C, Mach 2.17, 630 km, AA-2 Atoll AAMs, 2x30mm gun, 4000 kg. bombs, USSR
Su-24 Fencer C, Mach 2.18, 1800 km, 11,000 kg. bombs/AGMs including AS-7 Kerry AGM, one gun, USSR
Su-25 Frogfoot, 880 km/h., 556 km, AA-2 Atoll/AA-8 Aphid AAMs, 30mm guns, maximum armament and bomb load 4 tons, USSR
TA-4 KU, USA--see A-4; designation of advanced two seater training aircraft for Kuwait
Tornado (Panavia Tornado) IDS, Mach 2.2, 1390 km with heavy weapons load, AIM-9, AGM-65/AS-30 AGM/CBU-15, 2x27mm gun, maximum armament and bomb load 8.1 tons, Britain, FRG and Italy (joint production); see also Aircraft, Interceptors

Aircraft, Tanker

(aerial refuelling) (designation, derivation, fuel load, country of origin)
Boeing 707 Tanker, USA--see KC-135; also a Boeing 707 made in USA, converted to aerial refuelling role in Israel
KC-135A Stratotanker, Boeing 707, USA
KC-130H, C-130H Hercules, 23,923 liter, USA
KE-3A, similar to KC-135A, USA; designation of aircraft for Saudi Arabia

Aircraft, Training and Liaison

(designation, jet, turboprop or piston engine, ground attack capability if relevant, country of origin)
Aermacchi MB-326 B/KT/LT, jet, ground attack capability, Italy
Aermacchi MB-339, jet, ground attack capability, Italy
al-Gumhuriya, piston, Egypt (German/Spanish model)

Alpha Jet, jet, ground attack capability, France & West Germany/Egypt-assembly
Alpha Jet MS-2, same as Alpha Jet, licensed production in Egypt with improved ground attack and naval attack capabilities
AS-202/18A Bravo and AS-202/26A, piston, Switzerland
BAC-145 Jet Provost, jet, ground attack capability, Britain
BAC-167 Strikemaster Mk.82/Mk.83, jet, ground attack capability, Britain; development of BAC-145
BAe Jetstream 31, turboprop, Britain; a transport aircraft employed for cockpit training for Tornado aircrews
BAe-SA-3-120 Bulldog series 125/126, piston, Britain (formerly Scottish Aviation B-125 Bulldog and Beagle B-125 Bulldog)
Beechcraft Bonanza F-33A and V-35B, piston, USA
Beechcraft T-34C Turbo Mentor, turboprop, USA
Broussard, piston, France
Cessna 172 G/H/L, piston, USA
Cessna 182 Skylane, piston, USA
Cessna 185 Skywagon, piston, USA; same as Cessna U-206
Cessna 318 (T-37), jet, USA
Cessna U-206 Skywagon, piston, USA
CM-170 Fouga Magister, jet, ground attack capability, France/Israel (assembly)
Embraer EMB-312 (T-27), turboprop, Brazil; produced under license by Egypt and Britain; also designated Tucano T-27
FT-6, trainer, two-seat version of F-6 (interceptor), PRC; see interceptors
Galeb--see SOKO
Gepal IV (AMIN Gepal IV), turboprop, Morocco
Grob G-109B, ultra-light, FRG
Hawk, jet, ground attack capability, Britain
L-29 Delfin, jet, ground attack capability, Czechoslovakia
L-39 Albatross, jet, ground attack capability, Czechoslovakia
MBB-223 Flamingo/MBB-Flamingo, piston, FRG/Spain; produced in FRG by MBB or SIAT, and in Spain by CASA
MiG-15 UTI--see Aircraft, Strike and Multi-Role
Mushshak, (Saab Safari Supporter, Saab MF-17), piston, Pakistan; produced under license from Sweden (Saab)
Pilatus PC-6 Turbo-Porter, turboprop, Switzerland
Pilatus PC-7 Turbo-Trainer, turboprop, Switzerland
Pilatus PC-9, turboprop, Switzerland
Piper Cub/Piper/PA-18 Super Cub, piston, USA
Piper PA-44, USA
Piper Navajo (PA-31), USA
PZL-104 Wilga 35/80, piston, Poland
Rockwell T-6 (Texan, Harvard), piston, USA
SIAI-Marchetti SF-260M/WT/C/L Warrior, piston, Italy
SIAI-Marchetti S-208A, piston, Italy

SOKO G-2A/G-2AE Galeb, jet, ground attack capability, Yugoslavia; J-1 Jastreb derived from G-2A for light attack roles and advanced training
Strikemaster--see BAC-167 Strikemaster
T-33, jet, ground attack capability, USA
Tzukit, (French) CM-170 Fouga Magister upgraded by Israel (strengthened frame and new avionics)
YAK-11 Moose, piston, USSR
YAK-18 Max, piston, USSR

Aircraft, Transport & Executive

(designation, NATO codename if relevant, piston, turboprop or jet engine, maximum cruising speed, range, load, accommodation, paratroop dropping capability if relevant, country of origin)
An-2 Colt, piston, 200 km/h., 905 km, 1240 kg./14 paratroopers, USSR
An-12 Cub, turboprop, 670 km/h., 3600 km, 20 ton/100 paratroopers, USSR
An-24 Coke, turboprop, 450 km/h., 640 km, 5700 kg./ 38 passengers or 30 paratroopers, USSR
An-26 Curl, turboprop, 440 km/h., 1100 km, 5500 kg./ 38-40 passengers, USSR
Arava (IAI 101/201/202 Arava), turboprop, 319 km/h., 630 km, 2351 kg./24 passengers/16 paratroopers, Israel (IAI 202 data)
BAe-111 (BAC-111), jet, 870 km/h., 3013 km, 10,733 kg./119 passengers, Britain
BAe-125 (also known as HS-125), jet, 845 km/h., 5318 km, 1088kg./2 pilots + 14 passengers, Britain
Beechcraft Bonanza A-36, piston, 326 km/h, pilot + 4-6 passengers, USA; an executive aircraft
Beechcraft 1900C, turboprop, 435 km/h., 1469 km, 19 passengers/EW/CEW equipment, USA; a commuter aircraft employed in EW/CEW and/or maritime surveillance role in Egypt
Beechcraft King Air B-100, turboprop, 486 km/h., 2232 km, 13 passengers, USA
Beechcraft Queen Air, turboprop, 370 km/h., 2520 km, 1599 kg./9 passengers, USA; an executive aircraft
Beechcraft Super King Air, turboprop, 536 km/h., 3,658 km, 14 passengers, USA
Boeing 707/707-200/707-320, jet, 973 km/h., 7700 km, 43 ton/180 passengers, USA
Boeing 720/720B/720B-023B, jet, 897 km/h., 6690 km, 112 passengers, USA
Boeing 727, jet, 960 km/h., 14,740 kg./131 passengers, USA
Boeing KC-135--see Boeing 707, aerial refuelling aircraft
Boeing 737/737-200, jet, 943 km/h., 3521 km, 15 ton/115

passengers, USA
Boeing 747/747-200B/747-200C, jet, 967 km/h., 10,562 km, 160 ton/450 passengers, USA
Britten-Norman BN-2A Islander/Pilatus BN-2B Islander II, piston, 251 km/h., 1530 km, 10 passengers, Britain/Switzerland
C-47--see DC-3 Dakota
C-119, piston, 315 km/h. 725 km, 10 ton/67 troops, fewer paratroopers, USA
C-130H-30, stretched version of C-130H, see L-100-30
C-130 E/H Hercules, turboprop, 621 km/h., 3791 km (maximum payload), 19,685 kg./92 paratroopers, USA
C-140 Jetstar, jet, 885 km/h., 3185 km, 1360 kg./10 passengers, USA
C-212--see CASA C-212 Aviocar
Caravelle Super B, 835 km/h., 2,725 km, 9,265 kg./ 104 passengers, France
CASA C-212-5 series 100/C-212 series 200 Aviocar, turboprop, 365 km/h., 408 km, 2770 kg./24 passengers/23 paratroopers, Spain/Indonesia (licensed production)
CASA/Nurtanio CN-235 (also Airtech CN-235), turboprop, 454 km/h., 796 km, 3,575 kg./39 passengers/30 paratroopers, Spain/Indonesia; Airtech is company jointly owned by CASA (Spain) and Nurtanio (Indonesia)
Cessna 310, piston, 361 km/h., 2842 km, 6 passengers, USA
CN-235--see CASA/Nurtanio CN-235
DC-3 Dakota (C-47), piston, 220 km/h., 500 km, 2.5 ton/24 paratroopers, USA
DC-8, jet, Mach 0.8, 11,410 km, 30,240 kg./ 189 passengers, USA
DC-9, jet, 907 km/h., 3095 km, 14,118 kg./119 passengers, USA
DC-10, jet, 925 km/h.. 7,400 km, 43.3 ton/380 passengers, USA
DHC-4/DHC-4A Caribou, piston, 293 km/h., 2,103 km, 3965 kg./32 passengers/26 paratroopers, Canada
DHC-5/DHC-5D Buffalo, turboprop, 467 km/h., 1112 km, 8,164 kg./41 passengers, Canada
DHC-6 Twin Otter, turboprop, 338 km/., 1297 km, 1940 kg./20 passengers, Canada
Dornier Do-28 D/Do-28 D2 Skyservant, piston, 286 km/h., 2875 km, 1000 kg./13 passengers, FRG
Dornier Do-228-100, turboprop, 432 km/h., 1,970 km, 2.2 ton/15 passengers, FRG
EMB-110/EMB-110 P2 Bandeirante, turboprop, 417 km/h., 1900 km, 1681 kg./21 passengers, Brazil
EMB-121 Xingu, turboprop, 450 km/h., 2,352 km, 1,477 kg./9 passengers, Brazil; an executive aircraft
Falcon 20--see Mystere-Falcon 20
Fokker F-27 Mk.400/F-27 Mk.600, turboprop, 480 km/h.,

1926/1935 km, 5727/5696 kg/40/44 passengers, Netherlands

Fokker F-27 Mk.400M, military version of F-27 Mk.400, 46 paratroopers, Netherlands

Fokker F-28, jet, 843 km/h., 1900 km, 10,478 kg./85 passengers, Netherlands

G-222L, turboprop, 439 km/h., 2409 km, 9000 kg./53 passengers/42 paratroopers, Italy

Gates Learjet 35, jet, 872 km/h., 4200 km, 8 passengers, USA

Gulfstream II, jet, 0.85 Mach, 6,579 km, 8 passengers, USA; an executive jet

Hawker Siddeley Dove, piston, 338 km/h., 620 km, 670 kg./11 passengers, Britain

IL-14 Crate, piston, 358 km/h., 2600 km, 5.3 ton/18 passengers/paratroopers, USSR

IL-18 Coot, turboprop, 675 km/h., 4,700 km, 13,500 kg./122 passengers, USSR

IL-76 Candid, jet, 800 km/h., 6700 km, 40 ton/over 100 passengers, USSR

L-100-20, turboprop, 581 km/h., 3889 km (maximum payload), 21,130 kg./92 paratroopers (optional), USA; civilian or military stretched Hercules

L-100-30, turboprop, 583 km/h., 3326 km (maximum payload), 23,014 kg./passengers--not less than L-100-20, USA; civilian or military stretched Hercules

L-410 UVP, turboprop, 360 km/h., 540km, 1300 kg./2 crew + 19 passengers, Czechoslovakia

MD-315 Flamant, piston, 147 km/h., 10 passengers, France

Merlin IV (corporate version of Metro III), turboprop, 524 km/h., 1805 km, 13-16 passengers, USA

Mystere Falcon 10, jet, 900 km/h., 3,370 km, 7 passengers, France; an executive jet

Mystere Falcon 20, jet, 855 km/h., 4170 km, 1180 kg./7 passengers, France; an executive jet

Mystere Falcon 50, jet, 800 km/h., 6480 km, 8 passengers, France; an executive jet

Sabreliner 75A, jet, Mach. 0.80, 3,173 km, 10 passengers, USA; an executive jet

Short SC-7 Skyvan Srs. 3M, turboprop, 327 km/h., 1075 km, 2358 kg./22 passengers/16 paratroopers, Britain

Tu-124/Tu-134 Crusty, jet, 885 km/h., 3020 km, 8,200 kg./84 passengers, USSR

Turbo-Commander 690B, turboprop, 532 km/h., 11 passengers, USA

Westwind I/Westwind 1124, jet, 872 km/h., 4490 km, 10 passengers, Israel; an executive jet

Yak-40 Codling, jet, 550 km/h., 2,000 km, 2,720 kg./ 32 passengers, USSR

Bombs, Advanced

(designation, function, weight, country of origin)

Belouga Dispenser Weapon (BLG-66) Cluster Bomb Unit (CBU), anti-personnel & AFV, 290 kg., France

BL-755 Cluster Bomb, France

Cardoen CBU, cluster bomb, Chile

CBU-7A Cluster Bomb, USA

CBU-55 Cluster Bomb, anti-personnel, USA

Durandal Penetration Bomb, anti-runway bomb, 195 kg., France

JP-233 anti-runway bomb, Britain

Rockeye Cluster Bomb Mk.20, anti-tank CBU, USA

Helicopters, ASW

A-109/AS-109--see Helicopters, Attack

AB-212/Bell 212--see Helicopters, Medium Transport

Kamov Ka-25 Hormone--see Helicopters, Medium Transport

Mi-14 Haze, USSR

SH-3D (=Westland S-61), USA--see Helicopters, Heavy Transport

Westland Sea King HAS Mk.1/S-61A/AS-61A--see Helicopters, Heavy Transport

Westland Sea King Mk.47--nearly identical to Westland Sea King HAS Mk.1

Helicopters, Attack

(designation, NATO codename if relevant, max. speed, range, armament, country of origin)

Agusta A-109A, 311 km/h., 583 km, 4-8 BGM-71C Improved TOW, 2-3x7.62mm MG., 1x12.7mm HMG, 12x68mm rockets, Italy; a variant employed in ASW and/or naval attack role

AH-1S/AH-1G/AH-1J/AH-1Q Huey Cobra, 333 km/h., 577 km, 8xBGM-71C Improved TOW, 2x20mm mini-gun pod/68mm rockets/grenade dispensers, USA

AH-64 Apache, 300 km/h., 689 km, 8xAGM-114 Hellfire, 30mm gun, 68mm rockets, USA

Alouette III--see Helicopters, Light Transport; armed with AS-12 AGMs

500 MG Defender/ TOW Defender/ Advanced Scout Defender, 244 km/h., 589 km range, 4xBGM-71C Improved TOW, 30mm chain gun, USA (derivative of Hughes 500D light transport helicopter, renamed McDonnell Douglas 500MD)

530 MG, armament equivalent to Hughes 500MD, USA (military derivative of Hughes 530F, renamed McDonnell Douglas 530MG); see above and Helicopters, Light Transport

MBB BO-105, 6xHOT--see Helicopters, Light Transport

Mi-24 Hind D/E 330 km/h., 4xAT-2 Swatter ATGM, 1x12.7mm MG, 4x32 57mm rockets, 8 troops, USSR

Mi-25 Hind--improved version of Mi-24

OH-58D, Combat Scout (AHIP), 22 km/h., 556 km, BGM-71C

Improved TOW, LGM/or 2 AAMS, USA; derived from Bell 206 light helicopter, also designated Bell 406

SA-342/SA-342K/L/M Gazelle, 310 km/h., 360 km, 4xHOT/6xHOT/4xAS-11/2xAS-12, 2x7.62 mm. MG, France

Westland Lynx, 259 km/h., 630 km, 8xBGM-71C Improved TOW/8xHOT/6xAS-11 AGM, 2x20mm gun/7.62mm MG, 18x68mm rockets, 10 troops, Britain

Helicopters, Heavy Transport

(designation, NATO codename if relevant, speed, range, accommodation, load, country of origin)

AS-61A/A4, Italy (licensed production of US-made S-61A); see S-61A

CH-47C Chinook, 304 km/h., 185 km radius (ferry range 2142 km), 44 troops/9843 kg., USA/Italy (licensed production)

CH-53/CH-53D, 315 km/h., 413 km, ca. 50 troops/5.9 ton/9 ton external payload, USA

KV-107/KV-107 IIA-17, 270 km/h., 1097 km, 25 passengers/12 passengers and 2268 kg, Japan (licensed production of USA-Boeing Vertol 107, Model II)

Mi-6 Hook, 300 km/h., 1450 km ferry range, 65 passengers/12,000 kg. internal payload/ 9000 kg. external payload, USSR

S-61 A/S-61 A4 (Sikorsky SH-3 Sea King), 267 km/h., 1005 km, 25 passengers/3630 kg., USA; employed mainly in ASW role, and in search and rescue with sonar, navigation Doppler radar

SA-321 Super Frelon (SA-3200--earlier aircraft), 275 km/h., 1020 km, 27-30 troops/5000 kg. external/internal load, France; can carry AM-39 Exocet AGM

SH-3 (AS 61A) VIP version of S-61 or AS-61, Italy; licensed production of S-61

Westland Commando Mk.2 (=S-61A & Westland Sea King transport version), 28 troops, Britain

Westland Sea King HAS Mk.1, 211 km/h., 1110 km, 22 passengers/2720 kg. internal load/3630 kg. external load, Britain; employed mostly in ASW role or in search and rescue role; equipped with Plessey dipping sonar, navigation Doppler radar system and search radar (licensed production of S-61A)

Helicopters, Light Transport

(designation, NATO codename if relevant, speed, range, accommodation, country of origin)

AB-47G/3B-1, 196 km/h., 367 km, pilot + 3 passengers, USA/Italy; licensed production of Bell 47

AB-206 (=Bell 206), Italy

Alouette II (early versions designated Sud-Aviation SE

313/3130; later version designated Aerospatiale SA-318), 205 km/h., 720 km, pilot + 4 passengers/600 kg., France
Alouette III (early version designated Sud-Aviation SE-316/3160; later version designated Aerospatiale SA-316/319), 210 km/h., 540 km, pilot + 6 passengers/750 kg., France
AS-350 Ecureuil, 230 km/h., 700 km, pilot + 5 passengers, France
Bell 206/206B JetRanger II/III, 225 km/h., 608 km, 2 pilots + 4 passengers, USA
Bell 206L LongRanger, improvement of Bell 206, 2 pilots + 5 passengers, USA
BK-117 (MBB/Kawasaki BK-117), 248 km/h., 493 km, pilot + 6 passengers, FRG/Japan
Hiller UH-12E, 154 km/h., 565 km, pilot + 3 passengers, USA
Hughes 500D, 282 km/h., 531 km, pilot + 4 passengers, USA (=Hughes 500MD attack helicopter for civilian or observation tasks); renamed McDonnell Douglas 500D
Hughes 530F, improvement of 500D, renamed McDonnell Douglas 530F, USA
Hughes 300C, 169 km/h., 370 km, pilot + 2 passengers, USA
MBB BO-105, 270 km/h., 1112 km, pilot + 4 passengers /ca. 300 kg., FRG (=Nurtanio MBB NBO 105, Indonesia); can be fitted with HOT ATGM and used as attack helicopter; licensed production in Spain and Indonesia
Schweizer Model 330, 185 km/h., 470 km, pilot + 2 passengers, USA/licensed production in Jordan; a Hughes 300C with a turboshaft engine

Helicopters, Maritime Attack

(designation, maximum cruising speed, range, armament, country of origin)
AS-365 Dauphin=SA-365
HH-65A Dolphin, 257 km/h., USA (licensed production of French Aerospatiale SA-366 Dauphin 2)
SA-365N/365F Dauphin 2, 252 km/h., 4xAS-15TT air-to-ship missiles, France
SA-366--improved SA-365

Helicopters, Medium Transport

(designation, NATO codename if relevant, speed, range, accommodation, load, country of origin)
AB-205 (=Bell 205), Italy; production under USA license
AB-212 (=Bell 212), Italy; production under USA license
AB-214/214A (Bell 214), 250 km/h., 654 km, 16 passengers, Italy; production under USA license
AB-412 (=Bell 412), 226 km/h., 461 km, 14 troops, Italy; production under USA license

AS-332 Super Puma, 296 km/h, 644 km, 20 passengers, France
Bell 205, 204 km/h., 511 km, 14 troops/1759 kg., USA (AB-205 in Italy)
Bell 212/212B, 259 km/h., 420 km, 10 troops/2268 kg. external load/1814 kg. internal load, USA (AB-212 in Italy)
Bell 222, 259 km/h., 532 km, 8-10 passengers/3,810 kg. external load/3,742 kg. internal load, USA
Bell 412, 259 km/h., 695 km, 14 troops/2268 kg. external load/1814 kg. internal load, USA; a four blade derivative of the Bell 212
HH-34F (S-58), 158 km/h., 450 km, 16 troops, USA
IAR-330 Puma, Rumania; licensed production of French SA-330 Puma (see below)
Kaman HH-43F Huskie (also Kaman model 600-3/5/43B), 193 km/h., 445 km, 10 passengers/1760 kg., USA; employed as maritime rescue or VIP helicopter
Kamov Ka-25 Hormone, 209 km/h., 650 km, in ASW role--search radar and dipping sonar, 12 passengers in search and rescue role, USSR; see Helicopters, ASW
Mi-2 Hoplite (also PZL Swidnik), 210 km/h., 580 km, 8 troops/2372 kg., Poland (designed in USSR)
Mi-4 Hound, 210 km/h., 400 km, 14 troops/1740 kg., USSR
Mi-8 Hip, 250 km/h., 425 km, 24 troops/ 4000 kg. internal/ 3000 kg. external load, USSR
S-76, 269 km/h., 1112 km, 12 troops/1814 kg. external payload, USA
SA-330 Puma, 263 km/h., 550 km, 16 equipped troops/3,200 kg., France
UH-60A Black Hawk (also designated S-70), 268 km/h., 600 km, 14 troops/3630 kg. external load, USA
Westland Lynx--see Helicopters, Attack
Westland Whirlwind Series 3, 159 km/h., 480 km (ferry range--834 km), 10 troops/ca. 1000 kg., Britain

Radars

(designation, effective range, country of origin)
AN/FPS-110, USA
AN/FPS-117, 350 km, USA
AN/TPS-32, 556 km, USA
AN/TPS-43, 408 km, USA
AN/TPS-59, 370 km, USA
AN/TPS-63, 296 km, USA
AN/TPS-70, 350 km, USA
AR-3 D, 24 km, Britain
AR-15, Britain
ELTA-2220/2206 148 km, Israel
Long Track, USSR
S-713 Martello 3-D, 500 km, Britain
Spoon Rest (P-12) 275 km, USSR
Square Pair, USSR

S-600, Britain
Tiger S (TRS-2100), 110 km, France
Watchman, Britain

RPVs and Mini-RPVs

(designation, type, country of origin)
DRC-30, USSR
Mastiff, mini-RPV, Israel
Pioneer, mini-RPV, Israel
R4E-50, Skyeye, mini-RPV, USA
Scout, mini-RPV, Israel
SD-3 RPV, USSR
Teledyne Ryan model 124 Firebee, mini-RPV, USA
Teledyne Ryan model 324 Scarab, RPV, USA

Target Drones

(designation, type, country of origin)
Aerospatiale CT-20, target drone, France
Beech AQM-37A, target drone, USA
Beech MQM-107B, target drone, USA
MQM-74C Chukar II (also Northrop MQM-74C), target drone, USA
TTL BTT-3 Banshee, target drone, Britain

SAMs, Long Range

(designation, NATO codename if relevant, SP if relevant, range, country of origin)
HAWK, 35 km, USA
HQ-2J (CSA-1), PRC; copy of SA-2
MIM-23B Improved HAWK, 40 km, USA
SA-2 Guideline, 40-50 km, USSR
SA-3 Goa, 25-30 km, USSR
SA-5 Gammon, 250 km, USSR
SA-7, SA-9, Crotale, Crotale/Shahine, Rapier, Redeye, Stinger--see Army AA Defense--Missiles

NAVY

Advanced AA & Anti-Missile Guns

(caliber, designation, guidance and task, country of origin)

30mm Vulcan-goalkeeper, radar-controlled AAG and anti-missile gun, Netherlands (system and radar) and USA (gun)

20mm Vulcan-Phalanx, radar-controlled AAG and anti-missile gun, USA

Air-to-Surf./anti-Ship Missiles

(designation, guidance system, range, launching aircraft, country of origin)

AM-39 Exocet, inertial + active homing, 70 km, Super Etendard and Mirage F-1 EQ5 fighters, SA-330, SA-321 helicopters, France; a derivative of MM-38 Exocet SSM

AS-15TT, radar, 14.8 km, AS-365 helicopter, France

Gabriel 3 AGM, active, 52.9 km, F-4E, Kfir, A-4, Seascan, Israel; a derivative of Gabriel 3 SSM

See also Air Force AGMs; the following can be employed against naval targets: AGM-62A Walleye; AGM-65A/B/C Maverick; AS-11; AS-12; AS-1 (Kennel); AS-5 (Kelt)

Armament, Advanced

(excluding missiles) (designation, type of weapon, guidance system, country of origin)

Mk.37, anti-submarine torpedo, acoustic homing, USA

NT-37E, anti-submarine torpedo, acoustic homing, USA, improvement of Mk.37

Stingray, anti-submarine torpedo, acoustic homing, Britain

ASW Vessels

(designation, standard displacement, full load displacement, speed, AS weapons, guns, missiles, country of origin)

Chinese ASW vessel, PRC

Koni class ASW frigate, 1700 ton, 2000 ton, 32 knots, 2x12 barrelled RBU 6000, 4x3", 4x30mm, SA-N4 SAM (in Algeria)/SS-N-2C SSM (in Libya), USSR

Le Fougeux class, 325 ton, 400 ton, 18.5 knots, 2x anti-submarine mortar, 1x76mm, 2x40mm, France

Petya II class, 950 ton, 1160 ton, 32 knots, 4x16 barrelled RBU, 2 depth charge racks, 4x3", USSR

Shanghai III, 120 ton, 155 ton, 30 knots, 8 depth charges and variable depth sonar, 2x5mm, 1x25mm, PRC; similar to Shanghai II, see Gunboats/MTBs

Sirius class--see patrol craft

SO-1 class, 170 ton, 215 ton, 28 knots, 4x5 barrelled RBU, 4x25mm, USSR

Auxiliary Vessels

(designation, function, displacement, speed, country of origin)

Amphion class, repair ship, 14,490 ton full load, 16.5 knots, USA

Armed fishing vessel, coast guard & fishery protection, Algeria

Brooke Marine, 900 ton, royal yacht, 900 ton, 12 knots, Britain

Cargo vessel (765 DWT), Pakistan

Cargo ship, 1500 GRT, 11 knots, Norway

Cheverton type tender, 3.3 ton, 8 knots, Britain

Conoship Groningen coastal freighter, 1380 DWT, 11 knots, Netherlands

Durance class, tanker/supply ship, 10,500 ton full load, 19 knots, France

Harbor craft, 746 ton, 14 knots (former royal Iraqi yacht)

Harbor tanker, 1700 ton full load, Italy

Jansen research vessel (named Ekteshaf), 1,250 ton, FRG

LSD-1 type, logistic support ship, 2470 ton full load, 15 knots, Britain

Luhring Yard, supply ship, 3250 DWT, 16 knots, FRG

Maintenance and repair craft, ex-British LCT, 900 ton full load, 9 knots, Britain

Mala midget submarine (2-man vessel, 7.6 meter), Yugoslavia

Mazagon Docks, water tanker, 9430 ton, 15 knots, India

Niryat diving tender--see Patrol Craft

Okhtensky tugs, USSR (assembled in Egypt)

P-6, employed as training vessel--see Gunboats/MTBs

PN-17 support tanker, 650 ton full load, Yugoslavia

Poluchat I class, employed as torpedo recovery vessel--see Patrol Craft

Ro-ro transport ship, 3100 ton full load, Italy

Royal Yacht, 1450 DWT, 22.5 knots, Denmark; carries a helicopter

Royal yacht, 650 ton, 26 knots, Netherlands

Spasilac, salvage ship, 1300 ton, 15 knots, Yugoslavia

Sekstan survey ship (also training ship), 345 ton full load, 10 knots, USSR

Stromboli class, support ship, 8706 ton full load, 20 knots, Italy

Survey craft, 23.6 ton, 13.5 knots, Britain

Survey ship, 240 ton, Yugoslavia

Swan Hunter replenishment ship, 33,014 ton full load, 21.5 knots, Britain

Swimmer delivery vehicles

Training craft, 109 ton full load, 22 knots, FRG

Training frigate, 1850 ton full load, 27 knots, can carry SSM, 1x57mm gun, 2x20mm gun, Yugoslavia
Training ship, 350 ton, FRG
Training ship (former royal yacht), 4650 ton, 16 knots, Britain
Water carrier boat, 125 DWT, Yugoslavia
Water tanker, 9430 ton, 15 knots, India--see Mazagon Docks water tanker
Yelva class, diving support ship, 295 ton, 12.5 knots, USSR
YW-83 water tanker, 1250 ton, 10 knots, similar to Italian harbor tanker, USA
"108" class, target craft, 60 ton full load, 26 knots, Yugoslavia

Gunboats/MTBs

(designation, gunboat or MTB, length, speed, torpedo tubes if relevant, guns, country of origin)
Brooke Marine gunboat, 123 ft., 25 knots, 1x76mm, 1x20mm (=Brooke Marine 123 ft. MFPB), Britain
Fredrikshavn Vaerft gunboat, 45.8 meter, 20 Knots, 1x40mm, Denmark
Hainan class gunboat, 59 meter, 30.5 knots, 2x2x57mm, 2x2x25mm, 4xRBU 1200 ASW and depth charges, PRC
Jaguar class MTB, 139.4 ft., 42 knots, 4x21" torpedo tubes, 2x40mm, FRG
Kebir, see Brooke Marine 123 ft; same vessel, licensed production in Algeria, 2x23mm gun instead of 1x20mm
Lurssen FPB/gunboat, 38 meter, 126.3 ft., 32 knots, 1x76mm, 1x40mm, 3x7.62mm MG, FRG
P-4 class MTB, 62.3 ft., 55 knots, 2x21" torpedo tubes, 2x14.5mm, 8x122mm MRL, USSR
P-6 class MTB, 84.2 ft., 43 knots, 2x21" torpedo tubes, 4x25mm, USSR
PR-72 class gunboat, 57.5 meter, 28 knots, 1x76mm, 1x40mm, France
Shanghai II class gunboat, 128 ft., 30 knots, 4x37mm, 4x25mm, PRC
Shershen class MTB/gunboat, 118.1 ft., 40 knots, 4x21" torpedo tubes, 4x30mm, USSR

Gun Corvettes

(designation, standard displacement, full load displacement, speed, guns, country of origin)
C-58, 560 ton, 36 knots, 1x76mm, 2x40mm, Algeria; with assistance from Bulgaria
PF-103 class, 900 ton, 1135 ton, 20 knots, 2x3", 2x40mm, 2x23mm, USA
Vosper Thornycroft Mk.1B (Tobruk), 440 ton, 500 ton, 18 knots, 1x4", 2x40mm, Britain

Gun Frigates

(designation, standard displacement, full load displacement, speed, guns, country of origin)

Savage class, 1200 ton, 1490 ton, 19 knots, 2x3", 2x20mm, USA

Hovercraft

(designation, gross weight, disposable weight, speed, guns, country of origin)

BH-7 (Wellington) class, 50 ton, 14 ton, 60 knots, 2 Browning MG or 4xRGM-84A Harpoon SSM, Britain

Sealand Mk.2/Mk.3 class, 3 ton,

1 ton, 42 knots, Britain

Skima 12 class, Britain

SRN-6 (Winchester) class, 10 ton, 3.6 ton, 52 knots, 1x7.62mm MG, Britain

Tropmire Ltd., 6.4 ton, 4.2 ton, 45 knots, Britain

Landing Craft, Logistics (LCL)

(designation, full load displacement, speed, country of origin)

Siong Huat 40 meter, Singapore

Vosper 320 ton, 9.5 knots, Singapore

Landing Craft, Mechanized (LCM)

(designation, full load displacement, speed, country of origin)

150 ton Fairy Marine, 150 ton, 8 knots, Britain

Loadmaster, 350 ton (max. load 150 ton), 10.5 knots, Britain (also designated as LCT)

LCM-6, 62 ton, 9 knots, USA

T-4, 94 ton, 9 knots (unconfirmed--10 knots), USSR

US type LCM, 60 ton, 11 knots, USA

26 ton LCM, FRG

Landing Craft, Tank (LCT)

(designation, full load displacement, speed, guns, country of origin)

Ash class, 730 ton, 10.5 knots, 2x20mm, Israel

C-107 class, 600 ton, 8.5 knots, 2x20mm, Turkey

DTM-221 class, 410 ton, 9 knots, 1x20mm, 2x12.7mm HMG, Yugoslavia

EDIC class, 670 ton, 8 knots, 2x20mm, 1x120mm mortar, France

Loadmaster, 150 ton, 10.5 knots, Britain

Polnochny class, 1150 ton, 18 knots, 4x30mm, 2x140mm rocket launchers, USSR

750 ton LCT, 750 ton, 9 knots, Netherlands

48.8 meter LCT, no details

Landing Craft, Utility (LCU)

(designation, full load displacement, speed, guns, country of origin)
250 ton LCU, Iran
Cheverton 45 ton, 7 knots, Britain
Cheverton 30 ton, 6 knots, Britain
Impala Marine 75 ton, 9 knots, Britain
Lewis Offshore, 85 ton, 8 knots, Britain
Ondatra class, 93 ton, 10 knots, USSR
SMB-1 class, 360 ton, 10 knots, USSR
Swiftships, 390 ton, USA
US LCU 1431 class (similar to LCU 510 class), 320 ton, 10 knots, 2x20mm, USA
US LCU 1466 class, 360 ton, 10 knots, 2x20mm, USA
US LCU 1610 class, 375 ton, 11 knots, 2x12.7mm HMG, USA
Vosper Thornycroft 170 ton, 10 knots, Britain
Vydra class, 600 ton, 11 knots, USSR

Landing Ship, Logistics (LSL)

(designation, full load displacement, speed, guns, country of origin)
Batral class, 1409 ton, 16 knots, 2x40mm, 2x81mm mortars, France
Brooke Marine, 2000 ton class, 12 knots, 1x76mm, 2x20mm, Britain; can be employed as LST;
Brooke Marine, 2200 ton, 15.5 knots, 2x2x40mm, Britain (also an LST)
Hengam class, 2540 ton, 14.5 knots, 4x40mm, Britain; can be employed as LST

Landing Ship, Mechanized (LSM)

(designation, full load displacement, speed, guns, country of origin)
LSM-1, 1095 ton, 12.5 knots, 2x40mm, 4x20mm, USA

Landing Ship, Tank (LST)

(designation, full load displacement, speed, guns, country of origin)
3500 ton, 15.5 knots, Denmark
Bat Sheva class, 1150 ton, 10 knots, 2x20mm, Netherlands
LST (South Korean), South Korea
PS-700 class, 2800 ton, 15.4 knots, 6x40mm, 1x81mm mortar, France
Ropucha class, 4400 ton, 17 knots, 4x57mm, USSR

MFPBs

(designation, standard displacement, full load displacement, speed, missiles, guns, country of origin)

"400" Type, Yugoslavia

Aliya--see Sa'ar 4.5, below

Combattante II, 234 ton, 255 ton, 34.5 knots, 4xRGM-84A Harpoon or 4xOTOMAT 2, 1x76mm or 1x40mm, France

Combattante III, 395 ton, 425 ton, 38.5 knots, 8xMM-40 Exocet, 1x76mm, 2x40mm, 2x30mm, France

Dvora, 47 ton, 36 knots, 2xGabriel 2/3 SSM, 2x20mm, Israel; see also Patrol Craft

Hegu, 68 ton, 81 ton, 40 knots, 2 Hai Ying SSM (Chinese SS-N2 Styx), 2x25mm, PRC; copy of Soviet Komar

Komar, 68 ton, 81 ton, 40 knots, 2xSS-N-2 (Styx), 2x25mm, USSR

Lazaga (formerly Cormoran/Lazaga), 355 ton (full load), 36 knots, 4xExocet, 1x76mm, 1x40mm, Spain (licensed production of FRG's Lurssen Type-143); boats for Sudan to be armed with RGM-84 Harpoon SSM

Lurssen FPB-57, 353 ton, 398 ton, 38 knots, 4xMM-40 Exocet, 1x76mm, 2x40mm, FRG

Lurssen TNC-45, 228 ton (half load), 38 knots, 4xExocet, or 4xOTOMAT 2, 1x76mm, 1x40mm, FRG

October, 71 ton, 82 ton, 40 knots, 2xOTOMAT, 2x30mm, Egypt (electronics installed in Britain)

Ossa I, 160 ton, 210 ton, 36 knots, 2xSS-N-2 (Styx), 2x2x30mm, USSR

Ossa II--see Ossa I, stronger engine

P-48, 250 ton full load, 22 knots, 8xSS-12, 2x40mm, France/Belgium

PGG-1 class (Peterson), 384 ton full load, 38 knots, 4xRGM-84A Harpoon, 1x76mm, 2x20mm, 2x20mm Vulcan-Phalanx, USA

Province class, 311 ton, 363 ton, 40 knots, 6xMM-40 Exocet, 1x76mm, 2x40mm, Britain

Rade Koncar, 240 ton (full load), 40 knots, 4xSSN-2 (Styx), 1x76mm, 1x40mm, 2x30mm, Yugoslavia

Ramadan, 262 ton, 312 ton, 37 knots, 4xOTOMAT 2, 1x76mm, Britain

Reshef--see Sa'ar 4

Sa'ar 2 & 3, 220 ton, 250 ton, 40 knots, Gabriel 2/3 SSM, 1x76mm or 2x40mm, France

Sa'ar 4, 415 ton, 450 ton, 32 knots, 4xRGM-84A Harpoon, 5xGabriel 2/3, 2x76mm, 2x20mm, Israel

Sa'ar 4.5, 488 ton, 31 knots, 4xGabriel, 4xRGM-84A Harpoon, 1x76mm, Israel; carries a helicopter

Susa, 95 ton, 114 ton, 54 knots, 8xSS-12 (M), 2x40mm, Britain

Mine Warfare Vessels

(designation, standard displacement, full load displacement, guns, mines if relevant, country of origin)

Adjutant class minesweeper, 320 ton, 375 ton, 1x20mm, USA

Cape class minesweeper, 180 ton, 235 ton, 1x12.7mm HMG, USA

MSC 292/MSC 268 class, 320 ton, 378 ton, 2x20mm, USA

MSC 322 class, 320 ton, 407 ton, 2x20mm, USA

Natya class minesweeper, 650 ton, 950 ton, 4x30mm, 4x25mm, 10 mines, USSR

Nestin minesweeper, 65 ton (standard), 3x20mm, Yugoslavia

Sirius class minesweeper/patrol craft, 400 ton, 440 ton, 1x40mm, 1x20mm, France

Sonya class, 450 ton (full load), 2x30mm, 2x25mm, 5 mines, USSR

SRN-6--see Hovercraft; may serve as mine-laying vessel

T-43 class minesweeper, 500 ton, 580 ton, 4x37mm, 8x14.5mm, 20 mines, USSR

T-58 minesweeper corvette, 900 ton (full load), 4x57mm, 4x25mm, USSR

T-301 class, 159 ton, 180 ton, 2x37mm, 2xMMG, USSR

Tripartite type minesweeper, 510 ton, 588 ton, 1x20mm, Netherlands, Belgium and France

Vanya class minesweeper, 200 ton, 245 ton, 2x30mm, 5 mines, USSR

Yevgenia class minesweeper, 70 ton, 80 ton, 2x14.5mm HMG, USSR

Yurka class minesweeper, 400 ton, 460 ton, 4x30mm, 10 mines, USSR

Missile-Armed Hydrofoils

(designation, displacement, speed, missiles, guns, country of origin)

Flagstaff (=Shimrit), 91.5 ton, 52 knots, 4xGabriel, RGM-84A Harpoon, 2x30mm, USA/Israel (licensed production)

Missile Corvettes

(designation, standard displacement, full load displacement, speed, missiles, guns, country of origin)

Assad class, 670 ton full load, 33 knots, 4xOTOMAT, 1x76mm, 2x35mm, Italy; formerly designated Wadi class

Lurssen 62 meter, 600 ton, 30 knots, 4xMM-40 Exocet/RGM-84A Harpoon, Aspide/Albatros SAMs (in Bahrain) or Sadral SAMs (in UAE) FRG

Nanuchka II class, 780 ton, 900 ton, 30 knots, 4xSS-N-2 SSM, 2xSA-N4, 2x57mm, USSR; in Syria--4xSS-N-9 SSM (unconfirmed)

PCG-1 class (Tacoma Boatbuilding 245 ft.), 732 ton, 815 ton, 30 knots, 8xRGM-84A Harpoon, 1x76mm, 1x20mm Vulcan-Phalanx,

2x20mm, USA
Wadi class--see Assad class

Missile Destroyers

(designation, standard displacement, full load displacement, speed, missiles, guns, country of origin)
Battle class, 2325 ton, 3360 ton, 31 knots, 4xStandard, 4x4.5", 2x40mm, Britain
Sumner class, 2200 ton, 3320 ton, 34 knots, 4x2xStandard, 4x5", USA

Missile Frigates

(designation, standard displacement, full load displacement, speed, missiles, guns, country of origin)
Descubierta, 1233 ton, 1479 ton, 26 knots, MM-38 Exocet or MM-40 Exocet, Aspide SAMs, 1x76mm, 2x40mm, Spain; in Morocco carrying MM-38/MM-40, in Egypt carrying RGM-84A Harpoon SSM
F-2000, 2610 ton full load, 30 knots, 8xOTOMAT 2, 1x100mm, 4x40mm, France; carries a helicopter
Jianghu, 1568 ton, 1900 ton, 26.5 knots, 4xHY-2 (Hai Ying 2), 2x100mm, 4x2x37mm, 2xRBU 1200 ASW rocket launcher, 2 depth charge racks, PRC; planned: RGM-84A Harpoon SSMs
Koni, see ASW Vessels
Lupo class, 2208 ton, 2500 ton, 35 knots, 8xOTOMAT 2, 1x5", 4x40mm, Italy; carries a helicopter
Vosper mk.5 class, 1220 ton, 1540 ton, 34 knots, 5xSea Killer SSM, 3x Seacat SAM, 1x4.5", 2x35mm, Britain
Vosper Thornycroft Mk.7, 1325 ton, 1625 ton, 37.5 knots, 4x OTOMAT, 1x4.5", 2x40mm, 2x35mm, Britain, refitted and modernized in Italy

Patrol Craft

(designation, length in feet, speed, guns, country of origin)
Abeking & Rasmussen, 75.2 ft., 27 knots, 3x20mm, FRG
Abeking & Rasmussen, 26.2 meters, 40 knots, FRG
Acror 46, 14.5 meters, 32 knots, 2x12.7mm HMG, France
Aztec (Crestitalia), 9 meters, Italy
Baglietto type Mangusta, 98.4 ft., 32.5 knots, 1x40mm, 1x20mm, Italy
Baglietto type 20 GC, 66.9 ft., 36 knots, 1x20mm, Italy
Baglietto GC-23, 23 meter, 38 knots, 1x20mm, 2x12.7mm HMG, Italy
Bertram class (Egypt), 28 ft., 3x12.7mm, 4x122mm MRL, USA
Bertram class Enforcer (Jordan), 38 ft., USA
Bertram 20 ft., USA
Bertram (Jordan), 30.4 ft., 1x12.7mm HMG, 1x7.62mm MG, USA
Blohm & Voss 38.9 meters, 30 knots, 2x20mm, FRG
Boghammar, 13 meter, Sweden

Broadsword class, 105 ft., 32 knots, 1x75mm recoilless rifle, 1x12.7mm, USA
Byblos class, 66 ft., 18.5 knots, 1x20mm, 2xMG, France
Camcraft 77 feet, 25 knots, 2x20mm, USA
Camcraft 65 feet, 25 knots, 1x20mm, USA
Cantieri Posillipo, 65 ft., 24 knots, 1x20mm, Italy
Cape class (US Coast Guard)--see Mine Warfare Vessels
CG-27, 87.6 ft., 25 knots, Sweden
CH class, 130.8 ft., 16 knots, 2x20mm, France
Ch. Navals de l'Esterel, 124.7 ft., 27 knots, 2x40mm, 2x12.7mm HMG, France
Ch. Navals de l'Esterel, 104 ft., 30 knots, 1x20mm, France
Ch. Navals de l'Esterel, 83 ft., 23 knots, 1x20mm, France
Cheverton, 50 ft., 23 knots, 1x7.62mm MG, Britain
Cheverton, 27 ft., 8 knots, Britain
CMN, 40.6 meter, 25 knots, 2x40mm, 2xMG, France
Crestitalia, 70 ft., 35 knots, 1x30mm, 1x20mm, Italy
Dabur, 64.9 ft., 21.8 knots, 2x20mm, 2xMG, USA/Israel (licensed production)
de Castro (Nisr class), 1x20mm, Egypt
Damen "Polycat 1450", 14.5 meter, 26 knots, 1x20mm, Netherlands
Dvora=Dvora MFPB without missiles, Israel
Fairey Marine Interceptor class, 25 ft., 35 knots, Britain
Fairey Marine Spear class, 29.8 ft., 26 knots, 3x7.62mm MG, Britain
Fairey Marine Sword class, 44.9 ft., 28 knots, 1x7.62mm MG, Britain
Fateh, 18 meter, 35 knots, Iran
Garian class, 106 ft., 24 knots, 1x40mm, 1x20mm, Britain
Hyundai, South Korea
Kedma class, 67 ft., 25 knots, 2 MG, Japan
Keith Nelson, 57 ft., 19 knots, 2x20mm, Britain
Keith Nelson, 44 ft., 26 knots, 1x12.7mm HMG, 2x7.62mm MG, Britain
Keith Nelson (Dhafeer) class, 40.3 ft., 19 knots, 2x7.62mm MG, Britain
Le Fougeux (modified)--see ASW vessels
Lurssen, 23 meter, FRG/Spain (under license)
Magnum Sedan, 27.3 ft., 60 knots, USA
Naja 12 (Naja-ASD 12), 12 meter, 50 knots, 1x20mm, 2x7.62mm MG, France
Niryat II, 95.1 ft., 12 knots, USSR
Osprey, 55 meter, 20 knots (unconfirmed), Denmark
P-6--see Gunboats/MTBs (same craft with torpedo tubes removed)
P-32, 32 meter, 29 knots, 2x20mm, France
P-200D Vigilance, 60 meter, similar to Lazaga MFPB, Spain; armed with guns only
P-801 (Vosper Thornycroft), Britain/Algeria (assembly)

P-802 (Watercraft P-802), 30 Knots, Britain

P-1200, 39 ft., 21 knots, Britain

P-1903, 19.2 meter, 30 knots, 2x12.7mm, HMG, Netherlands

P-2000, 20 meter, 40 knots (unconfirmed), 1x20mm, Britain

PBR (Yatush), 32 ft., 25 knots, 2x12.7mm HMG, USA/Israel PBR (Yugoslavia), 115 ft., 20 knots, 1x40mm, 1x20mm, 2x7.62mm MG, Yugoslavia

Peterson Mk. II, 50 ft., 28 knots, 4x12.7mm, HMG, USA

PGM-71 (Improved PGM), 100 ft., 1x40mm, 2x20mm, 2x12.7mm HMG, USA

PO-2, 82 ft., 30 knots, 2x25mm or 2x12.7mm HMG, USSR

Police boat, 20 ft.

Poluchat I, 97.1 ft., 20 knots, 2x14.5mm, USSR

Rapier class, 50 ft., 28 knots, 2xMG, USA

SAR-33, 33 meter, 40 knots, 2x40mm, 2xMMG, Turkey (FRG design)

Seagull, 24 meter (aluminum boat), 30 knots, South Korea

Sewart class, 40 ft., 30 knots, 1x12.7mm HMG, USA

Sirius class, 152 ft., 10 knots, 1x40mm, 1x20mm, France

Skorpion class, 55.8 ft., 30 knots, 2x7.62mm MG, FRG

SO-1--see ASW vessels

Super Dvora (Improved Dvora), 21.6 meter, 40 knots, 2x20mm Oerlikon, 2x7.62mm MAG LMG, Israel

Swift FPB-20, 65 ft., USA

Swiftships, 28.3 meter, USA/Egypt

Thornycroft 100 ft., 12/18 knots, 1x3.7" howitzer, 2x3" mortar, 4xMG or 1x20mm, Britain (Libyan boats--18 knots, Iraqi boats--12 knots; Iraqi boats built under license in Yugoslavia)

Thornycroft 78 ft., 22.5 knots, 1xMG, Britain

Thornycroft 50 ft., Singapore

Thornycroft 45.5 ft., 23 knots, Singapore (similar to Vosper Thornycroft 46 ft.)

Thornycroft 36 ft., 27 knots, Britain

Thornycroft 21 ft., Britain

Timsah class, 31 meter, 25 knots, 2x20mm Oerlikon, Egypt

Tracker/Tracker II, 64 ft., 29 knots, 1x20mm, Britain

USCG type 95 ft.--see above, Cape class, and Mine Warfare Vessels

VC large patrol craft, 31.5 meter, 30 knots, 2x20mm (can carry SS-12 SSMs), France

Vosper 56 ft., 29 knots, Singapore, similar to Vosper Thornycroft 56 ft.

Vosper 25 meter, 25.8 knots, 1x20mm, 2x7.62mm MG, Singapore

Vosper 36 ft., Singapore; similar to British Thornycroft 36 ft.

Vosper Thornycroft 110 ft., 27 knots, 2x20mm, Britain

Vosper Thornycroft 103 ft., 27 knots, 2x20mm, Britain

Vosper Thornycroft 78 ft.--see Thornycroft 78 ft.

Vosper Thornycroft 75 ft., 24.5 knots, 2x20mm, Britain

Vosper Thornycroft 56 ft., 30 knots, 2xMG, Britain
Vosper Thornycroft 50 ft., Britain/Singapore (identical to Thornycroft 50 ft.)
Vosper Thornycroft 36.4 ft.--see Thornycroft 36 ft.
VT HAWK (Vosper Thornycroft), 30 meter, 2x30mm, 1x20mm, Britain
Wasp 30 meter, 22 knots, 1x25mm chain gun, 2x7.62mm MG, Britain
Wasp 20 meter (65.8 ft.), 37 knots, 2xMG, Britain
Wasp 11 meter, 24 knots, Britain
Watercraft & Shoreham 45.6 ft., 22 knots, 1xMG, Britain; in UAE--speed 25 knots, 2x7.62mm MG
Whittingham & Mitchell 75 ft., 2x20mm, Britain
Zhuk class, 80.7 ft., 34 knots, 2x14.5mm, 1x12.7mm HMG, USSR

SAMs (Shipborne)

(designation, guidance system, range, country of origin)
Aspide (Albatross/Aspide), semi-active radar, 18 km, Italy
Barak--see SSMs (Shipborne)
SA-N-4, radar-guided, 9.6 km, USSR
Sadral, infra red homing, 6km, France; maritime version of short range Mistral SAM
Standard, semi-active radar homing, 18.5 km, USA
Seacat, radio-command, radar/TV or visual, 6 km, Britain; can be employed as SSM or as shipborne SAM

SSMs (Shipborne)

(designation, NATO codename if relevant, guidance system, effective range, country of origin)
Barak (employed as SAM, SSM and anti-missile missile), 10 km, Israel
C-801, SSM, PRC; copy of French MM-38 or MM-40 Exocet
Gabriel 2, semiactive, 20.4 km, Israel
Gabriel 3, active, 36 km, Israel
Hai Ying-2 (HY-2, Silkworm), PRC; copy of Soviet SS-N-2
MM-38 Exocet, inertial and active homing, 42.6 km, France
MM-40 Exocet, inertial, 70.4 km, France
OTOMAT Mk.1/OTOMAT Mk.2, active homing radar, 183.3 km, joint French-Italian manufacture
RGM-84A Harpoon, active radar guidance, 111.2 km, USA
Seacat--see SAMs (Shipborne)
Seakiller, radio command, 25 km, Italy
SS-12, ATGM, France; employed on naval craft as anti-ship missile; see Army, ATGMs and Air Force, AGMs
SS-N-2/SS-N-2B (Improved Styx), autopilot, active radar homing, 40 km, USSR

SSMs (coastal defense)

(designation, guidance system, range, country of origin)
SSC-1B Sepal, radio command and active radar guidance, 250

km, USSR
SSC-2B Samlet, radar homing, 80 km, USSR
SSC-3, inertial and terminal homing, 80-90 km, USSR; coastal defense version of SSN-2 improved Styx shipborne SSM
Hai Ying-2 (HY-2, Silkworm), PRC; identical to Hai Ying-2 SSM shipborne
C-801, 70km (unconfirmed), PRC

Submarines

(designation/NATO codename if relevant, surfaced displacement, dived displacement, main armament, country of origin)
F class Foxtrot, 1950 ton, 2400 ton, 10x21" torpedo tubes, USSR
IKL type 209, 1260 ton, 1440 ton, 8x21", FRG
IKL/Vickers type 206, 420 ton, 600 ton, 8x21" torpedo tubes, Britain, FRG design
K class Kilo, 2500 ton, 3200 ton, 8x21" torpedo tubes, USSR
R class Romeo, 1400 ton, 1800 ton, 8x21" torpedo tubes, USSR
W class Whiskey, 1080 ton, 1350 ton, 6x21" torpedo tubes, USSR

CHRONOLOGY

Chronology of Key Strategic Events 1989-90

(January 1989 - June 1990)

January 4, 1989. US and Libya produce conflicting versions regarding large chemical plant at Rabta. The Libyans claim the plant is a pharmaceutical complex, while the US and others claim it produces agents for chemical warfare. A West German company is revealed to be aiding construction of the Libyan plant. As tension mounts between the parties, two US Navy F-14 fighter aircraft shoot down two Libyan MiG-23 fighters over the Mediterranean Sea.

January 7-11, 1989. An international conference in Paris, with 149 countries participating, deals with the use of chemical warfare and production of chemical agents. A unanimous resolution deplores the use of CW.

February 1989. Egypt, Iran, Jordan and Yemen (YAR) agree to form an economic and political entity, the Arab Cooperation Council (ACC). (It effectively ceased functioning in mid-1990.)

February 1989. The Maghreb countries — Algeria, Morocco, Tunisia, Mauritania and Libya — form the Arab Maghreb Union. This follows a June 10, 1988 resolution to unite.

February 8, 1989. The annual report on violations of human rights issued by the US Department of State expresses criticism of Israel's conduct in the Territories.

February 17-27, 1989. Soviet Foreign Minister Eduard Shevardnadze visits the Middle East, including stops in Syria, Jordan, Egypt, Iraq and Iran. In Iran, Shevardnadze confers with Ayatollah Khomeini. Shevardnadze confers with Israel's new Foreign Minister Moshe Arens in Cairo, as well as with Yasir Arafat, Chairman of the PLO.

February 28, 1989. Israeli fighter aircraft attack PFLP-GC and DFLP command posts and positions near Beirut, Lebanon, apparently in retaliation for two DFLP attempts to penetrate and attack Israel in recent weeks. 2-3 DFLP men killed, others wounded; 23 schoolchildren allegedly injured by a bomb that mistakenly hit their school.

March 1989. US government temporarily suspends $230 million in aid to Egypt, and demands that Egypt comply with IMF strictures.

March 1989. General Michel Aoun, prime minister of the Christian government in Lebanon, imposes a naval blockade on ports serving the Muslim militias, and orders Syrian troops to withdraw from Lebanon. Aoun's order is disregarded. Syrian and Christian-Lebanese armies shell each other and civilian targets. Syria imposes an effective maritime and air counterblockade on the Christian-controlled part of Lebanon.

March 15, 1989. Tabah, a disputed border area near Eilat, is returned by Israel to Egypt. This follows agreements signed by the two countries on November 26, 1988 and on February 26, 1989 (following border demarcation).

April 1989. Economic crisis and disturbances in Jordan. Eight persons killed by security forces. King Hussein cuts short a visit to the US; Prime Minister Zaid al-Rifa'i replaced by Sharif Zaid ben Shaker on April 27.

April 1989. The USSR revealed to be selling Libya 15 Su-24 advanced fighter aircraft, of which 6 already delivered.

April 7-11, 1989. Prime Minister Yitzhak Shamir of Israel visits the US, confers with President George Bush, and proposes a new four point plan, providing for elections in the Territories, to be followed by autonomy negotiations with the Palestinians elected. The PLO and Palestinian leaders in the Territories reject Shamir's proposal.

April 15, 1989. President Muhammad Husni Mubarak of Egypt relieves Field Marshal Muhammad Abd al-Halim Abu Ghazala of his posts as deputy prime minister and defense minister, and appoints General Youssuf Sabri Abu Talib to fill the positions.

May 1989. PLO leader Yasir Arafat on an official visit to France. Meets President Mitterand, and in a press conference says the Palestinian National Covenant (calling for the destruction of

Israel) is now "caduque," i.e., obsolete, no longer relevant.

May 3, 1989. Compromise reached in Lebanese crisis between the Aoun Christian government and Syrian Muslim coalition. Aoun ceases the naval blockade on anchorages and harbors serving the Muslim militias. Syria ceases shelling Christian controlled parts of Lebanon. A Kuwaiti general is appointed Arab League mediator between the parties.

May 5, 1989. General Adnan Khairalla, Iraq's minister of defense and deputy commander-in-chief of the armed forces, killed in a helicopter crash during a visit to Kurdish areas.

May 15, 1989. The government of Israel approves the Israeli peace initiative, including free elections in the Territories.

May 23-26, 1989. Arab summit conference convened in Morocco, with all Arab states participating, including Egypt, Libya and Syria. Most heads of state present. Egypt readmitted to membership in the League of Arab States.

May 28, 1989. IDF clashes with joint PFLP, PLF (Tal'at Ya'qub faction) and Hizballah team trying to infiltrate Israel from Lebanon after firing Katyusha rockets at Israeli village of Metula.

June 1989. Hashemi Rafsanjani, speaker of the Iranian Parliament and sole candidate for the August 1989 presidential elections, visits the USSR and confers with Soviet leaders. An agreement is signed on economic cooperation between Iran and the USSR, estimated to encompass $6 billion.

June 3, 1989. Ayatollah Ruhallah Khomeini, Iran's national and religious leader, dies. President Hojatoleslam Ali Khamenei succeeds Khomeini as national leader.

June 30, 1989. Coup d'etat in Sudan: the army overthrows the government. President al-Mirghani out of the country; Prime Minister Sadiq al-Mahdi arrested. New junta led by a Revolutionary Command Committee headed by Brigadier General Omar Hassan al-Bashir.

July 4, 1989. Likud Party Central Committee in Israel convenes. Unanimous approval of Prime Minister Shamir's peace plan, but with four constraining principles of "non acceptance" added. These reject: PLO as negotiating partner; independent Palestinian state; the right of Arabs residing in East Jerusalem to vote or be elected; and any suspension of Jewish settlement activity.

July 6, 1989. Israeli bus on the Tel Aviv-Jerusalem road driven into a ravine, after an Arab suicide terrorist overcomes the driver and takes control of the steering wheel. Sixteen passengers killed and 25 injured.

July 23, 1989. Israeli Cabinet votes to support the government's plan for elections in the Territories. No reference is made to Likud Party's four "constraints."

July 28-29, 1989. Israeli commandos kidnap Shi'ite Sheikh Obeid, Hizballah leader, from his village in Southern Lebanon. On July 31 Hizballah claims to have hanged US Marine Corps Lt. Colonel William Higgins as act of reprisal. US criticizes Israel for action undertaken without considering American interests. Later reports place Higgins' death at a much earlier date.

July 29, 1989. Ali Hashemi Rafsanjani elected president of Iran, replacing Ayatollah Ali Khamenei.

July 31, 1989. Arab Summit in Casablanca forms Arab Tripartite Committee to recommend solution for Lebanon crisis.

August 4, 1989. Saudi Arabia deposits $1 billion in Jordan's central bank to bolster the faltering Jordanian dinar.

August 9, 1989. A Shi'ite suicide carbomb near Marj Ayoun, in Israel's Southern Lebanon security zone, injures five Israeli soldiers and one SLA soldier.

August 15, 1989. UN Security Council appeal to all parties to the conflict in Lebanon to cease fire.

August 17, 1989. Explosion in a military industrial plant in Iraq causes fatalities. Iraq claims 19 persons dead, while most reports mention around 700, including Egyptian laborers and/or experts.

August 13-18, 1989. Heavy fighting at Souq al-Gharb, Lebanon, between Aoun forces and pro-Syrian militias. As many as 60 dead, including Syrian troops.

August 19, 1989. Israel protests, through US good offices, to Jordan, concerning Iraqi reconnaissance flights along Jordanian-Israeli border beginning in July.

September 9, 1989. President Shadli Bendjedid of Algeria dismisses Prime Minister Kasdi Merbah. Mouloud Harmouche appointed new prime minister.

September 15, 1989. President Husni Mubarak of Egypt presents a ten-point peace plan, hoping to satisfy both the PLO and Israel.

September 19, 1989. An 8,000 dunam (2,000 acre) forest preserve near Haifa is torched, apparently by *intifada* activists.

September 28, 1989. US decides to sell Saudi Arabia 300 modern M-1 A2 tanks, and to compensate Israel by prepositioning ammunition worth $100 million there.

October 1989. IDF ends months-long tax revolt in Beit Sahur — the most significant non-violent manifestation of the *intifada* to date.

October 6, 1989. Israeli Cabinet discusses Egyptian initiative to meet in Cairo and confer with Palestinian representatives. Labor Party favors the initiative, but the government rejects it.

October 10, 1989. US Secretary of State James Baker comes forward with a plan to promote an Israeli-Palestinian meeting in Cairo. Israeli Cabinet accepts the plan on November 5, but asks for several assurances, including that Israel will not be forced to negotiate with the PLO.

October 11, 1989. A Syrian pilot flying a MiG-23 ML defects and lands in Israel.

November 1989. Resolution by Arab Tripartite Committee to

resolve the Lebanese crisis is accepted by vote of Lebanese Parliament meeting in Ta'if, Saudi Arabia. Ta'if Accord recommends new elections, with new allocation of parliamentary seats to increase Muslim representation. General Michel Aoun rejects the resolution.

November 5, 1989. Rene Muawad elected president by Lebanese Parliament at a session at Klei'at Air Force Base, under Syrian control.

November 8, 1989. First free elections in Jordan after 22 years produce significant achievement for fundamentalist Muslim candidates. Mudar Badran appointed prime minister on December 6.

November 22, 1989. Rene Muawad, president-elect of Lebanon, assassinated by a carbomb in West Beirut.

November 24, 1989. Elias Harawi elected president by Lebanese Parliament at a session at Klei'at Air Force Base, under Syrian control.

December 5, 1989. Five armed Palestinian infiltrators from Egypt killed in a clash with Israel forces.

December 7, 1989. Iraq announces that on December 5 it launched a 48-ton, three stage missile intended in future to carry an Iraqi satellite, and to be employed as an IRBM with a range of 2000 kilometers. Satellite launching rocket designated al-Abd, its IRBM derivative Tammuz-1.

December 27, 1989. Full diplomatic relations renewed between Egypt and Syria.

January 1, 1990. Nearly 25,000 new immigrants came to Israel during 1989. Over 100,000 Soviet immigrants expected in 1990.

January 6-7, 1990. Tension along the Israeli-Jordanian border. After three incidents of firing at Israelis in the Hamat-Gader area, a Jordanian soldier who infiltrated Israel is killed by Israeli forces.

January 22, 1990. Israel Embassy reopened in Ethiopia, following the renewal of diplomatic relations severed 16 years earlier.

February 4, 1990. Palestinian terrorists attack a bus with Israeli tourists near Ismailiya, Egypt. Ten Israelis killed, 20 wounded. The terrorists escape. Egyptian President Mubarak expresses condolences to the families of the victims.

February 17, 1990. Jordan and Iraq announce the formation of a joint Jordanian-Iraqi squadron of fighter aircraft, to be stationed in Iraq, near the Jordanian border.

March 10-15, 1990. Farzad Bazoft, an Iranian-born British citizen working as a journalist for the British paper *The Observer,* is tried for espionage for Israel, condemned to death, and executed in Baghdad despite worldwide protest.

March 14, 1990. Fire at Libyan chemical plant at Rabtah that allegedly produces chemical weapons. Later, CIA and other sources claim the fire was a Libyan hoax.

March 15, 1990. Prime Minister Yitzhak Shamir dismisses Vice Premier Shimon Peres. Labor Party leaves the government, which resigns after a vote of no-confidence. Israel now led by a transition government.

March 20, 1990. Shimon Peres nominated by Israel's President Herzog to form a new government. When ultimately he fails, Yitzhak Shamir is nominated by the president on April 25 to form a government.

March 28, 1990. Forty capacitors seized by Scotland Yard at London Heathrow, in the course of being smuggled from the USA via London to Iraq.

April 2, 1990. President Saddam Hussein of Iraq threatens to incinerate half of Israel with chemical weapons if Israel attacks targets within Iraq. Saddam Hussein claims Iraq has binary chemical weapons.

April 3, 1990. Israel launches Ofek 2 satellite into orbit.

May 1990. President Mubarak of Egypt visits President Saddam Hussein of Iraq, delivers a message from Israel that Israel has no intention of attacking Iraq.

May 1, 1990. Israel claims 30,000 Soviet Jews arrived during the first four months of 1990.

May 2, 1990. Egyptian President Mubarak visits Damascus and confers with Syrian President Hafiz al-Assad.

May 20, 1990. An Israeli civilian murders seven Palestinians and wounds more than ten by gunfire at Rishon Le-Zion. In ensuing unrest in the Territories, seven Palestinians killed and many Palestinians wounded, with 12 Israelis wounded.

May 22, 1990. Yemen (YAR) and South Yemen (PDRY) proclaim their union.

May 28-30, 1990. Arab Summit Conference at Baghdad, presidents of Syria, Lebanon, and Algeria do not participate.

May 30, 1990. A squad from the Palestine Liberation Front (PLF Abu al-Abbas faction) launches a naval raid against Israel, with assistance from Libya. One terrorist speedboat lands 400 meters from a crowded bathing beach. Four boats are destroyed or captured by IDF, four Palestinians killed, 12 captured.

June 11, 1990. Yitzhak Shamir presents new Likud-led government to the Knesset. Shamir is prime minister; Moshe Arens, minister of defense; David Levi, foreign minister; Ariel Sharon, in charge of housing and coordinating immigration absorption. Government supported by 62 out of 120 members of Knesset.

June 18, 1990. President Saddam Hussein of Iraq threatens to attack Israel if Israel attacks Iraq or any other Arab country, from Mauritania to Syria.

June 20, 1990. US President George Bush suspends dialogue with PLO until the PLO deplores the May 30 PLF terrorist attack against Israel and takes disciplinary measures against Abu al-Abbas.

ABBREVIATIONS

AA	anti-aircraft
AAG	anti-aircraft gun
AAM	air-to-air missile
AEW	airborne early warning
AFV	armored fighting vehicle
AGM	air-to-ground missile
AP	anti-personnel
APC	armored personnel carrier
AR	assault rifle
ARV	armored reconnaissance vehicle
ASW	anti-submarine warfare
AT	anti-tank
ATGM	anti-tank guided missile
ATRL	anti-tank rocket launcher
AWACS	airborne warning and control system
batt.	battalion
bil.	billion
bty.	battery
CBU	cluster bomb unit
CLGP	Cannon-launched guided projectile
CW	chemical warfare
div.	division
DWT	dead weight tons
ECM	electronic countermeasures
ECCM	electronic counter-countermeasures
EW	electronic warfare
FLIR	forward-looking infrared
ft.	feet
GCC	Gulf Cooperation Council
GDP	gross domestic product
GHQ	general headquarters
GPMG	general purpose machine gun
GRT	gross registered tons
h.	hour
HMG	heavy machine gun
HQ	headquarters
IAF	Israel Air Force
IAI	Israel Aircraft Industries
IDF	Israel Defense Forces
kg.	kilogram
km	kilometer
laser	light amplification by stimulated emission of radiation
LCM	landing craft, mechanized
LCT	landing craft, tank

LCU	landing craft, utility
LMG	light machine gun
LSM	landing ship, mechanized
LST	landing ship, tank
LT	light tank
m.	meters
MBT	main battle tank
MFPB	missile fast-patrol boat
MG	machine gun
mil.	million
MLRS	multiple launch rocket system
mm	millimeter
MMG	medium machine gun
MRL	multiple-rocket launcher
MTB	motor torpedo boat
Naval SSM	sea-to-sea missile
NCO	non-commissioned officer
PGM	precision-guided munition
PLA	Palestine Liberation Army
PLO	Palestine Liberation Organization
port.	portable
reg.	regular
res.	reserve
RPV	remotely piloted vehicle
SAR	semi-automatic rifle
SAM	surface-to-air missile
SDV	swimmer delivery vehicle
SLAR	sideways-looking airborne radar
SMG	submachine gun
SP	self-propelled
sq.	square
SSM	surface-to-surface missile
STOL	short take-off/landing
TOE	table of organization and equipment

MAPS

Map no. 1

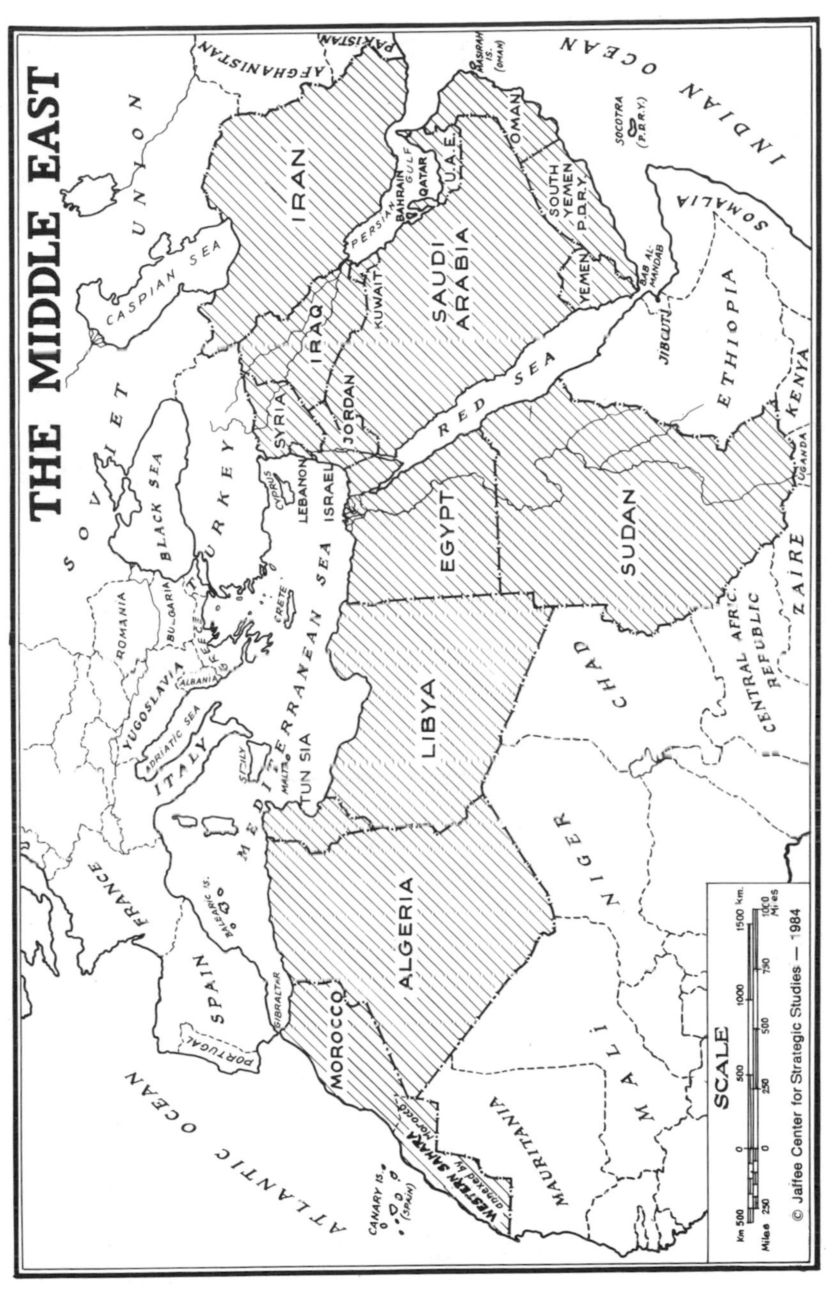
THE MIDDLE EAST
SOVIET UNION
CASPIAN SEA
AFGHANISTAN
PAKISTAN
IRAN
PERSIAN GULF
BAHRAIN
QATAR
U.A.E.
OMAN
MASIRAH IS. (OMAN)
INDIAN OCEAN
SOCOTRA (P.D.R.Y.)
SOUTH YEMEN P.D.R.Y.
YEMEN
SAUDI ARABIA
KUWAIT
IRAQ
SYRIA
JORDAN
LEBANON
ISRAEL
CYPRUS
TURKEY
BLACK SEA
ROMANIA
BULGARIA
GREECE
ALBANIA
YUGOSLAVIA
ADRIATIC SEA
ITALY
SICILY
MALTA
TUNISIA
CRETE
MEDITERRANEAN SEA
RED SEA
BAB AL-MANDAB
JIBOUTI
ETHIOPIA
SOMALIA
KENYA
UGANDA
SUDAN
EGYPT
LIBYA
CHAD
ZAIRE
CENTRAL AFRICAN REPUBLIC
NIGER
ALGERIA
MOROCCO
MALI
MAURITANIA
WESTERN SAHARA annexed by Morocco
CANARY IS. (SPAIN)
ATLANTIC OCEAN
SPAIN
PORTUGAL
GIBRALTAR
FRANCE
BALEARIC IS.
SCALE
Km 500 0 500 1000 1500 km.
Miles 250 0 250 500 750 1000 Miles
© Jaffee Center for Strategic Studies — 1984

Map no. 2

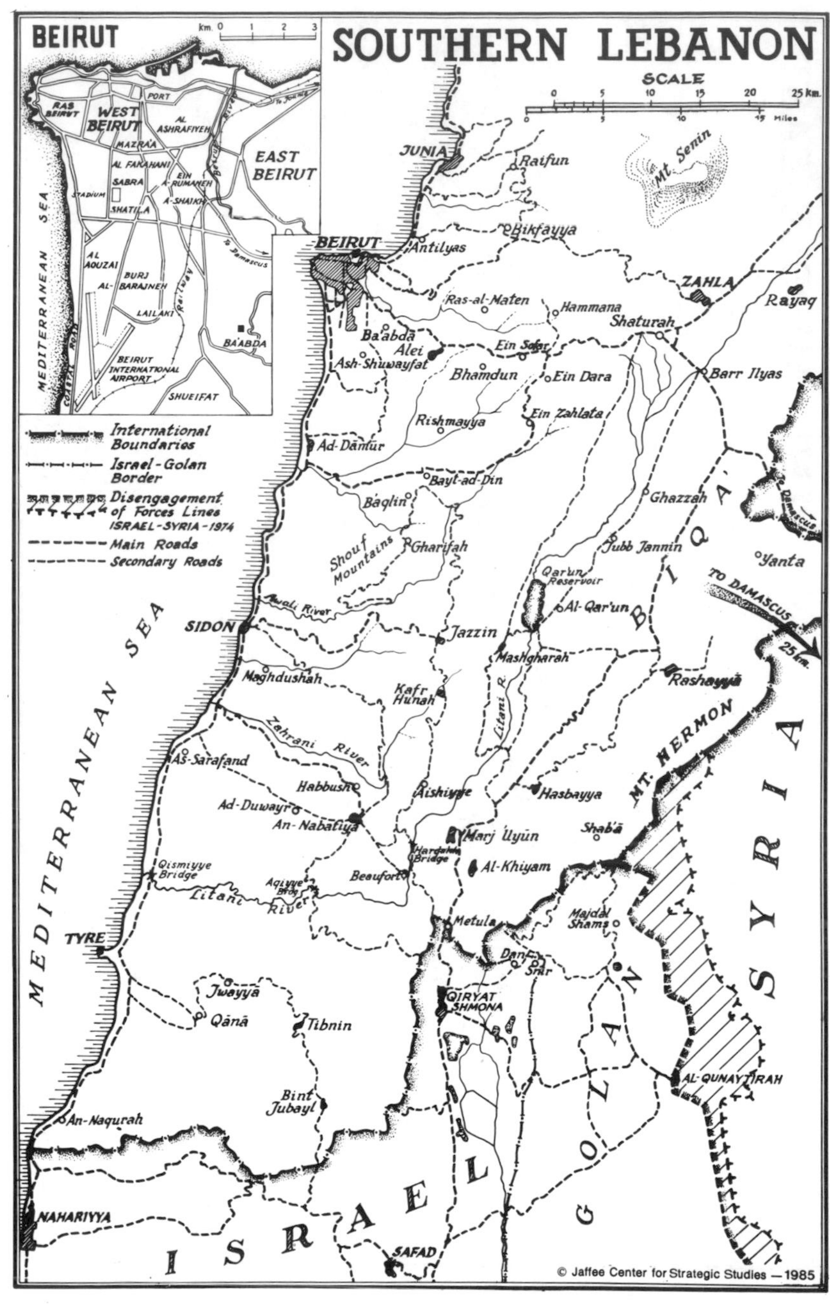

SOUTHERN LEBANON
SCALE
0 5 10 15 20 25 km.
Miles
BEIRUT
km. 0 1 2 3
PORT
RAS BEIRUT
WEST BEIRUT
AL ASHRAFIYEH
MAZRA'A
AL FAKAHANI
SABRA
EIN A-RUMANEH
A-SHAIKH
SHATILA
EAST BEIRUT
To Damascus
STADIUM
AL AOUZAI
BURJ AL-BARAJNEH
LAILAKI
BA'ABDA
BEIRUT INTERNATIONAL AIRPORT
SHUEIFAT
MEDITERRANEAN SEA
International Boundaries
Israel-Golan Border
Disengagement of Forces Lines ISRAEL-SYRIA-1974
Main Roads
Secondary Roads
JUNIA
Raifun
Mt. Senin
Bikfayya
Antilyas
Ras-al-Maten
Hammana
ZAHLA
Rayaq
Shaturah
Ba'abda
Alei
Ash-Shuwayfat
Ein Sofar
Bhamdun
Ein Dara
Barr Ilyas
Ein Zahlata
Rishmayya
Ad-Damur
Bayt-ad-Din
Ghazzah
Baqlin
Shouf Mountains
Gharifah
Jubb Jannin
Yanta
Qar'un Reservoir
Al-Qar'un
TO DAMASCUS
25 km.
BIQA'
Awali River
SIDON
Jazzin
Mashgharah
Rashayya
Maghdushah
Kafr Hunah
Litani R.
MT. HERMON
Zahrani River
As-Sarafand
Habbush
Aishiyye
Hasbayya
Ad-Duwayr
An-Nabatiya
Marj Uyun
Shab'a
Hardalah Bridge
Al-Khiyam
Qismiyye Bridge
Aqiyye Bridge
Beaufort
Litani River
Metula
Majdal Shams
TYRE
Dan
Snir
Jwayya
Qana
Tibnin
QIRYAT SHMONA
GOLAN
SYRIA
AL-QUNAYTIRAH
Bint Jubayl
An-Naqurah
NAHARIYYA
ISRAEL
SAFAD
© Jaffee Center for Strategic Studies —1985

Map no. 3

ISRAEL: NORTHERN FRONT
SCALE
Km. 10 5 0 10 20 50 100 Km
Miles 10 0 10 20 30 40 50 60 Miles
International Boundaries
West Bank & Gaza Strip Boundaries („Green Line")
Israel - Golan Border
Disengagement of Forces Lines ISRAEL - SYRIA - 1974
HOMS
TRIPOLI
LEBANON
BA'ALBEK
BEIRUT
BA'ABDA
ZAHLA
ALEI
BEIRUT-DAMASCUS ROAD
DAMUR
Litani River
SIDON
JAZZIN
NABATIYA
MARJ UYUN
DAMASCUS
SYRIA
TYRE
QUNEITRA
GOLAN
NAHARIYA
ACRE
SAFAD
HAIFA
TIBERIAS
AFULA
IRBID
DER'A
MEDITERRANEAN SEA
ISRAEL
HADERA
JENIN
NATANYA
TULKARM
Jordan River
MAFRAK
HERZLIYA
NABLUS
TEL-AVIV YAFO
PETAH TIQVA
BAT YAM
LOD
RAMLE
REHOVOT
RAMALLAH
JERICHO
KINGDOM OF JORDAN
AMMAN
ASHDOD
JERUSALEM
ASHQELON
BETHLEHEM
HEBRON
GAZA
DEAD SEA
BEERSHEBA
© Jaffee Center for Strategic Studies — 1984

Map no. 4

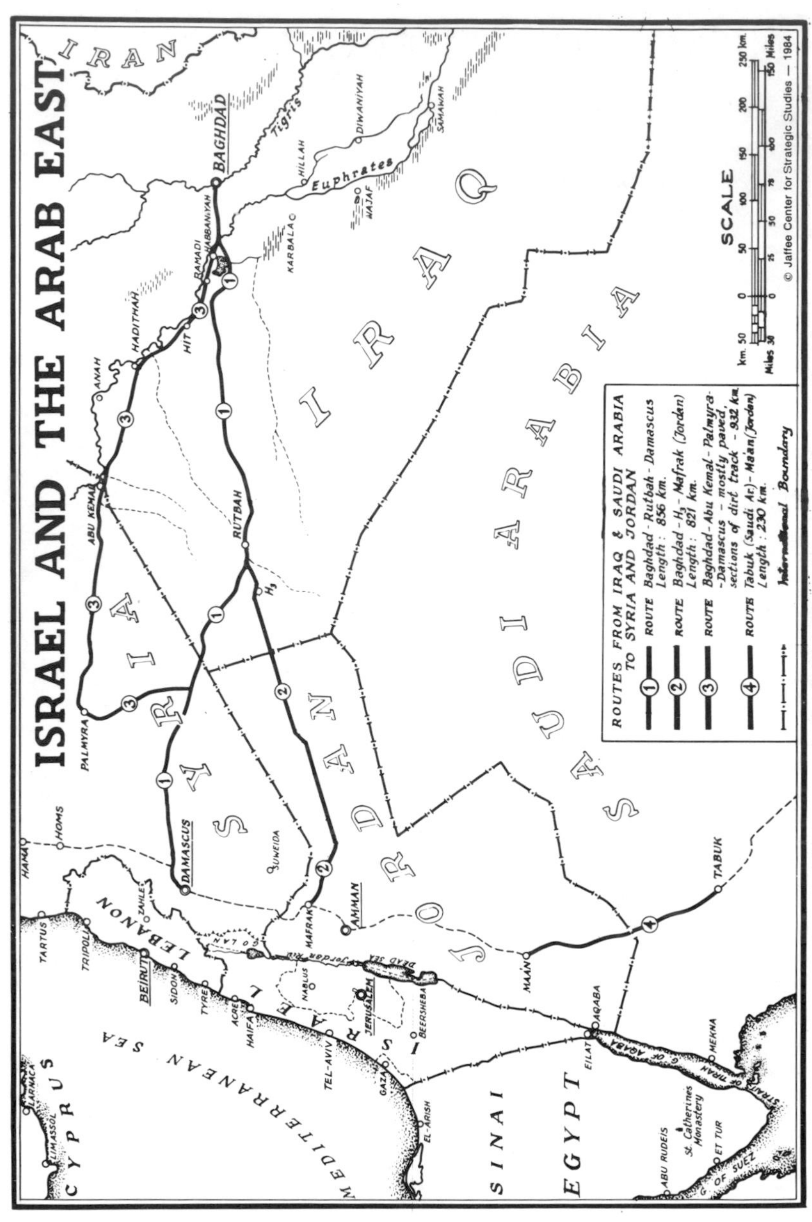

ISRAEL AND THE ARAB EAST
ROUTES FROM IRAQ & SAUDI ARABIA TO SYRIA AND JORDAN
1 ROUTE Baghdad - Rutbah - Damascus Length: 856 km.
2 ROUTE Baghdad - H3 - Mafrak (Jordan) Length: 821 km.
3 ROUTE Baghdad - Abu Kemal - Palmyra - Damascus - mostly paved, sections of dirt track - 932 km.
4 ROUTE Tabuk (Saudi Ar.) - Maan (Jordan) Length: 230 km.
International Boundary
SCALE
© Jaffee Center for Strategic Studies — 1984
IRAN
IRAQ
SYRIA
JORDAN
SAUDI ARABIA
LEBANON
ISRAEL
SINAI
EGYPT
CYPRUS
MEDITERRANEAN SEA
BAGHDAD
DAMASCUS
AMMAN
BEIRUT
JERUSALEM
Tigris
Euphrates
DIWANIYAH
SAMAWAH
HILLAH
NAJAF
KARBALA
HABBANIYAH
RAMADI
HIT
HADITHAH
ANAH
ABU KEMAL
RUTBAH
PALMYRA
HOMS
HAMA
SUWEIDA
MAFRAK
ZAHLE
TARTUS
TRIPOLI
SIDON
TYRE
ACRE
HAIFA
NABLUS
TEL-AVIV
GAZA
BEERSHEBA
EL-ARISH
DEAD SEA
MAAN
AQABA
EILAT
TABUK
MEKNA
St. Catherines Monastery
ABU RUDEIS
ET TUR
G. OF SUEZ
G. OF AQABA
LARNACA
LIMASSOL

Map no. 5

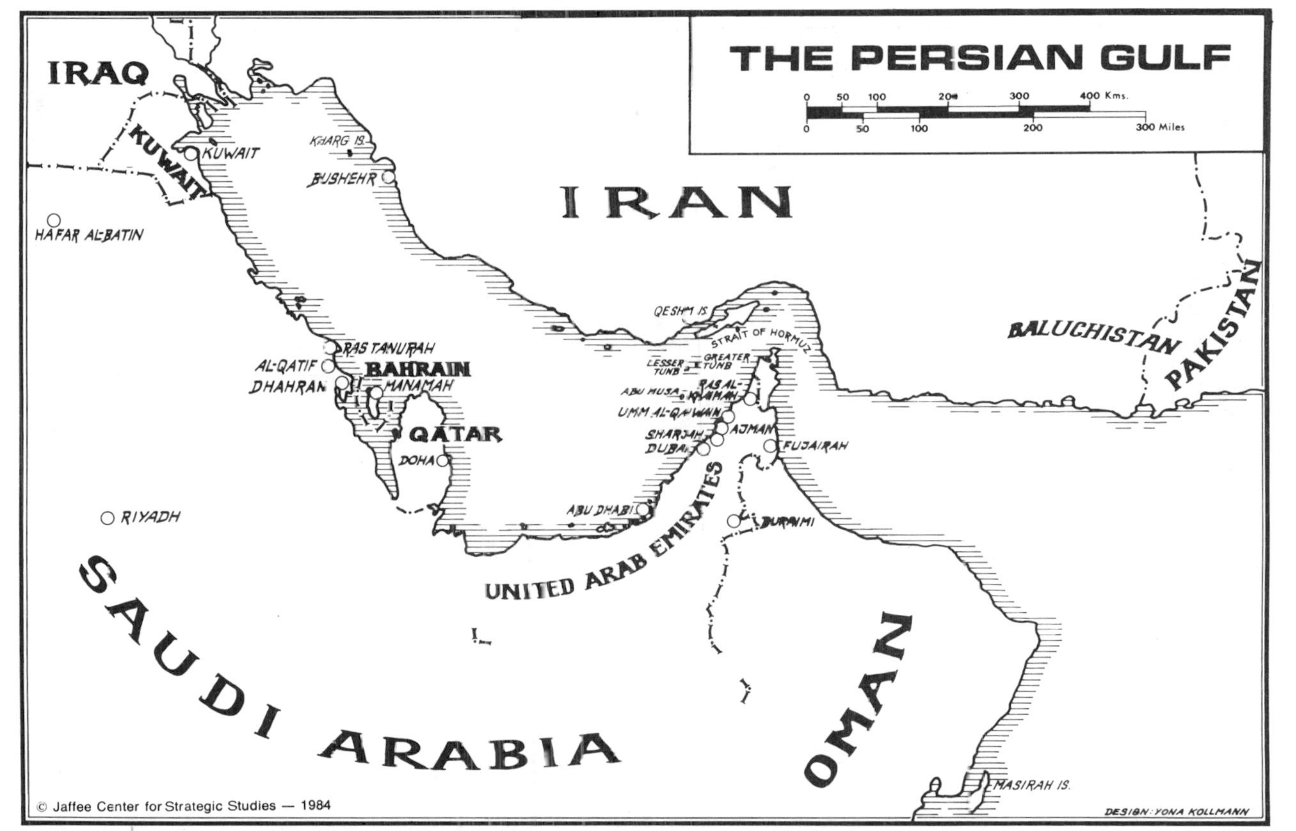
THE PERSIAN GULF
0 50 100 200 300 400 Kms.
0 50 100 200 300 Miles
IRAQ
KUWAIT
KUWAIT
HAFAR AL-BATIN
KHARG IS.
BUSHEHR
IRAN
QESHM IS.
STRAIT OF HORMUZ
LESSER TUNB
GREATER TUNB
ABU MUSA
RAS AL-KHAIMAH
UMM AL-QAIWAIN
SHARJAH
AJMAN
DUBAI
FUJAIRAH
BALUCHISTAN
PAKISTAN
RAS TANURAH
AL-QATIF
BAHRAIN
DHAHRAN
MANAMAH
QATAR
DOHA
ABU DHABI
BURAIMI
RIYADH
UNITED ARAB EMIRATES
SAUDI ARABIA
OMAN
MASIRAH IS.
© Jaffee Center for Strategic Studies — 1984
DESIGN: YONA KOLLMANN

Map no. 6

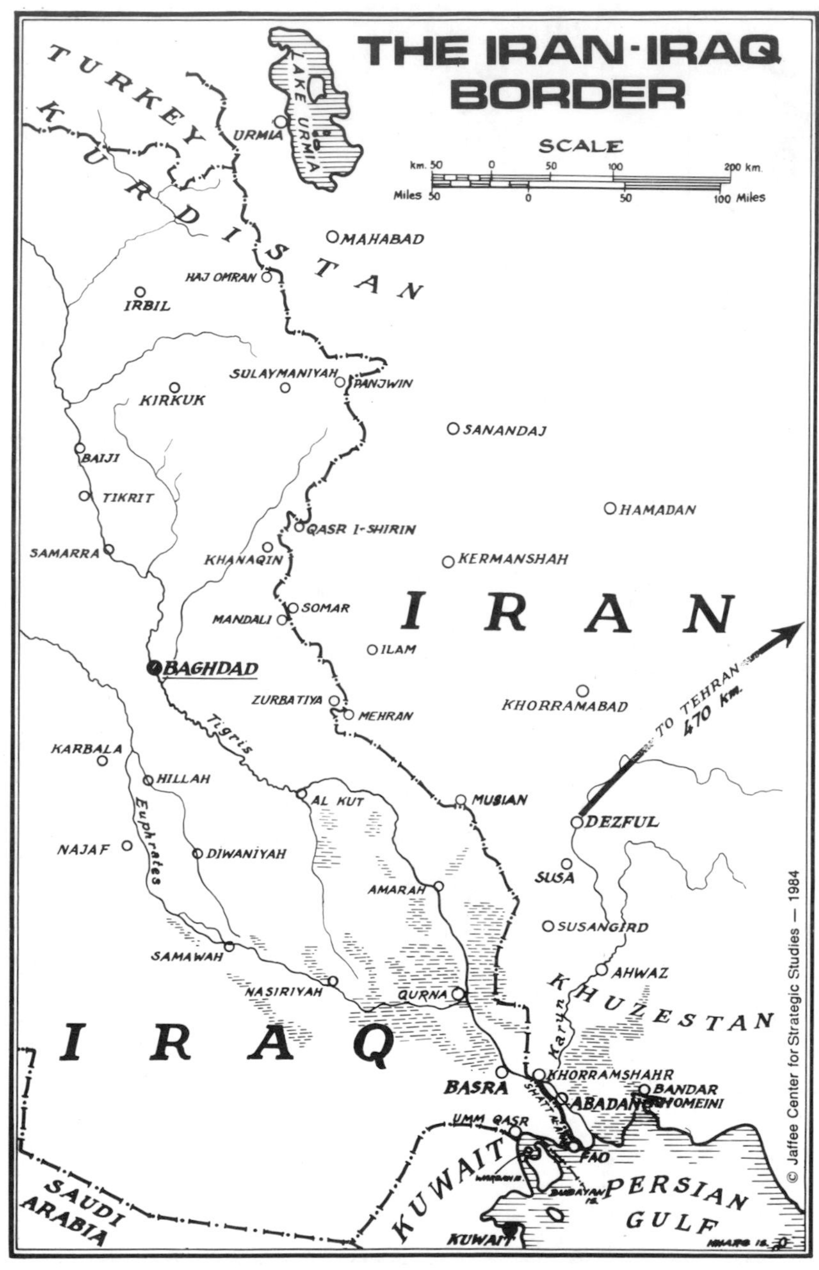
THE IRAN-IRAQ BORDER
SCALE
km. 50 0 50 100 200 km.
Miles 50 0 50 100 Miles
TURKEY
KURDISTAN
LAKE URMIA
URMIA
MAHABAD
HAJ OMRAN
IRBIL
SULAYMANIYAH
PANJWIN
KIRKUK
SANANDAJ
BAIJI
TIKRIT
HAMADAN
QASR I-SHIRIN
SAMARRA
KHANAQIN
KERMANSHAH
IRAN
SOMAR
MANDALI
ILAM
BAGHDAD
ZURBATIYA
MEHRAN
KHORRAMABAD
TO TEHRAN 470 Km.
Tigris
KARBALA
HILLAH
AL KUT
MUSIAN
DEZFUL
Euphrates
NAJAF
DIWANIYAH
SUSA
AMARAH
SUSANGIRD
SAMAWAH
AHWAZ
NASIRIYAH
QURNA
KHUZESTAN
Karun
IRAQ
BASRA
KHORRAMSHAHR
ABADAN
BANDAR KHOMEINI
UMM QASR
FAO
KUWAIT
PERSIAN GULF
SAUDI ARABIA
© Jaffee Center for Strategic Studies — 1984

Map no. 7

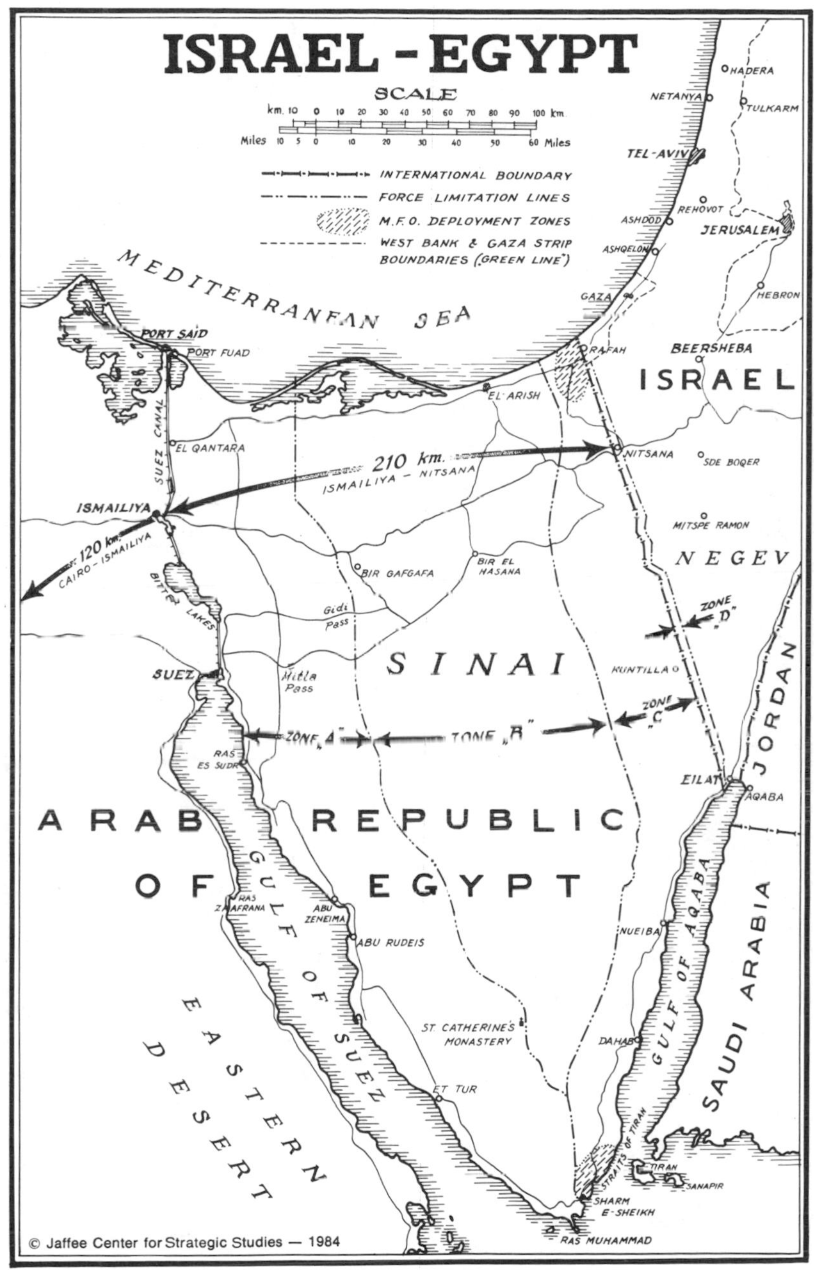

ISRAEL - EGYPT
SCALE
km. 10 0 10 20 30 40 50 60 70 80 90 100 km.
Miles 10 5 0 10 20 30 40 50 60 Miles
INTERNATIONAL BOUNDARY
FORCE LIMITATION LINES
M.F.O. DEPLOYMENT ZONES
WEST BANK & GAZA STRIP BOUNDARIES (GREEN LINE)
MEDITERRANEAN SEA
HADERA
NETANYA
TULKARM
TEL-AVIV
REHOVOT
ASHDOD
JERUSALEM
ASHQELON
GAZA
HEBRON
RAFAH
BEERSHEBA
ISRAEL
PORT SAID
PORT FUAD
EL ARISH
SUEZ CANAL
EL QANTARA
210 km.
ISMAILIYA - NITSANA
NITSANA
SDE BOQER
ISMAILIYA
MITSPE RAMON
120 km.
CAIRO - ISMAILIYA
BIR EL HASANA
BIR GAFGAFA
NEGEV
BITTER LAKES
Gidi Pass
ZONE "D"
SUEZ
Mitla Pass
SINAI
KUNTILLA
ZONE "C"
ZONE "A"
ZONE "B"
RAS ES SUDR
EILAT
JORDAN
AQABA
ARAB REPUBLIC OF EGYPT
GULF OF SUEZ
RAS ZAAFRANA
ABU ZENEIMA
ABU RUDEIS
NUEIBA
GULF OF AQABA
SAUDI ARABIA
EASTERN DESERT
ST. CATHERINE'S MONASTERY
DAHAB
ET TUR
STRAITS OF TIRAN
TIRAN
SANAPIR
SHARM E-SHEIKH
RAS MUHAMMAD
© Jaffee Center for Strategic Studies — 1984

Map no. 8

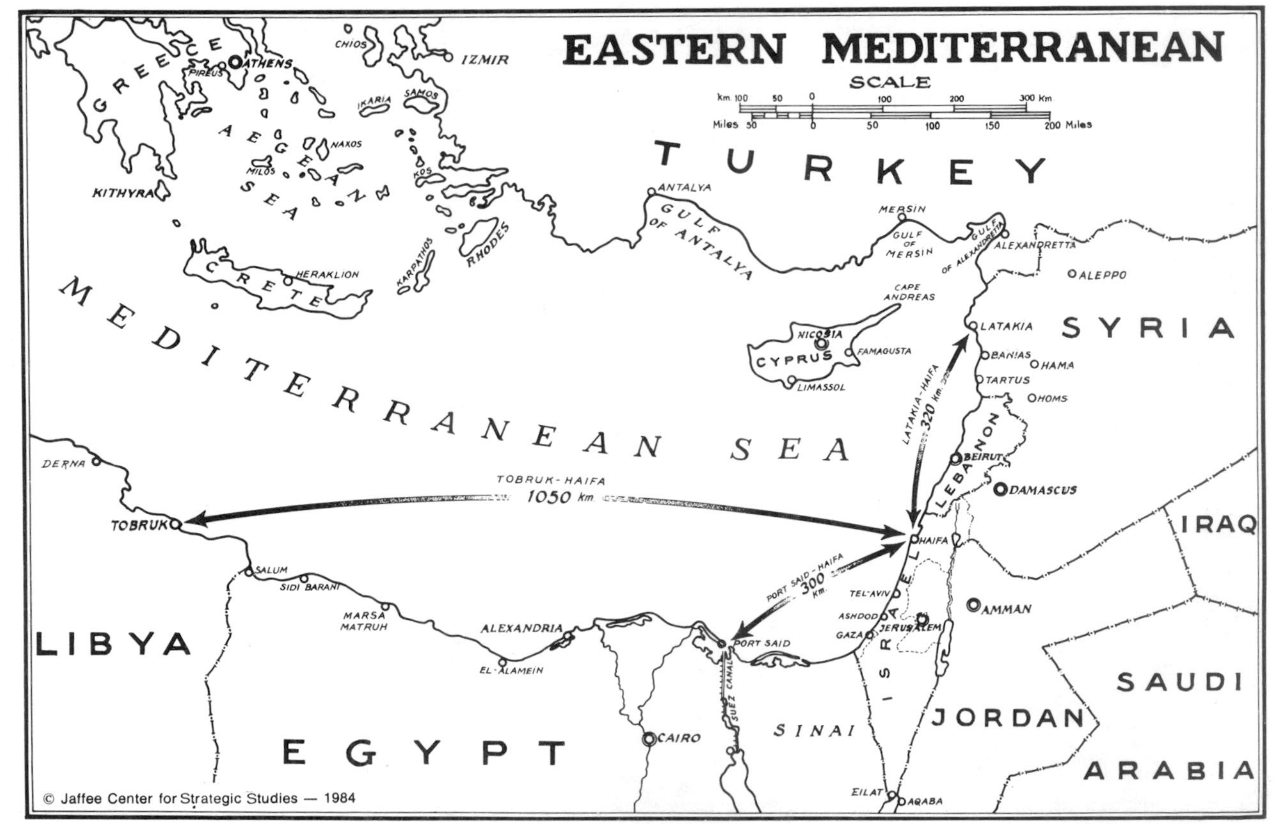
EASTERN MEDITERRANEAN
SCALE
Km 100 50 0 50 100 200 300 Km
Miles 50 0 50 100 150 200 Miles
TURKEY
SYRIA
IRAQ
SAUDI ARABIA
JORDAN
LEBANON
EGYPT
LIBYA
SINAI
GREECE
AEGEAN SEA
MEDITERRANEAN SEA
CRETE
CYPRUS
IZMIR
CHIOS
SAMOS
IKARIA
KOS
NAXOS
MILOS
ATHENS
PIREUS
KITHYRA
HERAKLION
KARPATHOS
RHODES
ANTALYA
GULF OF ANTALYA
MERSIN
GULF OF MERSIN
GULF OF ALEXANDRETTA
ALEXANDRETTA
ALEPPO
LATAKIA
BANIAS
HAMA
TARTUS
HOMS
DAMASCUS
BEIRUT
HAIFA
AMMAN
TEL-AVIV
ASHDOD
JERUSALEM
GAZA
EILAT
AQABA
CAPE ANDREAS
FAMAGUSTA
NICOSIA
LIMASSOL
PORT SAID
SUEZ CANAL
CAIRO
ALEXANDRIA
EL-ALAMEIN
MARSA MATRUH
SIDI BARANI
SALUM
TOBRUK
DERNA
LATAKIA-HAIFA 320 km
PORT SAID-HAIFA 300 km
TOBRUK-HAIFA 1050 km
© Jaffee Center for Strategic Studies — 1984

Map no. 9

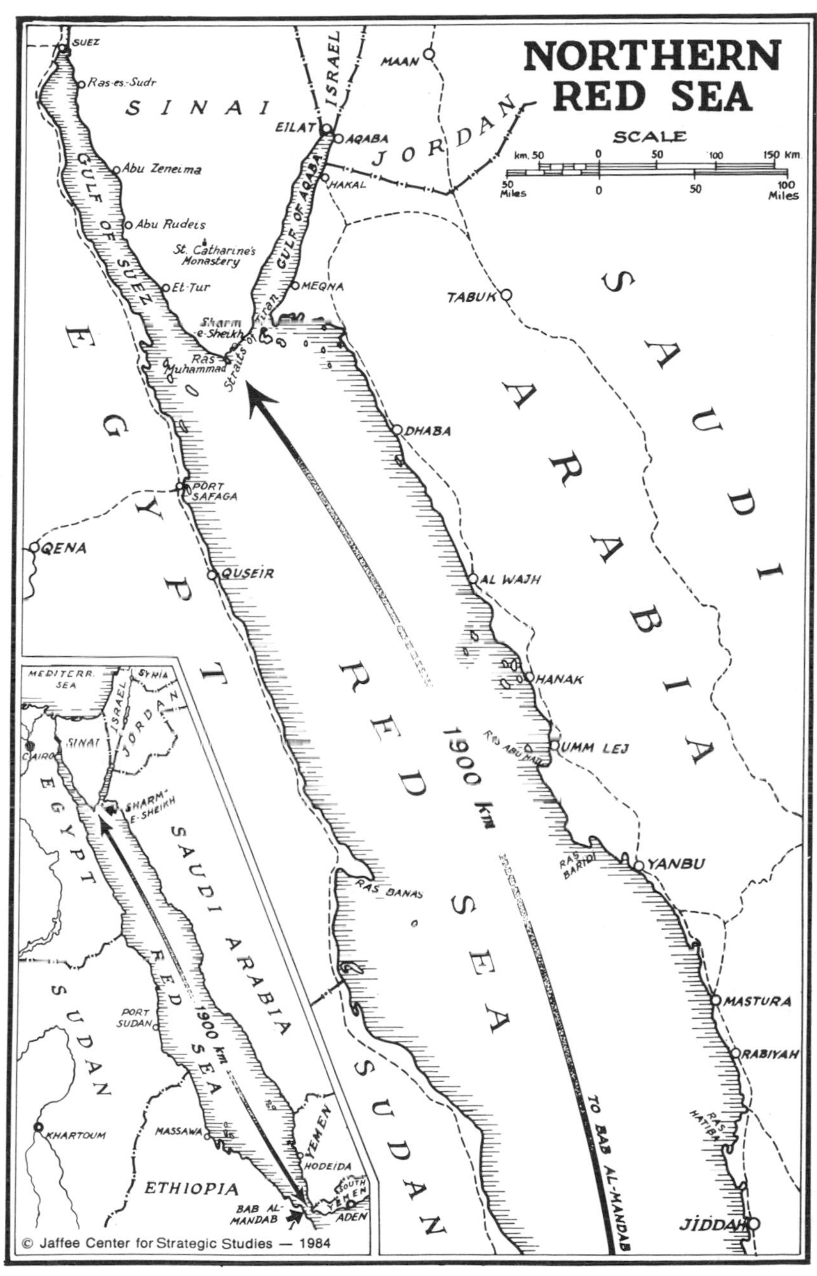
NORTHERN RED SEA
SCALE
km. 50 0 50 100 150 km.
50 Miles 0 50 100 Miles
SUEZ
Ras-es-Sudr
SINAI
EILAT
AQABA
ISRAEL
MAAN
JORDAN
GULF OF SUEZ
GULF OF AQABA
Abu Zeneima
HAKAL
Abu Rudeis
St. Catharine's Monastery
El-Tur
MEQNA
TABUK
Sharm e-Sheikh
Straits of Tiran
Ras Muhammad
EGYPT
SAUDI ARABIA
DHABA
PORT SAFAGA
QENA
QUSEIR
AL WAJH
RED SEA
HANAK
1900 km
UMM LEJ
RAS BARIDI
YANBU
RAS BANAS
MASTURA
RABIYAH
SUDAN
TO BAB AL-MANDAB
JIDDAH
MEDITERR. SEA
SYRIA
CAIRO
SHARM-E-SHEIKH
PORT SUDAN
KHARTOUM
MASSAWA
YEMEN
HODEIDA
SOUTH YEMEN
ETHIOPIA
BAB AL-MANDAB
ADEN

Map no. 10

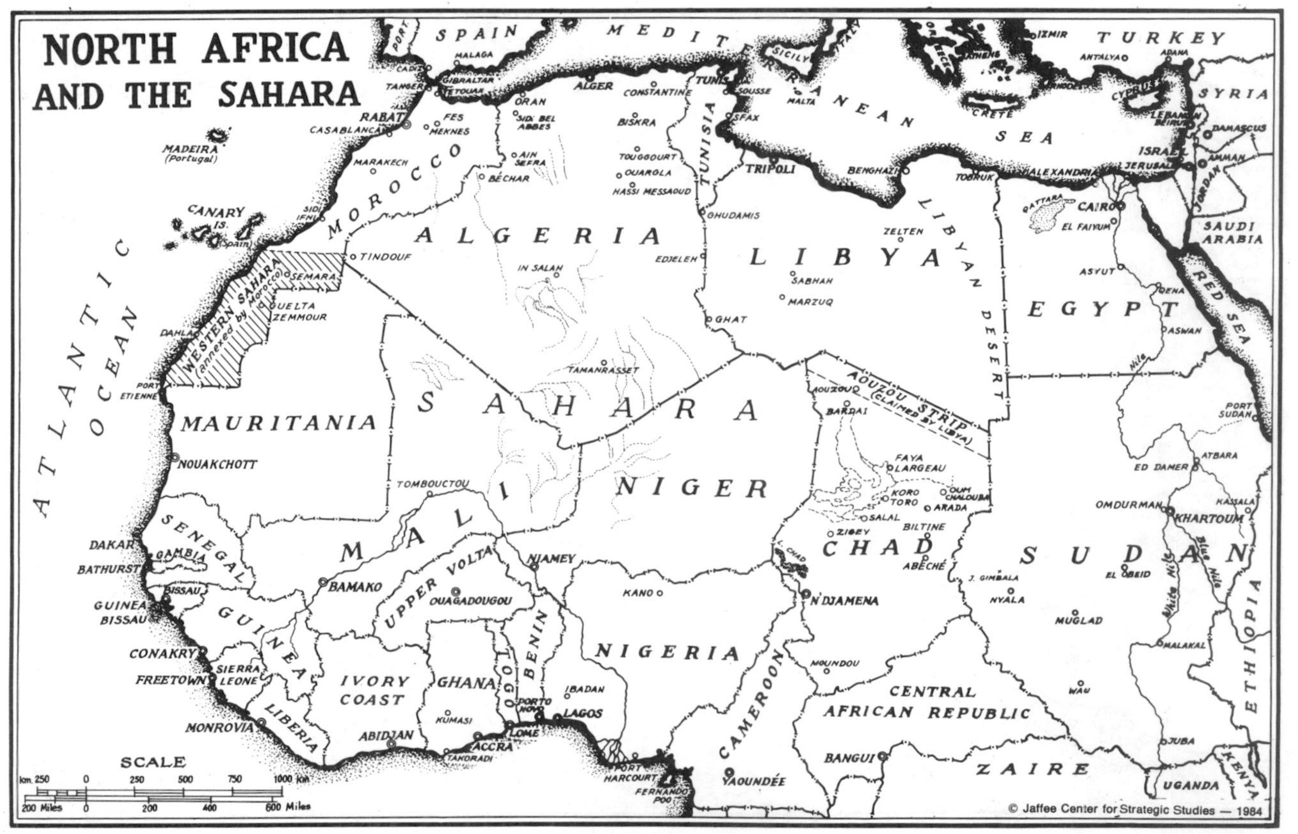
NORTH AFRICA
AND THE SAHARA
SPAIN
PORT.
MEDITERRANEAN SEA
TURKEY
SYRIA
SAUDI ARABIA
JORDAN
ISRAEL
LEBANON
CYPRUS
CRETE
SICILY
MALTA
RED SEA
ATLANTIC OCEAN
MADEIRA (Portugal)
CANARY IS. (Spain)
MOROCCO
WESTERN SAHARA (annexed by Morocco)
ALGERIA
TUNISIA
LIBYA
LIBYAN DESERT
EGYPT
AOUZOU STRIP (CLAIMED BY LIBYA)
SAHARA
MAURITANIA
MALI
NIGER
CHAD
SUDAN
ETHIOPIA
KENYA
UGANDA
ZAIRE
CENTRAL AFRICAN REPUBLIC
CAMEROON
NIGERIA
BENIN
TOGO
GHANA
UPPER VOLTA
IVORY COAST
LIBERIA
SIERRA LEONE
GUINEA
GUINEA BISSAU
GAMBIA
SENEGAL
MALAGA
GIBRALTAR
TANGER
TETOUAN
RABAT
CASABLANCA
FES
MEKNES
MARAKECH
SIDI IFNI
TINDOUF
SEMARA
GUELTA ZEMMOUR
DAHLA
PORT ETIENNE
NOUAKCHOTT
DAKAR
BATHURST
BISSAU
CONAKRY
FREETOWN
MONROVIA
ABIDJAN
TAKORADI
ACCRA
KUMASI
LOME
PORTO NOVO
LAGOS
IBADAN
PORT HARCOURT
FERNANDO POO
YAOUNDÉE
BANGUI
BAMAKO
OUAGADOUGOU
TOMBOUCTOU
NIAMEY
KANO
N'DJAMENA
MOUNDOU
ORAN
SIDI BEL ABBES
AIN SEFRA
BÉCHAR
ALGER
CONSTANTINE
BISKRA
TOUGGOURT
OUAROLA
HASSI MESSAOUD
IN SALAH
TAMANRASSET
EDJELEH
TUNIS
SOUSSE
SFAX
TRIPOLI
GHUDAMIS
GHAT
SABHAH
MARZUQ
ZELTEN
BENGHAZI
TOBRUK
ALEXANDRIA
CAIRO
EL FAIYUM
QATTARA
ASYUT
QENA
ASWAN
Nile
AOUZOU
BARDAI
FAYA LARGEAU
KORO TORO
OUM CHALOUBA
ARADA
SALAL
BILTINE
ZIGEY
ABÉCHÉ
L. CHAD
PORT SUDAN
ATBARA
ED DAMER
KASSALA
OMDURMAN
KHARTOUM
Blue Nile
White Nile
EL OBEID
J. GIMBALA
NYALA
MUGLAD
MALAKAL
WAU
JUBA
IZMIR
ANTALYA
ADANA
RHODES
ATHENS
GREECE
ITALY
BEIRUT
JERUSALEM
AMMAN
DAMASCUS
SCALE
km. 250 0 250 500 750 1000 km
200 Miles 0 200 400 600 Miles
© Jaffee Center for Strategic Studies — 1984